# Successful Fiber Optic Installation

## -The Essentials

*Version 7.0*

Eric R. Pearson, CPC, CFOS

Pearson Technologies Inc.

Acworth, GA

Disclaimer

All instructions contained herein are believed to produce the proper results when followed exactly with appropriate equipment. However, these instructions are not guaranteed for all situations.

Notice To The Reader

The publisher does not warrant or guarantee any of the products described herein or perform any independent analysis in connection with any of the product information contained herein. Publisher does not assume, and expressly disclaims, any obligation to obtain and include information other that provided to it by the manufacturer.

The reader is specifically warned to consider and adopt any and all safety precautions that might be indicated by the activities herein and to avoid any and all potential hazards. By following the instructions contained herein, the reader knowingly and willingly assumes all risks in connection with such instructions.

The publisher makes no representation or warranties of any kind, included but not limited to, the warranties of fitness for particular purpose or merchantability, nor are any such representations implied with respect to the material set forth herein, and the publisher takes no responsibility with respect to such material. The publisher shall not be liable for any special, consequential, or exemplary damages resulting, in whole or part, from the readers' use of, or reliance upon, this material.

The procedures provided herein are believed to be accurate and to result in low installation cost and in high reliability. However, there is a possibility that these procedures may be unsuitable for specific products or in specific situations. Because of this possibility, the installer should review, and follow, the instructions provided by product manufacturers. The instructions contained herein are not meant to imply that conflicting instructions from manufacturers are in error.

Trademark Notice

All trademarks are the property of the trademark holder. Trademarks used in the installation documents include Kevlar™ (Dupont), Hytrel™ (Dupont), and ST-compatible (Lucent).

Cover photographs courtesy of Condux Corporation, Alcoa Fujikura Ltd. and Pearson Technologies Inc.

Published by

Pearson Technologies Inc.
4671 Hickory Bend Drive
Acworth, GA 30102
770-591-8921
800-589-2549
509-693-5670/fax
www.ptnowire.com
fiberguru@ptnowire.com

Version 7.0

Printed in the United States of America.

10 9 8 7 6 5 4 3 2 1

ISBN 0-9769754-0-8

# Table of Contents

## PART TWO: ESSENTIAL PRINCIPLES AND METHODS

## INTRODUCTION

## 10 CABLE INSTALLATION PRINCIPLES

## 11 CONNECTOR INSTALLATION PRINCIPLES

## 12   SPLICING PRINCIPLES

## 13   TESTING PRINCIPLES

## 16   CONNECTOR INSTALLATION: EPOXY

## 17   CONNECTOR INSTALLATION: QUICK CURE ADHESIVE

## 23   PIGTAIL SPLICING

## TABLE OF FIGURES

## TABLE OF TABLES

## AUTHORS PREFACE

This book has three parts: essential information, principles and methods, and procedures. In the first part, Essential Information, I present the 'language' of fiber optic network components. This language is of the products with which the installer will work, of the types of such products and their advantages, and of the performance numbers that the installer can expect. With the foundation created by this part, the installer can understand the principles in the second part and follow the procedures in the third part.

This first part acts as a comprehensive textbook for those studying fiber optic technology with the intent of involvement in field installation. In addition, this first part includes most of the information that the reader needs to become certified by the Fiber Optic Association (FOA, www.thefoa.org) as a Certified Fiber Optic Technician (CFOT).

The second part, Principles And Methods, is a presentation of the rules, or basic characteristics, that give rise to the procedures. These rules are rarely included in installation procedures from manufacturers. Such inclusion would complicate those procedures and distract the installer from his prime focus on successful installation. Knowledge of these principles will make the installer sensitive to the importance of the procedures. With this sensitivity, the installer will be able to follow the procedures and achieve low power loss, low installation cost and high reliability. In addition, this second part includes additional information required for CFOT certification and for advanced FOA certification, the Certified Fiber Optic Specialist) in splicing (CFOS/S), testing (CFOS/T) and connector installation (CFOS/C).

The third part, Procedures, is a series of installation procedures that, when followed, result in the three goals of low power loss, low installation cost and high reliability. The reader can use these procedures as training procedures, as field procedures and as a reference, when there is a long time between fiber activities.

This book evolved from our work in training people in installation and testing of fiber optic products. Some of the elements of this book have come from manufacturers' instructions. Some have come from professional associates, for whose continuous generosity of time and information I am grateful. Some have come from watching the errors made by the 6800 trainees who have attended our training programs. Some have come from trainees, who have asked practical questions and shared their observations. Finally, some have come from testing we have performed in our laboratory to identify methods to improve, simplify and speed up the installation and learning processes. This evolution resulted in the subtitle of this book "-The Essentials." We included much information in this book because its lack results in increased power loss, increased installation cost or reduced reliability.

The result of this process of evolution is a series of procedures that work well. 'Working well' means the procedures will result in low power loss, the prime concern of the installer, low installation cost (through reduced rework) and maximum reliability, through avoidance of the common and subtle errors.

Whether you are studying fiber optics for the first time or you are a field installer, you will find this book highly useful and an investment that will pay back many times its cost. Finally, this book will help you can set up field installation and patch cord assembly operations.

As this book will remain a work in progress, we encourage your comments and observations.

Eric R. Pearson, CPC, CFOS

Pearson Technologies Inc.
800-589-2549
509-693-5670/fax
www.ptnowire.com
fiberguru@ptnowire.com
July 2005

# PART ONE
# ESSENTIAL INFORMATION

# 1    INTRODUCTION TO NETWORKS

Chapter Objectives: in this chapter you will learn the basics of networks. These basics will allow you to put fiber transmission in its proper context.

## 1.1    NETWORK FUNCTION

A data network, or short haul local area network (LAN), exists to enable communication between its parts. These parts, or nodes, include computers, servers, hubs, switches, routers, multiplexers, gateways, printers, modems, scanners, hard drives, and CD-ROM drives.[1]

## 1.2    TRANSMISSION TYPES

This communication can be of two types: analog or digital. Analog communication is communication with a signal, in which continuous signal amplitude indicates the information.

Examples of analog transmission include cable TV (CATV) networks and closed circuit television links (CCTV) use communication to distribute video signals over a cable TV (CATV) network.[2] Closed circuit TVs transmit an analog signal.

Digital communication is with a signal, in which the information is indicated by one of two power levels. These two levels indicate the zeroes and ones that are the digital form of the information. Most data communication over local area networks (LANs) is with digital signals.

## 1.3    TOPOLOGIES

Topology refers to the method of arrangement. Data networks have two topologies, a logical topology and a physical topology. The logical topology refers to the path in which data move through the network. The physical topology refers to the manner in which the cables are placed. A logical topology can run on more than one physical topology. For example, a logical

ring topology can operate on either a physical ring topology or a physical star cable topology.

The most common topology in data networks is a multi-level logical star with a physical star cable topology. The most common topology for telephone networks is a logical ring with a physical ring cable topology.

Five logical topologies are common:

- ➢ Point-to-point
- ➢ Multipoint (or common bus)
- ➢ Star
- ➢ Ring (or loop)
- ➢ Mesh

### 1.3.1    POINT-TO-POINT

In a point-to-point network, the network provides a link, or connection, between two nodes (Figure 1-1). The telephone line is an example of a point-to-point topology.

- ➢ With few exceptions, most fiber data networks and fiber telephone networks consist of a series of point-to-point links.

Figure 1-1: Point-To-Point Topology

Exceptions are some CATV networks, passive optical networks (PON) for fiber-to-the-home (FTTH), and 10BASE-F (1.5.3).

### 1.3.2    MULTIPOINT

In a multipoint, or common bus or shared medium, topology, all nodes are connected to a common transmission medium (Figure 1-2). Whenever any node transmits, all nodes on the bus receive the same signal. The node to which the signal is addressed processes the signal. All other nodes ignore the signal.

---

[1] This chapter is not intended to provide a comprehensive overview of networks. For such an overview, see the references (1.8).

[2] The CATV industry is converting some of its channels to digital.

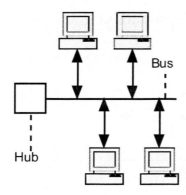

Figure 1-2: Multipoint Topology

The first Ethernet networks were multipoint networks. Cellular telephone networks and CATV networks are multipoint networks.

### 1.3.3    STAR

In a star topology, data are transmitted from one central node on the network to multiple second level nodes. Each second level node is directly connected to the central node (Figure 1-3). Each of these second level nodes can be connected to additional nodes. In a star network, the data can be switched or routed along one of the output paths from each node. The return signal from any node on the network will follow the same topology, but in reverse.

The passive optical network (PON) design for some fiber-to-the–home (FTTH) networks has a star topology (Figure 1-4). With such a topology, a single transceiver serves up to 32 customers.

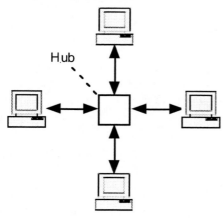

Figure 1-3: Star Topology

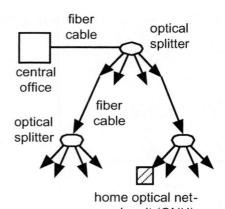

Figure 1-4: A Simplified FTTH PON Network

### 1.3.4    RING

In a ring topology, nodes are arranged to form a ring (Figure 1-5). One node transmits data, in the form of a token, to the adjacent node. At this adjacent node, the data are either stripped from token or passed onto the next node in the ring. The data are stripped at a node when that node is the destination of the data. A ring can operate in one direction (unidirectional) or in both directions (bi-directional), as in FDDI.

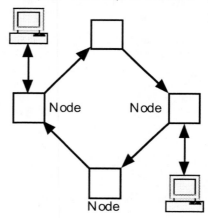

Figure 1-5: Ring Topology

### 1.3.5    MESH

In a mesh topology, all nodes have multiple links to each other (Figure 1-6). These multiple connections provide improved reliability in the event of a link failure. In addition, these multiple links enable load balancing to reduce transmission delays and lost transmissions due to congestion along specific links.

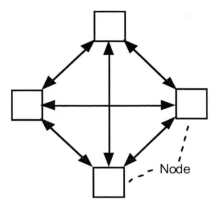

Figure 1-6: Mesh Topology

## 1.4    COMPONENTS

Each of these topologies requires creation of a link between the nodes. These nodes and links have components. These components include hubs, switches, bridges, routers, network interface cards (NICs), media converters, cables, or another communication media, and connectors.

### 1.4.1    HUBS

Hubs, or concentrator hubs, are network devices that collect signals from multiple LAN segments (Figure 1-7) or from multiple PCs (nodes) (Figure 1-8) for transmission onto a single back plane or single LAN segment.

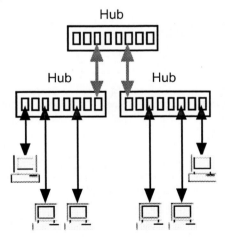

Figure 1-7: A Hub Connecting Multiple LAN Segments

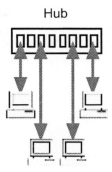

Figure 1-8: A Hub Connecting Multiple PCs

### 1.4.2    SWITCHES

While hubs enable concentration of signals from multiple sources, they are subject to simultaneous arrival of signals from multiple nodes. In this situation, all signals are corrupted by their 'collision'. Such collisions require retransmission of the signals that collided. Retransmissions result in significantly reduced effective, or real, bandwidth.

The switch places signals on its back plane one at a time, eliminating collisions and the necessary retransmissions.

### 1.4.3    BRIDGES

Bridges provide connection between two LANs that run the same protocol, such as Ethernet or FDDI. With a bridge, all signals from one LAN are repeated on the bridged LAN. As such, bridges are relatively simple, but provide inefficient use of network bandwidth.

### 1.4.4    ROUTERS

Routers address this inefficiency of bridges by forwarding, or routing, the data to the output port appropriate for the node to which the data is addressed. Routers read the address and route the signal to the appropriate output port according to an internal table.

### 1.4.5    NETWORK INTERFACE CARDS

Network interface cards (NICs) are cards that fit into the slot of a PC or a switch (Figure 1-9). NICs provide the ability to communicate with the device on the other end of the link.

Today, many PCs and switches do not have separate NICs, in that the communication function is built into the PC. Today, most PCs incorporate Fast Ethernet or Gigabit Ethernet chips. Such chips eliminate the need for a NIC.

Figure 1-9: Fiber Network Interface Card[3]

## 1.4.6    MEDIA CONVERTERS

In place of NICs, some switches enable communication through media converters (Figure 1-10). The media converter converts the signal from a form suitable for one transmission medium to that suitable for a different medium. This device is external to the computer. Media converters are used in place of NICs when the labor cost of opening a computer to install a NIC is high. In the context of this book, the term media converter will mean a device that converts an electrical signal to an optical signal.

Figure 1-10: Fiber Media Converter[3]

## 1.4.7    COMMUNICATION MEDIA

All of the aforementioned components must communicate through some medium. These media can be four types of copper cable (thick coax, thin coax, UTP and STP), two forms through air (radio frequency and infrared light), and optical fiber.

CATV networks use a 75-Ohm coaxial cable. The original data networks used a large 50-Ohm, coaxial cable with 'Vampire' taps as a connector. This cable is thick and somewhat difficult to handle. The handling difficulty resulted in use of a smaller coax, nicknamed 'Thinnet.'

The expense of coax cable and its termination and the relative low cost of unshielded, twisted pair (UTP) cable resulted in UTP becoming the cable of choice for subsequent data networks.

While most data networks use UTP, IBM designed its token ring system for use with shielded, twisted pair (STP). Because STP is more expensive and more difficult to install and terminate than is UTP, use of UTP dominates data networks.

While most networks use cable as the communication medium, some use air. Some networks use radio frequency (RF) signals to carry data. Wireless networks, such as Wireless Fidelity (WiFi), Bluetooth and cell phone networks are examples. Some short distance computer networks use infrared light (IR). With IR, transmission distance is limited.

The final transmission medium is optical fiber. Fiber offers advantages not found in other media (1.5.1).

## 1.4.8    CONNECTORS

With the exception of transmission by air, connectors are required. As this book has fiber as its focus, we will present information on fiber connectors only (5).

## 1.5    THE FIBER NETWORK

A fiber network includes fiber as the transmission medium. Fiber may be the only transmission medium, as in SONET, ESCON or FDDI networks. Alternatively, fiber may be one of several media, as in Ethernet, Fast Ethernet, and Gigabit Ethernet networks.

---

[3] Courtesy IMC Networks

## 1.5.1    NINE ADVANTAGES

Fiber is the medium of choice because of its nine advantages:

> ➢ Nearly unlimited bandwidth
>
> ➢ Long transmission distance
>
> ➢ EMI immunity
>
> ➢ RF immunity
>
> ➢ Low cost per bit
>
> ➢ Dielectric construction
>
> ➢ Small size
>
> ➢ Light weight
>
> ➢ Ease of installation

### 1.5.1.1    UNLIMITED BANDWIDTH

Optical fiber has essentially unlimited bandwidth. While 'unlimited bandwidth' may sound like a salesperson's exaggeration, it is a realistic and reasonable description of the capacity of the fiber. A study by Lucent Technologies indicated the theoretical capacity of a single, singlemode fiber is on the order of 200 Tbps, or 200 million Mbps. Such a capacity deserves the term 'essentially unlimited bandwidth'.

Part of this high capacity results from the ability to transmit multiple wavelengths simultaneously. Such transmission is called wavelength division multiplexing (WDM), coarse wavelength division multiplexing (CWDM), or dense wavelength division multiplexing (DWDM, Chapter 7).

WDM is the transmission of two widely spaced wavelengths, such as 850 nm and 1300 nm on multimode fibers or 1310 nm and 1550 nm on singlemode fibers. CWDM is the transmission of 3-8 moderately spaced wavelengths on singlemode fibers. CWDM operates in the wavelength range of 1310 nm to 1560 nm. DWDM is the transmission of many closely spaced wavelengths, such as 64-200 wavelengths spaced around a wavelength of 1550 nm or from 1310 nm to 1560 nm.

### 1.5.1.2    TRANSMISSION DISTANCE

Optical fiber allows extremely long transmission distance without return to the electrical regime. While not a current 'champion' result, Williams Communications demonstrated the ability to transmit 5000 km (3100 miles) in the optical regime. 5000 km is approximately the distance between Boston MA and Los Angeles CA!

This long transmission distance is the advantage that drives CATV providers to the use of fiber. This long transmission distance enables reduction in the number of satellite 'farms' necessary to support a service area. In addition, this advantage enables CATV companies to reduce the number of coax amplifiers between the satellite down link and the set top boxes. This reduction results in reduced costs for equipment and maintenance and in improved signal quality.

### 1.5.1.3    EMI AND RFI IMMUNITY

While long distance transmission capability results primarily from low attenuation rate (3.3.3) and low pulse dispersion (3.3.1), it also results from immunity to electromagnetic interference (EMI) and radio frequency interference (RFI). Since optical fibers are immune to interference from such energy, optical signals can travel long distances without the need for signal correction.

### 1.5.1.4    LOW COST PER BIT

The combination of low power loss, low pulse dispersion, and EMI/RFI immunity results in low cost per bit. This low cost has made fiber the medium of choice for long distance communication.[4] This low cost has resulted in the displacement of satellites as the 'king' of long distance communication. Now satellites are a back up for optical fiber transmission!

At the present time, many LANs with centralized back bone networks, also known as fiber to the desk networks (FTTD), have a total initial installed cost that is lower than that of traditional horizontal UTP, vertical fiber networks.[5] This cost advantage results from a reduction in the cost of telecommunication rooms that are required

---

[4] The telephone industry was able to justify use of optical fiber for long distance lines as early as 1978.

[5] See the Cost Model offered by the Fiber Optic LAN Section (FOLS) of the TIA at www.fols.org. The FOLS and Pearson Technologies co-developed this model.

within 300' of the nodes. Use of fiber reduces the cost of such rooms and the cost of support for such rooms.

Finally, the low cost of optical fiber has led to increased implementation of fiber-to-the-home (FTTH).

### 1.5.1.5    DIELECTRIC CONSTRUCTION

Optical fiber cables can be made without any conductive elements. Such dielectric construction eliminates the initial installed cost and maintenance cost of grounding and bonding.

Conductive cables must be grounded and bonded to prevent currents induced by lightning and ground potential rise from entering a building, injuring people and damaging electronics.

### 1.5.1.6    SMALL SIZE

The small size of optical fibers and their cables results in reduced system cost. For example, large cities with filled underground conduit systems have two methods of increasing telephone capacity: dig up the streets to install more conduits or replace copper cables with fiber cables. The replacement ratio is 100, 3" diameter, 900 pair cables to one 1" diameter fiber cable with single wavelength transmission. With dense wavelength division multiplexing (DWDM) allowing at least 200 wavelengths per fiber, this replacement ratio is 20,000, 3" diameter cables with the same 1" diameter fiber cable. With 1000 wavelengths per fiber, this ratio is 100,000 3" diameter copper cables! The cost advantage of using fiber instead of digging up streets is extremely large.

### 1.5.1.7    LIGHT WEIGHT

Optical fiber cables are significantly lighter than copper cables. As a result, fiber finds use in field tactical, shipboard and aircraft applications. In field tactical applications, this reduced weight enables solders to carry increased cable lengths. Such increased lengths enable placement of electronic monitoring equipment at the front line while the monitoring personnel are in a safe location. In addition, the non-radiating nature of optical fibers prevents the enemy from detecting the equipment location.

In shipboard applications, the lightweight of optical fiber cables increases the stability of the ships by reducing the weight above the waterline. Finally, in aircraft applications, the lightweight increases mission endurance.

Because of their lightweight and small size, fiber cables are easy to install. In addition, fiber connector installation methods have advanced sufficiently to enable installation by junior and senior high school students with minimal training.

## 1.5.2    LINKS CREATE NETWORKS

Networks consist of a series of links. To the installer, this term 'link' is the most important term.

> All installer actions are on the link. Incorrect procedures reduce both the optical power delivered to the receiver on a link and the reliability of the components of a link.

Many networks allow for full, two-way, or 'duplex' communication. Duplex fiber communication requires a pair of fibers.

The word 'pair' has different connotations in UTP and fiber networks. In a UTP network, two pairs of wires create duplex communication. If fiber networks, two fibers create duplex communication.

## 1.5.3    FIBER NETWORKS

### 1.5.3.1    ETHERNET

The IEEE 802.3 committee developed the Ethernet standard. From this committee comes its technical name, 802.3. Ethernet operates at an electrical data rate of 10 Mbps. Ethernet is the dominant networking protocol, with estimates of its dominance at 95 %.

There are three fiber Ethernet standards: 10BASE-FB, 10BASE-FL, and 10BASE-FP. 10BASE-FB creates a backbone link between switches or hubs (Figure 1-11). 10BASE-FL creates a ling between a node and a switch or hub (Figure 1-12). 10BASE-FP creates a link between a switch or hub and multiple nodes (Figure 1-13). The 10BASE-FP configuration requires a passive coupler and splitter and allows for collisions (1.4.2).

10BASE-FB, and 10BASE-FL allow transmission to 2000 m. Because of the power lost in the coupler and splitter, 10BASE-P allows transmission to 1000 m.

Hub                Hub

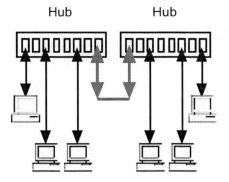

Figure 1-11: The 10BASE-FB Configuration

Hub

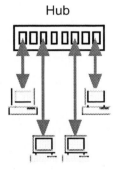

Figure 1-12: The 10BASE-FL Configuration

Hub

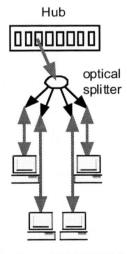

optical splitter

Figure 1-13: The 10BASE-FP Configuration

### 1.5.3.2     FAST ETHERNET

Fast Ethernet operates at an electrical data rate of 100 Mbps.[6] There are two fiber Fast Ethernet standards: 100BASE-FX and 100BASE-SX.[7] The original Fast Ethernet fiber standard, 100BASE-FX, was developed as a backbone technology, onto which Ethernet signals would feed. As a backbone technology, a reasonably long distance, up to 2000 m, was desirable. The combination of 125 Mbps data rate and the 2000 m distance forced designers to use optoelectronics that operate at a wavelength of 1300 nm. These optoelectronics are more expensive than those that operate at a wavelength of 850 nm. In addition, the use of 1300 nm meant that networks would need a forklift upgrade, since 850 nm and 1300 nm optoelectronics cannot communicate. Finally, the evolution of networks resulted in Fast Ethernet becoming the protocol of choice for links between PC and switches.

These facts resulted in relatively little use of 100BASE-FX. After recognizing this cost and upgrade disadvantage, the Fiber Optic LAN Section (FOLS) of the TIA initiated a development effort that resulted in the 100BASE-SX standard, which has reduced cost, 850 nm optoelectronics, a distance limitation of 300 m,[8] and auto negotiation. Auto negotiation allows for the preferred, node-by-node upgrading of the network from 10 Mbps to 100 Mbps.

### 1.5.3.3     GIGABIT ETHERNET

As we all know, network bandwidth requirements increase with time. In acknowledgement of this well-established trend, the data communications industry developed the Gigabit Ethernet (GbE) standard. This standard allows transmission at an electrical data rate of 1000 Mbps (1

---

[6] This standard transmits four electrical bits with five optical bits, resulting in an optical data rate of 125 Mbps.

[7] 100BASE-F is defined in the 802.3 standard. 100BASE-SX is defined in TIA/EIA-785.

[8] This 300 m limitation allows an FTTD network to function in a 43-story building. If the main cross-connect is in the middle of the building, the building can have 86 stories.

Gbps).[9] As a change from the two lower speed Ethernets, GbE allows use of both 50 µm and singlemode fibers, as well as the 62.5 µm fiber allowed by the Ethernet and Fast Ethernet standards. These three fibers, 850 nm and 1300 nm wavelengths, and multiple bandwidth distance product ratings enable transmission to eight distances from 220 m to 5000 m.[10]

### 1.5.3.4    10 GIGABIT ETHERNET

In recognition of the trend of ever-increasing network bandwidth requirements, network designers developed the latest, and perhaps, the last, Ethernet standard, the 10 Gigabit Ethernet (10GBASE-X) standard. This standard enables transmission over multimode and singlemode fiber to various distances, depending on the rating of the fiber.

### 1.5.3.5    FIBER DISTRIBUTED DATA INTERFACE

Fiber Distributed Data Interface (FDDI) was the first data standard developed as a fiber backbone. Developed as a high reliability, token passing, counter-rotating ring protocol, FDDI allowed transmission at 100 Mbps (data rate) and 125 Mbps (optical rate) over link or segment distances of 2000 m on a ring with a 100 km circumference (Figure 1-14).

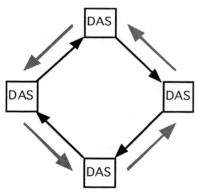

Figure 1-14: The FDDI Ring

The devices on the rings were Dual Attached Stations (DAS) or Dual Attached Concentrators (DAC) that were interconnected by two fibers. Data travels on the two fibers in opposite directions (Figure 1-14). The use of two fibers enabled automatic loop back in the event of a link failure (Figure 1-15).

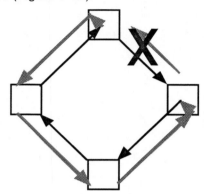

Figure 1-15: The FDDI Ring In Loop Back

The DAS could be a discrete device, such as a PC, or a concentrator (DAC). As concentrators, a DAC could be connected to Single Attached Stations (SAS) or to Single Attached Concentrators (SAC), which, in turn, could be discrete devices or concentrators (Figure 1-16).

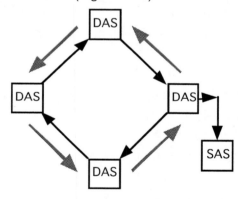

Figure 1-16: The FDDI Ring With SAS

Because FDDI development occurred prior to general awareness of the ever-increasing bandwidth requirements of networks, FDDI was designed for a single data rate, 100 Mbps. This lack of scalability limited FDDI to applications in which reliability is of utmost importance and scalability is of little importance. Such applications include military command, control and communication (C3) networks.

---

[9] As in the Fast Ethernet standard, the GbE optical data rate is 25 % higher than the electrical date rate.

[10] The maximum transmission distance of GBE is limited by the protocol, not by fiber performance.

### 1.5.3.6    TOKEN RING

IBM developed 4- and 16-Mbps token-passing ring networks as its answer to Ethernet. Token Ring transmission is considered to be deterministic, in that each station has a determined opportunity to transmit. In this characteristic, token ring networks differ from Ethernet networks, in that stations on Ethernet networks do not have a determined opportunity for transmission.

Network planners perceived this network to have four disadvantages. This network was proprietary, expensive, required STP instead of lower cost UTP cable, and was not scalable in the manner in which Ethernet has been. Fiber optic token ring networks operated at both 850 and 1300 nm.

### 1.5.3.7    ENTERPRISE SYSTEM CONNECTION

IBM developed Enterprise System Connection (ESCON) as a fiber optic technology to enable connection of mainframes to remotely located peripherals, such as tape drives. Peripherals are connected in a physical star topology to a switch, called a 'director'. The director switches signals from the mainframe to peripherals, with transmission over either multimode or singlemode cables. Transmission distances are up to 60 km. Connection is with ESCON connectors (5.5.3.3). Electrical transmission rates are 80 and 136 Mbps. With coding, the optical rate is up to 200 Mbps.[11]

### 1.5.3.8    ASYNCHRONOUS TRANSFER MODE

Asynchronous Transfer Mode (ATM) is a switch technology that transmits voice, video and data on the same network. Data rates are 155.52 Mbps, 622.08 Mbps and 2.488 Gbps, with additional lower speed rates defined. Transmission is of 53 byte cells, with 5 bytes of overhead. For rates of 155.52 Mbps and below, multimode fiber is used. For rates above, singlemode fiber is used.

ATM was touted as the successor to FDDI and Ethernet. High expense, complex implementation and the competition from reduced-cost Fast Ethernet and Gigabit Ethernet solutions defeated this expectation.[12]

### 1.5.3.9    SONET

Synchronous Optical Network (SONET) and Synchronous Digital Hierarchy (SDH) were the first two international digital communications standards for optical telephone networks, also know as long haul networks. Both of these standards were developed to enable interoperability between equipment made by different manufacturers. SONET is the North American Standard. SDH is the international standard.

These two standards are essentially the same. Their differences are small and mainly of terminology. Their differences are small enough to allow for the efficient and seamless communication between both types of networks.

Prior to SONET, there were many telephone communication protocols used worldwide. Their incompatibilities resulted in expensive and inefficient conversion of one protocol so that it could be transmitted across a network designed for a different protocol.

SONET networks can be configured as linear links, meshes, or rings. The most common implementation is a ring, similar to that shown for FDDI (Figure 1-14).

SONET has a base optical transmission rate, OC-1, of 51.84 Mbps. SDH has a base transmission rate, STM-1, of 155.52 Mbps, equivalent to the SONET OC-3 rate. Both have a practical, single wavelength limit of approximately 10 Gbps, corresponding to OC-192 and STM-48.

While telephone networks comply with the SONET standard, they can also carry Internet Protocol (IP) by mapping the IP packets into the SONET base rate 'container'.

---

[11] Fiber Optics Technician's Manual, 2nd Edition, 2001, Jim Hayes, Editor, p 38.

[12] As Category 5e and Category 6 UTP cables can support transmission rates of up to 1 Gbps, ATM can support this same rate. However, fiber supports ATM rates of up to 10 Gbps.

### 1.5.3.10 STORAGE AREA NETWORKS AND FIBRE CHANNEL

Storage area networks (SANs) are networks of high-speed storage devices.[13] Storage devices, such as hard drives, tape drives, CD-ROM drives, are high speed data devices that function by transmitting a relatively small number of large files. In this characteristic, storage area networks differ from local area networks, which function by transmitting a large number of small files.

The use of a storage area network allows separation of these two different functions. With this separation, each network can be optimized for the size of files and the number of files to be transmitted. In addition, this separation reduces latency on the local area network. Fibre Channel is the protocol used for communication on storage area networks.

### 1.5.3.11 CATV

The use of singlemode fiber in CATV networks reduces costs of capital equipment, of maintenance and of upgrades. In addition, such use improves signal quality through elimination of many coax signal amplifiers.

While some CATV networks transmit digital signals, most transmit analog signals. While such analog transmission has been possible since the early 1980s, it did not become common until the mid 1990s. At that time, the arrival of low cost, linear, analog, distributed feed back (DFB) laser diode systems made CATV fiber networks cost effective. In addition, the development of the erbium doped fiber amplifier (EDFA) allowed a single laser transmitter to transmit to 8 or 16 receivers, significantly reducing the cost per subscriber.

### 1.5.3.12 TIA/EIA-568 B

TIA/EIA-568 B, the Building Wiring Standard, describes the physical structure of standard-based fiber and UTP data networks. This standard allows the use of 50 μm, 62.5 μm and singlemode fiber. This standard allows use of SC and small form factor (SFF) connectors. It defines the performance requirements for fiber, cables and connectors, color-coding of fiber connectors, testing requirements and power loss limits.

### 1.5.3.13 FIBER TO THE HOME NETWORKS

While the previous types of fiber networks are well developed, the newest type of network, the fiber to the home (FTTH) network, is in its infancy. Such networks provide voice service, Internet access, data transfer, and digital and analog video service.

In the mid-1980's, companies began installing FTTH networks. At the time of this writing, there are 94 FTTH communities in the US.[14] The slow increase in the number of such networks is a result of four conflicting factors: uncertain definition of services for which the consumer is willing to pay, the fees the consumer is willing to pay for such services, relatively high cost of the network components, and regulatory conditions that are uncertain and unfavorable to investment in FTTH networks.

In spite of these factors, FTTH networks seem poised for significant growth in the near future. This growth is a result of reduced component costs, definition of at least two network designs that result in low cost per node and removal of some of the uncertain regulatory issues.

## 1.5.4 FIBER COMPONENTS

All fiber networks contain fiber links between transmitters and receivers. In most cases, the duplex communication requires two fibers per link. Each link contains fiber, cable, connectors, a transmitter, a receiver, and hardware (Figure 1-17). Some networks include splices and passive devices. Each of these components has specific functions.

### 1.5.4.1 FIBER

The function of the fiber (Figure 1-18) is to carry, or guide, the light between a transmitter and a receiver with minimum signal distortion and minimum power loss. With this function, the pulse dispersion

---

[13] ESCON is a SAN.

[14] Source: The FTTH Council, www.ftthcouncil.org.

(3.3.1) and attenuation rate (3.3.3) become important performance parameters.

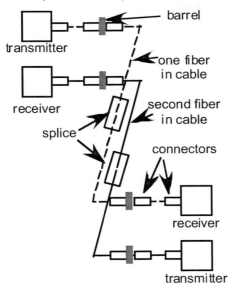

Figure 1-17: Functional Diagram Of A Duplex Fiber Link

Worldwide, all data communication fibers are glass fibers with a glass diameter of 125 µm (approximately 0.005").[15] These small glass fibers cannot be used without protection.

Figure 1-18: Optical Fiber With Cladding Darkened

### 1.5.4.2    CABLE

The cable (Figure 1-19) is the package that provides this protection. The cable protects the fiber during both installation and use.

The cable protects the fiber from degradation of optical and mechanical properties as long as the cable is used within the limits for which it has been designed. These limits include installation limits and environmental limits. The network designer defines both types of limits. However, the installer controls the conditions imposed on the cable during installation. Therefore, the installer must be

---

[15] The conversion factor is 25.4 µm to 0.001".

aware of the installation specifications of the cables he is installing.

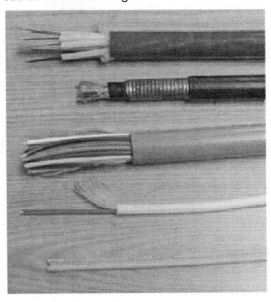

Figure 1-19: Optical Cables

### 1.5.4.3    CONNECTIONS

The light travels in the central region of the fiber. This region, with a diameter of one half to one twelfth the diameter of the glass, is small enough to require precise alignment whenever light enters or leaves a fiber. Connections, either connectors (Figure 1-20 and Chapter 5) or splices (Chapter 6), provide precise alignment to minimize power loss along the link. By minimizing power loss, the connections contribute to adequate power level at the receiver.

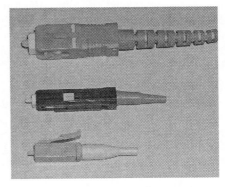

Figure 1-20: Optical Connectors

### 1.5.4.4    OPTOELECTRONICS

Jointly, the transmitter and receiver are called optoelectronics (Figure 1-21). The transmitter converts an electrical signal to an optical signal. The receiver performs the reverse conversion. The function of both devices is conversion with maximum signal accuracy. In digital systems, this accuracy specification is the 'bit error rate' (BER). The BER the ratio of error bits to total bits. In a fiber data network, each end of each link contains a transmitter and a receiver. This combination is known as a 'transceiver'.

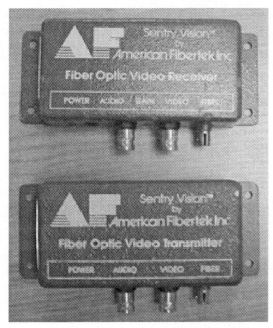

Figure 1-21: Video Transmitter-Receiver Pair

### 1.5.4.5 HARDWARE

While the fiber, cable, connections and optoelectronics allow the link to function optically, these components require protect-ion to provide reliable operation. The function of hardware (9) is provision of reliability to the network.

Hardware includes all products other than passive devices and those addressed. Hardware products include conduit, inner duct, enclosures, splice trays, splice covers, cable hangers, pedestals, cable raceways, and cable trays.

### 1.5.4.6 PASSIVE DEVICES

Passive devices (7) are couplers, splitters, wavelength division multiplexers and de-multiplexers, rotary joints, optical amplifiers, fiber switches, and rotators. Passive devices are used in some networks, such as CATV,

those based on 10BASE-FP, and fiber-to-the-home (FTTH) networks. These devices manipulate light as light. They do not require conversion of the optical signal into an electrical signal in order to perform this manipulation.

While passive devices simplify network design and can reduce network cost, they have a price: optical power loss that can be significant. As an example of this loss, consider a 32 port optical splitter: the power drop from input to output port is 16-17 dB. In contrast, the maximum power loss allowed between some data communication transmitters and receivers is between 2.38 dB and 16 dB (Table 8-1).

From the installer's perspective, the passive device creates power loss and a potential for reflectance (5.3.4). These two characteristics will be of concern to the installer.

## 1.6   SUMMARY

Networks enable communication between computers and peripherals. Optical networks offers advantages over other networks using other media. The optical network consists of a series of links arranged in a logical and physical topology. Each link consists of fibers enclosed in a protective cable structure, connectors and/or splices, and optoelectronics. In some networks, such as advanced optical telephone networks and CATV networks, the links will include passive devices.

## 1.7   REVIEW QUESTIONS

1.  How may advantages does optical fiber transmission offer?

2.  What are these advantages?

3.  Define WDM

4.  Define CWDM.

5.  Define DWDM.

6.  Why is a passive device called passive?

7.  What is the advantage of a passive device?

8. What are the disadvantages of a passive device?

9. In what two types of networks are you likely to find a passive device?

10. What is the most common topology for a fiber data network?

11. What is the most commonly used network standard?

12. True of false: the technical name for FDDI is 802.3.

13. What is the most common topology for a fiber telephone network?

14. Define a transceiver.

15. What type of communication does a transceiver enable?

16. True of false: Ethernet uses an analog transmission.

## 1.8   ADDITIONAL REFERENCES

Local Area Networks, The Next Generation, Thomas W. Madron, Wiley and Sons, 1991, ISBN 0-471-52250-3

LAN Tutorial, Patricia Schnaidt (Ed.), Miller Freeman Publications, 1990

Data Network Design, Darren L. Spohn, McGraw- Hill, 1997, ISBN 0-07-060363-4

Data and Computer Communications, William Stallings, 1988 MacMillian Publishing Company, ISBN 0-02-415454-7

Fast Ethernet, Dawn Of A New Network, Howard W. Johnson, 1996, Prentice-Hall PTR, ISBN 0-13-352643-7

Networking For Dummies, Douglas Lowe, 1999, IDG Books Worldwide, ISBN 0-7645-0498-3

Data Communication Technology, James Martin, 1988, Prentice-Hall International, ISBN 0-13-196643-X

The Business Guide To Local Area Networks, William Stallings, 1990, Howard W. Sams & Company, ISBN 0-672-22728-2

Understanding Local Area Networks, Stan Schatt, 1990, Howard W. Sams & Company, ISBN 0-672-27303-9

Handbook of Data Communications And Computer Networks, Dimitris N. Chorafas, 1991, TAB Professional and Reference Books, ISBN 0-8306-9690-3

Gigabit Ethernet Handbook, Stephen Saunders, 1998, McGraw-Hill, ISBN 0-07-057971-7

How Networks Work, Frank J. Derfler, Jr. And Les Freed, QUE Corporation, ISBN 0-7897-1595-3

The McGraw-Hill High-Speed LANs Handbook, Stephen Saunders, 1996, McGraw-Hill, ISBN 0-07-057199-6

# 2    A LIGHT OVERVIEW

Chapter Objectives: from this chapter, you will learn the language of light. With this language, you will be able to understand the behavior of light in fibers and connectors and understand the significance of the different types of fiber (3).

## 2.1    LIGHT LANGUAGE

Before we can present any concept of the behavior of light in a fiber, we must present the language of light.

## 2.2    BEHAVIOR

Light can be described by at least three different concepts: rays, particles, and waves or energy fields.

Often, light is described as a 'ray' since it travels in a straight line. In addition, light is described as a particle, since light reflects in a manner similar to that in which a particle bounces. Finally, light is described as a wave in that it behaves in the manner of waves. For example, when light from one source interferes with light from another source, an overlapping of the peaks of the waves from one source with the troughs of the waves from the second source can result in cancellation, or no light. Waves carry energy, as we all know from being in the water during a windy day. These concepts of light as a wave and as an energy field become important in understanding the importance of singlemode mode field diameter (3.2.3).

## 2.3    LIGHT PROPERTIES

As applied to fiber optic transmission, light has the characteristics of wavelength, spectral width, speed, power, reflection, dispersion and refraction. We use these characteristics to describe the behavior of light in optical fibers. In this section, we examine those characteristics.

### 2.3.1    WAVELENGTH

When people think about light, they tend to think of color. If we speak with technical terms, we use the term, 'wavelength'.

Light has a periodic, or wave-like nature. This nature has a period of repetition, which we call its wavelength. A stone dropped in a pond creates ripples with a circular form.

The distance from peak to peak, or from trough to trough, is the 'wavelength' of the waves in the water. Similarly, light exhibits behavior that indicates its wave-like nature. The wavelength of light, $\lambda$, is the measure, in nanometers (nm), of the distance between the peaks, or between successive troughs.

The wavelength of the light in a fiber is important, because the behavior of the light in that fiber depends upon its wavelength.

### 2.3.2    SPECTRAL WIDTH

When we use the term 'wavelength' in fiber optics, we imply, incorrectly, that light has a single wavelength. In almost all cases, the opposite state is true: the light used in optical fiber communication systems, includes a range of wavelengths centered around a 'central', or 'peak' wavelength (Figure 2-1). The measure of this range is the 'spectral width' of the light. Each wavelength in the output of the light source travels at a slightly different speed in the fiber. As you will learn (3), the spectral width of the light is one factor that determines the accuracy with which the fiber will transmit the light.

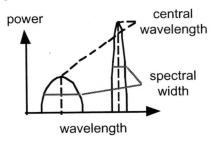

Figure 2-1: Central Wavelength and Spectral Width

### 2.3.3    LIGHT SPEED

We all learned about the speed of light in school: the speed of light, c, is the speed at which light travels in a vacuum.[1] However,

---

[1] c= 2.994 x10$^8$ m/sec.

the speed of light in any material is less than that in a vacuum. The technical term for speed of light in a material is 'index of refraction,' also know as the 'refractive index'.[2] This term is abbreviated as RI, IR and $\eta$.[3]

The RI is defined as:

RI= (speed of light in vacuum/speed of light

in a material)

Equation 2-1

With this definition, the RI is always greater than 1. The RI of optical fibers ranges from approximately 1.46 to 1.52 (Appendix 1). The IR is used to calibrate the OTDR for accurate fiber length measurements.

### 2.3.4   OPTICAL POWER

We all know that light has intensity, also known as power. For example, when a strobe light is flashed at us, we blink because of the high intensity. However, when a traffic signal changes color, we do not blink, because the low intensity does not overload the receptors in our eyes.

In fiber optics, power is measured in two ways: by absolute power level and by relative power level. When we measure intensity as an absolute power level, we use two terms: milliwatts (or microwatts) and dBm (or dBµ).

A milliwatt is one one-thousandth of a watt. A dBm is a power level relative to one milliwatt. Similarly, a dBµ is a power level relative to one one-millionth of a watt.

dBm is defined as:

dBm= 10 log (power level/one milliwatt)

Equation 2-2

Here are several examples:

   1 milliwatt = 0 dBm

   10 milliwatt = +10 dBm

   One tenth of a milliwatt = –10 dBm

   1 microwatt = 0 dBµ and

10 microwatt = + 10 dBµ

We use the terms dBm and dBµ as measures of the power level launched into a fiber by a transmitter and the power level required by the receiver for proper functioning.

When we measure intensity as a relative power level, we use the term dB. A dB is defined as:

dB= 10 log (new power level/arbitrary

reference power level)

Equation 2-4

We use the term dB to indicate: the power loss of a component in a fiber network; the total loss in a fiber link; and the maximum loss that can occur between a properly functioning transmitter and receiver pair.

For example, fiber optic connectors are commonly specified with a maximum loss of 0.75 dB/pair. Transmitter-receiver pairs can be specified with a maximum allowable loss of 12 dB (Table 8-1).

### 2.3.5   REFLECTION

We all recognize reflections. They occur in our daily life. For example, we see the sky reflected in a lake and we can see ourselves dimly reflected when we look through a closed window.

Both of these types of reflections play an important part in optical links. Let us reflect upon these two commonly occurring reflective events in order to understand the behavior of light in fibers and connections.

When we see the sky reflected in a lake, we are seeing a phenomenon that results from a change in the speed of light at the air-water boundary. This change results in nearly total reflection as long as the angle of reflection is proper. In the terms of physics, we see the sky as long as the rays of light strike the water within a 'critical angle' (Figure 2-2). If we look at the water closer and closer to our feet, we notice that, at some angle, we stop seeing the sky. Instead, we see into the water. Temporarily, we call the maximum angle at which the

---

[2] The term group index is also used.

[3] $\eta$ is the Greek letter 'eta'.

reflection occurs, the critical angle.[4] This concept of reflection within a critical angle becomes important in understanding the operation of step index multimode fibers (3.2.1).

We might be tempted to use the term 'critical angle.' However, the technical term for critical angle is 'numerical aperture' (NA). The NA, a measure of the critical angle, is defined:

NA= sine (critical angle)

Equation 2-3

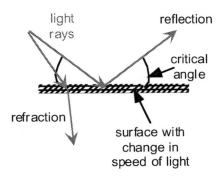

Figure 2-2: Reflection At An Interface

Since the sine of an angle, in degrees, is a dimensionless[5] number, the NA is dimension-less (Table 2-1).

| Critical Angle, ° | NA |
|---|---|
| 8.05 | 0.14 |
| 11.53 | 0.20 |
| 15.96 | 0.275 |

Table 2-1: Nominal NA Values

When we see our dim reflection on the surface of a closed window, we are seeing a partial, or 'Fresnel' reflection. A Fresnel reflection can occur any time light moves from one medium to another. More precisely, such a reflection will occur if the speed of light in the two media, air and glass, are different. Such reflections are important in fiber communication systems because connectors and splices create

---

[4] For more technical detail, review a physics text for 'Snell's Law'.

[5] Dimensionless means that we define a characteristic without units of measure. Most characteristics, such as weight, height, speed etc. requires units, such as pounds, inches, miles per hour.

locations at which the speed of light will change. As such, connector and splice reflections can occur, resulting in signal transmission errors (5).

### 2.3.6    REFRACTION

We have all seen refraction, or bending of light. When we look at a pen in a glass of water from the side, the pen appears to be bent (Figure 2-3). This bending occurs whenever light moves from a material with one speed of light to a material with another speed of light. This bending becomes important in under-standing the operation of graded index multimode fibers (3.2.2).

Figure 2-3: Refraction of Light

### 2.3.7    DISPERSION

Light that enters a fiber end enters the fiber at approximately the same time. The same cannot be said of the light that exits the opposite end. As light travels through a fiber, the optical power disperses, or spreads, with time. This phenomenon, known as 'pulse dispersion' pulse spreading and pulse broadening, determines the accuracy with which a fiber transmits data (3.3.1).

When light is described as an energy wave or field, it has two orthogonal axes, the E, or electromotive force, and the H, or magneto motive force. The energy in these two axes can travel at different speeds in a fiber, resulting in additional dispersion, known as polarization mode dispersion (PMD).

---

## 2.4   SUMMARY

Light has characteristics, with terms and units of measure. We use wavelength and spectral width with units of nanometers (nm); power, with units of dBm or dB; speed of light in an optical material with the dimensionless index of refraction; and critical angle with the dimensionless numerical aperture.

We know that light reflects and refracts, has behavior that can be described with the terms rays, particles, waves, and energy fields; and that optical power disperses as it travels through a fiber.

With these basic concepts, you will easily understand the behavior of light in optical fibers (3).

## 2.5   REVIEW QUESTIONS

1. What are the units of absolute power measurement?

2. What are the units of relative power measurement?

3. Why do you need to understand the two types of reflection?

4. Why is dispersion important?

5. What is the technical term for critical angle?

6. What are the units of measure of this technical term?

7. What are the units of measure for the index of refraction?

8. Where is a Fresnel reflection important?

9. Express 100 mW in terms of dBm.

10. Express 1000 µW in terms of dBm.

11. The transmitter of a link launches 1 mW into a fiber. The receiver requires at least 100 µW for accurate operation. Express the optical power budget in dB for this transmitter-receiver pair.

# 3    FIBER

Chapter Objectives: from this chapter, you will learn the types of fiber, the advantages of these types, the language of fibers, and the numbers that describe fibers and their performances.

## 3.1    STRUCTURE

The fiber is the medium through which light travels. The fiber's function is to guide the light between the transmitter and receiver with minimum signal distortion. Minimum signal distortion means of minimum power loss and minimal difference between the input and output signals.

The fiber provides this function through its structure. The structure consists of at least two, but usually three, regions. These regions are the core, the cladding, and the primary coating (Figure 3-1 and Figure 3-2).

A= core= 8.2-62.5 µm

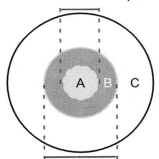

B=cladding= 125 µm
C= primary coating

Figure 3-1: Fiber Structure

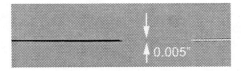

Figure 3-2: An Optical Fiber With Darkened Cladding

The core is the central region of the fiber in which most of the light energy travels. The cladding surrounds the core, confines the light to the core, and increases the fiber size so that the fiber is easily handled. The primary coating, formerly called the buffer coating, protects the cladding from mechanical and chemical attack so that the fiber retains its intrinsic high strength.[1] The installer removes, or strips, this coating for connector installation and splicing.

These three regions are characterized by their diameters, stated in microns (µm). In telephone and data networks, the core diameter can range from a small as 8.3 microns (µm) to 62.5 microns.

Beginning in 1985, data network, or short-haul LAN, standards specified the 62.5 µm core diameter fiber. As a result, this fiber has dominated data networks.

The latest of these standards, Fiber Channel, 1000BASE-SX, 10GBASE-SX, and TIA/EIA-568 B, allow use of both the 62.5 µm and the 50 µm fibers. In the future, we expect to see increasing use of this reduced core diameter, increased bandwidth fiber. As a practical matter, the core diameter is related to the fiber NA (Table 3-1).

| Core Diameter | NA |
|---------------|-------|
| 8.3-10 | 0.14 |
| 50 | 0.20 |
| 62.5 | 0.275 |

Table 3-1: Nominal Fiber NA Values

For data and telephone networks, the cladding diameter is always 125 microns, although there are fibers for other applications with cladding diameters between 140 and 1,000 microns

The primary coating[2] is usually 245 microns in diameter but can be as high as 500 microns in diameter. As a practical matter,

---

[1] A common misconception is that the coating provides strength to the fiber. The reality is that the coating protects the cladding from mechanical and chemical damage, thus allowing the fiber to retain its intrinsic high strength.

[2] Most fibers have an ultra violet (UV)-cured acrylate primary coating. This coating has two layers, a soft, low modulus inner layer and a hard outer layer.

---

the installer rarely need concern himself with the diameter of the primary coating.

As a matter of designation, fibers are referred to by their core diameter, cladding diameter, and, occasionally, by their coating diameter. For instance, a fiber might be called a 62.5/125 fiber or a 62.5/125/250 fiber. Occasionally, the core and cladding diameters are reversed, as in 125/62.5.

## 3.2   TYPES AND CHARACTERISTICS

The core and cladding can be glass or plastic. There are fibers with glass cores and glass cladding; fibers with plastic cores and plastic cladding; and fibers with glass cores and plastic cladding. Since fibers used in data and telephone networks have glass core and glass cladding, we shall focus this book on these all glass fibers. For all-glass fibers, the core and cladding are fused and inseparable.

There are three fundamental types of fibers:

> Step index multimode[3]

> Graded index multimode

> Singlemode

The term 'multimode' indicates that rays of light can travel multiple paths in the core. The term 'singlemode' indicates that rays of light behave as though they are traveling along a single path in the core.

The fiber type depends upon the core diameter and the structure of the core. Each of these three types has advantages.

### 3.2.1   STEP INDEX MULTIMODE

The first type of optical fiber produced was a large core, plastic optical (POF) step index (SI) multimode fiber.[4] Step index fibers have a relatively large core with a single chemical composition, and limited bandwidth.[5] SI

---

[3] The term 'mode' can be crudely translated to mean 'path'.

[4] While graded index POF fibers exist, most are step index.

[5] The correct technical term is bit-rate, since data systems transmit digital signals. However, the analog term 'bandwidth' is commonly used to

fibers are not used in data networks. They are not included any of the U.S. data standards.

Because the SI fiber has a single composition in the core, the speed of light throughout the core is constant (Figure 3-3). Because the composition changes at the core-cladding boundary, rays of light can be reflected at that boundary.

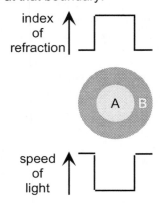

Figure 3-3: Core Profile Of Step Index Fiber

Rays of light that enter the core at an angle less than or equal to the critical angle, which is determined by the NA of the fiber (2.3.5), will be reflected at the cladding boundary and remain in the core (Figure 3-4). Rays of light that enter the core at an angle greater than the critical angle enter the cladding and do not reach the receiver (Figure 3-5).

Rays of light reflected at one side of the fiber core travel to the opposite side of the core. At the opposite side, the rays are again reflected, as long as the rays remain within the angle defined by the NA of the fiber (Figure 3-6). The name of this process is 'total internal reflection.'

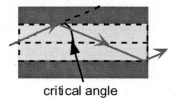

critical angle

Figure 3-4: Reflection of Rays In SI Fiber

---

mean digital bit-rate. Reluctantly, we bow to this misuse to avoid confusing our readers.

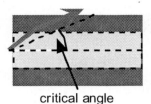

Figure 3-5: Escape of Rays Outside Critical Angle

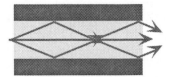

Figure 3-6: Ray Paths In A Step Index Fiber

In a SI fiber, rays of light in the same pulse can travel both parallel to the axis and at any angle to the axis up to the maximum angle defined by the NA. While these two rays will enter the fiber at the same time, they will travel different paths, different path lengths and can arrive at the output end of the fiber at significantly different times. This difference in time of arrival results in a significant amount of dispersion (2.3.7). This dispersion results in a SI bandwidth that is too low to be of much use. For this reason, the SI fibers are not used in data networks.

## 3.2.2    GRADED INDEX MULTIMODE

The second type of multimode fiber, a graded index (GI) fiber, has a relatively large core with up to 2500 different chemical compositions, and an increased bandwidth. It is difficult and expensive to make, because it contains roughly 2500 different chemical compositions in the 0.00125" radius of the core. All of the data transmission standards for local area networks[6] (LANs) require the use of GI multimode fibers.

The information carrying capacity of multimode fibers is specified by two terms, the "bandwidth distance product" (BWDP) and differential modal dispersion (DMD). The first term, bandwidth distance product, is measured in units of MHz-km, with typical values from 160 MHz-km to 500 MHz-km.

---

[6] LANs are also known as short haul networks.

This term is applicable to fibers that carry light from LEDs (8.2.1).

The second term, differential modal dispersion, is applicable to fibers that carry light from VCSELs (8.2.3). Fibers designed for use with VCSELs are 'laser optimized' fibers, a form of application specific fibers (3.3.2). Such fibers have a typical bandwidth distance product of 2000 MHz-km.

The GI fiber is constructed with many compositions in the core. These compositions are chosen so that the speed of light in the center of the core is lowest (Figure 3-7). The speed of light in the core increases as the radial distance from the axis increases. With this core structure, axial rays at the center of the core travel the shortest path length at the slowest speed. Critical angle rays travel the longest path length at the highest average speed.

This GI multimode fiber core structure allows for compensation of the different path lengths. This compensation allows rays that travel different path lengths to arrive at approximately the same time. This compensation reduces the amount of dispersion and increases the bandwidth to a level acceptable for use in data networks. For this reason, GI multimode fibers are specified for use in data networks.

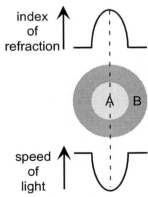

Figure 3-7: GI Core Profile

A second origin of reduced dispersion is refraction of rays. At each boundary between the layers, the rays bend back towards the axis. This bending reduces the difference between the path lengths. Thus, light tends to travel in what appear to be 'curved' paths in a graded index multimode fiber (Figure 3-8).

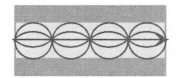

Figure 3-8: Curved Ray GI Paths

## 3.2.3    SINGLEMODE

While the GI multimode fiber provides increased capacity, or increased transmission distance, it does so at a significant manufacturing cost. This cost results from the need to create a fiber with 2500 different chemical compositions in 0.00125" (or less) and maintain those 2500 different compositions constant for the length of the fiber. This length is more than 600 miles! The manufacturing difficulty and the limitations on maximum possible GI BWDP restricted the usefulness of this fiber and led to a search for another fiber with increased capacity.

In the 1970's, the clever scientists and engineers working on fiber manufacturing found such a fiber. The design of this fiber arose from consideration of the quantum mechanics of light. This consideration indicated that all rays of light would behave as though they were traveling parallel to the axis of the fiber (Figure 3-9). Such propagation would result if the core were sufficiently small and the wavelength sufficiently long. With all rays traveling the same path, the multiple path dispersion of SI and GI fibers would be eliminated. Since light 'rays' in such a fiber would follow a single path, this fiber became known as 'singlemode' in North America and 'monomode', elsewhere.[7]

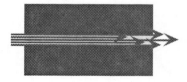

Figure 3-9: 'Apparent' Ray Paths In Singlemode Fiber

---

[7] Light in a singlemode fiber does not behave as a ray. Instead, it behaves as an energy field. For this reason, we use the phrase 'behave as though' and put the word rays in quotes.

Singlemode fibers have three important characteristics: very small core diameter, essentially unlimited bandwidth and a mode field diameter (MFD). This high bandwidth makes the singlemode fiber ideal for long haul, or inter-exchange telephone networks. The most common singlemode fiber core diameter is 8.3 µm.

We specify the capacity of singlemode fibers with the term 'dispersion rate' in units of picoseconds/nanometer/kilometer (ps/(nm-km)). A typical maximum dispersion rate for a single wavelength singlemode fiber at its optimum wavelength is 2.8 ps/(nm-km). The first singlemode fibers had a maximum dispersion rate of 3.5 ps/(nm-km).

The third singlemode characteristic, the mode field diameter (MFD), is the diameter within which most of the light energy travels. The MFD (Table 3-2) is larger than the core diameter by approximately 1 µm. Thus, some of the energy in a singlemode fiber travels in the cladding (Figure 3-10).

core≈ 8.2-10 µm

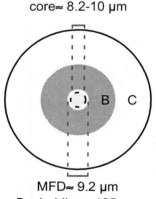

MFD≈ 9.2 µm
B=cladding= 125 µm
C= primary coating

Figure 3-10: Singlemode Core Diameter and MFD

| Fiber Type | MFD, µm |
|---|---|
| OFS Depressed Clad | 8.8 ± 0.5 @1310 nm |
| OFS Matched Clad | 9.3 ± 0.5 @1310 nm |
| OFS True Wave | 8.4 ± 0.6 @1550 nm |
| Corning LEAF ®: | 9.2-10.0 @ 1550 nm |
| Corning SMF-28 | 9.2 ± 0.6 @ 1310 nm |
| Corning SMF-28 | 10.4 ± 0.8 @ 1550 nm |
| Corning MetroCor | 8.1± 0.5 @ 1550 |

Table 3-2: Mode Field Diameters

To understand this phenomenon, we step away from fiber optics for a minute. Imagine that you are working with a son or daughter on a high school science fair project. The project is to build a model of a single mode fiber. You and your son or daughter have decided to use a piece of pipe to simulate the fiber. The center of the pipe simulates the core. The wall of the pipe simulates the cladding. You decide to use a ping-pong ball to simulate the photon traveling down the core of the fiber. You intend to shoot the ping-pong ball straight down the pipe. The ping-pong ball models, or simulates, the particle-like behavior of a photon. However, light has some of the properties of an energy field. At this time, you have not modeled the properties of an energy field. After additional consideration, you decide to rub the ping-pong ball with a piece of fur or silk in order to create a static charge on the ball. The static charge creates an energy field.

As the ball travels close to the inside wall down the pipe, some of the static field travels in the wall. Analogously, some of the optical energy in a singlemode fiber travels in the cladding of the fiber.

## 3.3    PERFORMANCE

As a pulse of light travels through a fiber, the pulse changes in two ways: the width of the pulse is increased[8] and the height of the pulse is reduced. These two changes give rise to the two main optical performance characteristics of the fiber, dispersion and attenuation.

## 3.3.1    DISPERSION

Four types of dispersion are important in data transmission systems:[9]

> Modal dispersion

> Chromatic dispersion

> Material dispersion

> Waveguide dispersion

---

[8] We present dispersion with the assumption of digital transmission. With the assumption of analog transmission, dispersion results in a 'smearing' of the signal, making the signal less precise.

[9] A fifth type, polarization mode dispersion (PMD) becomes important between 2.5 and 10 Gbps.

### 3.3.1.1    MODAL DISPERSION

Modal dispersion occurs when different rays of light arrive at the fiber output end at different times due to different travel paths. This dispersion occurs in multimode fibers, but not in singlemode fibers. Model dispersion is the largest of the four types.

### 3.3.1.2    CHROMATIC DISPERSION

Chromatic dispersion occurs in a fiber due to the nature of the light traveling in that fiber. Chromatic dispersion occurs because all commercial fiber optic light sources emit a range of wavelengths (spectral width, 2.3.2). Different wavelengths travel at different speeds in all materials. Each of these wavelengths within the spectral width of the light source travels at a slightly different speed. Even if all the rays in a pulse are traveling the same path length, as occurs in a singlemode fiber, rays with different wavelengths will arrive at different times at the output end of the fiber.[10] The spectral width of the light source creates chromatic dispersion in the fiber. This form of dispersion is active in both multimode and singlemode fibers. Chromatic dispersion is the second largest of the four types.

### 3.3.1.3    MATERIAL DISPERSION

Material dispersion occurs in the fiber core because of the nature of that core. Optical fibers are glass fibers. Glass fibers are amorphous materials. Amorphous materials have no crystal structure, no constant and repeating atomic level structure. Two rays of light traveling the same path length and having the same wavelength will travel in different regions of the core. Because of the amorphous structure, these different regions will not have the same exact atomic level composition and the same exact speed of light. Atomic level differences in composition in the core result in differences in speed, just as the difference between the compositions in the GI core and cladding result in different speeds. This form of dispersion occurs in

---

[10] Remember the experiment high-school physics in which you separated the different wavelengths of light from a white light source bypassing the white light through a glass prism. One of the reasons the wavelengths separated was the fact that different wavelengths travel at different speeds in all materials.

both multimode and singlemode fibers. Material dispersion creates the fundamental limit on bandwidth and transmission distance. We cannot eliminate or compensate for material dispersion, as we can for modal and chromatic dispersions.

### 3.3.1.4  WAVEGUIDE DISPERSION

Waveguide dispersion is the spreading of energy due to the different speeds of light in the core and the cladding. This form of dispersion is most important in singlemode fibers, since a significant amount of energy travels in the cladding.

These four types of dispersion create the total pulse dispersion. If we were sending a single pulse down the fiber, such dispersion would be irrelevant to accuracy. However, we send multiple pulses, each within its own time interval. Each of these pulses spreads. If multiple pulses spread sufficiently so that energy from a pulse arrives at the fiber output end in a time interval not its own, the input and output signals may not be the same. In other words, we will experience signal in accuracy (Figure 3-11).

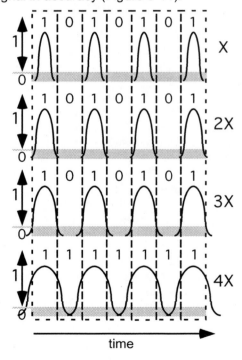

Figure 3-11: Pulse Dispersion Causes Signal Inaccuracy

Let us examine pulses of light during digital transmission (Figure 3-11). In digital

transmission systems, we have a threshhold power level. For power levels below the threshold, we call the signal 'zero'. For power levels above the threshold, we call the signal 'one'. This threshold may be at zero power or at some level above zero. [11]

In this figure, we transmit an alternating string of ones and zeros. Each of these ones (or zeroes) is created within a defined time interval. The size of this time interval is determined by many factors that are too complex for this book. Each of these ones is comprised of multiple rays of light that enter the fiber at the same time over range of angles. Each of these ones has a range of wavelengths. Each of these ones will experience material and waveguide dispersion.

Due to the four types of dispersion, the rays exit the fiber over a range of time. The first rays to arrive at the fiber output end are represented by the leading edge of each pulse; the last rays, by the trailing edge (Figure 3-11). The time difference between the leading and trailing edges is the pulse width.

As the fiber transmission distance increases, so does the pulse width at the output end. As pulse width increases, energy from one pulse will arrive at the output end of the fiber in the time interval of an adjacent pulse (Figure 3-11, 2X). If the pulse width is excessive, enough energy from one pulse will arrive at the fiber end in a time interval of an adjacent pulse. With excessive pulse width, a zero at the input end becomes a one at the output end (Figure 3-11, 4X).

From this presentation, you can see that the time interval for each bit at the receiver and the amount of dispersion that can occur without causing in signal inaccuracy both shrink as the bit rate increases. In addition, dispersion limits transmission distance.

In spite of the importance of pulse dispersion, the installer need not be concerned: dispersion is controlled by four factors- the size of the core, the manner in which light enters the core, the spectral

---

[11] To simplify this figure, we have ignored attenuation of the signal. In reality, the height of each pulse becomes less as the pulse travels further along the fiber.

width of the transmitter, and atomic level variations of the composition of the core. The installer can affect none of these factors to cause increased dispersion.

There is one exception. This exception occurs during troubleshooting of a high bit error rate (BER). If the power loss measurements all indicate proper installation and operation, the problem may be excessive transmission distance, which can result in differences between the input and output signals.[12]

## 3.3.2    APPLICATION SPECIFIC FIBERS

### 3.3.2.1    MULTIMODE

In addition to the standard GI multimode fibers, there is a number of application-specific fibers. These fibers, known as 'laser optimized,' are manufactured to meet the unique requirements of Gigabit Ethernet (1000BASE-SX) and 10 Gigabit Ethernet (10GBASE-SX, Table 3-3).

| Protocol | Product | Meters |
|----------|---------|--------|
| 1000BASE-SX | 160 MHz-km | 220 |
| 1000BASE-SX | 200 MHz-km | 275 |
| 1000BASE-SX | InfinicorCL1000 | 500 |
| 10GBASE-SX | 400 MHz-km | 66 |
| 10GBASE-SX | 500 MHz-km | 83 |
| 10GBASE-SX | Laser 150 | 150 |
| 10GBASE-SX | Laser 300 | 300 |
| 10GBASE-SX | Laser 500 | 500 |

Table 3-3: Standard And Application Specific Fiber Transmission Distances[13]

These fibers differ from the original, or standard, multimode fibers in that they have

a core profile (Figure 3-7) that is matched to the manner in which the transmitter launches light into the core. Through this matching, the fiber maximizes the transmission distance by minimizing dispersion. The basic advantage of these fibers is transmission distance in excess of those specified in the 1000BASE-SX and 10GBASE-SX standards (Table 3-3).

### 3.3.2.2    SINGLEMODE

Singlemode fibers have evolved. As a result, we have five different singlemode fibers:

- ➤ Non Dispersion Shifted (G.652)[14]
- ➤ Dispersion Shifted (DS, G.653)
- ➤ Dispersion Shifted, Non-Zero Dispersion (DS-NZD, G.655)
- ➤ Large Effective Area (LEAF™)
- ➤ Low Water/ Zero Water Peak

To understand the differences, we require a detailed knowledge of the behavior of singlemode fibers. For all fibers, attenuation rate and dispersion vary with wavelength. As wavelength increases, the attenuation rate becomes less (Figure 3-12). For this reason, operation of singlemode fibers at a wavelength of 1550 nm is desirable to achieve a reduced attenuation rate and increased transmission distance.

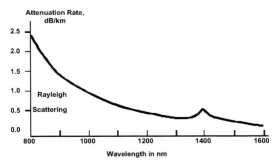

Figure 3-12: Attenuation Rate Vs. Wavelength for Silica Fibers[15]

However, singlemode fibers have an optimum wavelength for dispersion, the zero dispersion wavelength (ZDW). At this wavelength, the waveguide and material dispersions cancel out (Figure 3-13). With

---

[12] Imagine links from two locations to the same location (A to C and B to C). Image that a manager, not a fiber network designer, decides to transmit from location A to location C by cross connection at location B. While the individual links, A to B and C to B, may be sufficiently short to avoid excessive dispersion, the link A to C may have excessive dispersion.

[13] When the product is stated in 'MHz-km', the transmission distance is stated in the relevant standard. Otherwise, the manufacturer guarantees the transmission distance. Infinicor CL1000 is a trademark of Corning Inc. Laser 150, Laser 3000, and Laser 500 are trademarks of OFS.

[14] The G.65x is the designation of the ITU.

[15] Courtesy Corning Inc.

this cancellation, the fiber exhibits its minimum dispersion and maximum bandwidth or bit rate. The further the transmitter wavelength is from the ZDW, the larger will be the dispersion rate and the lower will be the bandwidth.

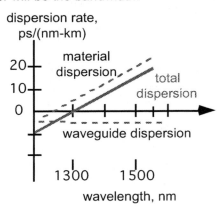

Figure 3-13: Dispersion Rate Vs. Wavelength For Singlemode Fibers[16]

The first singlemode fibers, called non-dispersion shifted (NDS) fibers, had a zero dispersion wavelength at approximately 1310 nm. These fibers could be used at a wavelength of 1550 nm to take advantage of the reduced attenuation rate at that wavelength. However, the dispersion rate at 1550 nm is 4-5 times that at 1310 nm. These two mechanisms work against each other: the reduced attenuation rate results in increased transmission distance, while the increased dispersion rate results in reduced transmission distance or reduced bit rate.

To provide both low attenuation rate and low dispersion rate, fiber designers created a second generation, singlemode fiber, the dispersion shifted fiber (DS). This fiber exhibits both low attenuation rate and low dispersion rate at 1550 nm through a design change that shifted the ZDW from 1310 nm to 1550 nm (Figure 3-14). This fiber behaves in a manner symmetrical to the NDS fiber: it exhibits low dispersion rate at 1550 nm and high dispersion rate at 1310 nm.

While the DS fiber extended transmission distances, it was best suited for use with only one or two wavelengths. To obtain

extremely high aggregate capacity on a single fiber, network designers wanted the ability to transmit multiple, closely spaced wavelengths. This process is known as dense wavelength division multiplexing (DWDM). When multiple, closely spaced, wavelengths travel on a DS fiber, they interact and interfere to create new wavelengths. This interaction creates noise, or signal errors, in wavelengths other than the two wavelengths that are interacting.

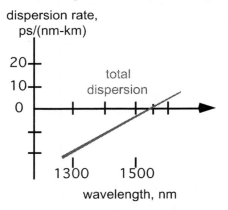

Figure 3-14: Total Dispersion For DS, G.654 Fiber

The cause for this interaction is the extremely low dispersion rate at 1550 nm. If there is a small level of dispersion, this interaction and interference become so low as to be inconsequential. The clever fiber designers developed a solution in the form of a third generation fiber: the dispersion shifted, non zero dispersion fiber (DS-NZD). This fiber has a ZDW close to, but not at, 1550 nm (Figure 3-15).[17] With a low level of dispersion, this interaction between multiple wavelengths was essentially eliminated. With this third generation, singlemode fiber, network operators could launch 200 different wavelengths into a single fiber.[18,19]

While this new fiber allowed for many wavelengths, each of approximately 10 Gbps and 1 mW of power, it created a new

[16] After Fiber Optics Handbook For Engineers and Scientists, (1990), Frederick C. Allard, p. 1.38.

[17] For example, the ZDW for Corning LS fiber is 1560 nm; that for OFS TrueWave™ Reach fiber, is less than 1405 nm.

[18] 200 is the number of wavelengths specified by the ITU.

[19] Lucent Technologies has demonstrated the ability to launch 1000 wavelengths into a single singlemode fiber.

problem. The process of shifting the ZDW resulted in a reduced MFD (3.2.3).[20] This reduction, in turn, resulted in an increased power density, in watts per square inch, which, in turn, resulted in non-linear optical effects that create transmission errors.

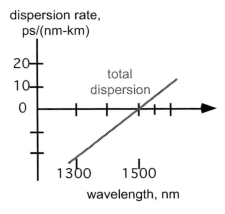

Figure 3-15: Dispersion For NZ-DSF Fiber

Corning Inc created the LEAF™ fiber, a DS-NZD fiber, in which the effective area in which the power is confined is larger than in standard DS-NZD fiber. This increased MFD results in reduced power density and level of transmission errors.

### 3.3.3    ATTENUATION

You have learned that dispersion limits the distance of transmission or the bit rate. The second major fiber characteristic, attenuation, or power loss, limits transmission distance, though in a different manner. If the power loss through a fiber is excessive, there be insufficient power delivered to receiver.

This power loss results from several mechanisms, the largest of which is 'Rayleigh scattering'. To understand Rayleigh scattering, let us step away from fiber optics. Imagine that you are in a dark dusty room, with a high intensity flashlight and a friend standing outside of the path of the beam. Your friend is able to see the dust in the air because the light from the

flashlight is scattered from its normal path by the dust in the air.

In an analogous manner, light traveling in the core of a fiber is scattered by the atoms in the core to the core-cladding boundary at an angle greater than the critical angle defined by the NA. Such light escapes from the core, reducing the power delivered to the receiver (Figure 3-16).

We refer to this power loss as "attenuation rate", which is specified in units of dB/km. The maximum and typical rates decrease as the core diameter decreases and as the wavelength increases (Table 3-4 and Table 3-5).

Figure 3-16: Rayleigh Scattering In Core

| Wavelength, nm | Core Diameter, μm | Attenuation Rate, dB/km |
|---|---|---|
| 850 | 62.5 | 3.5 |
| 850 | 50 | 3.0 |
| 1300 | 62.5 | 1.0 |
| 1300 | 50 | 1.0 |
| 1310 | 8.2 | 0.5 |
| 1550 | 8.2 | 0.25 |

Table 3-4: Maximum Cables Attenuation Rates

| Wavelength, nm | Core Diameter, μm | Attenuation Rate, dB/km |
|---|---|---|
| 850 | 62.5 | 2.8-3.0 |
| 850 | 50 | 2.5-2.7 |
| 1300 | 62.5 | 0.7 |
| 1300 | 50 | 0.7 |
| 1310 | 8.2 | 0.30-0.35 |
| 1550 | 8.2 | 0.20 |

Table 3-5: Typical Cable Attenuation Rates

The typical values are those that you should expect to see on properly installed cables. The network designer uses the maximum attenuation rate as a specification for cables. The network designer and installer use both the maximum and typical attenuation rates to calculate the acceptance value, which is the power loss value that the installer must not exceed for maximum reliability (14).

---

[20] For example, if 56 wavelengths, each with 1 mW of power, are launched into a fiber with a 9.2 μm MFD, and if 90 % of the power is within the MFD, the power density is 0.489 Megawatts /square inch.

➤ Power loss is the most important characteristic during installation, since installation mistakes can result in an excess power loss.

In addition to Rayleigh scattering, there are two causes of fiber-related excess power loss:

➤ Core offset, also called core-cladding non-concentricity, and

➤ Cladding non-circularity, also called ovality.

These two causes result in excess power loss at splices or connectors. Both conditions result in imperfect alignment of cores and subsequently excess power loss (Figure 3-17 and Figure 3-18).

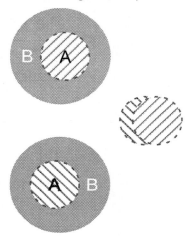

Figure 3-17: Core Offset And Excess Loss

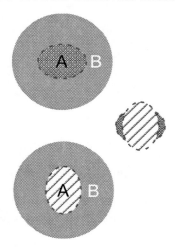

Figure 3-18: Cladding Non-Circularity and Excess Loss

Knowledge of these two characteristics becomes important during troubleshooting of excess connector loss that cannot be explained by any other reason. Fibers with low offset and ovality do not exhibit excess connection loss (Table 3-6).

| Fiber | Wavelength | Ovality | Offset, μm |
|---|---|---|---|
| Singlemode | 1310 nm | ≤ 1% | ≤ 0.6 |
| Singlemode | 1550 nm | ≤ 1% | ≤ 0.6 |
| Multimode | | ≤ 2% | ≤ 3.0 |

Table 3-6: Offset And Ovality Values[21]

## 3.4  SUMMARY

The installer needs to know the following fiber information:

➤ Wavelength(s), nm

➤ Core diameter, in μm

➤ NA, dimensionless

➤ Attenuation rate, dB/km, maximum

➤ Attenuation rate, dB/km, typical

➤ RI, dimensionless

The installer will match the wavelength of his testing light source to the wavelength in the transmitter. With such matching, the power loss measurement will simulate the loss that the transmitter-receiver pair will experience.

The installer will match the core diameter and the NA of the reference leads used in testing (13) to those characteristics of the fiber to be tested. Without such matching, the loss measurements will be higher than reality.

The installer will use the maximum and typical attenuation rates to calculate the acceptance value. This value is the maximum value at which the link can be accepted as being correctly and reliably installed (14).

The installer will use the RI to calibrate the OTDR. With such calibration, the OTDR length measurements will be accurate.

___

[21] These values are from Corning Inc. data sheets. Other manufacturers have similar values.

## 3.5    REVIEW QUESTIONS

1. Why should you know the core diameter?

2. Why should you know the NA?

3. Why should you know the wavelength?

4. Why should you know the attenuation rate?

5. Why should you know the IR?

6. What are the forms of dispersion?

7. Rate fiber types from low to high pulse spreading.

8. List common fiber core diameters from high pulse spreading to low pulse spreading.

9. Why should you know about pulse spreading?

10. Why should you know about power loss?

11. Can the installer affect pulse spreading of and installed a network?

12. What of the units of fiber diameters?

13. What are typical multimode core/cladding diameters?

14. What are typical singlemode core/cladding diameters?

15. What are the units of measurement for attenuation rate?

16. What are typical maximum attenuation rates?

17. What are typical wavelengths for multimode fibers?

18. What are typical wavelengths for singlemode fibers?

19. What are the units of measure of pulse spreading for multimode fibers?

20. What are the units of measure of pulse spreading for singlemode fibers?

21. What are typical values of pulse spreading for multimode fibers?

22. True or false: you can strip the cladding from the fiber.

23. True or false: the light energy travels in the core of all fibers.

24. True or false: the standards recommend the use of SI fibers.

# 4    CABLE

Chapter Objectives: from this chapter, you will learn the types of cables, the advantages of these types, the language of cables, and the numbers with which you will work.

## 4.1    STRUCTURE

While the fiber can easily perform the task of optical communication, it cannot, in and of itself, survive installation and use without additional protection.[1,2]

The structure, with its six elements, provides this additional protection. These elements are:

> ➢ Buffer tubes
> ➢ Water blocking materials
> ➢ Strength members
> ➢ Binding tapes
> ➢ Jacket(s)
> ➢ Armor

## 4.1.1    BUFFER TUBES

The buffer tube[3] is the first layer of plastic placed around a fiber by the cable manufacturer. This buffer tube can be a loose tube, with a diameter of 2-3 mm (Figure 4-1 and Figure 4-2)[4], or a tight tube, with a diameter of 0.9 mm (900 μm) (Figure 4-3 and Figure 4-4).

In a loose buffer tube, the inner diameter of the buffer tube is larger than the outside diameter of the fiber. As such, a loose buffer tube can contain one or more fibers. The usual number of fibers in a loose buffer tube can be 6, 12 or as high as 400.[5]

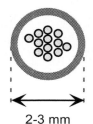

2-3 mm

Figure 4-1: Loose Buffer Tube Cross Section

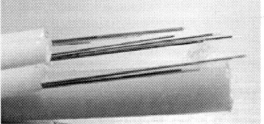

Figure 4-2: Loose Buffer Tube Cable

0.9 mm

Figure 4-3: Tight Buffer Tube Cross Section

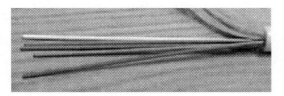

Figure 4-4: Tight Buffer Tube Cable

### 4.1.1.1    LOOSE BUFFER TUBE DESIGNS

Loose buffer tube designs were those used at the beginning of the development of fiber-optic cables. The loose buffer tube designs have four advantages:

> ➢ High reliability due to a 'mechanical dead zone'
> ➢ Relatively low cost

---

[1] Imagine five miles of directly buried glass optical fiber with a diameter of 0.010"!

[2] Some fiber-optic cable manufacturers refer to themselves as being " packaging houses".

[3] Caution: do not confuse the terms 'buffer coating' or primary coating, a fiber term, with 'buffer tube', a cable term.

[4] A central loose buffer tube cable or a ribbon cable can have a buffer tube diameter of 0.5 ".

[5] Fiber counts as high as 400 occur in a ribbon cable.

---

➢ Relatively small size

➢ Ease of achieving moisture resistance and

In these designs, the fiber is a longer than the buffer tube. This excess fiber length and the space between the fiber and the buffer tube create a 'mechanical dead zone' (Figure 4-5). This dead zone improves the reliability of the loose tube design over that of the tight tube design.[6]

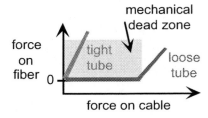

Figure 4-5: The Mechanical Dead Zone

The mechanical dead zone is a range of force that can be applied to the cable without imposing force on the fiber. This zone exists in tension, bending and compression.

Loose tube designs tend to have reduced costs because they have smaller sizes for a given fiber count than do tight buffer tube cables. This cost advantage increases as the fiber count increases.

The loose tube designs are preferred for outdoor cables. This preference is due to reduced cost for the fiber counts typical of outdoor cables and the ability to place stiff, tough jacketing materials over the loose buffer tubes. It is difficult to put such stiff materials around fibers in tight buffer tubes.

The loose buffer tube designs can achieve moisture resistance easily. Water blocking gels and greases can be placed inside of the buffer tubes and in all unfilled spaces outside the buffer tubes. Alternatively, super-absorbent polymer (SAP) tapes, yarns and powders can be placed inside the buffer tubes and under the jacket.

---

[6] In making this statement, we acknowledge various definitions of reliability   . With some definitions, loose tube cables are more reliable than tight tube cables. With one specific definition, tight tube cables are more reliable than the loose tube cables.

The loose buffer tube designs have three disadvantages:

➢ Reduced flexibility

➢ Increased cost for termination and

➢ Increased cost for end preparation, when gel filled and grease blocked[7]

The increased cost results from the needs to remove gel and grease water-blocking materials and to install a furcation tube on each fiber (Figure 4-6).

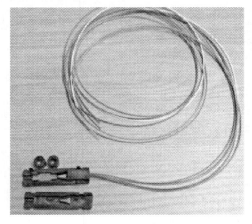

Figure 4-6: Furcation Kit For Loose Tube Fibers

4.1.1.2    TIGHT BUFFER TUBE DESIGNS

In a tight buffer tube, the inner diameter of the buffer tube is the same as the outer diameter of the fiber (Figure 4-3). As such, a tight buffer tube contains a single fiber.

Tight tube cable designs have two advantages:

➢ End alignment of a broken fiber and

➢ Sufficient strengthening of the fiber for connectorization

The primary advantage is end alignment of a broken fiber (Figure 4-7). Because there is no space between the outside of the fiber in the inside of the tight buffer tube, broken

---

[7] Pearson Technologies has measured the time to prepare gel-filled, grease-blocked cables. A 24-fiber cable requires 2.5 man-hours per end to prepare, for a rate of 0.11 man-hours per fiber per end. We estimate that the same cable with super-absorbent polymers requires less than one man-hour per end.

fiber ends cannot move laterally to create core offset, the major source of power loss in all connections. Thus, a broken fiber in a tight tube cable design can provide continuity of signal transmission. In the early 1980's, this advantage provided the incentive for use of tight tube designs in the field tactical, military applications.

The second advantage of tight tube designs is the strengthening provided by the tight buffer tube. The buffer tube strengthens the fiber sufficiently for connector installation. The typical tight buffer tube diameter is 900 µm (0.036"). This diameter creates a structure that is sufficiently rugged to allow repeated handling without fiber damage.

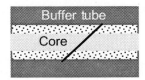

Figure 4-7: End Alignment Of A Broken Fiber In A Tight Buffer Tube

A 250 µm primary coated fiber is not sufficiently rugged to allow repeated handling. As such, the individual fibers in loose tubes must be strengthened with a furcation kit[8] (Figure 4-6) before connectors can be installed. A furcation kit to adds $2 to $3 per fiber end to the installation cost.

## 4.1.2    WATER BLOCKING MATERIALS

Fiber optic cables require moisture resistance. This resistance prevents cables channeling water into the electronics, fiber breakage from freezing water, and degradation of fiber strength from ground water

When they are gel filled and grease blocked ('filled and blocked'), loose tube designs have a relatively high cost for end preparation. Because of this disadvantage, most current moisture-resistant cables are made with the super-absorbent polymer (SAP) materials. These materials convert water to a gel. In conversion, the gel swells

to many times the original volume of the SAP. Such swelling blocks further moisture ingress.[9]

## 4.1.3    STRENGTH MEMBER MATERIALS

All fiber optic cables contain strength member materials. These materials prevent excessive stretching of fibers during cable installation. During this installation, the installer attaches the strength members to the pulling rope. In all dielectric, self-support cables (ADSS), the strength members allow the cables to withstand high long-term loads without fiber breakage.

Strength member materials include aramid yarns, such as Kevlar®, flexible fiberglass rovings, rigid fiberglass epoxy rods, and steel wires.[10] These strength members can be located in the center of the cable, as a central strength member, outside the buffer tubes and inside the jacket, or between jackets.

## 4.1.4    BINDING TAPES

Binding tapes, often Mylar, are placed outside loose buffer tubes to hold the buffer tubes together after stranding and during jacketing. In addition, such tapes provide a heat barrier so that the heat from jacket extrusion does not damage the loose buffer tubes. Finally, if the tape is a SAP, the tape provides moisture resistance.

## 4.1.5    JACKETS

All cables have one or more jackets. The jackets, the outer most layer of the cable structure, protect the core[11] of the cable and provide compliance with the National Electrical Code (NEC). The jacket materials provide this protection through resistance to the conditions imposed on the cable by the environment in which the cable is installed. Such conditions include exposure to UV light, abrasion, water, and chemicals.

---

[8] Also known as a splitter kit, a break out kit, a fan out kit and a spider kit. The term 'furcation' is a generic term meaning to separation and strengthening.

[9] SAP materials are the same family as the material used in disposable diapers.

[10] Steel wires are rarely used as strength members.

[11] The buffer tubes and the binding tape form the 'core' of the cable.

---

In the case of indoor-outdoor cables, multiple jackets provide different types of protection: an inner jacket provides compliance with the NEC; an outer jacket provides protection against degradation due to exposure to the outdoor environment.

Strength members may be placed between multiple jackets. Such a configuration is a 'strengthened' jacket. Such a configuration is used for the all-dielectric, self-support (ADSS) cables used by power utilities between widely spaced power transmission towers. Such cables are designed to withstand high long-term loads, up to 2000 pounds force.

Finally, jacket colors of indoor cables can indicate the type of fiber in the cable. By convention, a yellow indoor fiber cable contains singlemode fiber. Other colors, such as orange, are used for multimode cables.

### 4.1.6   ARMOR

Corrugated, plastic-coated, stainless steel armor provides both high crush resistance and rodent resistance (Figure 4-8 and Figure 4-9). Both resistances are required when the cable is directly buried. The corrugation provides a limited improvement in flexibility. The plastic coating allows the armor to be heat sealed to itself, providing a measure of moisture resistance. The stainless steel material does not corrode, so that the crush and rodent resistances remain constant with time. Armor always has an external jacket. Armor may have an internal jacket (Figure 4-9).

Figure 4-8: 168 Fiber Armored Cable Without Internal Jacket

Figure 4-9: 216 Fiber Armored Cable With Internal Jacket

## 4.2   TYPES

Fiber-optic cables can be characterized in four ways, by:

> The type of buffer tube (4.1.1)

> The specific design, of which there are seven

> The National Electrical Code (NEC) rating and

> Other performance requirements, such as armored, and dielectric design

While there are seven designs, only four are commonly used. We include a fifth design, the break out cable, because of its unique advantage.

### 4.2.1   MULTIPLE FIBER PER TUBE DESIGN

The multiple fiber per tube design (MFPT) consists of multiple loose buffer tubes around a central strength member (Figure 4-10 and Figure 4-11). Buffer tubes contain 6 or 12 fibers.[12] A binding tape surrounds the buffer tubes. Flexible strength members, either aramid yarn or flexible fiberglass rovings may be over the binding tape and under the jacket.

A ripcord is under a jacket or armor. The installer uses the ripcord to cut through a

---

[12] Other counts are possible, but not common.

jacket or armor. The ripcord eases jacket removal.

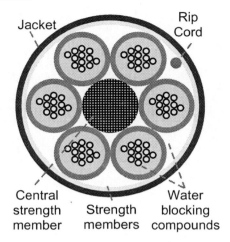

Figure 4-10: Multiple Fiber Per Tube Cross Section

Figure 4-11: MFPT Cable

Optional layers include additional flexible strength members, armor, and a second jacket (Figure 4-9). When present, the armor and additional jackets include a ripcord for ease of removal.

The MFPT design is one of the two most commonly used designs. The MFPT design has three advantages:

> Relatively low cost

> Relatively small size

> Easy mid span access

While not always true, this design has one of the lowest costs per fiber, particularly in high fiber counts. The small size of this design results in a relatively low-cost.

Mid span access refers to the situation in which some of the fibers are dropped off between the cable ends. In this situation, the installer can remove the jacket from the cable while still leaving some protection, the

buffer tubes, on the fibers. Because of the buffer tubes, it will be difficult to damage the fibers which are not terminated at the mid span location.

This design has two disadvantages:

> Relatively high labor cost for end preparation and

> A requirement for enclosures on the ends

The relatively high cost for end preparation is due to the existence of water blocking gels and greases. While not difficult, removal of these gels and greases is time consuming. In addition, removal of MFPT jackets is more difficult than that of tight tube cable designs.

The need for end enclosures increases link costs by a typical value is $3-$6 per fiber per end. For a 24-fiber cable, the enclosures will add $144-$288 per link.

## 4.2.2     CENTRAL LOOSE BUFFER TUBE DESIGN

There is no reason to limit the number of fibers to 6 or 12. We can place all the fibers in a single loose buffer tube. In this case, the buffer tube will reside in the center of the cable, resulting in a 'central loose tube' or 'central buffer tube' design.

In this design, fibers are arranged in groups of 6 or 12. A color-coded thread or yarn binds together the fibers in each group. Up to 216 fibers can reside in the buffer tube. The buffer tube can contain water blocking gel or SAP material.

Around the buffer tube are strength members, often flexible aramid yarns or fiberglass rovings (Figure 4-12).[13] The empty spaces outside the buffer tube can contain grease or SAP yarns to provide moisture resistance. An outer jacket surrounds the strength members.

As in the MFPT design, optional additional layers include additional flexible strength members, armor, and a second jacket.

---

[13] In early designs, strength members were rigid rods placed at 180° outside the buffer tube.

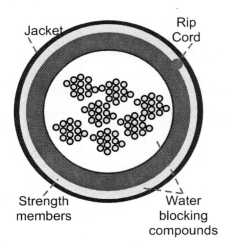

Figure 4-12: Central Buffer Tube Cross Section

This design has two advantages:

> Low-cost[14]

> Reduced cable size

A major disadvantage of this design is inconvenient mid span access. Imagine this design with 216 fibers. You wish to drop off 12 fibers at a mid span location. When you remove the jacket and the buffer tube, you expose all 216 fibers. Murphy's Law states that the fibers to drop at the mid span location will not be on the outside of the bundle. While digging through the bundle to access the desired fibers, the installer may break a fiber. Of course, Murphy's Law also states that the broken fiber will not be the one to terminate at the mid span location!

## 4.2.3    RIBBON DESIGN

The ribbon cable design, the third commonly used, loose tube design, is the ribbon cable, a cousin to the central loose tube design. A ribbon is a series of 4-24 fibers precisely aligned and glued to a thin tape substrate (Figure 4-13).

Ribbons can be stacked on one another to create a design with 416 fibers (Figure 4-14). The ribbons are enclosed in the central loose buffer tube. The buffer tube and the rest of the structure is the same as that of the central loose tube design (Figure 4-15). An alternative ribbon cable design

---

[14] As a practical matter, this design and the MFPT design have competitive prices.

consists of ribbons stacked in loose buffer tubes, which are stranded around a central strength member. This alternative design has the appearance of an MFPT design.

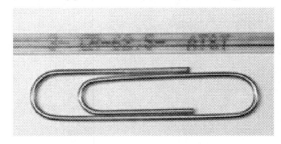

Figure 4-13: Twelve Fiber Ribbon

Figure 4-14: Central Buffer Tube, Ribbon Cable

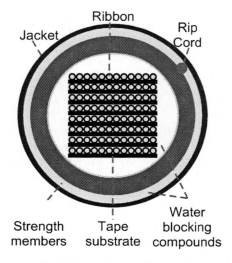

Figure 4-15: Ribbon Cable Cross Section

Ribbon cables have three advantages:

> Low cost

> Low splicing cost and time

> Small size

When filled with the optimum number of fibers, ribbon cables have low cost. The pre-alignment of fibers on the tape substrate allows simultaneous splicing of all fibers on the ribbon. This procedure, called mass fusion splicing, results in reduced splicing time and cost. Since all fibers are not individually aligned, ribbon splicing can result in unacceptably high losses on some fibers. Resplicing the ribbon is the solution. Finally, when the fiber count is very high, hundreds of fibers, ribbon cables have the smallest diameter and the highest fiber density.

## 4.2.4    PREMISES DESIGN

The premises cable, also known as the 'distribution' cable and the 'tight pack' cable, is the most commonly used tight buffer tube design in indoor networks. The premises[15] cable structure consists of a centrally located strength member surrounded by multiple, tightly buffered and stranded fibers (Figure 4-16 and Figure 4-17). Around the fibers is a layer of flexible strength members, usually aramid yarns, such as Kevlar®. A jacket is extruded over the aramid yarns. For moisture resistance, SAP tape or yarns is placed under the jacket.

This basic design (Figure 4-16) can be constructed with up to 24 fibers. For higher fiber counts, multiple structures can be stranded around a central strength member and covered with an outer jacket (Figure 4-17). Thus, a high fiber count premises design may have the appearance of the multiple fiber per loose tube design.

The premises cable design has four primary advantages:

> Low-cost for low to moderate fiber counts

---

[15] The correct term is premises, not premise. The word "premise" means hypothesis or assumption. The word "premises" means facility. Our thanks to John Highhouse for emphasizing the correct term.

> Low-cost and ease of end preparation

> Low-cost per end for termination

> High flexibility

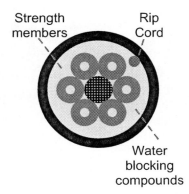

Figure 4-16: Premises Cable Cross Section

Figure 4-17: High Count Premises Cable

The low-cost for end preparation results from the lack of gel and grease and relatively soft jackets. In 15 minutes, an installer can prepare the end of a 24-fiber premises cable. In comparison, an installer would take two man-hours to prepare the end of a 24 fiber, gel filled, grease blocked loose tube cable.

Low cost per end results from the 900 μm buffer tube. This diameter provides strength sufficient to allow repeated handling without damage to the fiber. In comparison, the loose tube designs require a furcation kit (Figure 4-6) to increase the ruggedness of the 250 μm primary coated fibers.

The high flexibility of the premises cable simplifies installation in buildings, short dry conduit runs, and in riser and plenum runs. In all cases, the premises cable is allowed when the cable is terminated within a junction box or enclosure. This requirement results from the inability of the tight buffer tube to survive exposure to the working environment. Finally, this flexibility makes the premises preferred design for field tactical, military applications and electronic news and broadcasting applications.

Single fiber, tight-tube cables, or 'simplex' cables are used as jumpers or patch cords. Two fiber, or 'duplex', cables are used as patch cords. Some duplex cables have two channels that are attached by a thin web of jacket material. Such cables are 'zip-cord' cables, so named because of their similarity to lamp cord.

## 4.2.5    BREAK OUT DESIGN

The final design is the breakout cable design (Figure 4-18 and Figure 4-19). This design was the first design used in indoor networks until the mid 1980s. Break out cables were used in conduits, in risers and in air handling plenums.

The breakout structure starts with a tight buffer tube. Flexible strength members, usually aramid yarns, surround the buffer tube. An inner jacket surrounds the aramid yarns. This structure forms a 'sub cable' or 'sub element.' Multiple sub cables are stranded around a central strength member to form a cable core. Mylar tape and an outer jacket surround the cable core (Figure 4-19).

The breakout cable design has two advantages:

> Ruggedness

> Elimination of the need for end enclosures.

Figure 4-18: Break Out Cable

The ruggedness results from strength members associated with every fiber. The additional association of an inner jacket with each fiber results in a sub cable that can be exposed to the working environment.

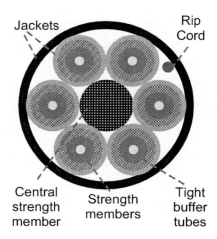

Figure 4-19: Break Out Cable Cross Section

The break out cable can be used for building cable runs, conduit runs, riser runs, and plenum runs. Since the individual fibers are fully protected by the inner sub cables, the break out cable need not be terminated inside an enclosure. Elimination of the end enclosures reduces the cost per link by $144-$288 per link. In comparison, all the other designs would expose fiber or tight buffer tube to the working environment.

The breakout cable has two major disadvantages:

> Large size and

> High cost.

The large size can restrict the use of break out cables to low fiber counts in small conduits. The high cost results from both the amount of materials in the cable and from the increased number of processing steps required by this design.

## 4.2.6    BLOWN PRODUCTS

### 4.2.6.1    BLOWN FIBER

A blown fiber system consists of proprietary fibers in a small diameter tube and a plumbing system of plastic tubes, elbows and couplings. Blown fiber is a group of fibers, typically up to 12, that is blown by air pressure into an airtight system of plastic tubes. The surface of the group is dimpled in the manner of a golf ball. This surface allows the fiber group to float in the plastic tubes, with a significant reduction in friction. This reduction in friction allows elimination of traditional strength members.

Blown fiber systems allow installation to lengths of 1000- 2000 m of fiber, removal of fibers for reuse in a new location, rapid installation of fibers, rapid restoration of damaged tubes, and low cost installation of additional fibers as needed.

A primary advantage of this system is a reduction in future installation cost: fibers can be added to the system as needed. In contrast, a traditional fiber optic cable system requires an initial investment in all the fibers needed for the lifetime of the network. This investment eliminates future installation costs.

A primary disadvantage is the cost of the plastic tube system. This cost makes the cost of the first installation higher than the cost of the first traditional cable system.

### 4.2.6.2    BLOWN CABLE

A blown cable is a small diameter, light duty, cable similar to the cables described in this chapter. Light duty indicates low installation load rating. The installation process allows this low rating.

This process involves attachment of a plug to the end of the cable and use of air flow and air pressure to blow the cable into an air tight conduit path. The airflow allows the cable to float in the conduit, resulting in a significant reduction in installation friction. This reduction in friction allows reduction in the amount of strength member materials and in the size of the cable.

## 4.3    NEC COMPLIANCE

The National Electrical Code (NEC) influences two aspects of fiber optics. In the first aspect, the NEC imposes flame spread and smoke generation requirements on all cables placed inside buildings.[16] The National Electrical Code identifies two groups of fiber optic cables and four ratings for each group (Table 4-1).[17,18] Each rating has a

different test procedure and different requirements.

| Rating | Can Replace |
|--------|-------------|
| OFNG, OFCG | --- |
| OFN, OFC | --- |
| OFNR, OFCR | OFN, OFC |
| OFNP, OFCP | OFN, OFC, OFNR, OFCR |

Table 4-1: Fiber Cable Ratings In The NEC

The two groups are: OFN and OFC. OFN stands for optical fiber cable non-conductive, OFC stands for optical fiber cable, conductive.

An OFC cable has at least one conductive element in its structure. A steel strength member, armor or conductor is conductive and would result in a cable designated as OFC.

Each group has three ratings, listed in order of increasing requirements: horizontal, riser rated[19] (R) and plenum-rated[20] (P). It is possible and legal to place a higher rated cable in a lower rated location. For instance, a riser rated cable can be used in a horizontal location or a plenum rated cable can be used in a riser or horizontal location. However, the reverse substitution does not comply with NEC requirements.

As a practical matter, OFNG and OFCG cables are not available in the US, as they are qualified with a Canadian test procedure.

As a second practical matter, most manufacturers do not make OFN or OFC cables, as the cost difference between these two ratings and the next higher ratings, OFNR and OFCR, is small enough to eliminate the need to maintain two types of inventories.

As a third practical matter, most indoor fiber optic cables are of the OFN series, since dielectric designs are easier to install in compliance with the NEC than are the OFC cables. As a general rule, indoor singlemode OFN cables are yellow.

---

[16] The federal government is the only organization that does not need to comply with any electrical code requirements. However, the federal government tends to implement its networks with cables that comply with the NEC.

[17] From Article 770 of the NEC.

[18] The Canadian Code differs slightly from the U.S. Code

---

[19] Riser rated cables are required for paths between floors.

[20] Plenum rated cables are required for paths that pass through air handling plenums.

In the second aspect, the NEC defines the language used to describe two types of fiber optic cables. As is to be expected, a cable containing only multimode fibers is a multimode cable. A cable containing only singlemode fibers is a singlemode cable. The NEC defines a cable containing both multimode and singlemode fibers as a 'hybrid' cable. The NEC defines a cable containing both fibers and conductors as a 'composite' cable.

With few exceptions, outdoor cables do not comply with the requirements of the NEC because their jackets are commonly HDPE, a member of the paraffin family. However, some indoor-outdoor cables are UV-resistant, moisture resistant and are either OFNR or OFNP rated.[21]

## 4.3.1    DIELECTRIC DESIGN

The OFN series is an example of an indoor dielectric design. Outdoor cables may be dielectric. Dielectric outdoor cables provide increased safety, since they cannot conduct lightning current or ground potential rise into a building.[22]

In addition, use of dielectric designs reduces installation and maintenance costs. Grounds and bonds are required on cables that are not dielectric. Such grounds and bonds do not last forever. As such, grounding and bonding increases both initial installation and maintenance costs. Because of these safety and cost advantages, outdoor designs tend to be dielectric.

## 4.4    INSTALLATION CHARACTERISTICS

Fiber optic cables are designed to meet two groups of requirements: environmental and installation. The system designer defines both. He defines the environmental requirements so that the cable survives the environment in which the cable is installed.

In addition, the designer defines the installation requirements so that the cable survives the installation process. Because the installer installs the cable, he needs to know the limits within which he must handle and install the cable without damage.

As presented (4.3), the installer must install a cable with an NEC rating appropriate to the location in which the cable is to be installed. In addition, the installer needs to know nine cable installation specifications:

> Installation load

> Use load

> Short-term bend radius

> Long term bend radius

> Outer jacket diameter

> Inner jacket diameter

> Buffer tube diameter

> Storage temperature range

> Installation temperature range

## 4.4.1    LOADS

As a material, glass does not support tension loads well. Because of this material characteristic, the cable is designed to limit the elongation of the fiber when a load is applied to the cable.

The cable is designed to withstand two types of loads:

> Short-term, or installation, load and the

> Long-term, or use, load.

The installation load is the maximum load that the installer can use while pulling the cable into location without damaging the cable. The use load is the maximum load that the installer can impose on the cable for the entire life of the cable without damage.

Damage can be of three kinds:

> Breakage of fiber

> Increased attenuation and

> Delayed breakage[23] of fiber

---

[21] Nexans, formerly Berk-Tek, was the first company to offer such products.

[22] Ground potential rise occurs when a conductive path connects two widely spaced locations. 0 volts in Chicago is not the same voltage as 0 volts in Atlanta. Because of this small difference in the voltage, current can flow, resulting in a potential hazardous condition.

---

[23] Delayed breakage is also known as delayed failure and static fatigue. Static fatigue is failure

Installation loads range from 110 pounds-force (490N) for single and dual fiber cables to 600 pounds-force (2700 N) for outdoor, high-fiber count cables. Use loads range widely, depending on the cable type.

The installation load is important in all installations in which the cable will be pulled into its final location. When the cable is pulled into underground conduits or building conduits, the load imposed on the cable can be high. If the cable is laid into a cable trough, cable tray, or raceway, the installation load applied to the cable will not be high. Because of this characteristic, the installer pulls in the cable in a manner that limits the load applied to the cable.

The long-term load is important in installations in which the cable is strung, without external support,[24] between widely spaced telephone poles, power transmission towers or buildings.

## 4.4.2    BEND RADII

As stated earlier, glass does not support tension loads well. Bending produces a tensile stress on the surface of the fiber. Because of this property, all fiber optic cables are designed with a limit on the radius to which the cable can be bent.

The cable is designed to withstand two types of bend radii: the short-term, or installation, bend radius and the long-term, or unloaded, bend radius. The short term, or installation, bend radius is the minimum bend radius to which the cable can be bent while the cable is under the maximum installation load. While defined precisely on the cable specification sheet, the installation bend radius is often specified as:

Short term bend radius = 20 x cable diameter

Equation 4-1

The long-term bend radius is the minimum bend radius to which the cable can be bent while the cable is under no load. This radius

of glass materials under relatively low, long-term stress.

[24] External support could be provided by a messenger or support wire, to which the cable is attached by a spirally wrapped wire.

is limited more by the cable materials than by the fibers. While defined precisely on the cable specification sheet, the installation bend radius is often specified as:

Long term bend radius = 10 x cable diameter

Equation 4-2

While the two rules of thumb may appear to be in reverse, they are not. When the cable is under the installation load and bent, the fiber surface in under two forms of tension: axial tension and bending tension. When the cable is under the installation load only, the fiber surface can withstand the same level of tension. Since there is no axial tension, the fiber can withstand a higher level of bending tension, which results from a bend radius smaller for the unloaded state than the loaded state.

## 4.4.3    DIMENSIONS

Three cable dimensions are important to the installer:

> ➢ Outer jacket diameter
> ➢ Inner jacket diameter
> ➢ Buffer tube diameter

The outer jacket is important whenever the cable is installed into a conduit or inner duct, since the cable must be smaller than the conduit or inner duct. The outer jacket of one-fiber cables and zip cord duplex cables must fit into the boot of the connector. The inner jacket of a break out cable must fit into the boot of the connector. The buffer tube must fit into the back shell of the connector.

## 4.4.4    TEMPERATURE RANGES

Two temperature ranges can be important to the installer:

> ➢ Storage temperature range and
> ➢ Installation temperature range

The cable is designed to withstand storage and installation within defined temperature ranges. If the cable is stored at an excessively high temperature, the cable materials can soften, degrade and shrink. Often, shrinkage of the cable materials results in an increased attenuation rate. If the cable is stored at an excessively low temperature, the cable jacket can crack. Cracks may expose the fibers to water and chemicals in the environment.

If the cable is installed at excessively low or high temperatures, the materials can be damaged. Flexing of the cable at an excessively low temperature can result in cracking of the jacket. Cracks in the jacket can expose the fibers to water and chemicals in the environment. Flexing of the cable at an excessively high temperature can result in a permanent stretching of the jacket. Such stretching can degrade the attenuation rate of the fibers.

## 4.5    STANDARDS

### 4.5.1    TIA/EIA-568-B

In its latest revisions, TIA/EIA-568-B.1-2001 and TIA/EIA-568-B.3-2000, this standard addresses many aspects of fiber network specifications. In Sections 11.3 and Annex A, TIA/EIA-568-B.1-2001 addresses testing requirements.

TIA/EIA-568-B.3-2000 addresses fiber cabling component specifications and field test instrument requirements. B.3 requires that indoor cables comply with ANSI/ICEA S-83-596-2001. B.3 requires that outdoor cables comply with ANSI/ICEA S-87-640-1999.

### 4.5.2    CABLE STANDARDS

#### 4.5.2.1    INDOOR CABLES

ANSI/ICEA S-83-596-2001 provides a comprehensive dimensional, performance and structural requirements for premises distribution cable. The dimensional requirements (Section 2.3) include tolerances on core and cladding diameters, NA, MFD, and ZDW. This standard requires fiber color-coding in compliance with TIA/EIA-598.

#### 4.5.2.2    OUTDOOR CABLES

ANSI/ICEA S-87-640-1999 provides a comprehensive dimensional, performance and structural requirements for outside plant communications cable. The optical and fiber requirements are consistent with those in ANSI/ICEA S-83-596-2001. The default

jacket material is high-density polyethylene (HDPE). Ripcords are optional.

### 4.5.3    COLOR CODING

#### 4.5.3.1    JACKET

Color-coding of cable jackets is optional. The colors are defined in TIA/EIA-598-B.

#### 4.5.3.2    BUFFER TUBES AND FIBERS

Color-coding of buffer tubes and fibers is defined in TIA/EIA-598. Table 4-2 contains the sequence for the first twelve units.

| Blue |
|------|
| Orange |
| Green |
| Brown |
| Slate |
| White |
| Red |
| Black |
| Yellow |
| Violet |
| Rose |
| Aqua |

Table 4-2: Color Coding Sequence

## 4.6    SUMMARY

In order to install a fiber optic cable without damaging the cable or fibers, the installer needs to know the:

➢ Short -term, or installation, load

➢ Long -term, or use, load

➢ Short term bend radius

➢ Long term bend radius

➢ Outer jacket diameter

➢ Inner jacket diameter

➢ Buffer tube diameter

➢ Storage temperature range and

➢ Installation temperature range

With this, and other, information, the installer can handle and install the cable without damage to the fibers.

## 4.7    REVIEW QUESTIONS

1. True or false: an installer can apply tension to a premises cable without applying tension to the fibers.

2. True or false: the long-term bend radius of 1 in. diameter cable is 20 in.

3. What are the three possible problems caused by a violation of the bend radius?

4. Why do outdoor tight tube cables not comply with the requirements of the NEC?

5. Most fiber optic cable manufacturers offer only two NEC compliant ratings. What are they?

6. True or false: OFN series cables need to be grounded.

7. True or false: tying the strength members of a jeep cable to the bumper of the jeep to pull a cable into an underground conduit is acceptable practice.

8. True or false: the latest water blocking technology is a super absorbent polymer.

9. True or false: super absorbent polymer cables cost more to prepare than gel filled, and grease blocked cables.

10. True or false: tight tube cables are always used only indoors.

11. True or false: loose tube cables are dominated indoor applications.

12. You are planning a network with a large number of fibers, 400-500. Your conduit system already exists, must be used and cannot be replaced. What cable design has the highest chance of meeting your needs?

13. True or false: to minimize splicing cost, used a MFPT or central loosed tube?

# 5    CONNECTORS

Chapter Objectives: from this chapter, you will learn the language of fiber optic connectors, the types, their advantages, and the performance concerns of the installer.

## 5.1    FUNCTION

Connectors provide four functions:

- Low power loss
- High fiber retention strength
- End protection
- Disconnection

Connectors achieve low power loss through precise alignment of the small fiber cores. Connectors achieve high fiber retention strength by gripping the fiber, either through an adhesive or mechanical crimp. Connectors achieve end protection by distribution of contact force over an area of increased size, thus reducing the pressure imposed on the end of the fiber. Finally, connectors enable disconnection, or detachment, of a fiber both from optoelectronics and another fibers. In short, connectors are used to create temporary connections and are installed in all locations in which permanent joints are not used.

## 5.2    STRUCTURE

All fiber optic connectors can be described by two attributes: the latching mechanism of the plug and the connection mechanism. While connectors, or plugs, have similar structures, most connectors follow one of two descriptions:[1]

- A ferrule, a key, a latching ring, a back shell, a crimp ring and a strain relief boot (Figure 5-1)
- A ferrule, a key, an inner housing, an outer housing, a back shell, a crimp ring and a strain relief boot (Figure 5-2)

The ferrule provides the precise alignment that results in low power loss. The back shell is the location to which a jacketed cable is attached. The crimp ring, also known as a crimp sleeve, grips the strength members of

the cable. The strain relief boot limits the bend radius of the cable or the tight buffer tube to increase the reliability of the connector.

In some connectors, the latching ring, such as that in the ST-compatible connector, is replaced with a latching mechanism. The inner and outer housings of the SC connector create this mechanism.

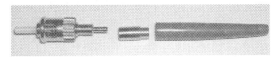

Figure 5-1: ST-Compatible Connector Design With A Latching Ring[2]

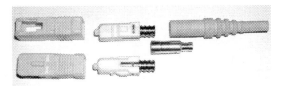

Figure 5-2: SC Connector Design With A Latching Mechanism[3]

Note that the inner housing in the second description replaces the latching ring in the first description.

There are two mechanisms by which two plugs[4] can be mated: use of a barrel, and a jack. When a barrel, also known as an adapter, feed through and bulkhead, is used, two mated plugs can be identical (Figure 5-3). When the connector plug connects to a jack, the plug and jack are different (Figure 5-4). The jack performs the functions of a plug and barrel, but in a single

---

[1] The exception is the Volition, also know as the VF-45, which has no ferrules.

[2] This structure includes, from left to right: the connector body, which includes the ferrule, retaining nut and back shell; a crimp ring; and the strain relief boot.

[3] This structure includes, from left to right: the outer housing; the connector body, which includes the ferrule, inner housing and back shell; the crimp ring; and the strain relief boot.

[4] The terms plug and connector are interchangeable.

---

structure. In general, jacks can be flush mounted, while barrels cannot. Flush mounting is an advantage in FTTD networks.

Figure 5-3: Connectors With Plugs And Barrel

Figure 5-4: Connector (Right) and Jack (Left)[5]

## 5.3    PERFORMANCE

The installer has four connector performance concerns:

- ➢ Maximum insertion loss, dB/pair
- ➢ Typical insertion loss, dB/pair
- ➢ Repeatability, or range, in dB and
- ➢ Reflectance, in - dB

### 5.3.1    MAXIMUM INSERTION LOSS

We begin by emphasizing the units "dB/pair".[6] The measurement of power loss in connectors is a measurement of power

loss from one fiber to another fiber.[7] Thus, the loss measurement requires a pair of fiber ends. Since power loss measurement is in units of dB,[8] the connector power loss measurement must be in units of "dB/pair".[9]

The maximum insertion loss, in dB/pair, is the maximum loss the installer will to see when he installs the connectors correctly.[10] However, he should not expect to see this value, any value close to this value, or a higher value, unless he makes errors during installation. Installers use this maximum value in certifying networks.[11]

When the installer installs connectors correctly, the loss is due to intrinsic causes, such as core and cladding diameter variations, core offset, cladding ovality, NA mismatch and offset of the fiber in the ferrule. When the installer makes errors, he introduces extrinsic causes of loss, such as damaged core, bad cleaves, dirt or contamination on the core, and air gaps due to excessive polishing. All connectors with which we are familiar, singlemode or multimode, keyed and contact, are rated at this maximum value.

- ➢ 0.75 dB/pair is a 'Magic Value' for maximum insertion loss.

### 5.3.2    TYPICAL INSERTION LOSS

The typical insertion loss, in the dB/pair, is the value the installer will see when he installs connectors correctly. Frequently, the installer will experience values lower than this value. The installer and the designer use this value in certifying networks. All singlemode or multimode, keyed and

---

[5] Courtesy of Panduit Corporation

[6] We emphasize the units to avoid errors on the part of the installer. Occasionally, a connecter data sheet will include the unit "dB/connector". There is no standardized test procedure for a unit "dB/connector".

---

[7] By this definition, there is no power loss from a transmitter source to a fiber or from a fiber to a receiver. In an absolute sense, power loss occurs at both locations. In a practical sense, field measurements need not include this loss. See Chapter 13.

[8] See Chapter 13 for power measurements.

[9] Many manufacturers use the term dB, with the implication that it means 'dB/pair'.

[10] Of course, if an installer installs a connector incorrectly, there is no limit to the power loss.

[11] In addition, the network designer uses this value.

contact, connectors, with which we are familiar, are rated at this typical value:[12]

> ➢ 0.30 dB/pair is a 'Magic Value' for typical insertion loss.

### 5.3.3    REPEATABILITY AND RANGE

Repeatability is the maximum increase in loss that a connector will exhibit between successive measurements.[13] Range is the maximum increase in loss that a link will exhibit between successive measurements. These successive measurements require disconnection and reconnection of both ends of a link. Thus, the range could be as high as twice the repeatability.

Connector data sheets contain the repeatability value, but not a range value. While range is infrequently discussed, it is essential for proper interpretation of trouble-shooting and maintenance insertion loss test results.

To understand the importance of the range measurement, we must go back to the basic function of connectors: core alignment. When we put two connectors together, we are aligning the cores of two fibers, each smaller than the human hair. We cannot expect to achieve exactly identical alignment each time we put together the same two connectors. Stated differently, we can expect to observe different insertion losses each time we measure loss of any cable link, even if there is no degradation of the link components.[14]

If we measure a loss that is higher than a previous measurement, are we measuring normal behavior or degradation of link components? In other words, how do we interpret an increase in insertion loss during maintenance or troubleshooting testing?

The answer is simple: we must know the value of the normal variation in insertion loss measurements. The range is a measurement of this normal variation. We

define range as the difference between the maximum insertion loss and the minimum insertion loss from multiple measurements of the same cable link.

When we know the range, we can answer the question: how do we interpret an increase in insertion loss during maintenance or troubleshooting testing? The answer is: if the increase in the insertion loss (from the initial value) is a larger than the range, the increase represents a degradation of the link. We present a method for determining the range (13.2.4.7). A typical value for the range of a link with keyed connectors is 0.2 dB/pair.[15]

Since the subject of range is infrequently presented, many installers do not have range test data. In this case, it is possible to derive a range value from connector data sheets that contain a repeatability value. Frequently, this repeatability value is ≤ 0.2 dB per end. Since then insertion loss test involves connecting and disconnecting both ends of a link, the loss of both ends could change. Thus, the installer could calculate a range by doubling the repeatability value. With this rule, a 0.2 dB repeatability value becomes a 0.4 dB range value. The use of this approach provides a range value that is less sensitive than the range value that the installer determines from multiple measurements of multiple links.

### 5.3.4    REFLECTANCE

Reflectance is a measurement of the relative optical power reflected backwards from a connector. This reflected power can travel back to the light source and be reflected back into the fiber. If this reflected power reaches the receiver with a power level above its sensitivity, the receiver will convert this optical power to a digital 'one'. If the time interval in which the reflected power arrived was a digital 'zero' at the transmitter, the output signal will differ from the input signal. Thus, reflectance influences the accuracy with which a fiber optic link will transmit. Minimizing reflectance results in maximizing signal accuracy. The objective of

---

[12] The equivalent value for cleave and leave connectors is 0.4 dB/pair.

[13] This is the definition used by some connector manufacturers.

[14] Link components are cables, connectors and splices.

[15] We have determined this value during training of more than 5000 novice installers. We expect that experienced installers will find the range to be lower than this value, typically 0.1-0.15 dB.

---

a reflectance requirement is to limit the reflected power at the receiver to a value less than the sensitivity of that receiver.

Reflectance occurs at a glass air interface. This interface, or any interface at which there is a change in speed of light, or index of refraction, can produce a reflection, called a "Fresnel reflection". This reflection occurs in fiber optic connectors because the end faces of mating connectors have surface roughness, which creates microscopic air gaps (Figure 5-5).

In connectors, this reflection is called reflectance. Reflectance is defined as

Reflectance =

10 Log (reflected power/incident power)

Equation 5-1

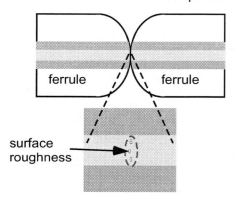

Figure 5-5: Air Gaps Create Reflectance

Reflectance is stated in units of negative dB, with values from -20 dB to -65 dB.[16]

Reflectance is qualitatively described by the terms PC, 'UPC' and 'APC'. Commonly, PC (physical contact) refers to reflectance of less than –40 dB; UPC (ultra physical contact), to less than –50 dB; and APC (angled physical contact), to less than –55 dB.

Historically, reflectance has been a concern for singlemode connectors. However, reflectance is now a concern in multimode connectors gigabit Ethernet and 10-gigabit Ethernet networks. The gigabit Ethernet

standard requires multimode connectors with reflectance below -20 dB.[17]

The Fresnel reflection between an optical fiber and air ranges between -14 dB to -18 dB. An installer would expect to see this range from a non-contact connector. An experienced installer could expect to obtain -50 dB, from a hand polishing singlemode connectors. Machine polished singlemode connectors exhibit values below -55 dB.[18] Only APC connectors provide consistent reflectance of less than -60 dB.

From these values, you can see that low reflectance is possible from contact connectors (Figure 5-5). Low reflectance is not possible from connectors with flat ferrule ends, because it is essentially impossible to achieve perfect perpendicularity and perfect smoothness on both fiber ends. Only with such dual perfection would air gaps, the cause of reflectance, be completely eliminated.

Two connector ferrule end geometries make low reflectance possible- radiused and angled physical contact connectors (APC). Radiused ferrules (Figure 5-5) eliminate the need to achieve perfect perpendicularity. With a radiused end, reflectance can be reduced through multiple polishing steps with successively finer polishing films. The principles are: as the surface becomes smoother, the air gaps become smaller; as the surface becomes smoother, the air gaps become fewer. As the air gaps become smaller and fewer, the reflectance becomes lower.[19]

The alternative to the radiused ferrule connector is the angled physical contact

---

[16] Angled Physical Contact (APC) connectors provide reflectance values better than (less than) -60 dB.

[17] Another relationship between reflectance and link performance is a relationship between bit rate or bandwidth and reflectance. The higher the bit rate, or the higher the bandwidth, the lower the reflectance requirement.

[18] Hand polishing of single mode connectors to -50 dB reflectance is not recommended, due to excessive cost. You will learn how to achieve this low reflectance (16).

[19] This process is time-consuming and thus, expensive. Factory installed single mode connectors are polished 24 at a time in a three minute cycle. This cycle time compares 3 to 6 minutes per connector for field singlemode polishing.

(APC) connector. This connector has a bevel on the tip of the ferrule at 8 degrees to the perpendicular of the fiber axis.[20] The angle on the end of the ferrule reflects light backwards at an 8° angle to the axis, which is outside of the critical angle of singlemode fibers. Such reflected light escapes from the core, resulting in the lowest reflectance possible for a connector. APC versions exist for SC (Figure 5-6), FC, LC and LX.5 connectors. By convention, APC connectors have green boots or housings.

Reflectance can be confused with two other terms: back reflection and return loss. Return loss is the power reflected backwards by a system or a link. As such, return loss includes reflectance and the backscatter from atoms in the core of the fiber (13). Back reflection is similar to reflectance, but differs in two ways. First, back reflection applies to all components in a link rather than to connectors exclusively. Second, back reflection ratio and is, therefore, a positive number (Equation 5-2).

Figure 5-6: The SC/APC Connector

Back reflection=

10 Log (incident power/reflected power)

Equation 5-2

## 5.4    CONNECTOR FEATURES

Connectors have five features that differentiate between styles and control their reliability and performance. These features are:

➢ Contact or non-contact

➢ Keyed or non keyed

➢ Axial load isolation (Pull proof or not)

---

[20] Some APC connectors sold in Europe have a 9 ° angle.

➢ Lateral load isolation (Wiggle proof or not)

➢ Ferrule material

## 5.4.1    CONTACT

Connectors can be contact or non-contact. Contact connectors exhibit lower power loss than do non-contact connectors. This reduced loss results from elimination of the expansion of the light as it exits a connector. This expansion results from the NA of the fiber: light exits from a fiber and expands within the cone defined by the NA. In a non-contact connector, the size of the spot on the receiving fiber is larger than the diameter of the receiving core. The light arriving on the cladding of the receiving fiber is lost (Figure 5-7).

In a contact connector, there is no expansion. At this time, all connectors are contact. In the early days of fiber optics, most connectors were non-contact.

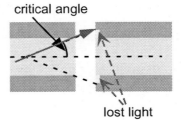

Figure 5-7: Increased Loss From Non-Contact Connectors

## 5.4.2    KEYED

Keying is a design feature that was absent on the early designs, but is an absolute necessity in current and future designs. The key prevents rotation of two ferrules relative to one another to provide consistent power loss from connection to connection (Figure 5-8).

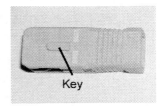

Figure 5-8: Key On Connector

This variability, referred to as 'repeatability' is specified commonly as a maximum of 0.2

dB[21]. We have tested repeatability for both keyed and unkeyed connector styles. For keyed connectors, we find typical repeatability closer to 0.1 dB than to 0.2 dB. For unkeyed connectors, we find typical repeatability to range from 0.5 dB to as high as 1.0 dB.[22]

This improvement from keying is obvious and significant in two situations: initial network certification and maintenance or troubleshooting. During initial network certification, the lack of high repeatability of non-keyed connectors could result in the need to tune connectors to bring link power loss into compliance with specification. Subsequent disconnection and reconnection of any connector could result in loss of the preferred ferrule orientation and in link failure.

During maintenance or troubleshooting, current loss measurements are compared to original measurements. There is a possibility that improvement in the alignment of non-keyed connectors could mask a degradation of link components. With this possibility, interpretation of changes is more difficult with non-keyed connectors than with keyed connectors.

The first two design characteristics, keying and contact, are common to both the popular styles, which dominate the industry, and the small form factor (SFF) types.

## 5.4.3   AXIAL LOAD ISOLATION

'Pull proof' behavior results from isolation of the ferrule from motion due to axial tension on the back shell. This isolation, which can be achieved by inclusion of a spring between the ferrule and the back shell, prevents an increase in power loss from tension applied to the cable.

## 5.4.4   LATERAL LOAD ISOLATION

'Wiggle-proof' behavior results from isolation of the ferrule from the motion due to lateral

pressure on the back shell. Such pressure will result in increased power loss if the ferrule tilts in response to such pressure. In summary, a pull-proof, wiggle-proof connector provides more reliable operation than one that is neither.

## 5.4.5   FERRULE MATERIALS

Ferrules can be of many different materials. Frequently used ferrule materials include:

> Ceramic
> Liquid crystal polymer
> Stainless steel[23]

As of this writing, ceramic ferrules are required for singlemode connectors, since only ceramic materials can be manufactured at a competitive price and with the precision required for singlemode core alignment. Unlike the softer ferrule materials, ceramic ferrules can be over polished, creating undesirable, excessive undercut (11.4.2.4).

Softer ferrule materials can be repolished without expensive diamond polishing films to remove damage from use. In addition, softer ferrule materials can be repolished without risk of undercutting. Through repolshing, an installer can restore original performance without replacement of the connector. In an apple-to-apple comparison, the softer ferrule materials provide a reduced initial cost and a reduced life cycle cost.

Early connector ferrule materials include nickel-plated brass, aluminum, zinc, thermoplastic polymer, and thermo set polymer. At this time, use of these additional materials is uncommon.

## 5.4.6   COLORS

By convention, the APC connectors are green, to distinguish them from the PC and UPC singlemode connectors, which are blue. Multimode connectors are beige. The blue and beige colors are requirements of TIA/EIA-568 B.

---

[21] We obtained this value from a survey of connector data sheets.

[22] Data are from SMA 906 connectors tested from 1990-1994.

[23] Other materials include nickel-plated brass, thermoplastic polymer, thermoses polymer, die case zinc, and die cast aluminum.

## 5.5 TYPES

We present connectors in three groups:

➤ Commonly used connectors

➤ Small form factor (SFF) connectors

➤ Legacy connectors

The commonly used types are the dominant at this time. The SFF connectors are expected to become dominant in the future. The legacy connectors were commonly used in the past but are infrequently used at this time.

### 5.5.1 TWO COMMON TYPES

The two most popular, or commonly used, connector types are the ST™-compatible[24] and the SC.

#### 5.5.1.1 ST-Compatible

First introduced in 1986, the ST-compatible (Figure 5-1) is keyed, contact, moderate loss connector that is not pull proof or wiggle proof. Installation of the ST-compatible is significantly easier and faster than installation of predecessor connector types.[25] The ST-™ compatible connector has a cost lower than that of the SC. However, the ST-™ compatible connector requires more space on a patch panel than does the SC. This space is required for rotation of the retaining nut. A consequence of this space requirement is increased patch panel and enclosure cost. In locations requiring more than 12 connectors, the ST-™ compatible can have a higher total installed cost than the SC connector.

#### 5.5.1.2 SC

First available in 1988, the SC (Figure 5-9 and Figure 5-10) was developed by Nippon Telephone and Telegraph (NTT) in Japan. The SC became commonly used after it became the connector type required for compliance with the Building Wiring Standard, TIA/EIA-568. Because of its exclusive recommendation in TIA/EIA-568

---

[24] ST is a trademark of Lucent Technologies.

[25] Such predecessor, or legacy, connectors are: 905 SMA, 906 SMA, biconic, mini-BNC, FDDI MIC, and FC types.

and TIA/EIA-568-A, the SC has dominated multimode installations during 1995-2000.

The SC is keyed, contact, moderate loss, pull proof and wiggle proof. Because of these latter two characteristics, the SC is more reliable than the ST-compatible.

This isolation results in a price higher than that of the ST-compatible connector. This isolation makes damage of the fiber end face difficult by controlling the force with which ferrules make contact. In contrast, the installer can apply excess contact force during the insertion of an ST-compatible connector.

A second benefit of this isolation is immunity to damage from 'pull and snap'. An SC connector cannot be pulled and allowed to snap back into an adapter. An ST-compatible connector can be pulled and snapped. Usually, such action results in damage to the fiber in an ST-™ compatible connector.

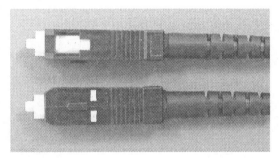

Figure 5-9: SC Simplex Connector

Figure 5-10: SC Duplex Connector

We have observed this improved reliability: during fiber optic connector installation training, we experience a damage frequency for ST-compatible reference leads that is 3-6 times that of SC reference leads. Thus, in spite of the increased price, the life cycle cost of the SC connector will tend to be lower than that of the ST-compatible connector.

The SC differs from the ST-compatible in two additional aspects: insertion method and ability to be duplexed. The SC insertion method is 'push on/pull off'. Because of this method, the SC connectors can be more closely spaced in a patch panel than can the ST-compatible, which requires space for rotation. In practice, this reduced spacing results in a connector density of two to four times that possible with ST-compatible connectors. This increased density results in a reduction in the total installed cost of SC connectors by reducing the number, or size, of enclosures required.

The SC can be duplexed, either through use of left and right outer housings[26] or an external clip (Figure 5-10). This capability results in increased network reliability because it is difficult to reverse the fibers in a duplexed SC connector. Thus, use of SC connectors results in three cost reductions:

> Reduced life cycle cost

> Reduced enclosure cost

> Increased reliability[27]

## 5.5.2    SMALL FORM FACTOR CONNECTORS

While the ST-compatible and SC connector types have had long, and successful lives, both have the same, significant drawback: large size. This size results in increased optoelectronics cost. The large size of the connectors forces optoelectronics manufacturers to space transmit and receiver electronics far apart. This large spacing results in half as many fiber ports in a fiber switch as in a UTP hub or switch.

The optoelectronics manufacturers request-ed a reduced size fiber connector that would enable them to reduce the per port cost of hubs and switches. Their goal was for cost parity of fiber switches with UTP switches. Connector manufacturers answered this

request with a series of small form factor (SFF) connectors.

Increased use of SFF connectors is guaranteed by the latest revision to the Building Wiring Standard, TIA/EIA-568 B. This standard states[28]:

"Various connector designs may be used provided that the connector design satisfies the performance requirements specified within annex A. These connector designs shall meet the requirements of the corresponding TIA Fiber Optic Connector Intermateability Standard (FOCIS) document."[29]

By the removal of the prior, exclusive recommendation for use of SC connectors in its earlier revisions, TIA/EIA-568-B guaranteed the increased use of SFF connectors. Such increased use has occurred and is expected to continue.

The request for reduced size fiber connectors resulted in six SFF connectors:

> MT-RJ

> Opti-Jack

> Volition

> LC

> LX.5

> MU

These SFF connectors obviously meet the need of increased density (Figure 5-11).

### 5.5.2.1    FIBER JACK

In January 1997, Panduit Corporation introduced the first duplex SFF plug and jack connector system, generically known as a Fiber Jack (Figure 5-4). This plug and jack connector system, trade name 'Opti-Jack™', introduced a new package based on four existing and well proven technologies: 2.5 mm ferrules, quick cure adhesive

---

[26] From TYCO

[27] The popularity of the ST-compatible connector, which is in large part a consequence of its reduced cost, is, probably, a result of lack of knowledge of these cost factors favorable to the SC.

[28] TIA/EIA-568 B.3, clause 5.1.

[29] From Clause 5.1 of TIA/EIA-568 B.3. The FOCIS standards are of a series labeled TIA/EIA-604-x, where x refers to a specific connector type.

installation,[30] split alignment sleeves, and an RJ-45 form factor.

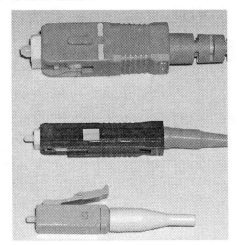

Figure 5-11: Size Comparison of SC (Top) And SFF Connectors

The 2.5 mm ferrules are the same as those in the ST-compatible, SC, FC, FDDI, and ESCON™ connectors. Quick-cure adhesives had been in use since 1992 and were well developed. The split alignment sleeves were commonly used in multimode adapters since 1986. The form was the same as that of the RJ-45, with which network installers and users were familiar.

The Opti-Jack™ is keyed, contact, moderate loss, pull proof and wiggle proof. It is a duplex connector with one ferrule per fiber. This structure allows separate alignment of each fiber for minimum power loss.

Panduit's use of these four well-proven technologies eliminated the risk of using this 'new' product. By its appearance, the Opti-Jack™ is the most rugged of the SFF connectors and is extremely well suited for fiber to the desk (FTTD) applications.[31]

### 5.5.2.2    MT-RJ

The MT-RJ is available in two versions, the plug and jack version from TYCO (Figure 5-12) and the plug, adapter and plug version from Corning Cable Systems and others

(Figure 5-13). The MT-RJ is keyed, contact, and pull proof with two fibers in a single ferrule. Installation is by the 'cleave and crimp' method.

Optoelectronics manufacturers offer more products with the MT-RJ interface than with any other SFF interface.[32] At this time, MT-RJ optoelectronics are available at bit rates up to 1 Gbps.[33]

Although the MT-RJ plug has a size smaller than those of other SFF connectors, the MT-RJ density in patch panels is the same as that of other SFF connectors.

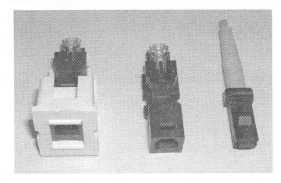

Figure 5-12: TYCO/AMP MT-RJ System

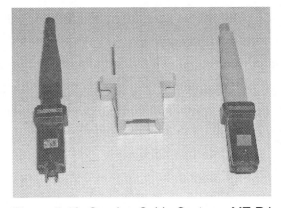

Figure 5-13: Corning Cable Systems MT-RJ System[34]

---

[30] Current products have pre installed and pre polished fibers. As such, they require the 'cleave and crimp' installation method.

[31] The author's FTTD network is based on the Opti-Jack™.

[32] We estimate that 22 manufacturers offer optoelectronics with the MT-RJ interface.

[33] We are aware of no 10 Gbps optoelectronics that use the MT-RJ interface.

[34] The plug on the left resides on the back side of a patch panel. The plug on the right is a patch cord plug. The barrel in the center provides the mechanism for connecting the two plugs.

### 5.5.2.3   LC

The LC is a simplex SFF connector that can be converted to a duplex form with a clip. The LC (Figure 5-14) was developed by Lucent Technologies, but is available from at least additional six manufacturers. The LC was developed as a telephone connector designed to enable telephone companies to increase the density of installed connectors. Dense wavelength division multiplexing (DWDM) is one of the technologies creating this need for increased density.[35]

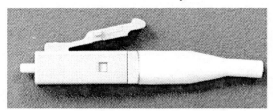

Figure 5-14: LC Simplex Connector

The LC is a keyed, contact, low to moderate loss, pull proof and wiggle proof design. The LC has a 1.25 mm ferrule, which is half the diameter of the ferrules used in ST-compatible, FDDI and ESCON connectors. This small ferrule size can cause problems for installers, until they realize that half the diameter means one quarter of the usual polishing pressure.

Many optoelectronics manufacturers provide products with the LC interface. These optoelectronics transmit at up to 10 Gbps. A large number of electronic and connector manufacturers support the LC type.

### 5.5.2.4   VOLITION™

The Volition™ duplex connector from 3M[36] is a plug and jack system (Figure 5-15, a jack open with darkened fibers in grooves, and Figure 5-16). The Volition incorporates a design feature that is both evolutionary

and revolutionary: 'V'-grooves instead of ferrules.

V-grooves are evolutionary, in that they have been used for alignment of fibers in fusion splicers since the late 1970's. V-grooves are revolutionary in that they have not been used in connectors prior to the Volition.

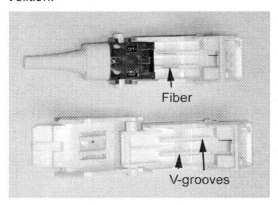

Figure 5-15: Volition™ Jack

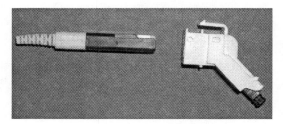

Figure 5-16: Volition™ Plug And Jack

3M used V-grooves for alignment of the fibers: in the jack, fibers rest in precision, molded, plastic V-grooves (Figure 5-15, top). In the plug, a custom fiber[37], floats in free space (Figure 5-16). The plug fibers slide into the V-grooves of the jack, with contact of the mating fibers maintained through pressure created by bent fibers.

The Volition plugs and patch cords are factory made. The jacks are field installable onto a custom Volition cable. This custom cable is required, since the jack requires fibers with a primary coating of 250 μm. This diameter is smaller than the 900 μm tight tubes of commonly used premises cables. Because of this requirement, it is not

---

[35] With DWDM, it is possible to launch up to 200 wavelengths onto the same singlemode fiber. With this level of multiplexing, the connector count, and patch panel space requirements at a telephone company location could rise 200-fold. The SFF was an obvious solution to telephone space requirements.

[36] The generic name of the Volition™ connector is SG. In addition, the Volition is known as the VF-45.

---

[37] This fiber, known as GGP, for glass/glass/polymer, has a glass core, a glass cladding to a diameter of 110 μm and a hard plastic over cladding to a diameter of 125 μm.

possible to retrofit existing fiber optic networks with the Volition system.

In spite of this limitation on retrofitting, the Volition system has proven popular because it provides the lowest cost fiber optic connection system available.[38] 3M achieved this low cost, approximately the same as that of a UTP jack, by eliminating the single, largest cost in the connector- the ferrule.

In addition, the Volition system provides and the lowest cost fiber optoelectronics. For example, the lowest cost Volition media converters are below $100. Use of media converters or switch blades with other SFF connectors are $150-$229.

### 5.5.2.5     MU

The MU is a simplex SFF connector with the appearance of an SC but with all dimensions reduced in half (Figure 5-17). Designed and developed in Japan, the MU is a keyed, contact, moderate loss, pull proof and wiggle proof design. It is unique in that it can be assembled to create a duplex, triplex or quadruple connector.

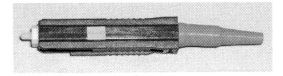

Figure 5-17: MU Connector

### 5.5.2.6     LX.5

ADC Telecommunications developed the LX.5 (Figure 5-18), similar to the LC, for use in telephone networks. The LX.5, available in radius and APC versions, has a unique feature: a built in dust cover (Figure 5-18, bottom). This cover lifts as the connector is installed into a patch panel.

Similarly, the LX.5 adapter has a built in dust cover (Figure 5-19). The dust covers on the connector and in the adapter increase the eye safety of the product. With multiple wavelengths on singlemode fibers in DWDM networks, the total power level at the connector can be as high as 0.2 watts.

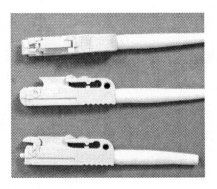

Figure 5-18: LX.5 Connector

Figure 5-19: SC And LX.5 Barrels

### 5.5.2.7     MTP/MPO

MTP/MPO connectors (Figure 5-20) have 6-24 fibers in a single, molded polymer ferrule. The fibers are incorporated in ribbons. These connectors reduce the size of enclosures and patch panels and enable rapid installation.

This connector has found acceptance in preterminated cable systems, often used in data centers. Such centers install preterminated cables, with modules on the ends. The modules break out the separate fibers to individual, single fiber connectors, such as SC or LC. This cable and module system reduces installation time significantly, although usually at increased cost.

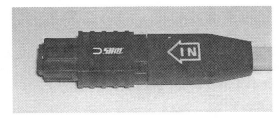

Figure 5-20: MTP® Connector[39]

[38] A Volition jack costs less than $6.60. This price is close to that of a Category 5e jack. At a minimum of $9.10, duplex SC plug and barrel costs at least 38 % more expensive than the Volition solution.

[39] Registered trademark of the US Conec Corp.

### 5.5.3 LEGACY CONNECTORS

In the previous two sections, we presented the connectors that are dominant now and those that are expected to become dominant in the future. In this section, we present the legacy connectors, those that have been, but no longer are, commonly used.

- ➤ SMA 905
- ➤ SMA 906
- ➤ Biconic
- ➤ Mini-BNC
- ➤ ESCON
- ➤ FDDI, MIC
- ➤ FC

#### 5.5.3.1 SMA, BICONIC AND MINI-BNC

Early connector types, such as the SMA 905 (Figure 5-21), SMA 906 (Figure 5-22), biconic (Figure 5-23), and mini-BNC (Figure 5-24) had flat end faces and deliberate air gaps, which resulted in high reflectance, −14 to -18 dB. These four types were non-keyed.

Figure 5-21: 905 SMA Connector

Figure 5-22: 906 SMA Connector

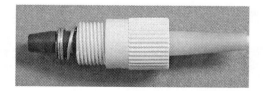

Figure 5-23: Biconic Connector

Figure 5-24: Mini BNC Connector

#### 5.5.3.2 FC AND D4

Originally developed in Japan, the FC (Figure 5-25) and D4 (Figure 5-26) connectors have some of the characteristics of both the ST-compatible and the SC connector types. Like the ST- compatible, the both have a rotational insertion method, which requires a relatively large spacing in a patch panel. Like the SC, both are keyed, contact, moderate loss, pull proof and wiggle proof. The FC/APC has a beveled end face and the same characteristics as the FC.

The D4 has a unique feature. During assembly, the key can be adjusted to achieve the lowest possible loss.

Figure 5-25: FC Connector

Figure 5-26: D4 Connector

#### 5.5.3.3 FDDI AND ESCON

All the previous connectors were simplex. The last two, FDDI (Figure 5-27) and ESCON (Figure 5-28) are duplex connectors. Both use the 2.5 mm ferrule, as do the ST-compatible, SC, and FC connectors. Both are very large, keyed, contact, pull proof and wiggle proof. The FDDI connector is has a fixed shroud at the ferrule end. In contrast, the ESCON connector has a movable shroud that makes cleaning of ferrules easy.

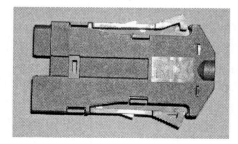

Figure 5-27: FDDI Connector

Figure 5-28: ESCON Connector[40]

## 5.6    INSTALLATION METHODS

Fiber optic connectors are installed by at least five methods. These methods were developed to address different concerns, such as reliability, convenience, time to install and cost to install.

Most of the development of methods has been to reduce one or more of the cost factors. In most cases, the effort to reduce the total installed cost resulted in increased connector cost. This development produced many installation methods, five of which have become well received:

> Epoxy

> Hot melt adhesive

> Quick cure adhesive

> Crimp and polish

> No polish, no adhesive

## 5.6.1    EPOXY INSTALLATION

The epoxy, pot and polish method was the first method used for installation of fiber optic connectors. These epoxies can required a slow cure at room temperature, a fast cure at room temperature, or a slow or fast cure at an elevated temperature.

___

[40] In this photograph, the shroud is pushed in to expose the ferrules for cleaning.

This method has four advantages:

> High resistance to degradation

> Loss stability over a wide temperature range

> High installation process yield

> Ability to be used with the lowest cost connectors

Epoxies are considered to have the highest resistance to the widest range of conditions. As such, epoxies can provide the highest reliability connectors. Other adhesive systems tend to have reduced resistance. As an example, fiber optic connector epoxies can resist degradation to temperature of 105°C., while the Hot Melt™ adhesive system is specified to 85°C.

The loss stability provided by epoxies is due to a good match of thermal expansion coefficients of epoxy, fiber and ceramic ferrules. This matching results in minimal relative movement of the fiber in the ferrule over a wide temperature range. Such limited movement results in stable power loss.

Use of epoxies tends to result in high process yield. This high yield is a result of the bead on the ferrule (Figure 5-29). This bead supports the fiber during polishing. This support nearly eliminates damaged ends, which represent 95 % of connector losses during installation.

Figure 5-29: Large Epoxy Bead Results in High Yield

Labor cost can be low for factory-installed connectors. The combination of low labor cost and low epoxy connector cost favors the use of epoxies as a factory installation method.

This method has three disadvantages. The first two disadvantages are related: inconvenience of use and low installation rate, which can translate to high installation hours. The third disadvantage is the need for power to heat curing ovens.

The use of epoxy requires mixing of two parts, transfer of the mixed epoxy into a syringe or automated injection mechanism, and clean up of excess epoxy. Because of these additional steps, the rate of installation of epoxy connectors is low, typically 6-8 per man-hour.

Two factors of field installation tend to result in high total installed cost: high labor cost and reduced utilization. During field installations, the total loaded hourly labor cost tends to be high. In addition, there is reduced labor utilization,[41] since field installations involve time spent in activities other than installation. For example, field installations involve the time factors of: travel to site, set up, pack up, clean up, and travel to the next installation location within the site.

Low labor utilization increases the cost impact of the low installation rate of the epoxy method. Because of the potentially high labor cost of the epoxy method, connector manufacturers developed other installation methods.

## 5.6.2    HOT MELT™ INSTALLATION

Because of the inconvenience and time impact of the installation with epoxy, 3M developed the Hot Melt installation method. In this method, a hot melt adhesive is preinstalled into the connector. The installer preheats the connector to soften the adhesive so that he can install the fiber. The installer installs the fiber and/or cable into the connector and allows the connector to cool in a heat sink (the cooling stand). Once cooled, the installer removes the excess fiber and polishes the end in a one step polishing procedure.[42] This installation method requires a 3M polishing film, which is not easily clogged by the hot melt adhesive.

The hot melt process eliminates the time factors of preparing and injecting the epoxy. In addition, this method eliminates the mess and inconvenience of epoxy. These eliminations allow an increased installation rate, 12-16 per hour.[43] This increased rate can result in a reduced installation cost.

However, the Hot Melt™ connectors are more expensive than epoxy connectors. In addition, the Hot Melt method requires power for the heating oven and proprietary oven, holders and polishing film. In spite of these factors, many installation situations can achieve a total installed cost with the hot melt method that is lower than the cost with the epoxy method.

## 5.6.3    QUICK CURE ADHESIVE INSTALLATION

Several manufacturers (Lucent Technologies and Automatic Tool and Connector[44]) addressed the disadvantages of the proprietary parts of the Hot Melt method and the inconvenience of the epoxy method through with 'quick cure' adhesive systems. These systems, either two part systems[45] (from Lucent Technologies, Automatic Tool and Connector) or one part (from TYCO), eliminate the need for power, resulting in an increase in the rate of installation. This increased rate, typically 15/hour, can result in a reduced installation cost.

---

[41] Utilization is the ratio of time spent in connector installation to total time required for connector installation. During field installation, the activities other than installation, such as travel to site, set up and clean up can reduce utilization from over 90 % to between 50 and 85 %.

[42] While the 3M instructions are for a single polishing step, some installers use a two or three step polishing process.

[43] 3M released a videotape demonstration of installation of an ST-compatible Hot Melt connector onto a single fiber cable in 4:45. this time indicates a rate of 12.63 / hour. The installation rate by this method onto premises cable will be higher, perhaps 14/hour.

[44] Now part of Suttle.

[45] Two part systems consist of an adhesive and a hardener or accelerator. A one-part system consists of a gel. Both tend to be edge-filling adhesives that harden in thin areas. Some refer to these adhesives as being 'anaerobic' but our information is that they are anaerobic like, but not true anaerobic adhesives.

A second advantage of quick cure adhesives is their compatibility with the low cost connectors with ceramic ferrules.[46] This combination of low cost connectors and high installation rate can result in a low total installed cost. Installers can achieve this low installed cost if they achieve a high process yield.

There are three disadvantages to the use of quick cure adhesives. The first two disadvantages of quick cure adhesives, premature hardening of the adhesive and minimal support of the fiber during polishing, contribute to a reduced process yield[47] and increased cost.

Premature hardening occurs when the fiber is coated with the hardener or accelerator and inserted into a connector loaded with adhesive. If the installer inserts the fiber slowly, the adhesive cures and the fiber locks up before it is fully inserted. In this situation, there is bare fiber inside the connector.

Such bare fiber can cause a reduction in the reliability of the connector. For example, SC[48] connectors allow the fiber inside the back shell to flex slightly during insertion into a patch panel or a receptacle. Repeated flexing of such bare fiber can result in breakage of the fiber. We have observed such failure in as few as 5 cycles.

The minimal support of the fiber during polishing occurs because the adhesive cannot produce a large bead on the tip of the ferrule. This inability is due to the nature of the adhesive: quick cure adhesives are edge-filling adhesives, not true anaerobic adhesives. Unlike the bead on epoxy connectors, the small bead on the tip of the ferrule can allow the fiber to break below the surface of the ferrule during removal of the excess fiber or polishing. Without extreme care during the end finishing steps, the installation yield can be low. For example,

typical yields during training of first-time novices installing epoxy and Hot Melt™ connectors are 80-90 %. Typical yields for these same novices with quick cure adhesives are 50-60 %. However, typical yields of quick cure adhesive connectors for experienced professionals are 95-98 %.

The third, and final, disadvantage of the use of quick cure adhesives is reduced reliability. Some of the quick cure adhesives exhibit degradation when exposed to a wide temperature range, a wide humidity range, rapidly changing temperature, or rapidly changing humidity. While there are exceptions, quick cure adhesives are suitable for indoor use.

## 5.6.4    NO ADHESIVE WITH POLISH INSTALLATION

Several manufacturers[49] have offered connectors that use a mechanical method of gripping the fiber and require polishing. These products are more susceptible to damage during polishing than are connectors installed with quick cure adhesives. This susceptibility to damage occurs because there is no bead supporting the fiber. Of the five methods, this method has the lowest acceptance.

## 5.6.5    'CLEAVE-AND-CRIMP' INSTALLATION

For all the installation methods presented, the major cause of reduced yield and increased cost is damaged or shattered fiber ends. This damage occurs during polishing. In addition, a significant amount of time is consumed by preparation, injection, and use of adhesives. The 'cleave and crimp'[50] installation method addresses both yield loss and time consumption by elimination of both adhesives and polishing. Such elimination offers the potential of increased installation rate and reduced installation cost. This increase in installation rate may be only a potential cost reduction, since the

---

[46] Some quick cure adhesives can be used on connectors with liquid crystal polymer ferrules.

[47] Yield is the ratio of the number of acceptable connectors to the total number of connectors installed.

[48] We expect the same type of failure to occur in any connector that is pull proof and wiggle proof, such as the FC, LC, and Opti-Jack.

---

[49] AMP, 3M and Automatic Tool and Connector

[50] This method is also known as 'prepolished/splice' and 'cleave-and-leave.'

cost of these connectors is higher than that of connectors installed by other methods.

'Cleave and leave' is a generic term for no epoxy, no adhesive, no polish connector products with the trade names LightCrimp™ Plus (TYCO/AMP), Opti-Crimp® (Panduit Corporation), Unicam™ (Corning Cable Systems), and others. All these products require cleaving the end of the fiber, inserting that fiber into a connector, and crimping or clamping the connector to the fiber. The connector contains a pre-installed fiber stub that has been polished by the manufacturer. In essence, this connector has a mechanical splice in its back shell.

The primary advantage of this installation method is reduced installation time, with the potential of reduced installation cost. Field installation rates can be 22-40/hour. A second, potential, advantage is reduced training cost.

The realization of reduced installation cost depends on five factors. Since the cost of connectors installed with this method is high and these five factors vary widely from installation to installation, the increased installation rate of this method may or may not result in reduced installation cost.

These five factors, total loaded hourly labor rate, labor time utilization, installation rate, installation yield, and connector cost, do not always combine to produce the lowest total installed cost. In spite of the complexity[51] of the cost analysis, we can develop some rough guidelines.

The higher the total loaded labor rate, the more likely the cleave-and-crimp method will result in the lowest total installed cost.

As the number of connectors per location drops, the labor time utilization drops. As this utilization drops, the probability of lowest total installed cost increases for the cleave and crimp method. Such situations include the desk locations in a fiber to the desk network (FTTD) but not necessarily a central equipment room in a vertical back bone or in an FTTD network.

In the last six months, our preliminary testing has indicated that the cleave and leave

method yields and power losses are close to those of epoxy, Hot Melt and quick cure methods.

## 5.7   SUMMARY

In summary, the installer needs to know the following information about the connectors he is to install.

➤ Connector Type
➤ Core diameter
➤ NA
➤ Maximum loss, dB/pair
➤ Average loss, dB/pair
➤ Repeatability, or range
➤ Reflectance

The installer needs to know the connector type, the core diameter and the NA to choose reference leads for testing. He needs to know the maximum and typical connector loss in order to calculate the acceptance for certification of network.

He needs to know the range, or the repeatability, for troubleshooting. The range will indicate the maximum increase in loss that he can accept as indicating normal behavior of the connectors. Finally, He needs to know the reflectance in order to certify the connectors.

## 5.8   REVIEW QUESTIONS

1. True or false: contact connectors have higher loss than non-contact connectors.
2. True or false: contact connectors have lower reflectance than non-contact connectors.
3. True or false: contact connectors dominate today's market.
4. True or false: non-contact connectors are common today.
5. True or false: a normal rating is a maximum of 0.75-dB/ connector.
6. True or false: more reflectance is better than less reflectance.

[51] For the detailed analysis, see Eye On Fiber, V.2, Issue 2 from Pearson Technologies Inc.

7. True or false: more reflectance provides lower BER than less reflectance.

8. True or false: small form factor connectors are legacy connectors.

9. True or false: SFF connectors drive network costs up.

10. True or false: a D4 is a SFF connector.

11. True or false: an MT-RJ is a simplex connector.

12. The diameter of an SC ferrule is:

13. The diameter of an LC ferrule is:

14. Is an LC connector a simplex or duplex?

15. True or false: There are two ferrules in a Volition connector.

16. What style of connector is this?

17. What style of connector is this?

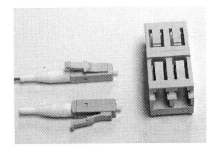

18. What style of connector is this?

19. What style of connector is this?

20. Why are the range and repeatability of connectors important?

21. True or false: when an installer installs connectors, he will often see the maximum loss value.

22. True or false: a normal experience is a measured value of 0.75 dB/connector.

# 6    SPLICES

Chapter Objectives: from this chapter, you will learn the types, advantages and language of fiber optic splicing. With this understanding, you will be able to understand the principles of splicing and achieve low loss and high reliability when splicing.

## 6.1    LOCATIONS

Splices are permanent joints between two fibers. A splice has two functions: provision of low loss and high strength.

Installers splice in two locations: mid span and pigtail. Installers perform mid span splicing whenever the following conditions exist:

> The cable cannot be obtained in a single length

> The cable cannot be installed in a single length

> The cable has experienced backhoe fade, posthole driller fade, rodent fade, shark fade or any other cause of broken fiber(s)

Pigtails are short length of cables or tight buffer tubes with a connector installed on one end. Installers perform pigtail splicing in order to reduce installation cost or installation time. Instead of field installing singlemode connectors, installers perform pigtail splicing.

## 6.2    TYPES

The two methods of splicing are fusion and mechanical. In both methods, two prepared fiber ends are core-aligned or cladding aligned to provide low power loss. Each splicing method has different characteristics, requirements and advantages.

The installer requires the same basic tool kit for both methods of splicing. This kit consists of cable end preparation tools and a precision cleaver.[1] Both methods require cleaving of the fiber ends to produce nearly perfect end faces. Such end faces are flat and perpendicular. Fusion splicing requires one additional tool, the fusion splicer.

---

[1] This basic kit costs approximately $2000 with a precision cleaver. With a low cost cleaver, the kit can cost $500-$1000.

## 6.2.1    FUSION SPLICING

Fusion splicing is the process of fusing, or welding together, two fibers. When two fibers are spliced together, the method is fusion splicing. When fiber ribbons are spliced together, the method is ribbon splicing, or mass splicing.

This method requires a fusion splicer. The fusion splicer provides two functions: the precise alignment of the fibers to each other prior to splicing and control of the splicing operation.

The fusion splicer provides precise fiber alignment in two ways: passive alignment and active alignment. The splicer provides passive alignment through the use of a precision 'V' groove (Figure 6-1). With such a groove, the splicer design operates with the implicit assumptions that 1) the fiber diameters and 2) the core-cladding concentricity are precise enough to achieve low power loss. These assumptions are valid for both the fiber made in North America and for much of the fiber made overseas.

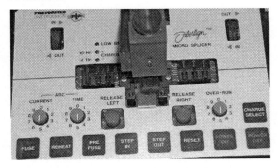

Figure 6-1: 'V-Groove' Splicer

The splicer can provide active alignment in two ways: profile alignment (PAL) and local injection and detection (LID). In order to provide profile alignment (Figure 6-2), the splicer incorporates a collimated light source, a microscope, image digitization and image analysis software. The collimated light allows the core-cladding boundaries of both fibers to be visible under a microscope. The digitized images are analyzed by software to define this boundary in two perpendicular axes. Control software adjusts one fiber so that the core offset is minimized in both axes.[2]

After the splice has been made, this same software analyzes the image to provide a value of the splice loss. This value is an estimate. The installer can measure the accurate splice loss only with an OTDR. In addition, accurate splice loss is an average of the loss in both directions (13.3.6.4.2).

Figure 6-2: Profile Alignment Splicer

In order to provide alignment by the local injection and detection method, the splicer includes a laser light source and a detector. Both source and detector are incorporated into structures that bend the two fibers being spliced. The bend at the source launches light into one fiber; the bend at the detector taps light from the second fiber. Control software adjusts one fiber so that the power at the detector is maximized.

After the splicer aligns the fibers, it controls the arc current, arc time and overrun. These parameters determine the power loss and strength of the splice.

The splice current and time control the energy provided to the fibers. The overrun

provides control of the diameter of the splice.

Installers use fusion splicing in most initial installations and in restoration. However, for rapid restoration and for splicing in manholes, installers use mechanical splicing.[3]

The four advantages of fusion splicing are low power loss, low to no reflectance, high strength[4] and low cost. Often, fusion splices result in 0 dB loss.[5] In contrast, mechanical splices rarely exhibit 0 dB loss. Because of this low loss, some applications, such as CATV, require fusion splicing exclusively.

Low reflectance results from the welding process: there is no change in index of refraction at a properly made fusion splice. Low cost per splice results from the low cost of the splice cover ($0.50-$1.20). High strength results from the welding process, since welds are always stronger than the base material.

Fusion splicing has two disadvantages: the high cost of the fusion splicer, ($5000-$30,000)[6] and potential for disruption of the profile of a multimode fiber. For a small number of splices, fusion splicing may be cost prohibitive, even with a rented splicer.

The disruption of the multimode core profile is a possibility with mixed data support. In December of 2001, FOTEC and Pearson Technologies Inc. performed such testing with a prototype FOTEC[7] multimode

---

[2] PAL splicers align the cores of singlemode fiber, but may align the cladding of multimode fibers.

[3] Manholes can collect methane, which could be ignited by the arc of a fusion splicer.

[4] When we compare splice strength of the fusion splice to that of a mechanical splice that uses compression for fiber retention, the fusion splice has the higher strength. The strength of a properly made fusion splice is higher than that of the base fiber.

[5] From our training experience, we estimate that 30 % of singlemode splices and 90 % of multimode splices have 0 dB loss.

[6] The more expensive the splicer is, the more capable the splicer and the higher will be the number of splices that the installer can make per hour.

[7] FOTEC was located in Medford, MA. FOTEC was purchased by Fluke Networks, which shut down FOTEC's operations and shelved development of the multimode bandwidth tester.

bandwidth tester. This testing demonstrated a reduction in bandwidth through mid span fusion splices of standard multimode fibers. The reduction was approximately 30 % on multimode links of 200-220 m. The same links exhibited high bandwidth when the mid span location contained mechanical splices and connectors. This testing suggested the possibility of failure of gigabit links with mid span splices when the links were near the maximum distance of the 803.2ae standard. However, recent testing by Corning indicates no significant bandwidth reduction on fusion spliced, laser-optimized fibers.[8]

## 6.2.2 MECHANICAL SPLICING

Mechanical splicing is the process of inserting two prepared fiber ends into a mechanical splice (Figure 6-3). The mechanical splice provides precise alignment of both fiber ends and the function of a cover.

Different methods create precise alignment. Some splices have a precision capillary tube for alignment. Other splices use a precision etched silicon substrate. Finally, one splice, the 3M Fibrlok®, has a precision 'V' groove that is unique.

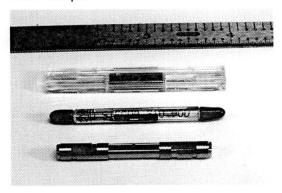

Figure 6-3: Mechanical Splices

All mechanical splices have index matching gel at their centers. This gel fills any air gap than may result from the end faces of either fibers being less than perfectly perpendicular. Such filling reduces loss. In some singlemode fibers, the index matching gel eliminates all reflectance.[9]

Mechanical splicing is used in fast restoration and by organizations that have a large number of splice teams.

A primary advantage of mechanical splicing is fast restoration. In fast restoration, both ends of a length of cable are prepared and inserted into mechanical splices. This cable, stored in a case, is a fast restoration kit. When a cable is broken, the installer brings the kit to the broken cable, prepares two ends, and inserts these ends into the fast restoration cable. Through this advance preparation, the installer reduces restoration time by approximately 50 %.

A second advantage of mechanical splicing is low tool cost: the installer requires no fusion splicer. Purchase or rental of a fusion splicer can increase the total cost above that of mechanical splicing.

A third advantage applies to multimode fibers: the melting of the fibers disrupts the core profile, resulting in reduced bit rate capacity. This reduction may not be significant for bit rates below 200 Mbps, but appears to be significant for Gigabit Ethernet data rate of 1.25 Gbps.[10]

Mechanical splicing has one major disadvantage and one minor disadvantage. The first major disadvantage is cost in large installations: at a price of $8-$15, a 1000 splice installation will consume $8000-$15,000. At $10,000, a fusion splicer becomes an attractive alternative.

A disadvantage is increased installation time: the fibers may need to be tuned to achieve acceptable loss. Tuning is the process of rotating one or both fibers to obtain the desired loss. Rarely do multimode mechanical splices require tuning. Some

[8] Private communication, Phillip Bell (Corning Optical Fiber) to the author, 3/3/05.

[9] Historical note: prior to 1996, all singlemode mechanical splices exhibited reflectance. After that date, some singlemode mechanical splices exhibited no reflectance, probably due to near perfect matching of the index of refraction of the gel to the index of refraction of the singlemode core.

[10] Gigabit Ethernet operates at an electrical data rate of 1 Gbps but an optical data rate of 1.25 Gbps.

singlemode mechanical splices require tuning.

## 6.3   STRUCTURE

A fiber splice consists of three primary components and secondary components. The primary components are the:

➤ Splice (Figure 6-4)

➤ Splice tray (Figure 6-5)

➤ Splice enclosure (Figure 6-6 and Figure 6-7)

The splice is the junction between two fibers. The tray protects the splices and houses the splice and excess fiber. The enclosure houses the trays and excess buffer tube.

The secondary components include: gaskets, internal, or integral, patch panels, strength member gripping mechanisms, moisture seals, splice covers, grounding strips, pressure valves, locking mechanisms and plugs.

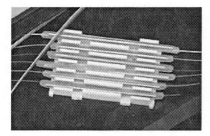

Figure 6-4: Fusion Splices in Splice Covers[11]

Figure 6-5: Half Length Splice Tray

[11] Figures 6-4 to 6-6 are courtesy of Preformed Line Products.

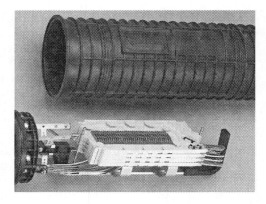

Figure 6-6: Outdoor Splice Enclosure

Figure 6-7: Indoor Splice Enclosure

### 6.3.1   SPLICE COVER

The installer places a splice cover over each fusion splice. This cover isolates the splice from the environment, and supports and protects the splice.

Splice covers can be heat shrinkable (Figure 6-8) or adhesive (Figure 6-9). The shrinkable splice cover consists of two layers of plastic separated by a steel rod. The rod prevents the fiber from bending when the cover shrinks. The installer places the heat shrinkable cover on the fiber prior to splicing.

In contrast, the installer places the adhesive splice cover on the fiber after splicing, or, when he realizes he forgot to place the heat shrinkable cover of the fiber prior to splicing!

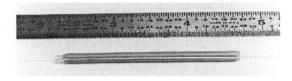

Figure 6-8: Shrinkable Fusion Splice Cover

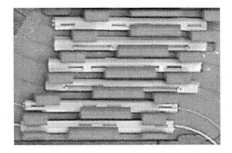

Figure 6-9: Adhesive Splice Covers

## 6.3.2    SPLICE TRAY

The splice tray houses and protects the splice and excess fiber (Figure 6-10). Excess fiber is required to allow making the splice outside of the tray. While not a rule of thumb, outdoor splices require 3-4' of fiber for each end of each splice. In contrast, indoor splices may require only 1-2 ' of fiber for each end of each splice.

Trays tend to be of two sizes, half (Figure 6-5) and full (Figure 6-10). Full trays tend to be used in outdoor enclosures. Half trays tend to be used in indoor enclosures and in FTTH enclosures.

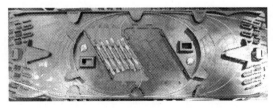

Figure 6-10: Full Length Splice Tray

Trays are designed for the number and type of splice. Most trays will allow 6 or 12 splices. In addition, the trays will contain a splice holder designed for either fusion splices or a specific type of mechanical splice.

Trays retain the splice with a splice holder, which can be integral to the tray (Figure 6-5)

or an insert (Figure 6-10).[12] The splice holder must be compatible with the splice cover or the mechanical splice.

## 6.3.3    SPLICE ENCLOSURE

The enclosure houses and protects the splice tray(s) and excess buffer tube length. An inside enclosure can include an internal patch panel, complete with barrels. Excess buffer tube allows the splice tray to be outside of the splice enclosure while the installer makes the splice. While not a rule of thumb, outdoor splice enclosures require four to five feet of buffer tube per cable per end.

Indoor (Figure 6-7) and outdoor (Figure 6-6) enclosures have functions that are similarities and differences. One similarity is the provision for one or more mechanism(s) to grip the cable strength members, so the cable cannot be easily pulled from the enclosure (Figure 6-11 and Figure 6-12). Another similarity is incorporation of an integral patch panel. Not all indoor enclosures provide space for splice trays. Not all outdoor enclosures incorporate patch panes.

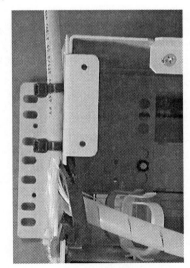

Figure 6-11: Gripping Mechanism For Indoor Splice Enclosure

---

[12] In the past, the fusion splice holder was a rubber pad with grooves. After all splices in a tray were completed, the grooves were filled with RTV (silicone). Today, this method is uncommon, as removal of a single splice for repair could result in damage to adjacent splices.

Figure 6-12: Gripping Mechanism For
Outdoor Splice Enclosure

Different functions include isolation of the
interior from the environment, including
moisture and dust.[13] Unlike outdoor
enclosures, indoor enclosures rarely provide
such isolation.

Some outdoor enclosures that are to be
installed below ground level provide for
internal air pressure to prevent moisture
ingress (Figure 6-13). Such enclosures have
a set of gaskets to prevent both such
ingress and internal pressure release.

Unlike most outdoor enclosures, indoor
enclosures include an internal patch panel
for direct connection of the fibers in the
enclosure to patch cords (Figure 6-7).

Figure 6-13: Valve For Internal Pressure

---

[13] Some outdoor, aerial enclosures do not
provide moisture isolation. Instead, they provide
weep holes so that condensed moisture can
drain.

## 6.4    PERFORMANCE

Splice loss is measured in dB. Splice loss of
both fusion and mechanical splices is less
than 0.15 dB, though some organizations
allow higher and lower values. Properly
installed fusion and mechanical splices
achieve this value, although fusion splices
tend to have lower loss than mechanical
splices.

The Fiber Optic Association advanced
certification process requires all splices to
be a maximum of 0.15 dB. The Building
Wiring Standard, TIA/EIA-568 B allows
splices to be up to 0.3 dB. Some
organizations allow splices to be as high as
0.5 dB, probably for cost reasons. Finally,
some organizations, such as CATV
organizations, require maximum values as
low as 0.08 dB, in order to achieve the
maximum signal to noise ratio, a
performance characteristic important in
analog transmission systems. In summary,
the choice of a maximum splice loss may be
more of a political or cost decision instead of
a technical decision.

## 6.5    SUMMARY

The installer needs to know the following
characteristics of splices:

> ➤ Splice type

> ➤ Cladding diameter

> ➤ Mode type

> ➤ Maximum loss, in dB

> ➤ Instructions for installing mechanical
> splices

> ➤ Instructions for installing splices into
> the enclosure.

## 6.6    REVIEW QUESTIONS

1. From the figures below, identify a
fusion splice.

2. From the figures below, identify a
mechanical splice.

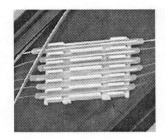

Figure 6-14: Review Figure 1

Figure 6-15: Review Figure 2

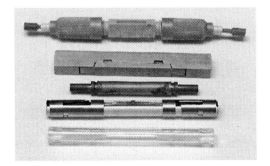

Figure 6-16: Review Figure 3

3. True of False: a splice has a higher maximum loss than a connector pair.

4. True of False: a splice has a lower typical loss than a connector pair.

5. What is the function of a splice cover?

6. Under what conditions will fusion splicing be less expensive than mechanical splicing?

7. Under what conditions might mechanical splicing be preferred?

8. Provide two reasons that mechanical splicing can be more expensive per splice than fusion splicing.

9. Why is there excess fiber in the splice tray?

10. Why is there excess buffer tube in the splice enclosure?

11. You are placing 12 fibers in an outdoor splice tray. What is the total length of fiber that might be in the splice tray?

12. You are placing buffer tubes into an outdoor splice enclosure. Each buffer tube contains 12 fibers. The cable contains 96 fibers. What is the total length of buffer tube that might be in the enclosure?

13. What is the total length of jacket that you might remove from a cable end in order to splice one outdoor cable to another?

14. Provide one reason that fusion splicing can be more expensive than mechanical splicing.

# 7    PASSIVE DEVICES

Chapter Objectives: from this chapter, you will learn the types of, functions of and installation concerns for passive devices.

## 7.1    TWO INSTALLATION CONCERNS

With the increased growth in the number of installations of 'fiber to the home' (FTTH), 'fiber to the curb' (FTTC), 'fiber to the premises' (FTTP) or, more generally, 'fiber to the x' (FTTx), the need for knowledge about passive devices has increased.

For the installer, passive devices create two concerns: power loss and reflectance. Any component in the optical signal path has a power loss. As a result, all passive devices reduce the power delivered to the receiver. Excessive power loss in a passive device can result in link failure.

In addition, all passive devices are connected to other network components, such as cables. Such connections create the potential for reflectance. Excessive reflectance can result in inaccurate signal transmission (5.3.4).

Passive devices have three types of power loss: connection loss,[1] intrinsic loss and extrinsic loss. Connection loss occurs in all passive devices, as they have connectors or splices on the inputs and outputs.

Intrinsic loss occurs due to the function of the device. For example, a 1x2 splitter must have a power drop of at least 50 %, or 3.01 dB, between input and output ports (Equation 2-2). For a 1x4 splitter, the power drop is at least 75%, or 6.02 dB.[2]

Extrinsic power loss is in excess of the intrinsic loss. The extrinsic loss is a result of our inability to make perfect passive devices.[3] For example, the typical power loss through a 1x2 splitter is 3.5-4.0 dB. Since the intrinsic loss is 3.01 dB, the extrinsic loss is the difference, or 0.49-0.99 dB.

Passive devices include:

- ➢ Couplers
- ➢ Splitters
- ➢ Wavelength division multiplexers and demultiplexers
- ➢ Wavelength and optical switches
- ➢ Optical amplifiers and
- ➢ Rotary joints

## 7.2    COUPLERS

Couplers (Figure 7-1) combine different optical signals, each with a unique wavelength, onto the same fiber. Coupling can be in one direction (Unidirectional, Figure 7-2) or in opposite directions (bi-directional, Figure 7-3).

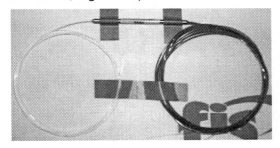

Figure 7-1: Coupler

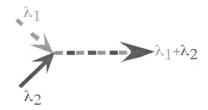

Figure 7-2: Unidirectional Coupler Function

---

[1] Connection means either a connector or a splice.

[2] Each 50 % reduction in loss corresponds to an additional 3.01 dB power drop. For example, a 1 x 16 splitter includes 4 reductions of 50%, for an intrinsic loss of 12 dB.

[3] In connectors, extrinsic loss is due to all causes that are not intrinsic, such as dirt, defects on the core surface, and undercutting.

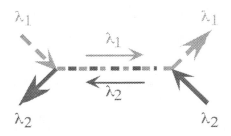

Figure 7-3: Bi-Directional Coupler Function

## 7.3    SPLITTERS

Splitters perform the function of splitting or separating a single input signal to multiple outputs (Figure 7-4). The outputs can contain all the wavelengths from the input (Figure 7-5). Such a device is a simple splitter. Splitters can operate uni-directionally (Figure 7-5) or bi-directionally (Figure 7-3).

Figure 7-4: A Splitter[4]

Figure 7-5: All Wavelengths In Output of Splitter

## 7.4    WAVELENGTH DIVISION DEMULTIPLEXER

A splitter that splits and separates multiple wavelengths is a wavelength division demultiplexer (Figure 7-6). Wavelength division multiplexing (WDM) and demultiplexing refer to the combining and separating of two wavelengths that are

---

[4] Photograph courtesy of Preformed Line Products.

widely separated. As such, multimode multiplexing refers to combining wavelengths of 850 nm and 1300 nm. Singlemode multiplexing refers to combining wavelengths of 1310 nm and 1550 nm.

WDM, CWDM (7.5), and DWDM (7.6) can be implemented in the same direction (Figure 7-2) or in opposite directions (Figure 7-3).

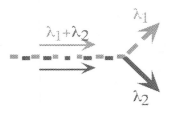

Figure 7-6: Wavelength Division Demultiplexer Function

## 7.5    CWDM

Coarse wavelength multiplexing and demultiplexing (CWDM) refers to the joining and separating of more than two wavelengths that are moderately separated. In its general usage, CWDM is a singlemode technology, with separations of at least 20 nm between adjacent wavelengths. Typical implementations of CWDM are three to eight wavelengths in a range that depends on the number of wavelengths. For four wavelengths, the range is 1510-1570 nm. For eight wavelengths, the range is 1470-1610 nm. For sixteen wavelengths, the range is 1310-1610 nm.

CWDM can have a central wavelength of 1550 nm or can operate through the range of 1310 nm to 1550 nm, as in fiber to the home (FTTH) networks.

The primary advantage of CWDM is reduced optoelectronics cost. The moderate wavelength separation allows use of uncooled lasers. Such lasers are lower in cost than cooled lasers, which are required for the closely spaced wavelengths of DWDM (7.6).

## 7.6    DWDM

Typically, dense wavelength division multiplexing (DWDM) and demultiplexing refers to the combining and separating more than eight wavelengths that are closely spaced. In its general usage, DWDM is a singlemode technology, with separations of as small as 0.4 nm between adjacent wavelengths.

According to the ITU standard G.692[5], as many as 200 wavelengths can be launched into a single fiber. These wavelengths can be unidirectional (Figure 7-2) or bi-directional (Figure 7-3). In 1999, Lucent announced a DWDM demonstration of 1000 wavelengths launched into a single fiber.

## 7.7    SWITCHES

Optical switches move optical power from one input path to one or more output paths. Such switches can reroute all wavelengths or individual wavelengths. While optical switches are not common at this time, they are used in FDDI and telephone networks.

## 7.8    ROTARY JOINTS

The rotary joint (Figure 7-7) is a passive optical device that allows transmission of an optical signal from a rotating structure to a stationary structure. Such a function is needed for sensor arrays and for undersea, remotely operated vehicles (ROV). Such ROVs are used for inspection of the underside of ships, for repair and maintenance of undersea fiber optic cables, and for undersea exploration at depths unattainable by a manned vehicle. Finally, such a function is needed for sensor arrays dragged behind ships for submarine detection.

## 7.9    OPTICAL AMPLIFIERS

Although optical amplifiers require power for operation, they are considered passive devices. Optical amplifiers are so considered because they manipulate light in the optical regime without an optical-electrical-optical conversion process.

Optical amplifiers provide amplification of an optical signal. Such amplification is most commonly performed with an erbium-doped fiber amplifier (EDFA).[6] The atoms in the

erbium-doped fiber are excited by laser power at a wavelength of 980 nm or 1480 nm. Incoming photons from the signal fiber strike these excited atoms. These excited atoms respond to the disturbance by emitting a photon at the same wavelength as the incoming photon. This process repeats itself as the original photons and the emitted photons travel through the amplifier fiber (Figure 7-8). This process results in gains of 20 dB.

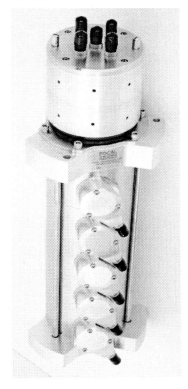

Figure 7-7: Five Fiber Rotary Joint[7]

Most amazing and useful of the EDFA properties is its ability to amplify a wide range of wavelengths simultaneously. This ability simplifies the design of DWDM networks by allowing a single amplifier instead of multiple amplifiers for amplifying multiple wavelengths. While a wide range is possible, the gain throughout the wavelength range is not uniform and is adjusted with attenuating filters.

---

[5] The title for this standard is "Optical Interfaces for Multichannel Systems with Optical Amplifiers."

[6] The alternate type of optical amplifier is a Raman amplifier. In a Raman amplification system, the amplification occurs in the transmission fiber.

---

[7] This is a Focal Model 242 from Kaydon Power & Data Technologies. Photograph is courtesy of Kaydon Power & Data Technologies.

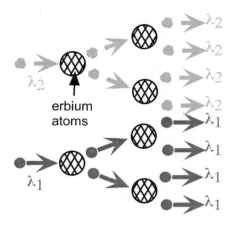

Figure 7-8: The EDFA Amplification Process

## 7.10   **SUMMARY**

The installer may install passive devices. As such devices introduce power loss and reflectance to the link, the installer will need to know maximum and typical power losses of such devices. With this knowledge, the installer will be able to interpret link power loss measurements. In addition, the installer will need to ensure that the connectors on all passive devices remain low loss and low reflectance.

## 7.11   **REVIEW QUESTIONS**

1.  What are the two most important installation concerns for passive devices?

2.  What is the proper name for a splitter that routes each wavelength to a separate output port?

3.  Define WDM.

4.  Define CWDM.

5.  Define DWDM.

6.  Why is an optical amplifier considered a passive device?

7.  What is the acronym for an optical amplifier?

8.  What element is used to create the amplification in an optical amplifier?

9.  Calculate the intrinsic power drop for a 1x16 splitter.

10. If the actual power loss in Question 9 is 14 dB, what is the extrinsic power loss?

11. Calculate the intrinsic power loss through the combination of a 1x4 splitter and a 1x8 (Figure 7-9).

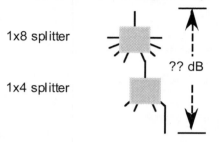

Figure 7-9: Splitter Network For Question 11

# 8    OPTOELECTRONICS

Chapter Objectives: in this chapter, you will learn the language, types and numbers for optoelectronics. With this knowledge, you will be able test the link in a manner that reflects the characteristics of the optoelectronics and recognize power loss values that represent conditions under which the optoelectronics may not function.

## 8.1    INSTALLATION CONCERN

The term optoelectronics describes both the transmitter and receiver, since both function with electrical and optical signals. The transmitter converts an electrical signal to an optical signal; the receiver performs the reverse conversion. The key installation concern is accuracy of signal transmission. The optoelectronics achieve high accuracy when the power level at the receiver is proper and the pulse dispersion is sufficiently low.

Proper power level means enough power and not excessive power. The only impact an installer can have on the optoelectronics is reduced power at the receiver. Such power reduction will occur if the installer allows dirt into the ports of the transmitter or receiver.

## 8.2    TRANSMITTER TYPES

In this chapter, we limit our presentation to types of light sources used for transmitting data. We exclude other types that may be used for testing. There are three types of light sources in transmitters:

> LEDs

> Laser diodes

> Vertical cavity surface emitting laser diodes (VCSELs)

These types differ in the manner in which they produce light and in the manner in which light is launched into a fiber.

### 8.2.1    LIGHT EMITTING DIODES

LED sources have the characteristics of:

> Large spot size (150-250 μm)

> Circular spot shape

> Relatively large angle of divergence (0.20-0.25 NA)

> Relatively low bit rate/ bandwidth capability (< 200 Mbps)

> Relatively low launch power (1-10 μW)

> Relatively low cost

> Multimode operation at 850 nm and 1300 nm

The large spot size, circular spot shape and large angle of divergence result in light filling most of the cross section of the core and most of the angle of acceptance defined by the NA (Equation 2-3). Under such launch conditions, the light experiences a large amount of modal dispersion, the maximum fiber attenuation, and maximum connector loss.[1] These characteristics make the LED best suited for use with multimode fiber in short distance data links.[2]

### 8.2.2    LASER DIODES

Laser diode (LD) sources have the characteristics of:

> Small spot size

> Rectangular spot shape (2 μm x10 μm)

> Small angle of divergence

> Relatively high bit rate/ bandwidth capability (<10 Gbps)

> Relatively high launch power (>1 mW)

> Relatively high cost

---

[1] Chapter 3.

[2] Singlemode LEDs exist, but they do not launch as high power levels as do singlemode LDs.

---

Singlemode LDs are common at 1310 nm and 1550 nm. Multimode LDs are uncommon in transceivers.

The small spot size, small angle of divergence, high bandwidth, high launch power and high cost make the LD well suited for use with singlemode fiber in long distance links.[3] However, the rectangular spot shape makes alignment to the singlemode core relatively expensive.

### 8.2.3    VERTICAL CAVITY SURFACE EMITTING LASERS

1 Gbps VCSELs have the characteristics of:

➢ Medium spot size (30 μm)

➢ Annular spot shape (Figure 8-1)

➢ Small angle of divergence

➢ Relatively high bit rate/ bandwidth capability

➢ Relatively high launch power

➢ Relatively low cost[4]

➢ 850 nm multimode VCSELs common

The annular spot shape (Figure 8-1) of 1 Gbps VCSELs was developed to avoid a potential splitting of pulses when the highly collimated light of a laser diode enters the center of the core of some 'old' multimode fibers.[5] This source emits most of the optical power in an annular ring with an inner diameter of 9 μm and an outer diameter of 30 μm. This annular launch condition and the small angle of divergence results in low dispersion in multimode fibers. This low

---

[3] Multimode LDs exist, but are used in test equipment, such as OTDRs.

[4] Typical prices (10/2003) for VCSEL–based, Gigabit Ethernet converters range from $150-$400 per end. Typical prices for LED-based Fast Ethernet (100 Mbps) converters range from $100-$150 per end. These prices result in a cost per 100 Mbps of $15-$40 for GBE and $100-150 for Fast Ethernet. A typical price for 1 Gbps, singlemode GBE converter is $1000/ end. The cost benefit of the VCSEL is obvious.

[5] Multimode VCSELs were developed for use in data communication networks operating at 850 nm.

dispersion enables gigabit transmission to significant distances on multimode fiber. In summary, the VCSEL combines the performance advantages of a LD with the cost advantage of an LED.

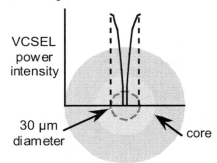

Figure 8-1: VCSEL Annular Launch Area

## 8.3    RECEIVER TYPES

There are two types of receivers: photodiodes and avalanche photodiodes. Photodiodes are used for relatively high receiver power and relatively low bandwidths. Avalanche photodiodes are used for relatively low receiver power and relatively high bandwidths.

Rarely does the installer need to know details of the receiver. However, in the event of reduced transmitter output power, the installer will need to know the sensitivity of the receiver. The sensitivity of the receiver is the minimum power level at which the receiver will function at the specified level of accuracy. If the power at the receiver is less than the sensitivity of the receiver, high error rates are possible.

Note that we have used the term 'bandwidth.' This term is a characteristic of the optoelectronics and is different from the term bandwidth-distance product, which is a measure of the capacity of multimode fiber. While bandwidth is an analog term, common convention is use of this term as a measure of the capacity for both analog and digital systems.

## 8.4    PERFORMANCE CHARACTERISTICS

For troubleshooting purposes, the installer needs to know the wavelength and the optical power budget of the optoelectronics, in dB, which we shall call the optical power budget available (OPBA).[6] The OPBA is the maximum power loss that can occur between a transmitter and receiver while still allowing the pair to function at the specified level of accuracy. If the link loss exceeds the OPBA, the optoelectronics and the link loss are mis-matched. We present typical OPBA for fiber standards in Table 8-1.

In addition, the installer may need to know the sensitivity of the receiver, in dBm, in order to troubleshoot transmitter and receiver problems.

| Standard | Core, µm | λ, nm | OPBA, dB |
|---|---|---|---|
| 10BASE-FB | 62.5 | 850 | 12 |
| 10BASE-FL | 62.5 | 850 | 12 |
| 10BASE-FP | 62.5 | 850 | 16-26 |
| 100BASE-F | 62.5 | 1300 | 11 |
| 100BASE-SX | 62.5 | 850 | 4.0 |
| 1000BASE-S | 62.5 | 850 | 2.33 |
| 1000BASE-S | 62.5 | 850 | 2.53 |
| 1000BASE-S | 50 | 850 | 3.25 |
| 1000BASE-S | 50 | 850 | 3.43 |
| 1000BASE-L | 62.5 | 1300 | 2.32 |
| 1000BASE-L | 50 | 1300 | 2.32 |

Table 8-1: OPBA For Fiber Standards

## 8.5   SUMMARY

The installer is concerned with optoelectronic characteristics:

➢ The wavelength or wavelengths and

➢ The optical power budget available (OPBA), in dB.

## 8.6   REVIEW QUESTIONS

1. What are common testing wavelengths?

2. For the installer, what are the two most important optoelectronics characteristics?

3. What is a typical optical power budget available from a transmitter-receiver pair?

4. Why is the installer concerned with the optical power budget?

5. Why is the installer concerned with the wavelength?

6. A 62.5 µm link has a power loss of 2.54 dB. According to Table 8-1, on which protocols will not run on this link?

7. A 50 µm link has a power loss of 3.44 dB. According to Table 8-1, which protocols will not run on this link?

---

[6] The OPBA is different from the optical power budget requirement, OPBR, which is the total loss due to fiber attenuation, connector loss, splice loss, and passive and device loss.

# 9    HARDWARE

Chapter Objectives: in this chapter, you will learn of the types, locations and functions of hardware commonly used in fiber optic networks.

## 9.1    FUNCTIONS

All hardware in fiber optic networks increases the reliability or convenience of use of the network. Hardware increases the reliability by protecting network components or limiting what can be done to such components during use. For example, many hardware components, or portions of those components, limit bend radius of cable to reduce fiber breakage, excess power loss and delayed failure.

## 9.2    TYPES

### 9.2.1    ENCLOSURES

Enclosures are either indoor or outdoor enclosures (Figure 9-1 and Figure 9-2). Both protect cable ends, buffer tubes and fibers.

Figure 9-1: Indoor Enclosures[1]

Figure 9-2: Outdoor Splice Enclosure

---

[1] Courtesy of Panduit Corporation

Enclosures are required because termination and splicing require removal of cable structural materials. Such removal eliminates the protection provided by these materials.[2]

Both types of enclosures can accept multiple cables, although outdoor enclosures require a minimum of two cables. Both types include one or more mechanisms for gripping the cable strength members.

Indoor enclosures can be rack or wall mounted (Figure 9-1 and Figure 9-3). They can provide front and/or rear access to the interior. The front of the enclosure can be flush with the front of the rack or recessed to create an integral patch cord shelf. Enclosures can allow side, top or bottom cable entrance.

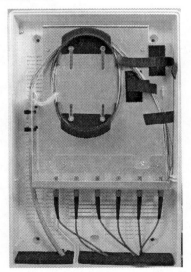

Figure 9-3: Wall Mounted Enclosure

Some indoor enclosures allow space for splice trays. Some include mechanisms to restrict bend radius (Figure 9-3).

---

[2] The one exception is the break out cable design, which provides protection with an inner jacket and strength members with each fiber. See Chapter 4.

Indoor enclosures are sized to the number of fiber ends. The use of SFF connectors doubles the number of connectors in an enclosure. With SFF connectors, the number of fiber ends in a 1U enclosure can be as high as 48.[3] This increase in end count increases the total length of fiber and/or buffer tube, in an enclosure. With 48 ends in a 1U enclosure and 3' of fiber per end, the total fiber length would be 144'. Such a large amount of fiber can result in increased maintenance cost.[4] In short, packing enclosures with as much fiber as possible may increase maintenance cost, and therefore, be counterproductive.

Outdoor enclosures can be single shell or multiple shells. The shell can be a single piece (Figure 9-4) or multiple pieces (Figure 9-5). With a single piece shell, moisture seals are provided at the ends. With a multiple piece shell, moisture seals are provided at the ends and along the perimeter.

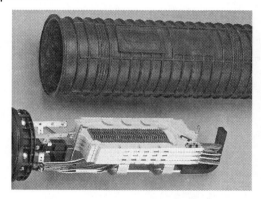

Figure 9-4: Single Piece Enclosure Shell

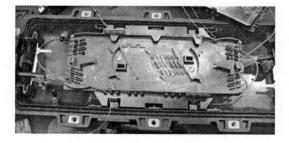

Figure 9-5: Multiple Piece Enclosure Shell

---

[3] 1U is 1.75" high; 2U, 3.5" high, and so forth.

[4] According to Murphy's Law, the fiber in need of repair will be the fiber on the bottom. In addition, repair of one fiber may result in damage to another.

Some outdoor enclosures have two shells. The space between the shells may be filled with a re-enterable moisture blocking gel. Outdoor enclosures are sized to the number of splices and the number of cables.

## 9.2.2    PATCH PANELS

Patch panels are metal or plastic plates that are formed to accept connector barrels. Although these panels can be independent of an enclosure, they are more commonly inserts, or modules, that are installed into indoor enclosures (Figure 9-6). The module form allows for convenient access of an individual connector or a group of connectors from the front of the enclosure.

Figure 9-6: Patch Panel Modules[5]

## 9.2.3    INNER DUCT/SUB DUCT

Installers use inner duct (Figure 9-7) in two situations: for underground, cable systems and for indoor cable systems. In outdoor systems, the inner duct, or flexible conduit, is used to create a crush resistant, rodent resistant, dielectric cable plant without armor. The inner duct provides a crush resistance that armor would provide. In addition, the inner duct is large enough that rodents cannot chew through the duct to damage the cable. Finally, elimination of armor reduces the cable cost and the installation cost. With the elimination of armor, the installer need not ground and bond the cable. Grounding and bonding are initial installation costs and maintenance costs.

In indoor cable systems, inner duct segregates and protects fiber cable that is placed in cable trays, cable troughs and cable raceways with other, heavier, copper cables. Such segregation increases network reliability in two ways. First, cable segregation reduces the possibility that the

---

[5] Courtesy Panduit Corporation.

SUCCESSFUL FIBER OPTIC INSTALLATION

fiber cable is cut for rerouting. Second, such segregation eliminates the placement of heavy copper cables on top of the fiber cables. When the fiber cables are on the bottom of a cable ladder tray, such placement can result in bend radius violation, in fiber breakage and in excess power loss.

Figure 9-7: Inner Duct

Installers use sub duct inside of conduit to utilize conduit volume efficiently and prevent installation problems. Unless installed at the same time, fiber cables are restricted to one per sub duct.

This restriction helps avoid two problems. The first problem occurs when the pull rope snakes around the first cable installed. In this situation, the second cable will experience high friction and high installation load. Such a load may violate the installation load rating of the cable.

The second problem occurs when the second cable is forced to violate its bend radius by snaking around the first. Both violations can result in fiber breakage, increased power loss and reduced reliability.

## 9.2.4    CABLE TRAYS

Cable trays house and protect splices. Outdoor enclosures always include internal cable trays (Figure 9-8). Indoor enclosures can include internal cable trays (Figure 9-9) when the main cable is spliced to pigtails. Trays are sized to the number of splices and to the enclosure housing the trays.

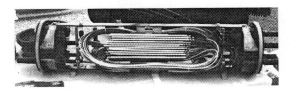

Figure 9-8: Cable Trays in Outdoor Enclosure

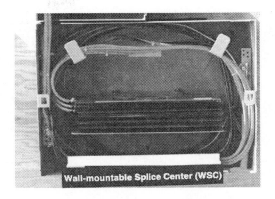

Figure 9-9: Cable Trays in Indoor Enclosure

## 9.2.5    STORAGE LOOP HOLDERS

The storage, or service, loop allows an aerial cable to be rerouted to a new pole location without breaking and splicing. Storage loop holders (Figure 9-10) are devices that control the bend radius of the cable while creating storage of service. Usually placed in pairs at a fifty-foot spacing, the storage loop holder creates a 100-foot service loop.

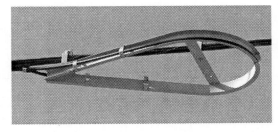

Figure 9-10: Storage Loop Holder

## 9.2.6    CABLE HANGING HARDWARE

Cable handing hardware includes all products that enable an aerial cable system to be installed in a reliable manner. At its simplest, cable hanging hardware consists of a stranded steel wire, called a messenger or strand cable. The installer attached the fiber optic cable to the messenger wire by wrapping a smaller wire around both the fiber cable and the messenger.

© PEARSON TECHNOLOGIES INC.

Figure 9-11: ADSS Pole Cable Grip

Figure 9-12: Mid Span Tap Cable Grip

Figure 9-13: End Cable Support

At its most complex, cable-hanging hardware includes the products in Figure 9-11 to Figure 9-13.[6] Each of these products serves a specific function based on its location.

### 9.2.7    CABLE ROUTING HARDWARE

Cable routing hardware consists of the hardware used indoors to control and route the cables.[7] Figure 9-14 demonstrates the bend radius control of cables from an overhead trough system into racks. Figure 9-15 demonstrates the bend radius control in the trough. Figure 9-16 demonstrates bend radius control within the rack.

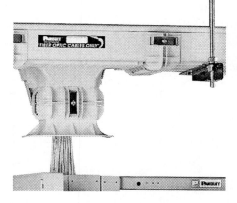

Figure 9-14: Bend Radius Control From Trough to Rack

## 9.3    SUMMARY

The prime function of hardware is provision of reliability. Hardware provides this protection by confining cables and connectors to a restricted access volume and by limiting the bend radius of cables placed in the hardware. While these functions determine the some of the design features of such hardware, ease of use determines other, equally important design features.

Figure 9-15: Bend Radius Control In Trough

---

[6] Figure 9-11 to Figure 9-13 are courtesy of Preformed Line Products.

[7] Figure 9-14 to Figure 9-16 are courtesy of Panduit Corporation.

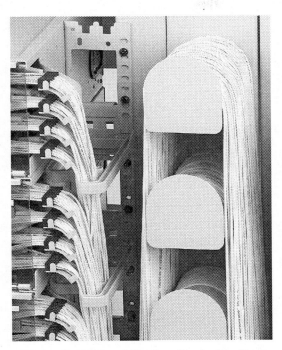

Figure 9-16: Bend Radius Control In Rack

## 9.4    REVIEW QUESTIONS

1.  What is the prime function of all fiber optic hardware?

2.  What are the reasons for use of inner duct?

3.  What are the reasons that fiber optic cables are not normally installed into an inner duct that has previously installed cables?

4.  If there is one specific function that most hardware provides, what is that function?

# PART TWO

# ESSENTIAL PRINCIPLES AND METHODS

# INTRODUCTION

A definition of principle is: "an essential element, constituent, or quality, especially one that produces a specific effect; as, the active principle of a medicine."[1] This definition applies to the information in Part 2. All the principles in this part result in the specific effects, or goals, of low power loss, low installation cost or high reliability.

We have highlighted the principles, or specific effects and the methods by which the installer achieves these effects. To highlight the principle, we have used one symbol (▶) before the Principle and another (▶▶) before the Method. These principles and methods support the three goals and result in the procedures in Part 3.

---

[1] Webster's New Twentieth Century Dictionary, Unabridged.

# 10    CABLE INSTALLATION PRINCIPLES

Chapter Objectives:  from this chapter, you will learn the principles for installation and preparation of the ends of fiber optic cables.

## 10.1    INTRODUCTION

There are four goals of the process of cable installation:

> Avoid breakage

> Avoid reduced power at the receiver

> Avoid reduced reliability

> Proceed in a safe manner

To meet these four goals, the installer needs to conform to principles. We organize these principles into five groups:

> Environmental limitation principles

> Installation limitation principles

> Management concern principles

> Safety principles

> End preparation principles

## 10.2    ENVIRONMENTAL LIMITS

The fiber network designer is responsible for specification of a cable proper for the intended environment. With this definition of responsibility, the installer need not be concerned with environment limitations. However, network designers can fail to consider or recognize all environmental conditions. In order to be complete, and to reflect common field problems, we provide this first principle.

### 10.2.1    ▶RESPECT ENVIRONMENTAL LIMITS

The installer must install the cable in environmental conditions that are within its limits.  Should the cable be exposed the conditions in excess of its limits, the cable can fail to protect the fibers. Such failure can lead to fiber breakage and excessive attenuation rate.

While not exhaustive, five environmental conditions represent most of the conditions[1] that have caused installation problems:

> Moisture

> Operating temperature range

> Bend radii

> Crush load

> Use load and vertical rise distance

An installer can install a cable that is not moisture resistant in an environment that contains moisture. Such a cable can:

> Channel moisture into electronics

> Develop increased attenuation rate and fiber breakage due to frozen water, and

> Experience reduced fiber strength and breakage due to attack from the chemicals in ground water.

An installer can install a cable in an environment with a temperature outside of the operating range of the cable. Such a cable can develop:

> Increased attenuation rate[2] and

> Degradation of cable materials.

In the former case, there may be insufficient power at the receiver for proper link operation. In the latter case, the fibers may break.

During installation, the installer can bend a cable to less than either of the two bend radii (4.4.2). In this case, the cable can develop:

> Increased attenuation rate

---

[1] This is a statement of the author's experience, not a statement with statistical support.

[2] This increase occurs at both low and high temperatures. We are aware of such problems occurring in hospitals and other facilities with steam tunnels.

> ➢ Fiber breakage and
>
> ➢ Reduction of fiber strength

Such a situation can occur in an underground conduit path, in which the conduit sweep, or elbow, has a radius less than either bend radius of the cable. In this situation, the cable path (its' environment) is forcing a violation of the bend radius.

If installer installs a cable in an environment that imposes either a long term or short-term crush load in excess of the limit of the cable, the cable can experience increased attenuation rate and fiber breakage. Such a situation could occur when an indoor, tight tube cable is directly buried in the ground.

An installer can install a cable with a long term, or use, load on the cable in excess of the rating of the cable. The same two problems, increased attenuation rate and fiber breakage, can occur.

## 10.2.2    ▶LIMIT THE USE LOAD

The installer limits the long-term load to a value less than or equal to the rating of the cable. To do so, he obtains the use load from on a data sheet, a web page, or the manufacturer.[3] Such a condition occurs when the cable is installed between widely spaced buildings, widely spaced telephone poles, widely spaced power transmission towers, and up a long vertical rise.

## 10.2.3    ▶LIMIT THE VERTICAL RISE DISTANCE

The installer limits the cable to a vertical distance to a value less than the vertical rise limit. To do so, the installer obtains the vertical rise limit from the data sheet, a web page, or the manufacturer. The installer can achieve a total vertical rise distance in excess of this limit by supporting the cable, such as with cable ties, at a separation no greater than this limit.

A long vertical rise exists in a 50-story building and on the side of a tall TV

transmission tower. When installed up a long vertical rise, the cable is exposed to a long-term load. This load is related to the maximum vertical rise distance, which is the maximum distance at which a cable experiences its maximum use load.

## 10.2.4    ▶▶LOOSE TUBE SERVICE LOOPS

Loose tube cables installed vertically need service loops at separations of less than the maximum vertical rise distance to avoid creating a straight vertical path, through which the fiber can slide out of the cable.[4]

## 10.3    INSTALLATION LIMITS

There are two types of cable installation: pulling the cable into its path and placing the cable in its location. The installer installs the cable with installation conditions that are within the limits of the cable. In this section, we address the pulling of the cable.

Cables have three major and two minor installation limitations:

> ➢ No twisting
>
> ➢ Installation load
>
> ➢ Installation bend radius
>
> ➢ Installation temperature range
>
> ➢ Storage temperature range

## 10.3.1    ▶NO TWISTING

Avoidance of fiber breakage requires that fiber cables be installed without twisting.

### 10.3.1.1    ▶▶USE SWIVEL

In order to avoid twisting, the installer uses a pulling swivel between the pulling rope and the cable (Figure 10-1).

## 10.3.2    INSTALLATION LOAD

In order to comply with the installation load limit, the installer must know the load limit

---

[3] This principle applies to all products to be installed, including connectors, splices, enclosures and passive devices.

[4] Because indoor cables must comply with the National Electric Code, they have no gel or grease, which tends to hold the fibers in place, even when the cables are installed in a vertical riser. This feature of loose tube cables is one that reinforces the preference for tight tube cables in vertical risers within buildings.

and have a method for limiting the load applied to the cable. The installer will know the limit from the data sheet for the cable, creating two principles.

### 10.3.2.1   ▶LIMIT INSTALLATION LOAD

The installer limits the installation load applied to the cable. To do so, the installer obtains the limits from data sheets.

There are three methods by which an installer can limit the short-term, or installation, load applied to a cable. In addition, there is one additional method for reducing the applied installation load.

The three methods have the advantage of providing concrete evidence that the installation load has not been exceeded. These methods are use of a:

➢ Pulling eye with a swivel with a shear pin (Figure 10-1)

➢ Pulling device with a slip clutch (Figure 10-2)

➢ Pulling device with a load gage (Figure 10-3)

Figure 10-1: Swivel With Shear Pins[5]

### 10.3.2.1.1   ▶▶USE SHEAR PIN

The installer attaches the pull rope and the cable to the pulling eye. The swivel allows the installer to pull the cable without twisting, which can result in broken fibers.

The eye has a shear pin, which is rated at a load less than the maximum installation load rating of the cable. For example, a cable with a rating of 600 pounds-force would

---

[5] Figures 10-1 and 10-2 are courtesy of Greenlee/Textron.

require a shear pin rated at 500-550 pounds-force. If the installer exceeds the shear pin rating, it, not the cable, breaks.

Figure 10-2: Puller With Slip Clutch

Figure 10-3: Puller With Load Gage[6]

### 10.3.2.1.2   ▶▶USE SLIP CLUTCH

The installer can use a pulling eye with a swivel without a shear pin if he has some other method of limiting the load applied to the cable. Pullers have two methods to provide such limitation. These methods are a slip clutch and a load gage.

---

[6] Figure 10-3 is courtesy of Condux International.

An installer can set the slip clutch of a puller (Figure 10-2) to a level less than the installation load rating of the cable. Should the applied load exceed the level set, the clutch slips eliminating fiber damage.

### 10.3.2.1.3   ▶▶USE LOAD GUAGE

An installer can set the load gage of a puller (Figure 10-3) to a level less than the installation load rating of the cable. Should the applied load exceed the level set, the load gage stops the pulling motor without fiber breakage or damage. The load gage has an additional advantage: it allows attachment of a chart recorder, which provides proof that the installer did not load the cable in excess of it's rating.

### 10.3.2.1.4   ▶▶USE LUBRICANT

These three methods limit the load but do nothing to reduce the load. One method for reducing the load is use of a fiber optic cable lubricant.

The installer can use a cable lubricant to reduce friction and load on the cable. While copper cable lubricants exist, the installer should use a fiber optic cable lubricant, as such a lubricant is matched to the jacket of the cable.[7]

### 10.3.2.1.5   ▶▶USE FIGURE 8 INSTALLATION

The installer can pull the cable by hand in a single, long pull or in multiple, reduced length pulls. Breaking a long pull into multiple pulls of reduced length reduces the load placed on the cable during each of the segment pulls. If the installer installs the cable in multiple pulls, he will store the cable at intermediate locations in a 'Figure 8' pattern. The advantage of this method is reduced load. The disadvantage is increased labor cost.

During a 'Figure 8' pull, the installer pulls the cable into the first manhole[8] and out of a subsequent manhole (Figure 10-4). The subsequent manhole may be the next manhole along the cable path or the $n^{th}$ manhole along the path. The installer

determines this manhole by the load he is able and willing to impose on the cable.

As the installer pulls the cable from the manhole, he places the cable on the ground in a 'Figure 8' pattern (Figure 10-5). This pattern can be 12 feet high and 4-6 feet wide. For practical reasons, the pattern is rarely higher than 24 inches.

When the installer has pulled all the cable out of the manhole, he, and several helpers, pick up the 'Figure 8' and flip it over so that the cable end is on top.

The installer pulls the cable back into the same manhole and out another manhole along the cable path (Figure 10-6). At this manhole, the installer repeats the 'Figure 8' pattern on the ground. The installer can repeat this process as many times as desired, until the cable is installed along the entire path.

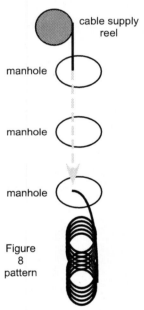

Figure 10-4: Installation Into Underground Conduit Path, Step 1

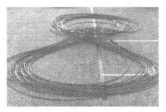

Figure 10-5: Cable Storage In A Figure 8 Pattern

---

[7] Fiber cables have jacket materials that are slightly different from those of copper cables.

[8] Or conduit segment.

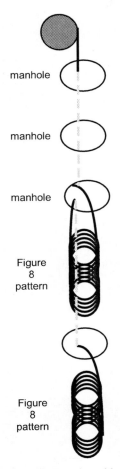

Figure 10-6: Installation Into Underground Conduit Path, Step 2

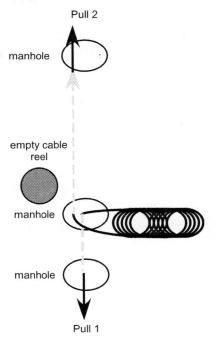

Figure 10-7: A Mid Pull

The installer can use the Figure 8 method for both unidirectional pulls (Figure 10-4 and Figure 10-6), and mid pulls, (Figure 10-7). In a mid pull, the installer pulls the cable in one direction, ('pull 1', Figure 10-7). He places the remaining cable in a figure 8 pattern on the ground. Finally, he pulls the cable from the figure 8 pattern in the opposite direction ('pull 2', Figure 10-7).

Some professional installers use a fourth method for limiting the load they apply during installation. This method requires installation of a 600 pound-force cable by hand pulling. The assumption is that it is essentially impossible to create a 600-pound load by hand pulling in a horizontal axis. This method does not have the advantage of providing concrete evidence that they have not been exceeded the installation load rating.

### 10.3.2.2  ▶DO NOT LOAD FIBERS

All four methods require attachment of a pull rope to the cable. The installer attaches a pull rope to a cable so that the cable strength members support the load and that no load is imposed on the fibers.

The installer has at least six attachment possibilities:

➢  Attachment of the pull rope around the outside of the cable jacket

➢  Attachment of the pull rope to a Kellems grip (Figure 10-8) that grips the cable through the jacket

➢  Attachment of the pull rope to strength members in the center of the cable

➢  Attachment of the pull rope to strength members outside a loose buffer tube

➢  Attachment of the pull rope to strength members under an outer jacket

➢  Attachment of the pull rope to strength members between multiple jackets

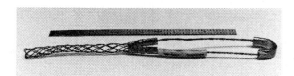

Figure 10-8: Kellems Grip

#### 10.3.2.2.1 ▶▶USE RECOMMENDED ATTACHMENT METHOD

With all these possibilities, the installer needs another principle. The best method of attachment is the method recommended by the cable manufacturer.

The manufacturer has designed the cable so that it can be installed without damage. He has done so by assuming that the installer will attach the pull rope to specific strength members. Attachment of a pull rope to any cable structural element other than these specific strength members may result in load imposed on the fibers.

#### 10.3.2.3 ▶▶USE LOOSE TUBE CABLE FOR HIGH LOAD INSTALLATION

There is one final principle that some installers follow. The installer uses a loose tube cable design for installations in which the installation load will be very high. The excess fiber (4.1.1.1) in this type of cable allows the fiber to move to reduce the stress on the fiber. This movement can be for hundreds of feet from the high stress area.[9]

## 10.3.3  ▶LIMIT BEND RADII

In order to avoid breakage and increased attenuation rate, the installer limits the bend radii of the cable to above the minimum value, such as those values in Equations 10-1 and 10-2.[10] This limitation means that each deviation from a straight path requires some form of control, such as a pulley or sheave. To ensure compliance with these limits, the installer obtains the values from the data sheet or other sources.

---

[9] An example of a high load installation: a professional installer applied a 1200 pound-force load to a loose tube cable rated at 600 pounds-force without experiencing fiber breakage or residual increase in attenuation rate.

[10] As a convenience, we repeat these equations from Chapter 4.

Short term bend radius = 20 x cable diameter

Equation 10-1

Long term bend radius = 10 x cable diameter

Equation 10-2

#### 10.3.3.1  ▶▶MONITOR SUPPLY REEL

The installer monitors the supply reel to avoid bend radius violations due to:

➢  Improper winding of cable on reel

➢  Loosening of cable

➢  Cable wrapping around the shaft supporting the reel

➢  Back wrapping when the pull stops

If the cable is improperly wound on the reel (Figure 10-9), the cable will attempt to pull a lower layer from under an upper layer. This situation results in the cable making a right angle as it leaves the reel- an obvious bend radius violation !

Figure 10-9: Cable Wound Incorrectly

If the cable loosens during the pulling process, it can ride over the top of the flange of the reel and wrap around the shaft that supports the reel. This situation is another example of bend radius violation.

If the installer does not stop the reel from rotating at the end of the pull, the cable can wrap backwards around the reel. Back wrapping provides a third example of bend radius violation.

#### 10.3.3.2  ▶▶COMMUNICATE AND COORDINATE PULLING

The installer communicates and coordinates the pulling actions. In advance of the stop, the installer in charge of the pulling equipment will inform the installer at the cable supply reel of the intent to. With this advance notice, the installer at the supply reel can don the heavy work gloves needed to avoid splinters as he grabs the rapidly spinning flange of the supply reel in order to stop the reel.

### 10.3.3.3 ▶▶3 PEOPLE PER PULL

The reality of the pulling operation is that the installer in charge of the pulling equipment can forget to alert the installer at the cable supply reel. Because of this possibility, each installation requires a minimum of three installers. The third installer coordinates the activity of the other two.

### 10.3.3.4 ▶▶MONITOR ALL PULLEYS

An installer monitors each pulley location (10.3.3). Should the cable jump from the pulley, the installer can have two problems: fiber damage due to bend radius violation and strength member damage.

Should the cable jump from a pulley, the bend radius is no longer under control. In addition, the cable may enter a metal conduit and scrape against a sharp edge at the entrance of the conduit. Should this sharp edge cut through the jacket, it may damage strength members that are under the jacket. Such damage will reduce the installation load capability of the cable, increasing the likelihood of fiber damage.

### 10.3.3.5 ▶▶ALWAYS PULL CABLE

During installation, the installer will pull, not push the cable. Pushing can cause a violation of the bend radius.

### 10.3.3.6 ▶LIMIT LONG TERM BEND RADIUS

At all times during the process, the installer must limit the long-term bend radius to a value larger than the minimum value, such as that in Equation 10-2.

## 10.3.4 INSTALLATION AND STORAGE TEMPERATURES

The installation temperature range is the range within which the installer can install the cable without damage. The storage temperature range is the range within which

the installer can store the cable without damage.

### 10.3.4.1 ▶COMPLY WITH INSTALLATION TEMPERATURE RANGE

The installer installs the cable at a temperature within the installation temperature range specified on the data sheet. At excessively low temperatures, the cable materials may be brittle enough to crack. At excessively high temperatures, the cable materials may stretch excessively, resulting in many problems.

### 10.3.4.2 ▶COMPLY WITH STORAGE TEMPERATURE RANGE

The installer stores the cable at a temperature within the storage temperature range specified on the data sheet. Storage of a cable at a temperature outside of its storage range will cause the same material problems previously mentioned (10.3.4.1).

## 10.4  CABLE PLACEMENT

In this section, we address the issue of cable placement. By placement, we mean installation without pulling. Such placement occurs in cable trays, cable troughs and cable raceways.

## 10.4.1  ▶▶BUNDLE CABLES

The installer bundles cables running along same path. Bundling reduces the risk of bend radius violation.

## 10.4.2  ▶▶ USE VELCRO™ BANDS

The installer uses Velcro™ bands to bundle cables. Cable ties can be tightened excessively, causing a bend radius violation and excess power loss under each tie. Velcro bands minimize the risk of bend radius violation.

## 10.4.3  ▶▶HAND TIGHTEN TIES

The installer tightens cable ties by hand, not with a cable tie tool, or gun. Excessively tight cable ties can deform the cable jacket, resulting in a localized bend radius violation and excess power loss.

### 10.4.4    ▶▶SEGREGATE FIBER CABLES

Whenever copper and fiber cables reside in the same tray, the installer places the fiber cables in inner duct. By segregating the two types of cables, the installer reduces the risk of crush load violations and bend radius violations of the fiber cables.

When fiber cables are in ladder trays, the installer places the fiber cables in inner duct. Ladder trays can cause localized bend radius violations in two situations: when heavy copper cables are installed on top of fiber cables and when small fiber cables[11] are on the bottom.

### 10.4.5    ▶▶LEAVE SERVICE LOOPS

The installer leaves service loops throughout the link. Service loops are lengths of excess cable that can be pulled into problem areas. Service loops are inexpensive insurance: they are less expensive than replacing the entire segment!

For indoor links, a common practice is a 10-12' service loop near the end of each link. This service loop may be coiled in the back of an enclosure or stored in a coil on a cable tray or above a ceiling.

For outdoor links, a common practice is a 100' service loop for each 1000' of cable. In addition, there is a 100' service loop for each street crossing, with no more than 200' feet of service loop per 1000' of cable. Finally, there will be a service loop of at least 10-12' at each cable end.[12] For aerial cable systems, service loop holders (Figure 9-10) will hold the service loop.

### 10.4.6    ▶▶MARK CABLE

In any location in which the cable can be accessed, the installer marks it as "Fiber Optic Cable". When the cables are so

marked, electricians will not be tempted to cut, reroute and splice them with black tape!

### 10.4.7    ▶▶LEAVE SAG

Installers install outdoor cables with sag to allow for thermal expansion and contraction. Failure to allow for expansion will result in fiber breakage. A 2.5-foot sag for 150-foot span is a common practice.

### 10.4.8    ▶NEC COMPLIANCE

Indoor cables must comply with the National Electric Code (NEC) and local electrical codes (4.3). Horizontal cable runs require OFN or OFC-rated cables. Cable runs between floors require OFNR or OFNC-rated cables. Cable runs in air handling plenums require OFNP or OFCP-rated cables. In addition, firewall penetrations must meet the requirements of the applicable fire code. As the NEC requires that compliant cables be printed with their rating and test number, the installer reads the printed information to determine compliance.

## 10.5    PLANNING AND MANAGEMENT ISSUES

Installers avoid many common problems through planning. Such planning will include the following twelve considerations. These considerations include management issues for connector installation and splicing.

> ➤ Identification of the equipment and supplies required

> ➤ Determination of the equipment locations

> ➤ Obtaining data sheets for all products to be installed

> ➤ Identification of the recommended installation techniques

> ➤ Determination of the installation methods to be used

> ➤ Determination of the people required

> ➤ Assignment of activities to people with appropriate knowledge and experience

---

[11] Somewhat arbitrarily, we define small at 12 or fewer fibers. The key parameter is the stiffness of the jacket material. The stiffer the jacket material, the less likely there will be such bend radius violations.

[12] This service loop is in addition to the length of cable that will be stripped for termination.

- ➢ Determination of the testing needs
- ➢ Creation of testing data forms
- ➢ Creation of As-Built Data Logs
- ➢ Identification of potential problem issues
- ➢ Identification of potential safety issues

Equipment and supplies include such items as pulling equipment, pulling ropes, cable lubricant, pulleys, cable ties, epoxy curing ovens, connector polishing films, etc.

After identifying the equipment required, the installer determines the equipment locations. For example, pulling equipment needs to be attached to a structure heavy enough to prevent movement (Figure 10-3).

The installer avoids problems with the information he obtains from data sheets for all products to be installed. For example, cable data sheets will include limits such as installation load, use load, and bend radii. Such information is essential to avoid damage due to violations of these limits.

The installer needs to identify the installation techniques recommended by the manufacturer of the cables, connectors, and splices to be used. Such information may be included in the data sheets. However, such information may be in application notes issued by the manufacturer. With such application notes, the installer will be able to avoid errors that damage the products.

Because the recommended installation method may not be best suited to all situations, the installer may need to use a method different from that recommended by the manufacturer. In this case, the installer must determine the specific installation method to use.

The supervisor will need to determine the number of installers required and the experience required for each activity. The experience of the installer will be appropriate for the activity to which he is assigned.

## 10.5.1 ▶▶TRAIN ALL PERSONNEL

The supervisor ensures that all installation personnel have the appropriate experience and training. All personnel who handle cables and connectors need some training. Even network technicians who install patch cords into patch panels and optoelectronics need to know about bend radius limitations, cleanliness of connectors, and caps on connectors and on optoelectronic ports.

Lack of adequate or appropriate training and experience is the single largest cause of fiber installation problems. For example, an installer with splicing experience should not be assigned to install connectors. As a second example, an installer who has had 1-hour of training in connector installation may have problems when assigned to install 500 connectors.

One method of verifying adequate experience is certification of personnel. The Fiber Optic Association offers a four-certification process based on written examinations and quantity of experience.[13] This examination is generic and not biased towards or against any products.

## 10.5.2 ▶▶CHECK CABLE BEFORE EACH OPERATION

The supervisor determines the testing needs. A common procedure is a check of continuity and attenuation before each operation. This procedure results in checks:

- ➢ As received or before installation
- ➢ After cable installation
- ➢ After splicing, and
- ➢ After all installation activities

## 10.5.3 ▶▶CREATE TEST FORMS

Before beginning the installation, the installer creates test data forms. Such data forms can be used to check the status of the installation. If the testing after one step is complete, the installers can proceed to the next step.

---

[13] Contact 760-451-3655 or www.thefoa.org.

## 10.5.4 ▶▶CREATE AS-BUILT RECORDS

The final testing results in a set of 'as-built' data records. These 'as-built' records greatly simplify troubleshooting. If current tests of the cable link reveal no changes in values from the 'as-built' values, any problems are in the optoelectronics, not in the cable link.

Good practices for 'as-built' records are:

➤ Creation of three copies

➤ Inclusion all information on the testing method

The three copies are: an archive copy; an open copy that is available to any who would need it; and a project manager copy.

The test information will include test technique, wavelength, spectral width, equipment used and direction of test and all information sufficient to enable exact reproduction of the test. Without the ability to exactly reproduce the test, the installer will not know whether changes in insertion loss and OTDR values are due to changes in the test technique or to degradation of the cable, connectors, or splices.

## 10.5.5 ANTICIPATE PROBLEMS

Before the start of the installation, the supervisor attempts to identify potential problems. In addition, he develops plans to avoid such problems and to solve such potential problems.

## 10.6 SAFETY ISSUES

Among potential problems are safety issues. The supervisor reviews the entire installation process to identify potential safety issues, with the goal of avoiding and solving such issues.

As optical fiber is small, and potentially dangerous, the installer uses procedures that minimize the possibility of fiber splinters.[14] In addition, there is the possibility of eye damage from the invisible light produced by high power lasers used in testing equipment and transceivers, such as OTDRs, reflectance test sets, Gigabit

Ethernet transceivers and 10 Gigabit Ethernet transceivers.

## 10.6.1 EYE SAFETY

### 10.6.1.1 ▶▶WEAR SAFETY GLASSES

The installer wears safety glasses. Should a fiber 'jump' towards his face, the glasses will prevent the fiber from landing in his eyes. Such a fiber will be very difficult to find and to remove without causing eye damage.

### 10.6.1.2 ▶▶NO LIGHT IN FIBER

The installer does not look into a fiber or connector without disconnecting all equipment from the opposite end of fiber. Should the fiber have high power laser light while the installer is inspecting the fiber with a microscope, the laser light can burn the rods and cones of the retina. Damaged rods and cones will not regenerate.[15]

### 10.6.1.3 ▶▶IDENTIFY MEDICAL SERVICE LOCATION

Before beginning an installation, the installer identifies a local hospital with the capability to find and remove optical fiber. Optical fibers fluoresce under high intensity lights. Such lights are not a part of every medical facility. Knowledge of which local hospitals can address the problem of fiber in eyes, in mouths or in hands. Such knowledge will reduce the time required to correct such problems. Finally, such a time reduction can result in reduced damage caused by such problems.

## 10.6.2 HAND SAFETY

### 10.6.2.1 ▶▶BARE FIBER DISPOSAL

The installer places bare fiber in a disposable container of as soon as he creates it. With this approach, the bare fibers are controlled as much as is possible and will not cause problems by becoming splinters in hands.

[14] A splinter is a fiber without the primary coating.

[15] Self-imposed laser eye surgery is not part of a normal installation!

### 10.6.2.2   ▶▶USE WORK MAT

The installer uses a work mat with a dark, dull surface.[16] The dull surface makes it easy to find fiber splinters. Use of any other surface may make the fiber difficult to see. Such fiber can be lost and find its way onto clothing or into other undesirable areas.

### 10.6.2.3   ▶▶WASH HANDS

The installer washes his hands before using the rest room. The reason for this principle is obvious. Just image the conversation at a doctor's office or hospital!

## 10.6.3   CLOTHING SAFETY

### 10.6.3.1   ▶▶WEAR SMOCK

The installer wears a smock that is washed separately from other clothes. Fibers that are caught on such a smock will not be washed onto other clothing.

### 10.6.3.2   ▶▶WEAR SMOOTH CLOTHING

While working with fiber, the installer wears smooth clothing. Smooth clothing is less likely to catch and retain fibers than rough clothing such as sweaters and sweatshirts.

### 10.6.3.3   ▶▶USE LINT ROLLER

After each session in which the installer generates bare fibers, he uses a lint roller.[17] He cleans his arms, chest and lap to remove any bare fiber.

### 10.6.3.4   ▶▶ISOLATE WORK AREA

The installer isolates the work area from unauthorized or untrained personnel. While the installer may know how to avoid getting fiber splinters, others may not know either the danger of or the methods of avoiding such splinters.

## 10.6.4   MOUTH SAFETY

### 10.6.4.1   ▶▶NO FOOD IN WORK AREA

The installer does not eat, drink or smoke in any area in which he is creating bare glass fiber. All items that can find their way to the his mouth should be removed from the area in which the installer creates such fibers.[18]

## 10.6.5   CHEMICAL SAFETY

Fiber installation activities may require the use of hazardous chemicals. Safe use of such chemicals requires knowledge of their dangers and of the treatment required after exposure. The Material Safety Data Sheet (MSDS), whch is available from the chemical supplier, provides this knowledge.

## 10.7   END PREPARATION

After pulling and placing the cable, the installer prepares the cable ends for either splicing or connector installation.

## 10.7.1   ▶PROTECT BUFFER TUBES AND FIBERS

The installer protects buffer tubes and fibers. This rule means that the jacket ends inside of enclosure, not outside of enclosure. The buffer tubes and fibers are not designed to withstand exposure to the working environment.

## 10.7.2   ▶SEAL ENDS

The installer seals the ends of grease filled, gel blocked cables with a fiber optic cable sealant. Water blocking compounds can, and will, flow from even a small vertical drop. Such flow will cause maintenance problems. An improper sealant can attack primary coating of the fiber.[19]

---

[16] The Clauss word mat, Fiber Instrument Sales part number F1-0024 is such a matt.

[17] Or pet hair roller, which may be less expensive than a lint roller.

[18] Bare glass fiber splinters are very difficult to find and to remove. Fibers fall down towards the floor, so such items, such as coffee cups, soda cans, fruit, cigarette packages, and candy should not be near or under a worktable. Being on a high fiber diet does not mean ingesting optical fiber!

[19] It is our understanding that some silicone sealants cure to produce acetic acid while others cure to produce water. Acetic acid can attack the primary coating of the fiber.

## 10.8   SUMMARY

The installer can damage fiber optic cables during their installation. This damage may be observed in the form of excessive power loss. However, this damage may be hidden in the form of reduced reliability. The installer can achieve the maximum possible reliability by following installation procedures that comply with the principles in this chapter.

## 10.9   REVIEW QUESTIONS

1. An installation team is planning to pull a cable through an underground conduit system. The system consists of conduits between manholes. There are no sweeps at locations at which the cable path changes direction or at which the conduit changes elevation. What must the installer do at these changes of direction?

2. Regarding Question 1: the manholes in this system have a cover diameter of 36". With the assumption that the installers have single piece pulleys only, what is the maximum cable diameter that the installers can install without violation of the short term bend radius?

3. The installer is planning to place a service loop of cable inside the back of an enclosure mounted on a 19" rack. The loop will be mounted vertically in the enclosure. The enclosure fills the full width of the rack. What is the maximum cable diameter that the installer can place in this enclosure?

4. Regarding Question 3: How high must this enclosure be?

5. Installers are installing the cable system shown in Figure 10-10. The cable changes direction by exiting one conduit and entering another in each of the manholes indicated. The supervisor believes that the cable can be installed in a single pull. A swivel-pulling eye with a shear pin will control the load. The swivel is between the cable and the pull rope. A truck will be used to pull in the cable. The

supervisor needs to determine the minimum number of installers he needs to send. Including the truck driver, what is this number?

6. You observe your installer tying a pull rope to the strength members of a fiber cable. Do you see any problems with this activity?

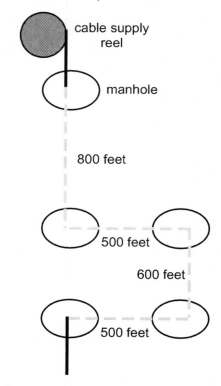

Figure 10-10: Map For Question 5

7. Make a list of the items needed to ensure safety of any cable and connector installation.

# 11   CONNECTOR INSTALLATION PRINCIPLES

Chapter Objectives: in this chapter, you will learn the principles for installation of fiber optic connectors. These principles result in the procedures of Part 3.

## 11.1   INTRODUCTION

In this chapter, we present the principles that result in the procedures for installation of fiber optic connectors. We present these principles for four installation methods:

➢ Epoxy and polish

➢ Quick cure adhesive

➢ Hot Melt™ adhesive

➢ Cleave and crimp

These methods are those most commonly used. These methods represent a majority of connectors installed in North America.

Taken as a group, these methods include combinations of the following five steps:

➢ End preparation of the cable

➢ Injection and curing of an adhesive

➢ Insertion of the fiber into the connector

➢ Crimping

➢ Connector end finishing

## 11.2   CABLE END PREPARATION

Cable end preparation involves:

➢ Removal of the jacket(s)

➢ Removal of water blocking compounds

➢ Trimming of strength members and

➢ Removal of buffer tube and primary coating (Figure 11-1, Figure 11-2 and Figure 11-3)

Figure 11-1: Single Fiber Cable End Prepared For Connector Installation

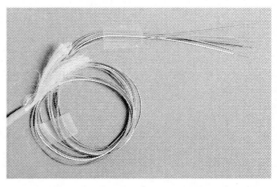

Figure 11-2: Eight Fiber Premises Cable End Prepared For Connector Installation

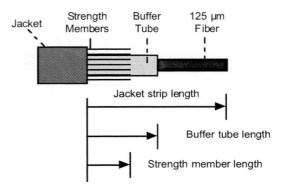

Figure 11-3: End Preparation Dimensions For Jacketed[1] Fiber

## 11.2.1   ▶DETERMINE DIMENSIONS

The cable end preparation dimensions depend on three factors:

➢ The nature of the installation

➢ The specific connector

➢ The specific enclosure in which the cable is to be installed

The installation can be either patch cord assembly or enclosure installation.

---

[1] Jacketed fiber means that each fiber has its own strength members and jacket.

### 11.2.1.1　PATCH CORD ASSEMBLY

For patch cord assembly,[2] the connector into which the cable is to be installed determines the end preparation dimensions. Six principles determine these dimensions (Figure 11-3).

#### 11.2.1.1.1　▶FIBER PROTRUDES THROUGH FERRULE

For connectors requiring polishing, two lengths, the jacket removal length and the bare fiber length, are long enough that:

> ➢ The bare fiber protrudes through the fiber hole in the ferrule

> ➢ The installer can remove the excess fiber easily

The fiber must protrude through the ferrule so that the fiber can be polished flush with the ferrule to create a round, clear, featureless, flush core (21).

For epoxy connectors, these two lengths may be increased to allow easy removal of the excess fiber. However, if the bare fiber length is increased excessively, the installer may break the fiber while installing the connector into a curing oven.

For some connector styles, such as the SC and the LC, the jacket removal length is increased. Such an increase enables a slight amount of flexing of the fiber when the connector is inserted into a patch panel. This flexing enables pull proof and wiggle proof behavior (5.4.3 and 5.4.4).

Excessive jacket removal length can result in two problems, long bare fiber and short jacket. Excessive bare fiber length can result in breakage during insertion through the ferrule. In some cases, this broken fiber can become jammed in the fiber hole, causing loss of the connector.

When the connector has quick cure adhesive, excessive fiber length can result

in premature adhesive curing and bare fiber inside the connector. Bare fiber inside a connector results in reduced reliability.

The SC connector installed with epoxy or quick cure adhesive provides an example of such reduced reliability: if there is bare fiber inside the connector or if the buffer tube is short, so that the buffer tube is not immersed in the epoxy or adhesive, bare fiber will remain inside the connector. The SC connector requires that the fiber in the back shell flex slightly whenever the connector is inserted into a patch panel. Repeated flexing of bare fiber results in breakage.[3]

The boot will not support a short jacket. A cable that is not covered by the boot is a condition of reduced reliability (Figure 11-4 and Figure 11-5).

Figure 11-4: Proper Jacket Removal Length

Figure 11-5: Improper Jacket Removal Length

#### 11.2.1.1.2　▶STRENGTH MEMBER GRIPPED

The strength member must extend beyond the end of the jacket enough to be gripped by the crimp sleeve.[4] For many connectors, the strength member length is 3/16" to 5/16".

Excessive strength member length can result in interference with proper operation of the connector. For example, excessive strength member length will prevent sliding

---

[2] We assume that patch cords contain one fiber in the jacket. This assumption means that the installer is installing connectors onto one fiber, zip cord duplex or break out cables. If the installer is creating a patch cord from a premises cable, the installer will install a break out, or furcation, kit on the end of the cable. After such installation, the installer will install a connector on each fiber as described herein.

[3] During training programs, we have observed such failure after 5-10 insertions.

[4] Some connectors have no crimp sleeve. Instead the strength member folds back over the jacket, which fits into the back shell of the connector. The back shell of the connector is crimped to both the strength member material and the jacket.

of the outer housing of an SC connector over the inner housing (Figure 5-2). Such sliding is necessary for both insertion and removal of the connector from a receptacle and a barrel.

### 11.2.1.1.3   ▶NO BARE FIBER

The buffer tube length must be long enough to butt against the inside of the ferrule, or to be completely immersed in an adhesive that hardens so the adhesive prevents motion of the bare fiber (Figure 11-6).

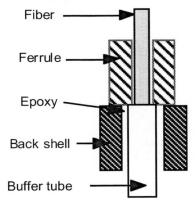

Fiber

Ferrule

Epoxy

Back shell

Buffer tube

Figure 11-6: Buffer Tube Butting Against Inside of Ferrule

The length of the buffer tube that remains after stripping must be sufficient to eliminate bare fiber inside the connector. Bare fiber in a connector is a condition that can result in reduced reliability.

### 11.2.1.1.4   ▶▶USE TEMPLATE

In order to comply with the principles in 11.2.1.1.1- 11.2.1.1.3, the installer uses a template for each connector type to control the stripping dimensions. This template has the form of Figure 11-3.

### 11.2.1.2   CRIMPING

This section applies to connectors that require adhesive. Connectors that require a cleaved fiber require a crimper that is unique to the connector. Crimping of such a connector grips the fiber and the buffer tube.

The installer performs crimping to attach the strength members in the cable to the connector back shell and to grip the jacket.[5]

_____

[5] Some cables experience jacket shrinkage, which is post extrusion shrinkage. Post extrusion

### 11.2.1.2.1   ▶USE PROPER NEST

An oversized crimp nest will not grip the strength members, allowing the connector to be pulled from the cable easily. An undersized crimp nest tends to destroy the crimp sleeve. In addition, the tolerance of the crimp sleeve is relatively tight.[6]

To avoid such problems, the installer uses the crimp nest size(s) recommended by the connector manufacturer (Figure 11-7).

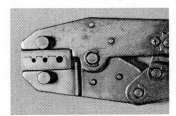

Figure 11-7: Crimp Nest In A Crimper

### 11.2.1.2.2   ▶▶LARGE CRIMP FIRST

The large diameter of the crimp sleeve attaches the strength members to the connector. Once this part of the crimp sleeve is attached to the connector, the connector cannot fall off the cable.

### 11.2.1.3   ENCLOSURE INSTALLATION

For installation of connectors onto a cable that is installed in an enclosure, both the enclosure and the connector determine the end preparation dimensions. These dimensions are determined by four principles.

### 11.2.1.3.1   ▶SUFFICIENT BUFFER TUBE LENGTH

For all connectors, the jacket removal length is long enough to enable the cable to be attached to the enclosure at a specific location (Figure 11-8 and Figure 11-9), to allow the buffer tube to extend outside the front of an enclosure for connector installation, and to allow the end of the buffer tube to reach the patch panel that is integral to the enclosure. Excess buffer tube

_____

shrinkage is similar to the insulation shrinkage observed the when a copper wire is soldered.

[6] For example, a 0.141" crimp nest may result in a loose crimp sleeve, while a 0.138" nest results in a tight sleeve.

length will be coiled inside of the enclosure (Figure 11-10).

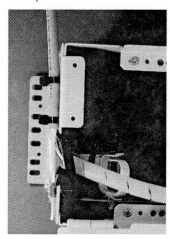

Figure 11-8: Indoor Cable Attachment Location

Figure 11-9: Outdoor Cable Attachment Location

This length must not be excessive, as excessive length can result in damage to the buffer tube when the volume of buffer tubes exceeds the capacity of the enclosure. As a practical matter, a practical tolerance on buffer tube length is ±1-2".[7]

Figure 11-10: Buffer Tube Coiled Inside Indoor Enclosure

---

[7] This is the author's estimate.

### 11.2.1.4　▶SUFFICIENT STRENGTH MEMBER LENGTH

The enclosure determines the strength member length. The enclosure is designed so that the strength members can be attached at a specific location (Figure 11-8 and Figure 11-9). In general, excessive strength member length is a cosmetic or workmanship concern, but not a performance or reliability concern.

For installation of connectors in an enclosure, the principles and methods in 11.2.1.1.1, 11.2.1.1.3 and 11.2.1.1.4 apply.

## 11.2.2　FIBER PREPARATION

In order to provide low power loss, the clearance between the cladding and the inside of the fiber hole is small. This small clearance requires prevention of both damage to and contamination of the cladding surface.

### 11.2.2.1　▶AVOID DAMAGE

Because the installer removes the primary coating in order to install the fiber into a connector, the cladding can become scratched or otherwise damaged.[8] Such damage can result in fiber breakage during installation.

### 11.2.2.2　▶AVOID CONTAMINATION

The installer cleans the fiber to remove contamination that would interfere with the fit of the fiber in the ferrule. After cleaning the fiber, the installer should not contaminate the fiber by placing the it down or against any surface prior to insertion.

### 11.2.2.3　THREE STEPS

To avoid such damage, breakage and contamination, the installer performs three steps in an uninterrupted sequence: he removes the last layer of protection from the fiber,[9] cleans the fiber and inserts the fiber into a connector.

---

[8] If the cladding is exposed to air for a significant length of time, moisture in the air can reduce the fiber strength.

[9] This last layer is either a primary coating from a fiber in a loose tube cable or the tight tube and primary coating from a fiber in a tight tube cable.

### 11.2.2.4 ▶▶LENS GRADE TISSUE

The installer cleans the fiber with lens grade tissues, which will not damage or contaminate the cladding. He uses 98 % isopropyl alcohol,[10] which leaves no residue (contamination) that would interfere with adhesive of the epoxy or adhesive.

## 11.3 ADHESIVES

We use the term 'adhesive' to mean any material that is used to glue, or fix in place, the fiber inside the connector. With this definition, we address three adhesive types:

➢ Epoxy

➢ Quick cure adhesive

➢ Hot melt adhesive

## 11.3.1 EPOXY

We define the term 'epoxy' to mean a one or two part chemical system that requires a minimum cure time of two minutes with heat or a minimum cure time of 6 hours without heat.[11]

### 11.3.1.1 THREE USE OBJECTIVES

Epoxy provides three functions:

➢ A strong bond between the fiber and the ferrule

➢ A strong bond between the buffer tube, or primary coating, and the connector back shell

➢ Support of the fiber protruding beyond the end of the ferrule during polishing

### 11.3.1.2 TYPES

We organize fiber optic epoxies into two main groups, each of which has three subgroups.[12] The two main groups are:

➢ Heat cured epoxies

➢ Room temperature cure epoxies

The three subgroups are based on curing time:[13]

➢ Fast cure (1-5 minutes)

➢ Medium cure (5-60 minutes)

➢ Slow cure (> 60 minutes)

Heat reduces cure time, but increases the chance of thermal cracking of the fiber. As the cure temperature increases, the likelihood of thermal cracking increases.

### 11.3.1.3 ▶PROPER STRENGTH

The curing time and temperature must be sufficient achieve adequate strength between the fiber and the ferrule. With insufficient strength, tension on the fiber can result in the fiber withdrawing into the ferrule. Pressure on the fiber can result in the fiber protruding from the ferrule. Both types of motion, called 'pistoning', are undesirable.

### 11.3.1.4 ▶USE PROPER COMBINATION

The combination of curing temperature, fiber core diameter, ferrule material and epoxy must result in sufficient strength. Heat curing can be used, as long as the combination of temperature, fiber core diameter, ferrule material and epoxy does not result in cracking.[14]

### 11.3.1.5 ▶AVOID CRACKING

Cracked fibers can result from excessive compressive stress during cooling to room temperature.[15] For singlemode, 62.5 µm fibers and 50 µm fibers, thermal cracking is rare. Cracks in fibers can divert the light from its proper path and cause in high connector loss.

---

[10] Isopropyl alcohol should be > 98 % pure. Rubbing alcohol is not suitable, as it contains oil that can prevent adhesion.

[11] These times are for convenience.

[12] This is grouping is for convenience.

[13] Again, these times are for convenience.

[14] When a heat cured connector is cooled to room temperature, the different thermal expansion rates of fiber, epoxy and ferrule can result in excessive compression of the fiber. This compression causes cracking.

[15] Cracked fibers can result from excessive force during end preparation. Such cracks are mechanical cracks.

### 11.3.1.6    ▶▶USE NO HEAT

Whenever practical, the installer uses an epoxy that cures at room temperature. Such an epoxy will not exhibit thermal cracking. In addition, there will be no thermostat to malfunction. Such a malfunction can result in cracking.

### 11.3.1.7    INJECTION

The installer injects epoxy into the back shell of the connector with a syringe. The amount he injects is critical to proper operation of the connector.

### 11.3.1.7.1    ▶NO INTERFERENCE

The epoxy is injected so that the epoxy does not interfere with proper operation of the connector.

### 11.3.1.7.2    ▶▶MINIMIZE EPOXY

Excessive epoxy can create connector malfunction due to expansion and displacement. When heated, excessive epoxy in the back shell will expand. Such expansion can cause the epoxy to flow out of the back shell onto other areas of the connector. Such epoxy can cause the connector to fail to function.

For example, the SC and LC connectors contain a tube inside the back shell (Figure 11-11 and Figure 11-12). This tube is mechanically independent of the back shell. Should epoxy flow between the tube and the back shell, the connector will lose its pull proof and wiggle proof performance.

In addition, such excessive, expanding epoxy can wick under a jacket via the strength members, making the cable rigid and extremely sensitive to handling.[16]

When the fiber and buffer tube are inserted into the back shell, excess epoxy will be displaced from the back shell. In the case of the SC and LC connectors, such displaced epoxy can flow between the central tube and the back shell. As stated earlier, the connector will lose its pull proof and wiggle proof performance (5.4.3 and 5.4.4).

To avoid excessive epoxy, the installer injects enough epoxy to fill the fiber hole in

---

[16] One trainee used so much epoxy that 6" of cable were rigid!

the ferrule and one additional drop in the bottom of the back shell (Figure 11-13). The additional drop bonds the buffer tube to the connector.

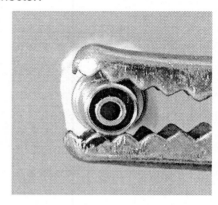

Figure 11-11: SC Inner Tube

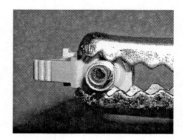

Figure 11-12: LC Inner Tube

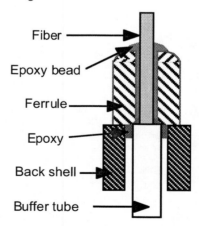

Figure 11-13: Sufficient Epoxy In Back Shell

### 11.3.1.7.3    ▶CONTROL BEAD SIZE

Connectors that use epoxy have a bead on the tip of the ferrule (Figure 11-13). During polishing, this bead supports the fiber. With this support, fiber shattering and mechanical cracks can be eliminated.

The size of the bead determines polishing time and process yield (through avoidance of shattering). As the bead size increases, the polishing time and cost increase. However, as the bead size increases, the incidence of shattering will decrease. Obviously, there is a trade off.

This trade off depends on the experience of the installer: the more experience the installer has, the smaller the bead can be. A practical strategy is a bead of approximately 0.020-0.030" high (Figure 11-14) for novice installers and a 0.015" bead for experienced installers (Figure 11-15).[17]

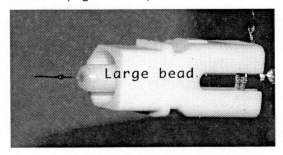

Figure 11-14: Large Bead For Inexperienced Installers

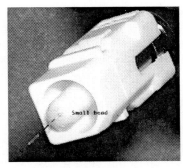

Figure 11-15: Small Bead For Moderately Experienced Installers

### 11.3.1.7.4    ▶▶REMOVE EPOXY

To control the bead size, the installer injects the epoxy. He wipes the epoxy from the tip of the ferrule. The size of the bead will be controlled by the epoxy forced through the fiber hole by the fiber and the length of the fiber. As long as the bare fiber length is consistent, this method results in a consistent bead size.

Highly experienced installers can follow a different method: after inserting the fiber,

they withdraw the fiber into the ferrule, wipe all epoxy from the tip of the ferrule and reinsert the fiber through the ferrule.[18] This method results in an extremely small bead, which is appropriate for hand polishing by highly experienced installers only.

Inexperienced installers can polish without damaging or shattering the fiber. They can add epoxy to the tip of the ferrule prior to curing the epoxy.

### 11.3.1.8    CURING

Curing[19] has three variables: expiration date, time and temperature. Epoxies may not cure after their expiration date. In addition, some epoxies will not cure if they have been exposed to freezing temperatures.

Epoxies will cure properly as long as the curing time exceeds a minimum time. Additional time will not cause degradation of the bond.

Temperature is a different matter. Low temperature will not result in full bond strength between the fiber and the ferrule. Without such a bond, the fiber can move into and out of the ferrule ('pistoning') during use. Such movement can result in link failure due to insufficient power at the receiver. Excessive curing temperature can result in degradation of the bond strength and in fiber cracks, as stated in 11.3.1.5.

### 11.3.1.8.1    ▶▶CONTROL OVEN

The installer controls the temperature at that recommended by the epoxy manufacturer. To ensure such control, he monitors the oven temperature with an accurate thermometer.[20]

To ensure the best possible temperature control, the installer chooses an oven with a thermostat that fails in the 'full off' mode. An

---

[17] As a visual reference, installers can use a paper clip. Paper clips have a diameter of approximately 0.030".

[18] A connector manufacturer recommended this technique in the mid 1980's.
We do not recommend this procedure.

[19] Some connector manufacturers recommend a cure time long enough to create a hard bead for polishing. However, this time does not cure the epoxy to full hardness.

[20] Oven thermostats do fail. Electronic thermometers seem to be more accurate than some glass and mercury or alcohol thermometers.

oven without such a thermostat will overheat and crack fibers.

## 11.3.2   QUICK CURE ADHESIVES

We define 'quick cure adhesive' to mean a one or two part chemical system that cures without heat in a relatively short time, typically less than two to five minutes.

### 11.3.2.1   TYPES

Quick cure adhesives can be a two part liquid product or a one-part gel product. In general, both are edge-filling adhesives: the hardening occurs when the adhesive fills a narrow space, such as that between the outside of the fiber the inside of the fiber hole in the ferrule.

### 11.3.2.2   INJECTION

Excess adhesive inside the connector can create the same problems as does excess epoxy. 11.3.1.8 applies to quick cure adhesives. In addition, two part, quick cure adhesives may not cure inside the back shell. Thus, excess adhesive inside the connector has no benefit.

#### 11.3.2.2.1   ▶▶DO NOT RUSH

By itself, two part, quick cure adhesive may cure very slowly. As a result of this characteristic, the installer need not rush the insertion of the fiber into the connector out of concern for premature curing of the adhesive. After being injected, the adhesive may not cure for five minutes.

### 11.3.2.3   PRIMER APPLICATION

The second part of some quick cure adhesive systems, called a primer, accelerator or hardener, is applied to the fiber prior to its insertion into the connector. This application can be by spraying, dipping or brushing.

#### 11.3.2.3.1   ▶▶BRUSH PRIMER

The installer applies the primer by brushing. We recommend against spraying, as spraying can create a mist of acetone, a carcinogen.

Dipping would seem to provide the most consistent and complete coverage of the fiber. However, dipping is not convenient when the primer bottle is partially empty. Brushing has proven convenient and without any observable problems.[21]

### 11.3.2.4   FIBER INSERTION

#### 11.3.2.4.1   ▶▶MINIMIZE DELAY

We have observed a problem with insertion of the fiber into the connector after wiping the primer onto the fiber. If the time between application of the primer and insertion of the fiber into the connector is excessive, the fiber may not fit into the fiber hole.[22] After wiping the primer onto the fiber, the installer inserts the fiber into the connector without delay.

#### 11.3.2.4.2   ▶▶INSERT QUICKLY

The primer on the fiber starts curing the adhesive in the connector as soon as the fiber is inserted into the connector. Quick-cure adhesives cure in less than two minutes, and, occasionally, in as little as 30 seconds. Because of this short cure time, the installer inserts the fiber into the connector reasonably quickly. To do otherwise would allow the adhesive to cure prior to full insertion of the fiber. Premature curing results in bare fiber inside the connector, a condition of low reliability. The installer installs the fiber quickly but without bending.

#### 11.3.2.4.3   TIP BEAD

Insertion of the fiber forces the quick cure adhesive from the fiber hole onto the tip of the connector. As the adhesive cures only when in thin sections, application of the primer to the fiber or to the tip of the ferrule results in a very small bead (Figure 11-16).

Repeated application of adhesive and primer to the tip of the ferrule does increase the bead size and increase the resistance to fiber shattering during polishing (Figure 11-17). However, the increase in bead size is not significant. In addition, application of

---

[21] In our training programs, we have used both dipping and brushing. We have observed no problems with brushing.

[22] Apparently, the acetone in the primer evaporates, leaving a residue layer that increases the fiber diameter to larger than that of the hole in the connector.

additional adhesive increases connector installation time, thus reducing the advantage of this method.

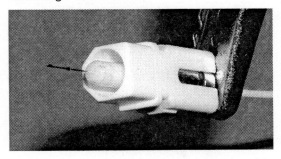

Figure 11-16: Bead Without Application Of Additional Adhesive Is Not Visible

Figure 11-17: Bead Size With Three Adhesive Applications

### 11.3.2.5    ▶▶USE OLD ADHESIVE

Curing begins as soon as the fiber is inserted into the connector. The older the adhesive is, the longer the cure time will be. Since 'old' adhesive cures slowly and provides increased time for fiber insertion, the installer in training will benefit from use of old, slow curing adhesive.

To verify full curing, the installer pulls on the cable. If the fiber protruding beyond the tip of the ferrule does not move into the ferrule, the adhesive has cured fully.[23]

## 11.3.3    HOT MELT ADHESIVE™

We define the term 'hot melt adhesive' to mean a one part adhesive with two

---

[23] Quick cure adhesive systems have expiration dates. We have used these adhesives at four years beyond their expiration dates for training novice installers. Cure time increases with adhesive age. Eventually, the adhesive fails to cure.

characteristics: it is preloaded in the connector and requires connector pre-heating prior to insertion of the fiber. 3M pioneered this system.

### 11.3.3.1    REHEATABILITY

Because the adhesive can be reheated, it is possible to salvage and repair damaged connectors. This characteristic results in reduced installation and maintenance costs.

### 11.3.3.1.1    ▶▶EXTRA FIBER

The installer inserts the fiber fully into the connector. He can withdraw the fiber by approximately 1/16". With this method of insertion, there will be the extra bare fiber buried in the adhesive. After the installer reheats the connector, he can push this extra fiber through the ferrule for a second polishing to repair a damaged core.

Because the adhesive softens with heat, reheating is possible to repair a damaged fiber. However, this repair is possible only if there is 'extra' bare fiber inside the connector.

### 11.3.3.1.2    ▶RE-USE

If a fiber is so badly shattered that it cannot be re-polished as in 11.3.3.1.1, the installer can reheat the connector, remove the fiber, prepare a new cable end and reinsert the new end into the connector. This method can result in 100 % yield and reduced maintenance cost.

This method works well with connectors installed on premises cable. This method can work once or twice with jacketed cable and the ST-™ compatible connector. This method will not work with installed on a jacketed cable and the SC connector.

### 11.3.3.2    ▶REDUCED POLISH TIME

The viscosity of the hot melt adhesive is so high that it tends to stick to the fiber as the installer inserts the fiber through the ferrule.

### 11.3.3.3    ▶▶INCREASE FIBER LENGTH

The experienced installer can reduce polishing time by increasing the bare fiber length by 1/2". By increasing the fiber length, the installer reduces the bead size and polishing time to 20-30 seconds for multimode connectors.

## 11.3.4   FIBER INSERTION

Regardless of the method of installation, the installer inserts a fiber into a connector. Low loss requires a small clearance between the cladding and the fiber hole in the ferrule. In addition, clearance and tolerances of singlemode connectors and fibers are smaller than those in multimode connectors and fibers. The installer will exercise more care inserting fibers into singlemode connectors than into multimode connectors.

### 11.3.4.1   ▶DO NOT BREAK FIBER

His objective is to insert the fiber without breaking the. If the fiber breaks, the installer may loose the connector.

### 11.3.4.1.1   ▶▶DO NOT BEND

During insertion of the fiber into a connector, the installer does not allow the fiber to bend. If the fiber does not bend, it cannot break.

### 11.3.4.1.2   ▶▶ROTATE CONNECTOR

During insertion of the fiber into a connector, the installer rotates the connector, or fiber, to avoid bending the fiber. Rotation allows the fiber to slip past lips or steps internal to the connector.

### 11.3.4.1.3   ▶▶HANDS TOGETHER

During insertion of the fiber into the connector, the installer rests his hands together. By resting his hands together, the installer will not accidentally break the fiber.

### 11.3.4.1.4   ▶▶FLUSH CONNECTOR

Difficulty during insertion of the fiber may be due to dirt in the fiber hole. The installer may be able to clean dirt from a fiber hole by injecting 98 % isopropyl alcohol through the ferrule with a syringe. The alcohol may flush the dirt from the connector.

## 11.4   END FINISHING

End finishing is the process of removing excess fiber from the end of the ferrule and creating a lens grade, or optical grade, surface on the end of the fiber. When properly performed, this process results in a core that is round, clear, featureless and flush with the surface of the ferrule (21, Figure 21-2, Figure 21-4, Figure 21-5 and Figure 21-6). This process includes three

steps: removal of excess fiber, air polishing and pad polishing.

## 11.4.1   FIBER REMOVAL

The installer removes the fiber protruding beyond the tip of the ferrule without causing the fiber to break below the surface of the ferrule. If the fiber breaks below this surface, the installer may not be able to polish the fiber so that the core is defect free and low loss (Figure 11-18 and Figure 11-19). A connector with such a core will have high loss. The installer removes the fiber by scribing and pulling the fiber.

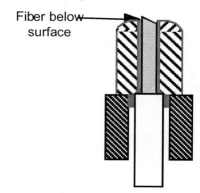

Figure 11-18: Fiber Broken Below Ferrule

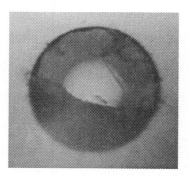

Figure 11-19: Fiber Broken Below Ferrule

### 11.4.1.1   SCRIBING

Scribing is the act of placing a single, small scratch on the fiber at the tip of the bead of epoxy or adhesive (Figure 11-20). Scribing is not sawing the fiber or breaking the fiber.

### 11.4.1.2   ▶FIBER ABOVE FERRULE

The objective of scribing is a fiber end above the surface of the ferrule. If the fiber end is below the surface of the ferrule, the installer may not be able to achieve low loss.

### 11.4.1.3   ▶▶USE WEDGE SCRIBER

The installer uses a scriber with a wedge shape, not one with a point (Figure 11-21). The installer will align the edge of a wedge scriber to the fiber more easily than the point of a 'pencil' type scriber.

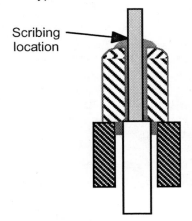

Scribing location

Figure 11-20: Ideal Location Of Scribe

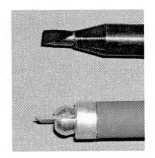

Figure 11-21: Wedge Scribers

### 11.4.1.4   ▶▶REST HANDS TOGETHER

During scribing, the installer rests his hands together. By resting his hands together, the installer will not accidentally hit and break the fiber with the scriber. If he hits the fiber, he may break the fiber below the surface of the ferrule (Figure 11-18).

### 11.4.1.4.1   ▶▶SCRIBE ONCE

The installer scratches the fiber once, and only once, with a light pressure. With a single scratch, the fiber breaks on a single plane. If the fiber breaks on multiple planes, the fiber may break below the surface of the ferrule (Figure 11-18).

### 11.4.1.4.2   ▶PULL FIBER

After scribing the fiber, the installer will pull the fiber away from the tip of the ferrule. To do so without breaking the fiber below the tip

of the ferrule, the installer must not bend the fiber to the side. To break the fiber, the installer slides his fingers up the ferrule, onto the fiber and pulls the fiber along its axis.

## 11.4.2   POLISHING

The goal of polishing is the creation of a lens grade, or optical grade, surface on the end of the fiber. This goal requires avoiding snagging the fiber on the polishing film.

### 11.4.2.1   ▶▶FLUSH FIBER, DULL EDGE

This avoidance, in turn, requires two characteristics: a fiber flush with the bead of epoxy or adhesive (Figure 11-22) and a fiber without a sharp edge (Figure 11-23).

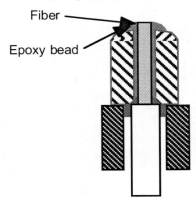

Fiber

Epoxy bead

Figure 11-22: Desired Condition For Problem Free Polishing

### 11.4.2.2   POLISHING TYPES

Polishing is of three types: air polishing, pad polishing and machine polishing. Air polishing is the rubbing of a relatively coarse polishing film[24] against the fiber. Pad polishing creates the desired low loss fiber end. Cable assembly facilities use machine polishing, as it results in reduced polishing cost. Machine polishing of up to 24 connectors to low loss and low reflectance can take as little as three minutes. In comparison, field polishing of a single connector can take thirty seconds (multimode) to 3 minutes (singlemode).

Air polishing achieves two goals: it brings the fiber flush with the bead and removes the sharp edge created by scribing and fiber removal.

---

[24] 12-15 μm.

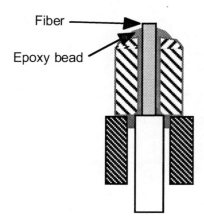

Figure 11-23: Undesired Condition

### 11.4.2.2.1 ▶▶ALWAYS AIR POLISH

The installer air polishes before both hand and machine polishing. The air polish reduces the frequency of shattered ends.

### 11.4.2.3 PAD POLISHING

Pad polishing is polishing with relatively fine polishing film(s)[25] placed on a resilient rubber pad.[26] The connector is aligned to the pad with a polishing tool, also known as a polishing puck and polishing fixture (Figure 11-24). Both hand and machine polishing require pads.

Figure 11-24: Polishing Fixtures[27]

---

[25] Usually ≤ 2 μm.

[26] Polishing is performed on rubber pads to allow the polished fiber to conform to the radius of curvature of the tip of the ferrule. This radiused tip allows contact connectors to achieve low loss.

[27] These polishing tools are for the following connectors, clockwise from upper left: duplex LC, SC/APC, FC/APC, ST-™ compatible, SC, SMA, and simplex LC.

### 11.4.2.4 POLISHING FILMS

All polishing films are harder than the fiber. Some films are harder than some ferrules. Diamond films are harder than the hardest ferrule material, which is ceramic. Alumina (aluminum oxide) films are harder than LCP[28] and stainless steel ferrules materials but softer than the ceramic ferrules.

Polishing with a diamond film results in removal of fiber and ferrule. During polishing, the fiber stays nearly flush with the ferrule (Figure 11-25). Polishing ceramic ferrules with alumina films results in removal of fiber and adhesive but not of ferrule. Excessive polishing with alumina films results in undercutting, which creates an air gap, high loss and high reflectance (Figure 11-26).

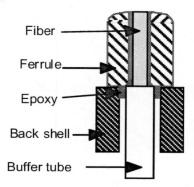

Fiber
Ferrule
Epoxy
Back shell
Buffer tube

Figure 11-25: Fiber Flush With Ferrule

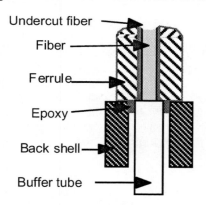

Undercut fiber
Fiber
Ferrule
Epoxy
Back shell
Buffer tube

Figure 11-26: Undercut Fiber

### 11.4.2.5 ▶AVOID AND REMOVE SCRATCHES

Scratches can be from contamination or from previous polishing steps. Scratches on the core can divert and block light from its

---

[28] LCP is also called 'composite'.

normal path, resulting in increased connector loss.

## 11.4.2.5.1  ▶▶USE DISTILLED WATER

The installer can perform wet or dry polishing. Cable assembly polishing tends to be wet. For wet polishing, the installer uses distilled or reverse osmosis water. These types of water are free from particles that can cause scratches on the core.[29] Such scratches divert the light from its proper path and can result in increased loss and reflectance. In addition, wet polishing increases film life, as the liquid tends to flush grinding materials from the films.

## 11.4.2.5.2  ▶▶DRY FIELD POLISH

In environments with dirty air, the installer uses dry polishing. Many field environments have significant amounts of particles in the air. In such environments, wet polishing is not the best choice, as the liquid can attract particles from the air.[30] These particles can cause scratches on the core.

## 11.4.2.5.3  ▶▶CLEAN EQUIPMENT

Prior to use, the installer cleans the connector, the polishing pad, the polishing films, and tool to avoid scratching the core.

In addition, the installer cleans the connector and fixture before he changes to a film with grit finer than that of the previous film.

The installer can clean with lens grade[31] gas, distilled water or isopropyl alcohol[32] and lens grade tissues. Gas is convenient, but relatively expensive. The isopropyl alcohol is less convenient and relatively inexpensive.

## 11.4.2.5.4  ▶▶FINAL MULTIMODE FILM ≤ 1.0 μm

With one exception, multimode connectors exhibit their specified loss[33] when polished

with a final film having a grit as fine as 1 μm. The installer can polish multimode connectors with films having finer grits. Such films improve the appearance of the connector when viewed at high magnification. Such films do not seem to reduce loss.[34]

## 11.4.2.5.5  ▶▶FINAL SINGLEMODE FILM ≤ 0.3 μm

Singlemode connectors exhibit their specified loss[35] and low reflectance[36] when polished with a final film having a grit as fine as 0.3 μm. The installer can polish singlemode connectors with films having finer grits.[37]

## 11.4.2.6  ▶CONFORMANCE

As almost all connectors have radiused or domed ferrule tips (5.3.4), and low loss requires contact of cores, the installer polishes the fiber end to conform to the radius of the ferrule tip.

## 11.4.2.6.1  ▶▶USE RUBBER PAD

Polishing a domed tip ferrule requires use of a rubber polishing pad. Glass polishing plates and hard plastic polishing plates will produce a flat fiber end, high loss and high reflectance. Such plates are no longer used except on legacy non-contact connectors, such as biconic and SMA connectors.

## 11.4.2.6.2  ▶▶USE 'FIGURE 8' POLISH

The installer will polish the connector with a 'Figure 8' motion. The Figure 8 motion avoids creation of a bevel on the end of the fiber (Figure 11-27). Such a bevel will create

[29] Tap water tends to be contaminated.

[30] This is the author's opinion.

[31] We use Stoner Gust, part number 94203.

[32] The purity of the isopropyl alcohol should be 98 % or better. Rubbing alcohol has oil, which can be difficult to remove after polishing.

[33] When properly installed, connectors that require polishing exhibit a typical loss of 0.3 dB/pair.

[34] This is the author's experience. We know of one exception. The 3M, 2 μm, Hot Melt film provides loss as low as other 1 μm films. However, the 3M film does not create a featureless core, complicating the interpretation of the connector when the installer views with a microscope.

[35] When properly installed, connectors that require polishing exhibit a typical loss of 0.3 dB/pair.

[36] We define low reflectance from hand polishing as less than -50 dB. Machine polishing results in lower and more consistent reflectance than does field polishing.

[37] This is the author's experience.

an air gap between mated connectors, which results in high loss and high reflectance.

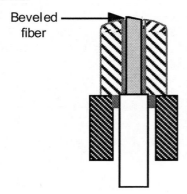

Beveled fiber

Figure 11-27: Bevel On End Of Fiber

### 11.4.2.6.3   ▶▶USE LIGHT PRESSURE ON BEAD

The installer performs polishing without breaking the fiber below the surface of the ferrule. Should the bead of epoxy or adhesive be sheared from the tip, the fiber will not conform to the radius.

To avoid shearing the bead, the installer uses a light polishing pressure until the fiber is flush with the ferrule. Once the fiber is flush, the installer cannot shatter the fiber below the ferrule. The fiber is flush when the bead is gone.

Hot melt connectors require less pressure than do epoxy connectors. Hot melt adhesive is gummy or rubbery. If the installer uses excessive pressure during polishing, the adhesive compresses but the fiber does not. In this case, the fiber can protrude beyond the bead of adhesive (Figure 11-23), snag on the polishing film and break below the surface of the ferrule (Figure 11-18 and Figure 11-19).

### 11.4.2.6.4   MINIMUM POLISH TIME

When polishing ceramic ferrules with films other than diamond, the installer polishes for a minimum time. Over polishing with alumina films can result in undercutting, high loss and high reflectance (11.4.2.4).

### 11.4.2.6.5   ▶▶USE REDUCED PRESSURE ON HOT MELT AND QUICK CURE CONNECTORS

Hot melt and quick cure adhesives can create a very small bead on the tip of the ferrule. This bead provides less support of the fiber during polishing than does a bead of epoxy. Because of this difference in support, the installer performs the air polish and the first pad polishing with less pressure than he would use on an epoxy connector. This reduced pressure is required until the fiber is flush with the ferrule.

### 11.4.2.6.6   ▶▶USE REDUCED PRESSURE ON 1.25 mm FERRULES

Connectors with the 1.25mm ferrule[38] have a cross section area that is 25 % of the area of 2.5 mm ferrules. In order to avoid excessive pressure and broken fibers, the installer reduces his polishing pressure to 25% the pressure he would use when polishing the larger ferrules.

### 11.4.2.6.7   ▶▶SCRATCHINESS REQUIRES SLOW, LIGHT POLISHING

The installer may detect 'scratchiness' as he polishes a connector. Scratchiness is caused by glass fiber with a sharp edge protruding beyond a bead on the tip of the ferrule (Figure 11-23). This fiber can snag on the polishing film, resulting in fiber broken below the tip of the ferrule.

The installer should start polishing all connectors slowly, with very light pressure and with a 1/2" high 'Figure-8' pattern until the scratchiness stops.

### 11.4.2.6.8   ▶▶SALVAGE WITH DIAMOND FILMS

To remove minor damage from the core of a fiber in a ceramic ferrule, the installer uses diamond polishing films. These films remove both fiber and ferrule.

### 11.4.2.6.9   SALVAGE WITH ALUMINA FILMS

To remove minor damage from the core of a fiber in a LCP or stainless steel ferrule, the installer can use either type of polishing film. Because alumina films are much less expensive than diamond films, they are

---

[38] LC, LX.5 and MU have this ferrule.

preferred for salvaging connectors with these two ferrule materials.

### 11.4.2.7   LOW REFLECTANCE POLISHING

Singlemode connectors may need polishing for low reflectance. The installer can achieve low reflectance by more than one method. One method requires use of dry polishing on ultra fine film (0.05 μm).

### 11.4.2.7.1   ▶▶ USE POLISHING LIQUID

A second method requires use of a polishing liquid. This liquid contains fine suspended abrasives that will enable the installer to achieve a reflectance of less than -50 dB by hand polishing. This solution may result in a reflectance of less than -55 dB by machine polishing.

### 11.4.2.8   MACHINE POLISHING

The prior polishing principles and methods apply to hand polishing. Machine polishing has one method that is different from those for hand polishing. All machine polishing requires grinding through the ferrule to produce a round cladding. Hand polishing may not produce a round cladding. For machine polishing, all films, except the final film, are diamond films.

## 11.5   CLEAVE AND CRIMP INSTALLATION

The 'cleave and crimp' connector has a preinstalled fiber stub that the manufacturer has pre-polished. This stub has index matching gel on the inside end of the fiber (Figure 11-28). Because of this structure, the connector is actually a mechanical splice in a connector.

### 11.5.1   CLEAVING

The performance of this connector is strongly determined by the quality of the cleave on the fiber that the installer installs. As the quality and cost of the cleaver increase, the cleave angle and connector loss become lower. In addition, as the cost of the cleaver increases, the cleave angle becomes increasingly consistent.

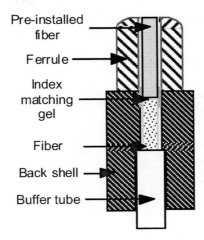

Figure 11-28: Internal Structure Of The Cleave And Leave Connector

### 11.5.1.1   ▶▶USE HIGH QUALITY CLEAVER

Obtaining low and consistent cleave angles requires a high quality cleaver. Such a cleaver can cost more than $1200. The installer will save more than the additional cost of this cleaver from improved yield and reduced labor cost.

### 11.5.1.2   ▶▶CONTROL CLEAVE LENGTH TIGHTLY

Connectors that have cleaved fibers grip the cladding and the primary coating or buffer tube. A long cleave length may prevent the crimp from creating a proper grip through the primary coating and/or buffer tube, resulting in high loss or slippage of the fiber from the connector. A short cleave length may prevent the cleaved end from contacting the preinstalled fiber.

The installer cleaves the fiber to the cleave length and tolerance indicated in the connector instructions. A typical cleave length is 8 mm with a range of 8 to 8.5 mm.

### 11.5.2   INSERTION

Contamination of the fiber end results in increased loss. Such contamination cab block light from its proper path or create a gap between the fiber ends. There are two methods for avoiding such contamination.

### 11.5.2.1   ▶▶MINIMIZE DELAY

After cleaving the fiber, the installer inserts the fiber into the connector without delay.

Delay can allow dirt and dust to collect on the end of the fiber, resulting in high loss.

### 11.5.2.2    ▶▶AVOID TOUCHING END

During insertion of the fiber, the installer does not touch the cleaved end against anything. Doing so may contaminate the fiber end, resulting in high power loss.

A common misconception is that the fiber should be cleaned after cleaving. Such cleaning is more likely to contaminate the cleaved end than to clean it.

### 11.5.2.3    ▶▶VERIFY CONTACT

After inserting the fiber, the installer verifies that the fiber has not slipped from its fully inserted position. Such slippage creates a gap between the fiber and the preinstalled fiber, which, results in high loss.

## 11.6   SUMMARY

The information, principles and methods presented in this chapter indicate the need for attention to detail. Such attention is necessary to address the subtleties of achieving low loss, low reflectance, high reliability, and low installation cost.

## 11.7   REVIEW QUESTIONS

1. Organize the following polishing films in the proper sequence of use: 3 µm, 12 µm, 0.5 µm, and 1 µm.

2. Organize the following polishing films in the proper sequence of use: alumina, diamond.

3. Is tap water the best source of liquid for wet polishing? Justify your answer.

4. Is cracking common in connectors using quick cure adhesive? Justify your answer.

5. Is wet polishing is preferred for all polishing? Justify your answer.

6. Does oven curing of quick cure adhesive takes less than 2 minutes? Justify your answer.

7. Should the strength members be cut longer than necessary if a connector requires that the strength members be

crimped to the back shell? Justify your answer.

8. Is undercutting is desirable? Justify your answer.

9. Should installation of a fiber into all connectors be done as slowly as possible to avoid breakage and other problems? Justify your answer.

10. What single action almost completely eliminates fiber breakage during insertion?

11. Your technician states that the cause of cracking in his room temperature cured connectors was the epoxy. Do you believe him? Justify your answer.

12. Your technician is terminating a 12 fiber premises cable with cleave and leave connectors. He has just finished cleaving all 12 fibers, which he has placed on a work mat. He is about to insert the first fiber into a connector. Is there anything wrong with this procedure? If so, what?

13. Your technician is polishing both multimode and singlemode connectors. To simplify his process, he plans to use the same polishing films. He plans to finish the polishing with a 1 µm film. Is there anything wrong with this procedure? If so, what?

14. Your technician states that the cause of high loss in his hot melt adhesive connectors was pistoning. Do you believe him? Justify your answer.

15. You are to make a decision on which cleaver to purchase for your cleave and crimp connectors. You plan to install 1200 connectors. The inexpensive cleaver costs $300. The expensive cleaver costs $1200. The connectors cost $15. You have been led to believe that you will lose 5 % of the connectors with the expensive cleaver and 13 % with the inexpensive cleaver. Which cleaver should you purchase?

# 12   SPLICING PRINCIPLES

Chapter Objectives: from this chapter, you will learn the principles of both fusion and mechanical splicing. These principles apply to both indoor and outdoor enclosures and to both mid span and pigtail splicing. These principles result in the procedures of Part 3.

## 12.1   INTRODUCTION

The principles in this chapter are relatively independent of the enclosure, the mechanical splice used, and the specific fusion splicer used. As such they are general principles that may not apply to all possible products.

The process of splicing requires nine steps:

> Ensure compatibility of the cable with the enclosure

> End preparation of the cable

> Attachment of the cable to the enclosure

> Tray preparation

> Cleaving of the fiber

> Making of the splice

> Placement of the splice and fiber into a tray

> Placement of the tray into an enclosure

> Testing

> Closing the enclosure

## 12.2   CABLE-ENCLOSURE COMPATIBILITY

While uncommon, some cables are incompatible with some enclosures. This incompatibility results from two limitations: buffer tube bend radius limitation and fiber bend radius limitation.

The buffer tube incompatibility is a result of the enclosure forcing the buffer tube into a bend radius that is too small for the buffer tube. At a small radius, the buffer tube may kink and break the fibers (Figure 12-1).[1]

Such kinking can occur many months after the installation of the splices.

The fiber incompatibility is a result of the dimensions of the enclosure and/or the splice tray. These dimensions force the fiber into a bend radius that results in increased fiber attenuation. Such increased attenuation may be evident from splice loss at a long wavelength that is higher than that at a short wavelength. For example, a multimode splice with a higher loss at 1300 nm than at 850 nm or a singlemode splice with a higher loss at 1550 nm than at 1310 nm is indication of this incompatibility.

## 12.2.1   ▶ENSURE COMPATIBILITY

To avoid this breakage, the installer must ensure that the cable and enclosure are compatible.

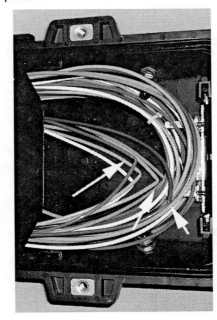

Figure 12-1: Six Kinked Buffer Tubes

---

[1] This kinking can result from incompatibility between the enclosure and cable or from improper buffer tube dimensions, improper buffer tube processing, or deformation of the buffer tube.

## 12.3    ATTACHMENT LOCATIONS

The installer prepares the cable end to dimensions (Figure 12-2) that enable attachment of all parts of the splice system at the proper locations (Figure 12-3). The enclosure and the splice trays determine these dimensions.

This preparation involves:

> Removal of cable jacket[2] and moisture blocking greases

> Trimming of strength members

> Removal of some of the buffer tube length

> Removing of water blocking gels from the fibers

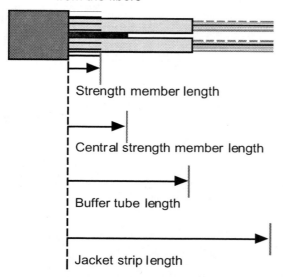

Strength member length

Central strength member length

Buffer tube length

Jacket strip length

Figure 12-2: Cable End Preparation Lengths

Figure 12-3: Enclosure Attachment Locations

---

[2] The installer will remove armor and multiple jackets, if they are part of the cable design.

## 12.3.1    ▶▶MATCH DIMENSIONS TO ENCLOSURE

The installer prepares the cable end to dimensions appropriate for the enclosure and trays. The length of the strength members beyond the end of the cable jacket allows these members the installer to attach the cable to the enclosure so that the cable cannot be pulled out (Figure 12-4). The lengths of the buffer tubes beyond the end of the cable jacket allow them to enter the splice tray when the tray is properly located in the enclosure. This buffer tube length is defined by the enclosure in that the buffer tubes must make an specific number of circuits in the enclosure (Figure 12-3). In addition, this buffer tube length allows the installer to place the trays outside the enclosure during splicing (Figure 12-5).

The length of the fiber beyond the end of the buffer tube allows the splice to rest in the splice holder in the center of the splice tray. As with the buffer tube length, the fiber must make an specific number of circuits in the splice tray. In addition this fiber length allows the splicing technician to place the fibers outside the tray and into the splicer (Figure 12-5) or into the mechanical splicing tool (Figure 12-6).

These lengths depend on the enclosure. For example, the jacket removal length can be 96". The buffer tube length can be 48". The central strength member and strength member lengths can be 2-4". In general, indoor cable enclosures require buffer tube and fiber lengths that are shorter than those required by outdoor enclosures.

Figure 12-4: Cable Attachment To Splice Enclosure

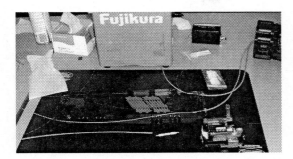

Figure 12-5: Buffer Tube Length Enables Splicing

Figure 12-6: Mechanical Splice Closing Tool

## 12.3.2 ▶▶GROUP FIBERS

If necessary, the installer installs fibers into tubing or spiral wrap in order to group them. After the installer prepares the cable end, he may need to group fibers for routing to a specific location, such as a splice tray. Some cable designs, such as the multiple fiber per tube design (4.2.1), provide this grouping.

Others, such as the central buffer tube, ribbon, and premises do not. For these designs, the installer creates groups of fibers or buffer tubes with spiral wrap or tubing, so that each group can be separately routed to its tray (Figure 12-7). For example, the central buffer tube cable design may have 216 fibers in 18 groups of 12. With such a cable, grouping with tubing or spiral wrap will be essential for a reliable enclosure.

## 12.4 ATTACHMENT

The splicing technician attaches the cable to the enclosure to prevent the cable being pulled from the enclosure. The method of attachment is unique to the enclosure. For example, the cable in Figure 12-4 is attached with a hose clamp, while the cable in Figure 12-8 is attached with cable ties and a metal clamp.

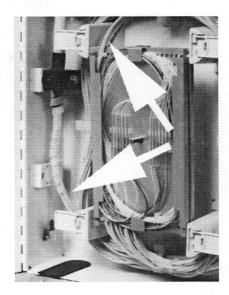

Figure 12-7: Fibers Grouped And Routed With Tubing

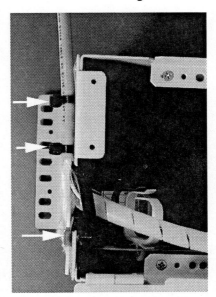

Figure 12-8: Indoor Enclosure Cable Attachment

## 12.4.1 SPLICING CONFIGURATIONS

There are two cable-splicing configurations:

➢ Butt

➢ In-line

In a butt configuration, the cables enter the enclosure from the same end of the enclosure (Figure 12-9). This configuration is most common. In an in-line configuration, the cables enter the enclosure from the opposite ends (Figure 12-10).

Figure 12-9: Butt Configuration

Figure 12-10: In-Line Configuration

### 12.4.1.1   ▶▶USE BUTT CONFIGURATION

The installer uses the butt configuration to attach the cables to the enclosure in accordance with manufacturer's instructions. The butt configuration is preferred as its use simplifies installation of trays into the enclosure. In addition, the installer uses the butt configuration to attach the buffer tubes to the splice tray (Figure 12-11).

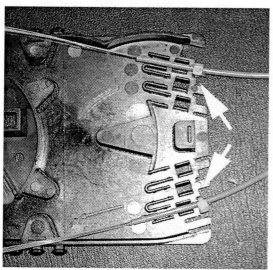

Figure 12-11: Buffer Tube Attachment To Splice Tray

## 12.4.2   GROUNDING AND BONDING

If an outdoor cable has conductive components, such as a stainless steel armor, steel strength members, or conductors, the installer bonds the cable. The installer bonds the cable by connecting together the conductive components of the two cables. Bonding requires hardware appropriate for the enclosure (Figure 12-12).

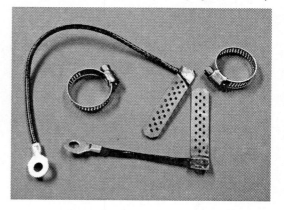

Figure 12-12: Grounding and Bonding Hardware

Bonding requires removal of the insulating materials from the conductive elements in the structure of the cable.

### 12.4.2.1   ▶▶GROUND CONDUCTIVE CABLES

If an outdoor cable terminates indoors, the installer grounds the conductive elements in accordance with the requirements of the relevant electrical code (Figure 12-13).

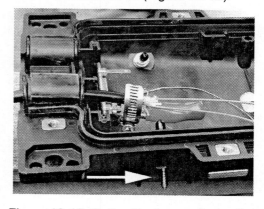

Figure 12-13: Splice Enclosure Grounding Location

## 12.5    TRAY PREPARATION

Some splice trays require insertion of splice holders (Figure 12-14).[3] Some splice holders accept heat shrink and adhesive splice covers but not mechanical splice covers (Figure 12-15). The installer inserts the holders appropriate to the splice type and splice cover type. Use of the incorrect insert can result in splices loose in the tray (Figure 12-15), a condition of reduced reliability.

Figure 12-14: Splice Holders

### 12.5.1    ▶▶USE PROPER INSERTS

The installer uses tray inserts appropriate for the splice.

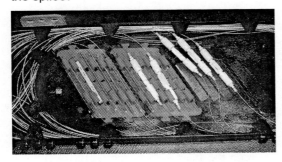

Figure 12-15: Incorrect Splice Holders[4]

## 12.5.2    BUFFER TUBE ATTACHMENT

The installer attaches the buffer tubes to a splice tray. The method of attachment can be cable tie (Figure 12-11), a press fit into a slot, or by crimping part of the splice tray onto the buffer tube.

If done improperly, such attachment could result in increased optical power loss due to bend radius violation. Such violation is less likely on loose tubes than on tight tubes, as the loose buffer tubes tend to be rigid.

At the location of the attachment, the buffer tube enters the tray for a short distance, approximately one inch. If the buffer tube enters the tray by an excessive distance, the fibers may experience a bend radius violation as they exit the tube. In addition, the excessive tube length may make placing fibers in the tray difficult.

### 12.5.2.1    ▶AVOID INCREASED LOSS CONDITIONS

The installer avoids any conditions that can increase loss. Such conditions include bend radius, crush load and twisting.

### 12.5.2.2    ▶▶AVOID VIOLATING BUFFER TUBE BEND RADIUS

The installer attaches buffer tubes to the trays in a manner that does not violate the bend radius.

### 12.5.2.3    ▶▶USE BUTT CONFIGURATION

For mid span splicing, the installer attaches one buffer tube from each cable to the same end of the tray (Figure 12-11). The installer uses this butt configuration, as it simplifies coiling of the buffer tube in the enclosure. Finally, attachment of more than one buffer tube per cable per tray results in significant difficulty in placement of the tray in the enclosure.[5]

---

[3] Some trays do not require such installation, as they have pre-installed splice holders.

[4] Since the holders in this figure were not compatible with the mechanical splices, the mechanical splices would not fit properly in their intended location. The holders in this figure were appropriate for either heat shrink or adhesive fusion splice covers.

[5] We are aware of exceptions to this principle. These exceptions were motivated by desperation: there was no other solution available.

### 12.5.2.4    ▶▶DO NOT TWIST BUFFER TUBES

The installer routes the buffer tubes from the enclosure to the splice tray without twisting them. Twisting will complicate the placement of a completed tray into the enclosure.

## 12.6    FIBER END PREPARATION

After attaching the buffer tubes to a splice tray, the installer routes these tubes out of the tray (Figure 12-14), strips the primary coating, or tight tubes and primary coatings, to exposes the fiber for cleaving.

## 12.6.1    ▶▶USE PROPER FIBER LENGTH

The cleaver determines the length of bare fiber. This length will be sufficient for the cleaver to produce a flat and perpendicular end. Such an end is essential for low loss.

The installer strips the primary coating or the buffer tube and the primary coating to the length required by the cleaver.

This length varies from cleaver to cleaver. For the CT04 and CT07 cleavers,[6] this strip length is 1.5-1.75". Other cleavers require different strip lengths, up to 4".

## 12.7    CLEAVING

## 12.7.1    CLEAVER FUNCTION

The cleaver produces a low loss, flat and perpendicular end. It does so by holding the fiber perpendicular to and at a tightly controlled distance from a scribing blade. The cleaver holds the fiber on both sides of the cleaving blade. The cleaver holds the fiber perpendicular to the path of the scribing blade. The cleaver places a single, narrow scratch of controlled depth. The breaking arm places a controlled bend on the fiber so that the fiber breaks at the scratch.

---

[6] These are products from Alcoa Fujikura Ltd.
The web site is:
http://www.alcoa.com/afl_tele/en/product_categor
y.asp?cat_id=81.

### 12.7.1.1    ▶LOW ANGLE, UNCONTAMINATED END

All steps with the fiber and cleaver have two goals, a flat, perpendicular end on the fiber and an end without contamination.

### 12.7.1.2    ▶▶CLEAN FIBER

In order that the cleaver holds the fiber properly, the splicing technician cleans each fiber and the cleaver. As dirt or dust on the fiber can change the angle at which the fiber rests in the cleaver, the installer cleans each fiber with isopropyl alcohol and lens grade tissues.

After cleaving, the splicing technician does not clean the fiber, since such cleaning can contaminate the end face of the fiber. However, cleaning of the fiber after cleaving is not fatal for a fusion splice. Prior to splicing, fusion splicers emit a pre-fuse arc across both fibers. This arc creates a electrostatic charge on both the fiber and dirt on the fiber. As like-charged materials repel each other, this charge results in removal of dust and dirt from the fiber.

### 12.7.1.3    ▶▶CLEAN CLEAVER

The installer cleans the cleaver with lens grade gas before cleaving the first fiber and periodically during the splicing operation. The frequency for cleaning the cleaver is determined by the environment in which the installer performs the splicing. As the dust level in the air increases, the frequency of cleaning increases.

### 12.7.1.4    ▶▶MOVE FIBER IMMEDIATELY

Immediately after cleaving, the technician places the fiber into a fusion splicer or into a mechanical splice. He does not place the fiber on any surface. Doing so can contaminate the cleave.

## 12.7.2    CLEAVE LENGTH

Two factors determine the cleave length:

➢ The fusion splicer or the mechanical splice and

➢ The coated diameter of the fiber

The cleave length must be long enough that the bare fiber fits into a v-groove holder that provides the positioning and final gripping of the fiber (Figure 12-16). If the cleave length is short, this final positioning will be on the primary coating or tight tube. With such positioning, the splicer may not have sufficient range of motion to align the fibers.

For a fiber with a 250 µm primary coating, a typical fusion splicer cleave length is 12 mm. For the same fiber, a typical mechanical splice cleave length is 7-12 mm.

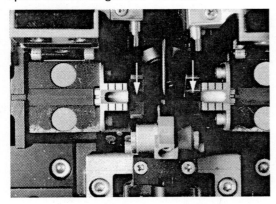

Figure 12-16: V-Groove On PAL Splicer

If the fiber has a 900 µm tight buffer tube,[7] the fusion splice cleave length may be increased to 15-20 mm. If the fiber has a 900 µm tight buffer tube, the cleave length for a mechanical splice may be increased.

#### 12.7.2.1    ▶▶USE RECOMMENDED CLEAVE LENGTH

The installer determines the cleave length, as specified in the instructions for the splicer or the mechanical splice.

## 12.7.3    CLEAVE QUALITY

For both fusion and mechanical splices, the cleaved fiber end must be smooth and perpendicular (Figure 12-17). If the fiber end has missing glass (Figure 12-17) or extra glass (Figure 12-19), or a large angle on the end (Figure 12-20), the splice will be high loss due to an air gap or a reduced core diameter in the splice.

The installer does not inspect the cleave quality for a mechanical splice. To do so might contaminate the fiber end, resulting in high loss.

Figure 12-17: Acceptable Cleave

Figure 12-18: Unacceptable Cleaves Due to Missing Glass

Figure 12-19: Unacceptable Cleave Due to Extra Glass

Figure 12-20: Unacceptable Cleave Due to High Cleave Angle

#### 12.7.3.1    ▶▶EVALUATE CLEAVES

Prior to fusion splicing, the installer will evaluate the quality of the cleave.

## 12.8    FUSION SPLICING

Before fusion splicing, the installer slides a heat shrinkable splice cover (Figure 12-21)[8] on one fiber. Alternatively, after splicing, he installs an adhesive splice cover (Figure 12-22).

Figure 12-21: Heat Shrink Splice Cover

---

[7] Most pigtails have 900 µm tight tubes.

[8] Preshrink, Top; Post shrink, Bottom

Figure 12-22: Adhesive Splice Cover[9]

## 12.8.1 FIBER ALIGNMENT

The installer places the fibers into the splicer and crudely aligns them. The precision of the initial of the fibers into the fusion splicer is not critical, as PAL splicers (6.2.1) examine this placement to ensure sufficient range of motion for both fibers. However, there are two principles of placement.

### 12.8.1.1 ▶▶PLACE FIBER ON ITS SIDE OF ELECTRODE

Each fiber is placed into the splicer on its side of the electrodes (Figure 12-23 and Figure 12-24).

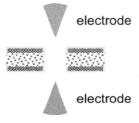

Figure 12-23: Correctly Placed And Aligned Fibers

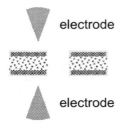

Figure 12-24: Incorrectly Positioned Fibers

The installer need not align the fibers precisely. Current generation splicers have active alignment (6.2.1). With such active alignment, the splicer will compensate for some misalignment due to dirt on the cladding or in the grooves of the splicer.

However, this compensation is limited. If there is excessive dirt on the fiber or in the splicer groove, the splicer will be unable to achieve the precise alignment required for low loss. In summary, fiber cleanliness is required to enable fiber alignment by the splicer.

Some passive alignment splicers have fiber holders that are integrated with the cleaver and splicer. With such integration, the holder controls the fiber placement. The installer has minimal concern for placement.[10]

### 12.8.1.2 ▶▶POSITION FIBER NEAR ELECTRODES

The installer positions both fibers close to the electrodes (Figure 12-23 and Figure 12-25). Such positioning places the fibers within the range of motion of the splicer.

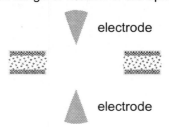

Figure 12-25: Excessive Fiber Separation

However, some passive alignment splicers require the installer to align the fibers. With manual alignment, the technician cleans the fibers and the grooves on the splicer so that the claddings of the fibers are aligned (Figure 12-23 and Figure 12-26).

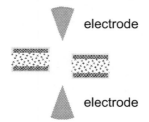

Figure 12-26: Fibers Misaligned In Splicer

### 12.8.1.3 ▶▶CLEAN GROOVES

If required, the technician cleans the fibers and the splicer grooves so that the fibers align.

---

[9] Open, Top; Closed, Bottom

[10] Some passive alignment splicers produced in the early 1990's required precise initial placement and alignment of the fibers. As such splicers are no longer in production, we will not address the principles of their use.

## 12.8.2    SPLICER OPERATION

The splicer fuses together the fibers by a procedure determined by the type of fiber being spliced. This procedure is defined by a 'recipe' or 'menu', which is built into all current-generation splicers.[11]

Most automatic splicers, such as PAL splicers manufactured by Alcoa-Fujikura, Corning Cable Systems, Ericcson and Sumitomo, perform eight operations:

> ➤ Check of z-axis motion
> ➤ Cleaning of fibers
> ➤ Measurement of the cleave angles of both fibers in two axes
> ➤ Alignment of fibers
> ➤ Control of arc current, arc time, and overrun
> ➤ Estimation of splice loss
> ➤ Splice strength check
> ➤ Shrinking of splice cover

### 12.8.2.1    Z AXIS CHECK

The check of z-axis motion ensures that the fibers are in acceptable initial locations and can be moved sufficiently out of the arc, into the arc, and past one another to provide overrun.

Overrun is the amount by which the ends of the two fibers move past one another (Figure 12-27). If the z-axis movement is insufficient, the splicer stops the process and alerts the splicing technician.

### 12.8.2.2    ▶UNIFROM DIAMETER CREATES LOW LOSS

The installer sets a proper overrun in order to achieve both a uniform fiber diameter and low loss. On passive alignment splicers, the installer may set the overrun. On active alignment splicers, the installer invokes the overrun through his choice of the splicing menu appropriate to the fibers he is splicing.

A bulge, which results from excessive overrun (Figure 12-28), or an hourglass

shape, which results from insufficient overrun (Figure 12-29), results in high loss.

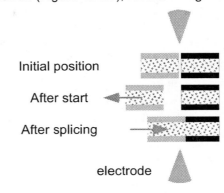

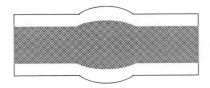

Figure 12-27: Overrun

Figure 12-28: Bulged Splice Due Excessive Overrun

Figure 12-29: Hourglass Splice Due Insufficient Overrun

### 12.8.2.3    ▶▶FIBER CLEANING

Prior to inspection of the cleave angles, the splicer passes a low level electrostatic arc across the fibers. This pre-fuse arc cleans the fibers of dust and dirt.

### 12.8.2.4    CLEAVE ANGLE MEASUREMENTS

After this cleaning action, the video microscope in the splicer creates two digitized images of the ends of the fibers. The two images are at 90° to each other. The images are analyzed for cleave angles. The splicer measures and compares the cleave angles to a maximum acceptance angle. If the cleave angles are greater than the acceptance angle, the splicer stops the process and alerts the splicing technician. A typical maximum cleave angle is 2°.

---

[11] Old splicers required manual setting of the splicing parameters (6.2.1).

### 12.8.2.5   FIBER ALIGNMENT

For singlemode fibers, the splicer analyzes the core boundaries of both fibers, which are visible due to the collimated light that the splicer uses. For multimode fibers, splicer analyzes and aligns the cladding of both fibers. The splicer adjusts the fiber positions so that the fibers are optimally aligned. With this alignment method, the splicer can achieve minimum splice loss even if the fibers that have different core or cladding diameters. This splicer performs this alignment in two planes at 90° to each other.

### 12.8.2.6   FUSING

The splicer positions both fibers in their initial locations. The splicer moves one or both of the fibers out of and slowly into the arc. During this movement, the splicer controls the arc current, arc time, and overrun. These three values depend upon the fiber being spliced and the splicer.[12] The arc current may or may not be ramped from zero to a maximum value (Figure 12-30).

The splicer controls the arc current and time as long as the electrodes are in good condition. These electrodes wear and need periodic replacement.[13]

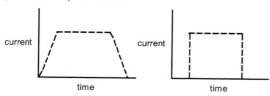

Figure 12-30: Ramped (Left) And Non-Ramped (Right) Splicing Currents

If the splicer controls the arc current and time properly, the location of the splice is not visible. Should the glass temperature during splicing be low, the joint will be visible.

---

[12] Most splicers have multiple menus for different fibers. For example, the Alcoa-Fujikura FSM30S has 25 built in menus some of which are fixed and some of which can be modified by the splicing technician.

[13] However, our experience indicates that the electrodes last much longer than indicated by the replacement frequency recommended by splicer manufacturers. One of our fusion splicers has a recommended electrode replacement frequency of 1000 arcs. We have experienced consistent, 0.05 dB singlemode splices up to 2500 arcs!

Occasionally, the splicing and end face conditions combine to create a gas bubble in the fiber. Such a bubble is unacceptable since it can cause high loss, high reflectance and low splice strength.

### 12.8.2.7   LOSS ESTIMATION

After completing the fusing process, the splicer may make an estimation of splice loss. The splicer makes this estimation by analyzing the microscopic image of the core alignments in two axes at 90° to one another.

### 12.8.2.7.1   ▶▶PLACE SPLICE IN TRAY BASED ON SPLICER LOSS

This splice loss is a calculated and estimated value. It is not the true value of the splice. The true value of the splice loss is the average the OTDR splice loss measurements in both directions (13.3.6.5).

This estimation allows the technician to place the fiber into the tray with confidence that the splice has acceptable loss. Without this estimation, the splicer must wait for a splice loss measurement from an OTDR technician, who has been sitting idly, waiting for the splicing technician to make the splice.

### 12.8.2.7.2   ▶▶ACCEPT SPLICE LOSS BASED ON OTDR MEASUREMENT

The installer uses the loss estimated by the splicer as an indicator of acceptance. The installer will use the OTDR splice loss for acceptance.

### 12.8.2.8   ▶SPLICE IS STRONGER THAN FIBER

Sophisticated splicers pull on the two fibers to check the strength of the splice. A properly made splice will be stronger than the base glass.[14] If the splice is sufficiently strong, it will not break. A properly made fusion splice is stronger than the base glass.

### 12.8.2.9   SPLICE COVER APPLICATION

After fusing, the splicing technician removes the splice from the splicer, and takes one of

---

[14] There is an equivalent rule in metal welding: a metal weld is stronger than the base metal.

two steps.  He centers a heat shrinkage splice cover over the center of the bare glass fiber, and places the splice cover in a heating oven, which will shrink the cover. This shrinkage starts from the center of the splice and moves towards the ends. After shrinking the splice cover, the splicing technician will place the fiber in the tray. Alternatively, the technician will place an adhesive splice cover on the splice.

## 12.9   MECHANICAL SPLICING

To install a mechanical splice, the installer inserts cleaved fibers into the splice, one at a time. The mechanical splice provides both functions of alignment and of a splice cover.

The installer inserts the first fiber to a specific location, which is dependent upon the splice. For example, the installer installs the first fiber into a 3M Fibrlok™ splice until it stops. As another example, the installer installs the first fiber into a Siemon Company ULTRAsplice™ splice until the fiber is in the center of the splice. The center of the ULTRAsplice™ splice has a glass capillary tube, which allows the installer to see the position of the first fiber.

The installer installs the second fiber in a manner that is dependent upon the splice. For example, the installer installs the second fiber into a 3M Fibrlok™ splice until the amount of bow of both fibers is the same (Figure 12-31). As another example, the installer installs the second fiber into a Siemon Company ULTRAsplice™ splice until it is in contact with the first fiber.

Figure 12-31: Equal Bow Results In Low Loss 3M Fibrlok™ Splice

The installer 'closes' the Fibrlok™ splice so that the splice grips the fibers properly. Closing may be by crimping, as in the 3M Fibrlok™ splice, or by sliding or rotating a cover or collar of the splice, as in the

ULTRAsplice™. Most mechanical splices grip the fiber by compression.[15]

### 12.9.1  ▶▶SPLICE TUNING

Some mechanical splices may require tuning. Tuning is the rotation of one or both fibers in order to achieve either an acceptably low loss or the lowest possible loss. The need for tuning is uncommon with some mechanical splices but common with others.

Tuning can be done three ways with:

 ➢  An OTDR

 ➢  An insertion loss test set

 ➢  A feature finder or fault finder[16]

When the installer uses an OTDR or insertion loss test set, he tunes the splice to the lowest loss value.

When the installer uses a feature finder or fault finder, he tunes the splice until the visible light from the feature finder disappears. With no visible light escaping from the fibers, the splice loss is minimum.

## 12.10  FIBER PLACEMENT

The installer places the fiber in the splice tray by coiling the fiber. He lays the fiber along the long sides of the tray from one end to the other. He twists the fiber at the end opposite the buffer tubes. He lays the fiber along the long sides of the tray back towards the end with the buffer tubes. At this end, he again twists the fiber, but in the direction opposite to the direction of the first twist (i.e., a 'reverse twist'). The installer repeats this process until all the fiber is in the tray.

The reverse twist prevents an accumulation of the twisting, which causes the fiber to pop out of the tray. In addition, the installer avoids repeated twisting in the same direction, which can result in fiber breakage (4.3.1).

---

[15] Some splices grip the fiber with epoxy or UV-cured adhesive. We do not address these types.

[16] Feature finders emit a visible laser light, at approximately 660 nm, which is visible from the outside of some splices.

### 12.10.1 ▶▶REVERSE TWIST

The technician coils the fiber in the tray with a reverse twist.

If the technician has prepared the fiber lengths properly, the splice cover, or mechanical splice, will be in the proper position for placement in the splice holder (Figure 12-32).

Figure 12-32: Coiled Fiber

After placing all the splices in the splice holder, the installer places a cover on the tray. If the splicing is pigtail splicing, the installer attaches the pigtails to the end of the tray opposite to that at which he attached the buffer tube (Figure 12-33).

## 12.11  TRAY PLACEMENT

The installer attaches the trays to the inside of the enclosure. This attachment can be by bolts (Figure 12-33), by Velcro straps (Figure 12-34) or by other mechanisms.

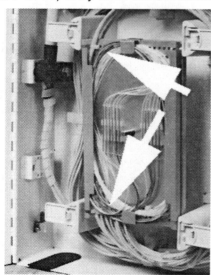

Figure 12-33: Pigtails and Tubing
Attachments Locations

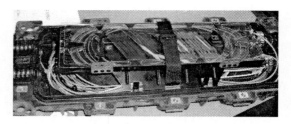

Figure 12-34: Velcro Strap Attachment

### 12.11.1 ▶▶ATTACH TRAYS

The installer attaches trays are to prevent damage due to tray movement.

### 12.11.2  TESTING

There is no single rule for the sequence of splice testing. However, there are two principles.

### 12.11.3  TEST EACH SPLICE

If the splicer does not provide automatic splice loss estimation, the OTDR technician can test each splice after it is made and after it is placed into the tray. Should a high loss splice be found after the installer makes each splice, the cost of repair is low.

## 12.12  TEST ALL SPLICES

If the splicer provides automatic splice loss estimation,[17] the OTDR technician can test all splices after all trays have been placed in the enclosure but before the enclosure is closed. Should a high loss splice be found before the installer closes the enclosure, the cost of repair is low.

For efficiency in testing, some organizations test all splices after the enclosure is closed. These organizations do so because of their confidence. The organization is confident in the ability of the splicer loss estimation function to indicate low loss and high loss splices. The organization is confident in the splicing technician's ability to place the fiber in the trays, the trays in the enclosure, and to close the enclosure without damaging fibers or buffer tubes.

---

[17] The assumption is that the estimation correlates with OTDR measurements. That is, the splicer estimation process and the OTDR measurement both indicate acceptable loss.

## 12.13 ENCLOSURE CLOSURE

Closing the enclosure requires cleaning of all gasket grooves, placing gaskets into the grooves, and installing moisture seals (Figure 12-35). Moisture seals are required on outdoor enclosures but not on indoor enclosures. Some outdoor enclosures do not require seals, but have weep holes so that condensed moisture can drip from the enclosure. This process may include checking the seals by pressurizing the enclosure (Figure 12-36).

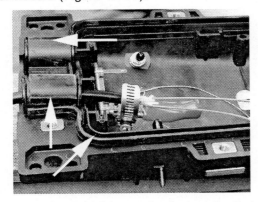

Figure 12-35: Moisture Seals And Gasket Grooves

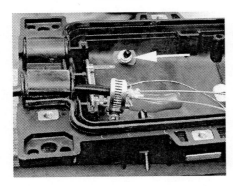

Figure 12-36: Pressurization Valve

Figure 12-37: Closed Enclosure

When the installer completes all steps, he places the enclosure in its final location (Figure 12-37).

## 12.14 SUMMARY

The process of splicing requires following a large number of principles and methods. Each principle, by itself, is relatively simple. However, the number is large. When properly completed, the splice enclosure (Figure 12-37 and Figure 12-9) will be reliable and require no maintenance.

## 12.15 REVIEW QUESTIONS

1. A splicing supervisor must make a decision: rent a splicer without the loss estimation feature at a reduced cost or rent a splicer with this feature at an increased cost. The difference between the two rental fees is $500. He owns an OTDR so there is no additional cost. He expects the splicing to take 3 man-days at eight hours per day. He expects that an OTDR technician could test all the fibers in no more than one day. The total loaded labor rate of the OTDR technician is $50/hour. Which piece of equipment should he rent?

2. Put the following steps in sequence:
   A. Place tray in enclosure,
   B. Pressurize enclosure,
   C. Clean grooves for gaskets,
   D. Place splice in splice holder,
   E. Attach buffer tube to tray,
   F. Test splice,
   G. Splicing,
   H. Cleaving,
   I. Coil fiber in tray,
   J. Place splice holder in tray,
   K. Attach cable to enclosure.

3. Are strength members cut flush with the jacket of the cable? Justify your answer.

4.  What is the purpose(s) of having several feet of fiber exposed beyond the end of the buffer tube?

5.  What is the purpose(s) of having several feet of buffer tube exposed beyond the end of the jacket?

6.  What consideration determines the length of bare fiber?

7.  What consideration determines the cleave length?

8.  Choose the most accurate statement. Justify your choice:

    A.  Cleaning of the fiber is more important to fusion splicing than to mechanical splicing.

    B.  Cleaning of the fiber is more important to mechanical splicing than for fusion splicing.

    C.  Cleaning of the fiber is equally important to fusion splicing and to mechanical splicing.

# 13   TESTING PRINCIPLES

Chapter Objectives: from this chapter, you will learn the principles of the methods of the three types of testing performed on fiber optic data LANs and networks.

## 13.1   INTRODUCTION

As you learned from Chapter 3, light experiences two changes as it moves through a fiber: pulses spread or disperse and the intensity is reduced. Thus, we would expect to need to perform testing of dispersion and of optical intensity, or optical power. Sophisticated fiber systems, such as DWDM networks, do require both types of testing. However, data networks do not require dispersion testing.

The reason for this elimination arises from the manner in which data standards are developed. Fiber optic local area networks (LANs) are designed and implemented within limits stated in the appropriate standard. In setting these limits, the standard committees have determined the maximum dispersion that can occur under worst-case conditions. As long as the network is implemented within the limits defined by these worst-case conditions, dispersion will not be excessive and signal accuracy will be acceptable.

Since installation errors increase the power losses of cables, connectors, and splices, networks require power measurements. Such measurements include:

➢   Insertion loss testing

➢   Optical time domain reflectometry

➢   Reflectance testing

## 13.2   INSERTION LOSS TESTING

Insertion loss testing is performed on each link in a network. Insertion loss testing is performed to verify the fact that power loss through the link is not greater than the maximum loss at which the electronics will function at the maximum acceptable error rate.

### 13.2.1   TWO TYPES

There are two types of insertion loss tests:

➢   Simulation tests

➢   'Multimode normalization' tests

#### 13.2.1.1   SIMULATION TESTING

If the characteristics of the testing light source are the same as those in the transmitter, the testing will simulate network operation. With simulation, the insertion loss measurement will closely match the loss that the transmitter-receiver pair will experience. Simulation seems to occur for singlemode loss measurements[1] and for some multimode loss measurements.[2]

➢   ▶The basic principle of insertion loss testing is measurement of the difference between the power level delivered to the input end of the link and the power level exiting from the output end of the link.

All details of the methods derive from this concept.

While this concept is simple, its application to multimode fibers is not, because the distribution of optical power[3] in the core of a multimode fiber strongly influences both the attenuation that occurs in the fiber and the power loss that occurs at connections.

➢   Thus, different light sources, both in transmitters and in testing light sources, can experience different power losses on the same link.

These differences result from differences in attenuation rates and differences in power at the boundary of the core.

---

[1] Most singlemode transmitters and singlemode light sources use the same type of laser diodes.

[2] If the LED in the transmitter and the LED in the testing light source have the same angle of divergence and the same spot size, testing will simulate operation.

Clause 2.2.1.1.1 of EIA-455-171 provides definition of simulation when the source overfills the core diameter and the NA.

[3] This term is also known as 'mode power distribution'.

### 13.2.1.1.1    ATTENUATION RATES VS. DIVERGENCE ANGLE

The attenuation of light in the core depends upon the travel path of the rays of light. The longer the travel path is, the higher will be the attenuation. Thus, rays of light that travel at a large angle to the fiber axis travel paths that are longer than those that travel parallel to the axis. The higher the percentage of rays that travel at high angles to the axis, the longer will be the travel path and the higher will be the attenuation. This technical term is 'differential modal attenuation'.

With this understanding, we can compare the attenuation rates of the same fiber with two different types of light sources: LEDs and VCSELs. LEDs tend to have a large portion of the optical power at high angles to the fiber axis (Figure 13-1). VCSELs tend to have a small portion of the optical power at high angles of the fiber axis (Figure 13-2).

▶From this comparison, we would expect attenuation rates experienced by a fiber with an LED testing light source to be higher than those measured with a VCSEL testing light source. Such is the case.

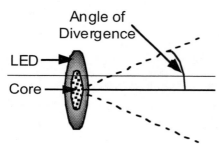

Figure 13-1: LED Angle Of Divergence

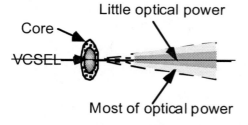

Figure 13-2: VCSEL Angle of Divergence

### 13.2.1.1.2    POWER AT THE CORE BOUNDARY

Power loss at connections is strongly influenced by the power at the core

boundary. The power at the core boundary is influenced by the angle of divergence, as indicated above, and by the spot size of the source.

Spot sizes can be larger or smaller than the core diameter. If the light source is larger, that light source is said to 'overfill' the core. An overfilled core has a significant fraction of the optical power at the core boundary.

▶Since the single largest cause of connection power loss is core offset, a relatively large amount of optical power at the core boundary will result in a relatively large power loss (Figure 13-3).

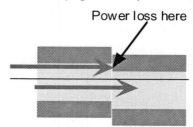

Figure 13-3: Increased Power Loss At Connection With Overfilled Core

850 nm LEDs tend to have a spot size larger than the core and a significant amount of power at the core boundary. VCSELs have spot sizes that are smaller than the core and relatively little optical power at the core boundary (Figure 13-4).

▶From this comparison we would expect connection losses measured with an LED light source to be higher than those measured with a VCSEL light source. Such is the case.

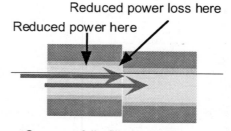

Figure 13-4: Reduced Power Loss At Connection With Under filled Core

Simulation of operating conditions in the insertion loss test procedure is desirable.

However, simulation will require multiple tests with different light sources. Multiple tests made simulation testing difficult, expensive, and unpopular.[4]

### 13.2.1.2    NORMALIZED TESTING

Testing procedure normalization is used because multimode transmitter light sources with a wide range of characteristics are used on a network. Normalization testing replaces multiple tests with a single test that provides angular and radial distribution of power in the core that are a compromise of those characteristics of LEDs and VCSELs.

This procedure was presented in TIA/EIA-568-B. This normalized procedure allows an installer to test with any light source that met a single set of requirements and obtain the same power loss measurements.

The term 'category' defines the ratio of the optical power in the center of the fiber to the total optical power in the core.[5]

▶TIA/EIA-568-B requires the use of Category 1 sources for multimode testing at both 850 nm and 1300 nm. A Category 1 source overfills both the core diameter and the NA of the fiber.

▶A second requirement is the use of a source reference lead wrapped around a mandrel (Figure 13-5) of a diameter determined by the core diameter and the cable diameter (Table 13-1).[6]

The mandrel removes some of the optical power at the core-cladding boundary and some of the power traveling at high angles to the axis. This removal results in a power distribution that is independent of the light source. With such normalization, insertion loss measurements made with different light sources will result in approximately the same value.[7]

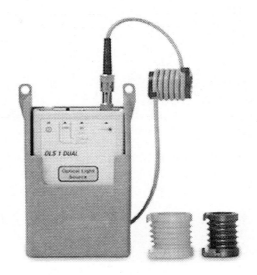

Figure 13-5: Category 1 Source With Mandrel Wrapped Reference Lead[8]

| Core diameter, μm | Mandrel diameter for 900 μm | Mandrel diameter for 3 mm |
|---|---|---|
| 50 | 1.0 in. | 0.9 in. |
| 62.5 | 0.8 in. | 0.7 in. |

Table 13-1: Mandrel Diameters For Testing Multimode Cables[9]

## 13.2.2    PRINCIPLES

Insertion loss testing has six basic principles:

> ➢ Determination of a reference power level

> ➢ Arbitrary reference power level

> ➢ Use of matched and qualified reference, or test, leads

---

[4] In addition, simulation testing was not part of TIA/EIA-568-A.

[5] The category is defined by the coupled power ratio (CPR). The CPR is defined as the ratio of the power in the central mode to the total power in the core. The CPR depends upon the wavelength and the core diameter. The CPR is defined in Tables A.1 and A.2 of Annex A of TIA/EIA-526-14-A.

[6] The requirement for use of a multimode mandrel is in Clause 7.1 of TIA/EIA-568 B.3.

[7] Pearson Technologies Inc. has performed testing that demonstrates the success of this normalization procedure. When links are tested with different light sources, the difference in insertion loss test results is less than 0.05 dB for multimode links from 2 m to 220 m. This testing, presented in Eye On Fiber, also demonstrates a troubling lack of linear increase of total insertion loss with increasing transmission distance.

[8] Photograph is courtesy of Alcoa Fujikura Ltd.

[9] From Table 11-15 of TIA/EIA-568-B.1.

➤ Cleaning and inspection of
connectors

➤ Unknown reference lead loss

➤ Power levels measured at the
detector in a power meter

### 13.2.2.1    ►MEASURE REFERENCE POWER LEVELS

In order to make power loss measurements, the installer must know the power delivered to the input of the cable link under test. As a practical matter, direct measurement of the output power of the testing light source is not possible. However, measurement of the output power from a reference cable that will be connected to the cable or connector under test is possible.

All insertion loss testing requires measurement of this 'reference power' level[10] at the end of a 'reference', or 'source', cable. The installer makes all power loss measurements relative to this reference power level. This power level at the output of the reference cable (Figure 13-6) is the power level delivered to the input of the cable or connector under test.

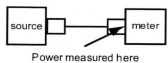

Figure 13-6: Reference Power Level

By convention, the term 'reference' cable is used for both insertion loss and reflectance measurements. The terms 'source' and 'receive' cable are used for insertion loss tests. The term 'launch' cable is used for OTDR measurements.

### 13.2.2.2    ►ARBITRARY REFERENCE POWER LEVELS

This reference power level is arbitrary. That is, the loss measurement will be the same for different initial, or reference, power levels.

While an arbitrary reference power level may seem wrong, it is acceptable for measurements of the power levels in data

networks. The power losses that occur in data fiber cables and connectors are linear with power level. That is, a cable or connector that exhibits a 1 dB power loss at an input power level of 1 mW (0 dBm) will exhibit the same power loss at 10 mW (+10 dBm) and at 0.1 mW (-10 dBm). The power losses become non linear only at the power levels that do not occur in data networks.

### 13.2.2.3    ► USE MATCHED AND QUALIFIED REFERENCE LEADS

The installer will match reference leads to the cable and connectors under test. The reference leads will contain the same fiber as that in the cable and connectors under test. 'Same' means the same core diameter or mode field diameter and the same NA. In addition, the reference leads will have the same connector type as that on the cable under test.[11]

The installer performs all testing with 'qualified' reference leads. For insertion loss and OTDR measurement, qualified means that the reference leads, or launch cable, must have low loss connectors. Low loss is not defined in FOTP-171-A,[12] but a value of 0.5 dB/pair is commonly used.[13]

Unqualified reference leads with high loss connectors will produce high losses when used to test low loss connectors. If the installer uses such unqualified or high loss reference connectors, he will reject low loss, properly installed connectors and cables.

---

[10] This term is also called 'launch power' level, and 'source power' level.

[11] It is possible to use reference leads with a connector style different from that under test, if the ferrule diameter is the same in both styles of connectors. For example, it is possible to test an SC connector with a reference lead that has an ST-compatible connector, as both have 2.5 mm ferrules. Similarly, FC, FDDI, ESCON styles can be tested with SC or ST-compatible connectors. Finally, LC, MU and LX.5 styles can be tested with one another, as all have a 1.25 mm ferrule.

[12] This standard is known as EIA/TIA-455-171-A.

[13] Pearson Technologies Inc. has tested 62.5 μm fibers in singlemode connectors. This testing indicates that most fiber and connector combinations result in losses less than 0.4 dB/pair, in reasonable agreement with the commonly used value of 0.5 dB/pair.

The installer will qualify the reference leads prior to use. Periodically, the installer will re-qualify reference leads, as they can become dirty and damaged.

Insertion loss reference leads form a qualified and matched set. The installer cannot replace one of the qualified leads without performing a re-qualification of both leads. As reference leads can become damaged, the installer will have multiple reference lead sets.

### 13.2.2.4 ▶▶REFERENCE LEAD MAINTENANCE

Prior to performing any testing, the installer will clean and inspect all reference leads with a microscope. Cleaning can restore reference leads to low loss and low reflectance.

In addition, the installer will clean the connectors on reference leads frequently. Use does result in contamination of connector tips with small particles of dirt and dust. Such particles can cause high loss measurements.

### 13.2.2.5 ▶UNKNOWN REFERENCE LEAD LOSS

To some extent, loss measurements are arbitrary, as they are relative to a reference lead with unknown, but low, loss. For example, the installer performs the insertion loss test with a set of reference leads that he qualifies. The insertion loss is relative to that set of reference leads.

The arbitrary loss is deliberate, if only because absolute, known measurements would be inconvenient and extremely expensive. To obtain reference leads with known loss, the installer would need reference leads, in which the core diameter, NA, cladding diameter, core offset, cladding ovality, fiber hole diameter, and fiber hole offset were all specified to be within tightly limited, tolerances. Such leads would be expensive, perhaps as high as $1000,[14] and would have a limited lifetime. In addition, such leads would not improve the primary function of the test: to indicate proper operation of the optoelectronics and proper installation of the link.

In spite of this characteristic, most reference leads with low loss connectors will produce loss measurements within ±0.2 dB of one another.[15] Measurements with this low level of variability will fulfill their primary function: to indicate proper operation of the transmitter-receiver pair on a link.

### 13.2.2.6 ▶LOCATION OF POWER LEVEL MEASUREMENTS

One of the subtleties that confuse many installers is the location of power level measurements. Power levels are always determined at the detector in a power meter. This is the only location at which power levels are measured. The detector converts photons to electrons. In most power meters, this detector is at the end of the reference lead (right connector in Figure 13-6).

## 13.2.3 EQUIPMENT

Insertion loss testing requires the following equipment:

> A stabilized light source
> A calibrated power meter
> Two qualified reference leads
> A multimode mandrel and
> Two low loss barrels[16]

### 13.2.3.1 ▶STABILIZED LIGHT SOURCE

The light source used in testing must be stabilized. A stabilized light source provides constant optical output power. With constant output power, the installer can perform tests on a large number of links with the same the reference output power level.

The light source will have a wavelength close to that of the transmitter to be used on the network. Of course, if the network will be used at more than one wavelength, the installer will test the links at all wavelengths

---

[14] This value is a guess.

[15] This is the author's experience. An installer can achieve this value through use of singlemode connectors on both singlemode and multimode reference leads.

[16] Barrels are also known as adapters, feed-throughs, and bulkheads. Barrels are not known as couplers as such use would cause extreme confusion with the couplers described in Chapter 7.

with different light sources. Many light sources have multiple wavelengths in a single package (Figure 13-5). As presented (13.2.1.2), the multimode source must be Category 1. Finally, the installer uses a singlemode source to test singlemode fibers.

### 13.2.3.2   ▶CALIBRATED POWER METER

The installer uses a calibrated power meter to make absolute or relative the power measurements. Three features are common to most optical power meters. The first feature is calibration that is traceable to the standards of the National Institute of Science and Technology (NIST). The second feature is calibration at multiple wavelengths. With this second feature, the installer can use a single meter to perform tests at more than one wavelength. The third feature is an 'offset' or 'zeroing' capability. This offset capability allows the installer to set the launch power level, also known as a reference power level, to 0 dB. With a zero dB reference power level, the meter reading is the loss of link.

A fourth feature, more common of power meters made in the early 1990's than in those made in the 2000's, is a changeable adapter (Figure 13-7). The changeable adapter allows the power meter to be used to make true Method B insertion loss measurements and to reduce the uncertainty of the measurement method.

Figure 13-7: Power Meter With Changeable Adapters

### 13.2.3.3   ▶USE QUALIFIED REFERENCE LEADS

The installer uses a pair of qualified reference leads. The reference leads must be 1-5 m long and have the same core diameter, NA and connector type as those of the cables to be tested.[17]

"Qualified" means that all connectors of the reference leads are low loss connectors. The process of qualifying reference leads is defined in FOTP-171-A. Low loss is defined as less than 0.5 dB.[i18]

The process of qualification creates a matched pair of reference leads. This process requires eight tests as described in Figure 13-8 to Figure 13-19.

Test 1. The installer connects a candidate reference lead, lead A, lead to a light source and power meter (Figure 13-8). The installer records the power level or uses the offset function to set the meter to 0 dB. Using a barrel (the black vertical bar in these figures), the installer connects a second candidate reference lead, lead B, between the first candidate reference lead and the power meter. The power meter should read a power level above -0.5 dB (Figure 13-9).

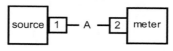

meter = 0 dB

Figure 13-8: First Reference

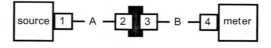

meter ≥ -0.5 dB

Figure 13-9: First Reference Lead Test

---

[17] These requirements are stated in TIA/EIA-526-14-A, Clause 3.3.

[18] This value is not required by TIA/EIA-526-14-A for insertion loss testing. However, it does appear in Clause A.2.3.3 of this standard as a requirement for test leads used to measure the coupled power ratio (CPR). While using this value for the last 15 years, Pearson Technologies and other organizations have found it to be a valid value for accepting reference leads.

Test 2. The installer reverses lead B (Figure 13-10). Again, The power meter should read a power level above -0.5 dB.

meter ≥ -0.5 dB

Figure 13-10: Second Reference Lead Test

Tests 3-8. The installer tests all combinations of connectors (Figure 13-11 to Figure). If all eight tests result in losses of less than 0.5 dB, these two leads are a qualified pair.

Note that this test procedure results in the creation of a matched reference lead pair. In addition, the power meter port must accept the type of connector to be tested. A consequence of the second requirement is a power meter with interchangeable adapters, each adapter for different connector style.

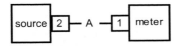

meter = 0 dB

Figure 13-11: Second Reference

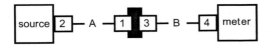

meter ≥ -0.5 dB

Figure 13-12: Third Reference Lead Test

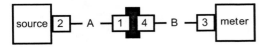

meter ≥ -0.5 dB

Figure 13-13: Fourth Reference Lead Test

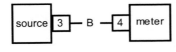

meter = 0 dB

Figure 13-14: Third Reference

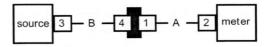

meter ≥ -0.5 dB

Figure 13-15: Fifth Reference Lead Test

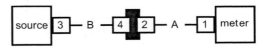

meter ≥ -0.5 dB

Figure 13-16: Sixth Reference Lead Test

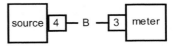

meter = 0 dB

Figure 13-17: Fourth Reference

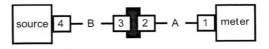

meter ≥ -0.5 dB

Figure 13-18: Seventh Reference Lead Test

meter ≥ -0.5 dB

Figure 13-19: Eighth Reference Lead Test

### 13.2.3.4  ▶USE LOW LOSS BARRELS

▶▶The insertion loss test requires pair of low loss barrels (Figure 13-20).

The barrels must be precise, not dirty or worn. Worn barrels result in insertion loss measurements that are higher than reality and cause properly installed links to be rejected. If the installer uses the same barrels in qualification of the reference leads as he uses in testing, the reference lead qualification process results in qualification of the barrels.[19,20]

---

[19] The author recommends the use of singlemode barrels for all testing. Singlemode barrels have ceramic precision alignment sleeves. Ceramic alignment sleeves do not wear out until 2000 to 3000 insertions. Worn alignment sleeves can

Figure 13-20: Barrels[21]

## 13.2.4 THREE INSERTION LOSS TEST METHODS

With the equipment specified in 13.2.3, the installer can make valid insertion loss tests. There are at least three insertion loss test procedures:

➤ Multimode Method B, as defined in EIA/TIA-455-14-A and TIA/EIA-568-B[22]

➤ Method A, as defined in EIA/TIA-455-14-A

➤ Modified Method B, as defined by several fiber product manufacturers

All three methods are 'double ended cable tests', in the tests include the connector loss of both ends, as specified in OFSTP-14 (TIA/ EIA 526-14-A). The qualification testing of reference leads (13.2.3.3) is single end testing.

### 13.2.4.1 METHOD B

Two standards, TIA/EIA-526-14-A and TIA/EIA-568 B, define the insertion loss test procedure known as 'Method B'. Method B is also known as the 'single reference lead' test.

The Method B loss approximates the loss that a transmitter-receiver pair will

experience through the backbone cable and both patch cords on the end of the backbone cable (Figure 13-21). However, the patch cords are not part of the test. Instead, reference leads take the place of the patch cords.

The Method B loss includes all loss in the link except the attenuation in the patch cord at the transmitter (Figure 13-22). As such, the measured loss is slightly less than the actual loss.[23]

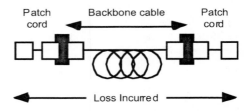

Figure 13-21: The Link Loss That Method B Estimates

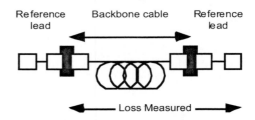

Figure 13-22: The Link That Method B Tests

### 13.2.4.1.1 ▶▶ USE MULTIMODE MANDREL

Method B requires the installer to wrap a qualified, multimode reference lead around a mandrel. The diameter of the mandrel depends upon the fiber core diameter and the cable diameter (Table 13-1).

---

result in insertion losses that are 0.5 dB higher than reality.

[20] Use of singlemode barrels to test multimode connectors results in a slight reduction in the insertion loss values. However, use of the multimode barrels on singlemode connectors results in a significant increase in insertion loss values. To avoid measurement problems, the author recommends only singlemode barrels in a test kit.

[21] From left to right: LC duplex, SC, SC duplex, and ST-compatible barrels.

[22] The equivalent singlemode method is Method A.1 in EIA/TIA-455-7-A.

[23] The underestimate results from exclusion of the attenuation in the patch cord at the transmitter and attenuation due the difference between the length of the patch cord at the transmitter and the length of the reference lead at the power meter. For example, the loss underestimate for a 10 m patch cord at the transmitter is 0.010 km x 3.5 dB/km, for a loss underestimation of 0.035 dB. If the difference between the lengths of the patch cord at the receiver and the reference lead at the power meter is 10 m, there will be an additional 0.035 dB underestimate. Thus, the total underestimate will be 0.07 dB. This value is on the same order of magnitude as the difference between measurements made with different reference leads.

### 13.2.4.1.2 ▶▶ USE SINGLEMODE LOOP

For singlemode testing, the installer makes a 2" loop in the singlemode reference lead attached to the source.[24]

The installer connects this source reference lead to a stabilized light source and a calibrated power meter (Figure 13-23). With this set up, the installer measures the launch, or reference, power level. If the meter has an off set capability, the installer sets the meter to 0.0 dB.

The installer disconnects this reference lead from the power meter, installs a barrel onto this connector and connects this reference lead to one end of the cable system under test. The installer installs a barrel onto a second qualified reference lead and plugs the other end of this lead into a power meter. He connects the second end of the cable under test to the second reference lead. If the meter has an offset capability, the meter reading is the Method B insertion loss of the cable system under test (Figure 13-24).

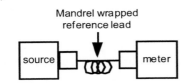

Figure 13-23: Method B Reference

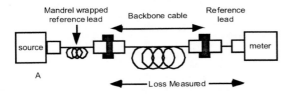

Figure 13-24: Method B Test

This test procedure sets the reference power level with zero connector pairs between the light source and the power meter. The insertion loss includes the attenuation in the fiber and the loss of at least two connector pairs. These pairs are formed with the connectors on the end of the cable under test.[25]

> ➢ Thus, the end plugs count as two pairs in a Method B test.[26]

### 13.2.4.2 METHOD A

FOTP-171 defines the insertion loss test procedure known as 'Method A'. The Method A loss is the loss of the backbone cable excluding the loss through the patch cords on the ends of the backbone cable (Figure 13-25). This measurement is made without the patch cords (Figure 13-26). Method A is also known as the 'two reference lead' test.

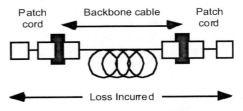

Figure 13-25: The Link Loss That Method A Estimates

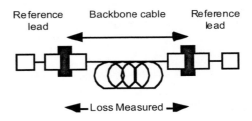

Figure 13-26: The Link That Method A Tests

To test according to Method A, the installer connects together two qualified reference leads[27] between a light source and a power meter (Figure 13-27). The leads are connected together with a qualified, low loss barrel. With this set up, the installer

---

[24] Singlemode fibers behave as multimode fibers for short distances. This requirement occurs in Clauses 2.2.2.1.1.2 and 5.1.3 of EIA-455-171, This loop eliminates the high order mode power than can exist in a short singlemode cable. Such power can result in increased power loss measurements.

[25] . All other connectors, other than the end connectors, are pairs and count as pairs.

[26] Method B was developed to test loss in relatively short links. However, The Method B test is of the backbone. Method B provides an estimate of the loss through the backbone and patch cords on the end of the backbone.

Short lengths are those typical within a building and in small campuses of closely spaced buildings.

[27] Method A does not require a mandrel.

measures the launch, or reference, power level. If the meter has an offset capability, the installer sets the meter readings to 0.0 dB. The installer disconnects two reference leads from each other.[28] The installer connects these two reference leads to the ends of the cable under test (Figure 13-28).

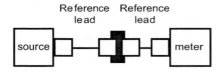

Figure 13-27: Method A Reference

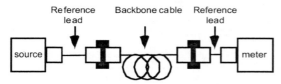

Figure 13-28: Method A Test

This test procedure sets the reference power level with one connector pair between the light source and the power meter (Figure 13-27). The insertion loss includes the attenuation in the fiber and the loss of at least two connector pairs (Figure 13-28). Stated differently, a single connector pair has been added to the reference conditions in a Method A test.

➤ In effect, the end plugs in a Method A test function as a single connector pair.

➤ A Method A loss measurement will be less than a Method B loss measurement by the loss of one connector pair.

### 13.2.4.3   MODIFIED METHOD B

A number of connector and test equipment manufacturers have recommended use of a modification to Method B. None of the test standards allow or define this modification. The modified Method B is used only when Method B cannot be used. This modification allows testing when the power meter has a connector type that is incompatible with the

connectors on the ends of the cable under test.

To test according to modified Method B, the installer wraps a qualified reference lead around a mandrel. The diameter of the mandrel depends upon the fiber core diameter and the cable diameter (Table 13-1). The installer connects this launch reference lead to a qualified receive reference lead (Figure 13-29).

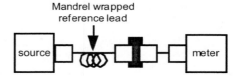

Figure 13-29: Modified Method B Reference

With this set up, the installer measures the launch, or reference, power level. If the meter has an offset capability, the installer sets the meter readings to 0.0 dB.

The installer disconnects the two reference leads from each other. The installer connects launch reference lead to one end of the cable under test. The installer connects the qualified receive reference lead to a third qualified reference lead, which, in turn, he connects to the other end of the cable under test (Figure 13-30).

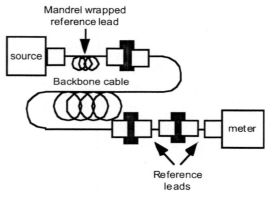

Figure 13-30: Modified Method B Test

Like the Method B test, the modified Method B insertion loss includes the attenuation in the fiber and the loss of at least two connector pairs.[29]

---

[28] Once the installer determines the reference power level, the installer does not remove the connectors attached to either the power meter or the source. To do so will result in loss of the known launch power level.

[29] The author's tests have shown a negligible difference between insertion loss values obtained by Method B and those obtained by the modified Method B (Eye on Fiber, Vol. 2, Issue 3, Part 2).

### 13.2.4.4   RELATIVE ADVANTAGES OF THE THREE METHODS

Method B has the advantage of reduced uncertainty. The Method B launch power is well known, as all the power exiting the source reference lead is measured.

The Method A launch power has increased uncertainty. This increased uncertainty is due to the somewhat arbitrary alignment of the mated connectors during the setting of the reference power level (Figure 13-27). It is possible that the mated reference connectors (Figure 13-28) will align with the connectors on the ends of the cable under test more precisely than they align with each other. In this case, the power delivered to the power meter through the cable under test can be higher than the power delivered to the power meter through the reference leads. In other words, the loss will be positive. A positive loss is a useless number, as the best possible loss is 0.0 dB. Positive losses can occur on short cable lengths.[30]

Method A has the advantage of allowing use of an imperfect, or lightly damaged, receive reference lead. Any excess loss due to imperfections in either reference lead will be reflected in the reference power level. A lightly damaged receive reference lead (right reference lead, Figure 13-24) will bias all Method B insertion loss measurements higher than reality. In this case, the installer may reject low loss links.

### 13.2.4.5   METHOD B VS. METHOD A

Neither Method A nor Method B biases the interpretation of the insertion loss measurement. As long as the test is performed properly, both methods will result in the same interpretation. That is, both methods will indicate that the loss is acceptably low or unacceptably high.

### 13.2.4.6   DIRECTIONAL DIFFERENCES

Insertion loss measurements can be different in opposite directions. There are five potential causes of such differences"

---

[30] During the Pearson Technologies' training programs, we see frequent positive losses on 1 m cable links. These positive losses are rarely above +0.2 dB when the reference leads have singlemode connectors.

➢ Core diameter differences

➢ NA differences

➢ Differential modal attenuation

➢ Core offset

➢ Cladding Ovality

➢ Fiber offset in connectors

Core diameter differences can create directional effects. When light travels from a small core to a large core there will be little power loss. However, when light travels in the opposite direction, there can be increased power loss.

NA differences can create directional effects in a manner similar to core diameter differences: when light travels from a small NA fiber to a large NA fiber, there will be little power loss due to such a difference. However, when light travels in the opposite direction, there will be an increased loss.

Differential modal attenuation (DMA) occurs in multimode fibers. DMA is the mechanism by which the ratio of the light in the center of the core to that at the core boundary becomes increasingly larger as the light travels further along a fiber. In other words, the light tends to become increasingly focused at the center of a multimode fiber as the light travels further along a fiber.

This mechanism is directly related to the travel path of the rays of light. The longer the travel path, the more attenuation the rays experience. As defined by the NA, the critical angle rays travel the longest path and experience the highest attenuation in the core. The critical angle rays will spend more 'time' near the core boundary than in the center of the fiber. The axial rays travel the shortest path and experience the lowest attenuation. The axial rays will comprise much of the power in the center of the core.

As light travels further along a fiber, the fraction of the total power in the central region of the core increases while the fraction of the total power at the core boundary drops. Connector loss is related to the amount of power at the core boundary, As the distance between the source and a connector pair increases, the power level at the core boundary becomes less and the loss of the connectors becomes less. In other words, multimode connectors exhibit reduced loss as the distance from the light increases.

One consequence of DMA is the directional effect of insertion loss measurements. To see this mechanism, consider a two-segment link with mid span connectors that are not equidistant from the ends (Figure 13-31). When the testing light source is on the end of the link that is close to the mid span connector pair, there will be some DMA which reduces the power at the core boundary of the connector pair. When the testing light source is on the end of the link that is far away from the mid span connector pair, there will be increased DMA which reduces the power at the core boundary of the connector pair to a level below the level of the source at the opposite end. Thus, the measured insertion loss will be less in the direction with the connectors closer to the source than in the opposite direction.

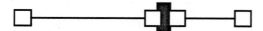

Figure 13-31: Connectors At Unequal Distances From Link Ends

Core offset, cladding non-circularity and fiber offset in connectors create directional differences in insertion loss tests in combination with DMA. The power distribution across the core is different in opposite directions due to DMA. As a result, the alignment of the region of the transmitting core that contains most of the power to the receiving core will differ in opposite directions due to these three characteristics.

13.2.4.7    REPEATABILITY AND RANGE

Repeated insertion loss measurements of the same link can be, and usually are, slightly different. Such differences result from several factors, including variations in ferrule diameters, in barrel inner diameters and the clearance in barrels. The small, but finite, clearance between the outside diameter of the connector ferrules and the inside diameter of the barrel used to connect two connectors can prevent identical alignment of two connectors for every insertion into the same barrel. To establish a range, the installer makes multiple tests on multiple fibers.

When the installer disconnects and reconnects one end of a cable system, he is testing the repeatability of the connectors on the end of system. Repeatability is the maximum change in loss, in dB, that will occur between successive measurements of the same connector pair. However, when the installer disconnects and reconnects both ends of the same cable system, he is testing the 'range' of loss.

The installer will use this value as the range for the network. The installer will use this value as a threshold to interpret insertion loss increases during maintenance and troubleshooting.

13.2.4.7.1    ▶▶MAKE MULTIPLE MEASUREMENTS

The installer makes multiple measurements of a small number of fibers in the network.[31]

13.2.4.7.2    ▶ESTABLISH RANGE

When the installer reviews these differences, he will find that most of them will be below a certain value. From these measurements, he can determine the difference between the minimum and maximum values for each fiber so tested.

13.2.4.7.3    ▶▶INTERPRET INCREASE IN LOSS WITH RANGE

If an insertion loss increase is less than the range, the installer will interpret the increase as normal behavior. If an insertion loss increase is less than the range, the installer will interpret the increase abnormal behavior caused by degradation of link components.

13.2.4.7.4    ▶CALCULATE RANGE

Connector manufacturers test the repeatability of their products. A typical repeatability for keyed and contact connectors is 0.2 dB. With this value, the installer might expect that the range, which involves disconnecting and reconnecting two ends, would be twice the repeatability, or 0.4 dB. However, the we find a range smaller than double the repeatability. Range testing for multimode, keyed and contact connectors indicates a typical range of less than 0.2 dB. In addition, testing indicates

---

[31] We find that six measurements on four to six links provides a good estimate of the range.

repeatability closer to 0.10 dB than to the 0.20 dB value of connector data sheets.

### 13.2.4.8   ADVANTAGES AND DISADVANTAGES

The three advantages of the insertion loss test are:

> ➢ Low-cost equipment

> ➢ Test procedure simplicity

> ➢ Simplicity of interpretation of the test results

The disadvantage of the insertion loss test is its blindness to the location and distribution of loss. For example, an acceptably low insertion loss can result from at least four situations:

> ➢ Nominal loss connectors and nominal attenuation rate cable

> ➢ Low loss connectors and slightly high attenuation rate cable

> ➢ Slightly high a loss connectors and low attenuation rate cable

> ➢ Low loss connectors, low attenuation rate cable, and a bend radius violation, or some other violation of the cable performance parameters

Since the insertion loss test is blind to the location of power loss, the insertion loss test cannot be used to indicate proper installation of all components. We define the word 'component' to mean a cable segment, splice, or connector pair. At best, the insertion loss test can provide a crude inference of proper installation.[32]

## 13.3   OPTICAL TIME DOMAIN REFLECTOMETRY

Optical time domain reflectometry (OTDR) is a test procedure that allows testing of almost every component in a fiber optic link. With such testing, the installer can verify proper installation of each component. If each component in a link is properly installed, the

link will have maximum reliability. This, maximum reliability, is the key advantage of, and reason for, OTDR testing.

There are three types of OTDRs: mainframe OTDRs (Figure 13-32), mini- OTDRs (Figure 13-33 and Figure 13-34), and OTDR modules that are controlled by an external computer, such as a laptop computer. All types have a computer processor for analysis of the trace data.

A mini-OTDR meets the needs of most field installation work. The battery-powered mini-OTDR has a reduced speed processor for extended battery life.

The AC-powered mainframe OTDRs, with their high-speed processors, are used in fiber and cable manufacturing facilities. The high speed of mainframe OTDRs justifies their cost.

OTDR modules are cost effective when the purchaser already has a computer or notebook computer than can be dedicated to use as an OTDR. Being battery powered, such OTDRs have reduced speed processors.

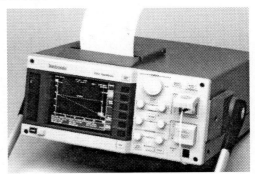

Figure 13-32: Mainframe OTDR (Courtesy Tektronix)

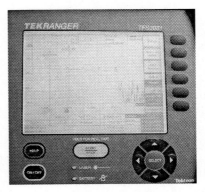

Figure 13-33: Tektronix Mini-OTDR

---

[32] In a legal sense, a low insertion loss measurement does not prove low loss of all components in a link.

Figure 13-34: EXFO Mini-OTDR

## 13.3.1 OTDR PRINCIPLES

In order to understand the method by which an OTDR functions, we must review the basics of attenuation (3). As light moves through an optical fiber, some of the light is scattered towards the core boundary at an angle greater than the critical angle. Such light escapes from the core, creating attenuation. However, some of the light is scattered backwards towards the input end of the fiber at an angle less than the critical angle. Such light experiences total internal reflection and travels backwards towards the input end of the fiber (Figure 13-35). Thus, whenever there is light moving in one direction in a fiber, there is a small amount of optical power moving in the opposite direction. [33]

### 13.3.1.1 ▶THE OTDR MEASURES 'BACKSCATTERED' POWER

Backscattered power

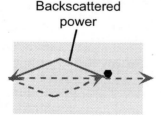

Figure 13-35: Rayleigh Back Scattering

---

[33] Because light moves in both directions, it is not possible to perform simultaneous, bi-directional communication at the same wavelength in the same fiber.

## 13.3.2 FUNCTIONAL DIAGRAM OF AN OTDR

In its simplest description, an OTDR consists of four parts: a high-power laser diode, a high sensitivity detector, a bi-directional coupler, and a connector on the front panel (Figure 13-36). The laser diode sends a pulse of light into a fiber. At each point along the fiber, some of the light is scattered backwards towards the OTDR. The directional coupler directs this backscattered optical power to the high sensitivity detector.

The OTDR measures the power scattered backwards as a function of time. When the correct index of refraction for the fiber under test is entered into the OTDR, the OTDR displays optical power level verses fiber distance. The OTDR displays this information in the form of a trace, often called the backscatter trace (Figure 13-37).

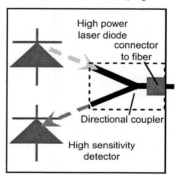

Figure 13-36: Functional Diagram Of OTDR

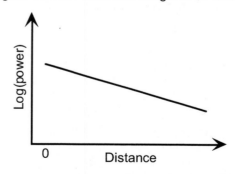

Figure 13-37: Basic Theoretical Backscatter Trace

The horizontal axis of an OTDR trace is a time axis, but is displayed as fiber distance. The fiber distance is calculated from the time measurements of the OTDR and the index of refraction. The vertical axis is a power axis, in dB, and is used to measure loss.

### 13.3.2.1 ▶OTDR MAKES MULTIPLE MEASUREMENTS

Because the backscattered power level is very low, the backscattered signal can contain significant electronic noise. In order to reduce the noise from the backscattered signal, the OTDR interrogates the cable many times.[34] With a large number of measurements, the OTDR averages the noise from the signal, providing accurate power measurements.

### 13.3.2.2 ▶ POWER DIFFERENCE IS LOSS

With this capability to measure backscattered power levels at different points along the cable link, we can interrogate almost every component in a cable link. For example, if we measure the power levels at the beginning and end of a cable segment, we can divide the power loss difference by the distance between these two locations to determine the attenuation rate.[35]

We measure the backscattered power level before and after a connection to determine its power loss. Finally, we can determine cable segment lengths. With these measurements, we can verify acceptably low power loss for almost all components and conformance of the installed cable distances to the design map. In short, the OTDR gives us the ability to verify proper and reliable installation of the link.

## 13.3.3 BACKSCATTER TRACE FEATURES

In this section, we use the symbols shown in Figure 13-38.

---

[34] During the author's fiber optic training programs, the minimum number of repetitions is 2000 for the Tektronix mini-OTDR. This OTDR allows for up to 64,000 repetitions, or pulses, in order to obtain noise-free traces from long, 1550 nm singlemode cables.

[35] The attenuation rate is also known as the attenuation coefficient.

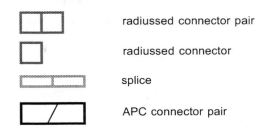

radiussed connector pair

radiussed connector

splice

APC connector pair

Figure 13-38: Symbols Used

Theory tells us, and millions of OTDR traces prove, that a plot of the logarithm of backscattered power (dB) verses distance produces a straight-line trace with a negative slope (Figure 13-37). This trace has a vertical axis of logarithm of power, which is the method of calculating 'dBs'. The horizontal axis is distance, which is calculated from time measurements and the index of refraction. This straight-line trace results from backscatter in the fiber. The slope of this trace is the attenuation rate of the fiber.

### 13.3.3.1 ▶ ENDS CREATE REFLECTIONS

In Chapter 4, we learned that connectors and splices can create reflections. The power from these reflections adds to the power backscattered by the atoms in the core. When the OTDR adds this reflected power to the backscattered power, the straight-line trace with a negative slope has peaks at the locations of connectors (or splices). The peaks are also known as spikes, but are most accurately called reflections (Figure 13-39).

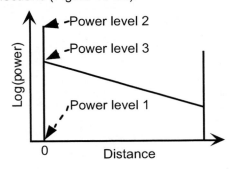

Figure 13-39: Trace With Backscatter And Reflections

The height of a reflectance, or peak, depends on a nature of the connection. The larger the difference in the index of refraction at the connection, the higher will be the reflectance. Reflectances of various types of connections, from highest to lowest, are:

> ➢ Air gap connectors
>
> ➢ Flat physical contact connectors
>
> ➢ Radiused physical contact connectors
>
> ➢ Mechanical splice
>
> ➢ Fusion splice or APC connectors

### 13.3.3.2   ▶ PEAK WIDTH CONCEALS FEATURES

In Figure 13-39, the peaks are vertical lines. These vertical lines imply an OTDR ability to measure three different power levels in zero time. This implication cannot be correct, since all electronics take time to respond to changes in power level. The OTDR cannot display a figure like Figure 13-39 because of this response time.

To reflect this response time, the OTDR creates a trace with peaks that have a forward slant and a finite width (Figure 13-40). This width can be from a few meters to thousands of meters.

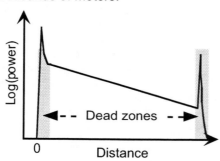

Figure 13-40: Basic Trace With Modified Peaks

The bandwidth limitation of the OTDR detector determines the width of these peaks. The width of these peaks obscures the true nature of the fiber in the peaks. As a result,

> ➢ These peaks are often called optical 'blind zones' or optical 'dead zones'.

Concealed features, i.e., reflectances or drops, occur whenever the features are more closely spaced than the width of the reflection. Imagine that we have two reflective components that are closely

spaced. The peak created by the first reflective component can be wider than the distance between the two components. In this case, the peak from the first component could conceal the second component (Figure 13-41).

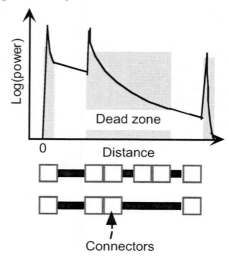

Figure 13-41: Two Closely Spaced Reflective Events In A Single Peak

Because a reflection from one reflective component can obscure the reflection from a second, closely spaced, reflective component, we may not be able to measure the loss of every event in a link.

This is one example of the fact that we may not be able to test and confirm proper installation of all components. Hence, at the beginning of Section 13.3, we were forced to use the phrase 'testing of *almost every element* in a fiber optic link'.

## 13.3.4   THREE BASIC TRACES

With this basic understanding of the OTDR and its traces, we can reduce thousands of different traces to three basic traces:

> ➢ A reflective loss
>
> ➢ A non- reflective loss
>
> ➢ A bad launch

### 13.3.4.1   REFLECTIVE LOSS

A reflective loss will have the appearance of Figure 13-42.

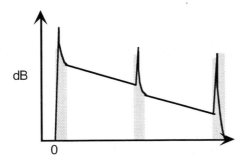

Figure 13-42: Reflective Loss

This trace can result from at least five link configurations:

> Two segments connected by radiused connectors

> Two multimode segments connected by mechanical splice

> Two singlemode segments connected by a mechanical splice

> A broken fiber and a tight tube cable

> A single cable segment that is demonstrating 'multiple reflections', also known as 'ghost reflections'

Radiused connectors always create reflectance. The OTDR trace of two cables segments connected by radiused connectors will exhibit reflectance at the location of the connectors (Figure 13-43). This reflectance results from the imperfectly smooth surfaces of the mated connectors (5.3.4). This lack of perfect smoothness creates air gaps, at which the IR changes.

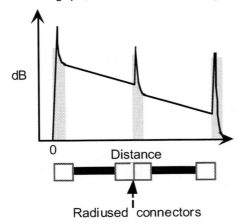

Figure 13-43: Reflective Loss Trace From Radiused Connectors

Multimode mechanical splices always create reflectance (Figure 13-44). Reflectance results from the difference in the IR of the index matching gel of the mechanical splice and the speed of light in the core of the multimode fiber. Since the multimode core has a multiple indices of refraction (3.2.2), the single index of refraction of the gel will be mismatched to most of the indices of refraction of the multimode fiber core.

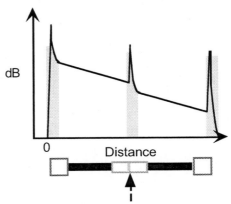

Figure 13-44: Reflective Loss From A Multimode Mechanical Splice

Singlemode mechanical splices may create reflectance (Figure 13-45). The cause of this reflectance is a difference between the index of refraction of the core and that of the gel.

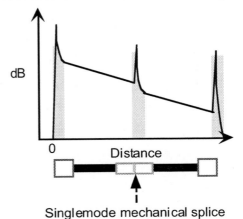

Figure 13-45: Reflective Loss Trace From A Singlemode Mechanical Splice

A broken fiber in a tight tube cable creates reflectance. The OTDR trace of such a break (4.1.1.2) exhibits a reflectance at the break (Figure 13-46). The cause of this reflectance is air between the fiber ends. Air has diffused into the break.

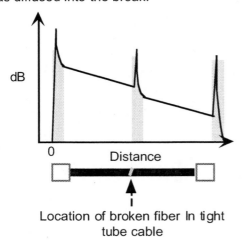

Figure 13-46: Reflective Loss Trace From Broken Tight Tube Cable

A single segment of cable with a high reflectance connector may create two reflectances (Figure 13-47). Light scattered backwards from the atoms of the core and reflected by the far end connector can be partially reflected back into the fiber for a second round trip, before entering the OTDR and registering as a peak (Right peak of Figure 13-47). This type of reflection is a 'multiple reflection', or more commonly, a 'ghost'. In 13.3.6.4.2, we discuss ghosts in more detail.

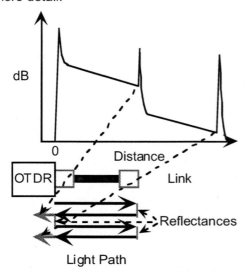

Figure 13-47: Reflective Event From Multiple Reflection

A comparison of Figure 13-42 to Figure 13-46 reveals that different link components can create identical traces. This comparison indicates an important rule:

### 13.3.4.1.1    ▶ INTERPRET TRACE FROM MAP

The trace must be interpreted with an accurate map; a map cannot be created from a trace.

### 13.3.4.2    NON-REFLECTIVE LOSS

The second basic trace is a non-reflective loss (Figure 13-48).

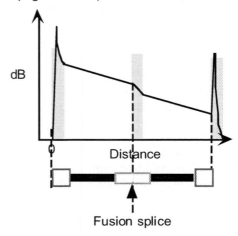

Figure 13-48: Non-Reflective Fusion Splice

This trace can result from four cable configurations:

> Two segments connected with a fusion splice

> Two singlemode segments connected with a mechanical splice

> Two segments connected by APC connectors and

> A cable with a violation of any cable performance parameter

Properly made fusion splices of the same fiber type create no reflectance but may exhibit a loss (Figure 13-48).[36] Because there is little or no change in the IR as light moves from one fiber to another fiber, there is no reflectance. Should the fusion splice

---

[36] A reflectance may result from a fusion splice if the indices of refraction are different.

exhibit a 0.0 dB power loss, the splice would be invisible to the OTDR (Figure 13-49).[37]

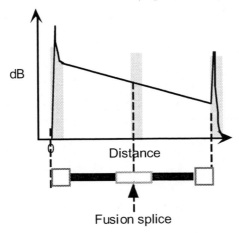

Figure 13-49: Trace For 0 dB Fusion Splice

Singlemode mechanical splices may create no reflectance. The single index of refraction in the core of the singlemode fiber may exactly match the index of refraction of the gel in the mechanical splice. Two singlemode segments connected with a mechanical splice may exhibit a loss without a reflectance (Figure 13-48). In this case, there will be no reflection, since there will be no change speed of light.

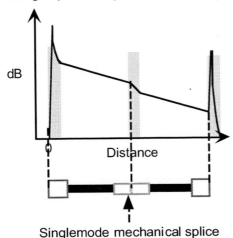

Figure 13-50: Non-Reflective Loss From Singlemode Mechanical Splice

Figure 13-45 and Figure 13-50 may create confusion. Both figures could result from the

same cable configuration. If the index of refraction of the gel does not exactly match the index of refraction of the fiber core, reflectance will result.[38] As stated earlier, the principle is:

> ➤ The trace must be interpreted with an accurate map; a map cannot be created from a trace.

Two segments connected by APC connectors can exhibit a loss without reflectance (Figure 13-51). The APC connectors reflect light backwards at an angle greater than the critical angle of the singlemode fiber. When this light crosses the core boundary, it escapes into the cladding. In this case, there will be no reflectance, and no peak.

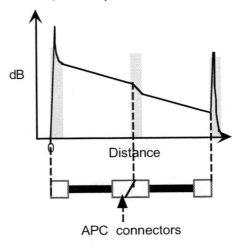

Figure 13-51: Non-Reflective Loss From APC Connectors

A violation of a cable performance parameter can be a violation of the bend radius, the crush load, the operating temperature range, the crush load, or any other cable performance parameter.[39] When

---

[37] The author's experience is that approximately 30% of fusion splices are 0.0 dB splices.

[38] The author has observed singlemode mechanical splices that exhibit both reflectance and non-reflectance when the same two singlemode fibers are repeatedly spliced with the same mechanical splice.

[39] By definition, the cable is designed so that the fiber experiences the lowest attenuation rate possible, as long as the cable is operated within its operating limits. When a cable is subjected to conditions that violate its operating limits, it can no longer allow the fiber to experience the lowest attenuation rate.

this violation occurs, power is lost at that location. We refer to this loss as an 'event', as it is not a connection. This violation results in an event with a non-reflective loss (Figure 13-52).

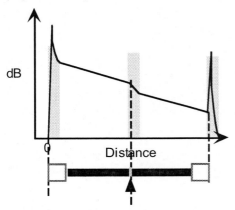

Location of violation of cable performance parameter

Figure 13-52: Non-Reflective Loss From Cable Parameter Violation

A comparison of these figures reinforces the important rule of trace interpretation: the trace must be interpreted with an accurate map; a map cannot be created from a trace.

### 13.3.4.3   THE BAD LAUNCH

The third basic trace is of a bad launch (Figure 13-53). A bad launch results from a broken connector at the OTDR or a break in the fiber within the dead zone. If no light moves through the break in the fiber, none will experience backscatter to the OTDR, resulting in no straight-line trace with a negative slope.

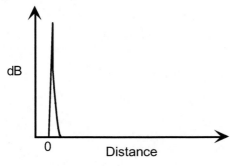

Figure 13-53: Trace From A Broken Fiber In The Dead Zone

In addition to the three basic traces, there is one unique trace that can occur: a trace without a far end reflection (Figure 13-54). This trace can result from three configurations:

➤   A cable with APC connector on the far end

➤   A fiber with a high angle cleave on the far end

➤   A singlemode fiber with a mechanical splice on the far end

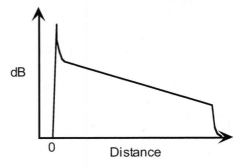

Figure 13-54: Trace Without End Reflection

The APC connector and a high angle cleave reflect light backwards at an angle greater than the critical angle. Thus, no reflection, or peak, is produced. In the case of the mechanical splice on the far end, exact matching of the index of refraction of the core to the index of refraction of the gel results in no power reflected backwards and no end reflection.

## 13.3.5   USING THE OTDR

### 13.3.5.1   SETTING UP THE OTDR

The purpose of using an OTDR is to make power loss measurements of all components in a link. In order to create valid measurements, the installer must provide the OTDR with certain information:

➤   Wavelength

➤   Pulse width

➤   Maximum length of cable to be tested

➤   Index of refraction

➤   Either the maximum allowed for the test or the number of pulses to be analyzed by the OTDR

The wavelength is same as the wavelength at which the transmitter will operate. The pulse width determines the amount of power launched into the fiber in each pulse. As the cable length increases, the pulse width must become longer to ensure adequate power from the far end of the cable. As the pulse width becomes wider, the dead zone becomes wider. As the dead zone becomes wider, the spacing between components must increase to be separately measured for loss.

The maximum length of cable to be tested limits the time the OTDR takes to complete test. The time of the test or the number of pulses to be analyzed determines the noise level in the final backscatter trace.

### 13.3.5.1.1 ▶IR ENABLES ACCURATE LENGTH MEASUREMENTS

When the installer enters the index of refraction in the OTDR, the OTDR makes accurate fiber length measurements. However, the fiber length is greater than the cable length (4.1.1.1).

### 13.3.5.1.2 ▶CABLE LENGTH IS LESS THAN FIBER LENGTH

### 13.3.5.2 ▶▶USE LAUNCH CABLE

In order to make an OTDR trace, the installer connects a launch cable[40] between the OTDR and the cable under test. With a launch cable, the trace will exhibit at least two segments (Figure 13-55).

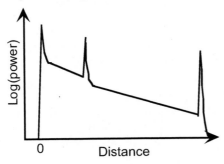

Figure 13-55: Trace Of OTDR With Launch Cable

The launch cable has a fiber with the same core diameter, or mode field diameter, the same NA, and the same connector as on the cable under test. An additional requirement is a low loss connector on both ends.

With a length longer than the dead zone, the launch cable serves two functions:

➤ Protection of the OTDR port

➤ Measurement of the loss of the near end connector

When testing a large number of fibers, the installer connects the launch cable to the cable under test. Occasionally, and eventually, the connector on the far end of the launch cable becomes damaged. The repair of the launch cable connector is much less expensive than repair of an OTDR port.

If the length of the launch cable is greater than the width of the dead zone, the installer will be able to measure the loss of the connector at the near end of the cable under test. Without this launch cable, the loss of the near end connector may not be measurable.[41]

In a manner similar to insertion loss testing, the installer makes the OTDR loss measurements with a launch cable that has a connector with unknown, but low, loss. The loss of that first connector on the cable under test is relative to the connector on the launch cable.

## 13.3.6    MEASUREMENTS

Once the installer sets up the OTDR, he is able to obtain a trace of the cable. From this trace, the installer can make loss and length measurements. To make these measurements, the installer can allow the software that runs the OTDR to determine all loss and length measurements. As we all well know, software is not perfect!

Because of this lack of perfection, the installer needs to know how to place cursors on the backscatter trace in order to make

---

[40] The launch cable is also known as a 'pulse suppressor'. This label is misleading, in that the cable does not suppress the pulse. Rather, the cable allows measurement of the near end connector by creating a straight-line trace before the near end connector of the cable under test.

[41] This statement is true for OTDR without an internal fiber. If the OTDR has an internal fiber, it is possible to measure the loss of the near end connector without using a launch cable. However, use of an OTDR without a launch cable can result in damage to the OTDR port.

accurate measurements. In this section, we will examine how to place cursors so that you need not curse at cursors!

One final note that applies to all measurements made by moving cursors to the proper location: the installer will make all measurements with both axes expanded enough to see fine details. If either axis is not sufficiently expanded, the installer may place the cursors on the trace incorrectly.

### 13.3.6.1   LENGTH MEASUREMENTS

The installer can make three types of OTDR measurements:

> Segment length

> Splice or connector loss

> Attenuation rate

Segment length measurements require placement of two cursors. Cursors are placed at the beginning and at the end of the segment. For the first segment attached to an OTDR, the beginning of the segment is at the OTDR front panel, which is at 0 m.

The end of the first segment is defined by either:

> A peak, for a reflective connection,

> Or a change in slope or drop off, for a non-reflective connection or event.

▶The principle for length measurement of the first segment with a reflective connection is:

> The curser is at the lowest point of the backscatter trace before the peak (Figure 13-56).

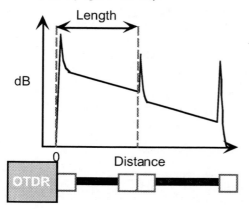

Figure 13-56: First Segment Length Measurement, Reflective Connection

The principle for first segment length measurement with a non-reflective connection or event is:

> The curser is at the lowest point of the backscatter trace before the change in slope, or drop off, that marks the end of the first segment (Figure 13-57).

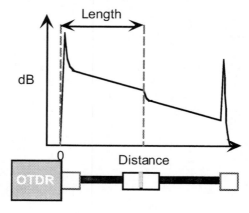

Figure 13-57: First Segment Length Measurement, Non-Reflective Event

For length measurements of a segment other than the first segment, the installer places two cursors on the trace. The installer places the first cursor at the end of the previous segment and the second cursor at the end of the segment of interest.

▶The principle for a length measurement with reflective connections is:

> The first cursor is at the lowest point on the straight line trace before the peak that marks the end of the previous segment (Figure 13-58).

> The second cursor is at the lowest point of a straight line trace of the segment before either the peak that marks the end of that segment (Figure 13-58) or the non-reflective drop that marks the end of the segment (Figure 13-59).

▶The principle for a length measurement with non-reflective connections is:

> The first cursor at the lowest point on the straight line trace before the drop that marks the end of the previous segment and

> The second cursor at the lowest point of a straight-line trace of the

segment being measured before the drop that marks the end of that segment (Figure 13-60).

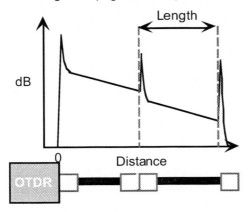

Figure 13-58: Segment Length With Reflective Ends

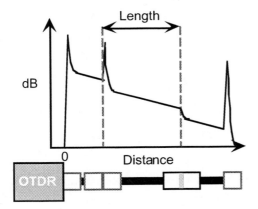

Figure 13-59: Segment With Reflective and Non-Reflective Ends

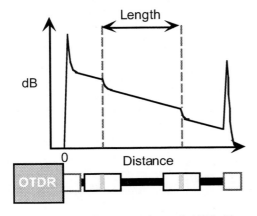

Figure 13-60: Segment Length With Non-Reflective Connections At Both Ends

▶The basic principle for all length measurements is:

➤ A length measurement includes a peak or a drop off at the beginning and excludes a peak or drop off at the end.

### 13.3.6.2   CONNECTION LOSS MEASUREMENTS

There two types of connection loss measurements: estimated and accurate. The installer makes estimated measurements; the computer in an OTDR makes accurate measurements.

### 13.3.6.2.1   ESTIMATED CONNECTION LOSS MEASUREMENTS

Estimated connection loss measurements require placement of two cursors that straddle the connection, but are in the backscatter, or straight lines, on both sides of the peak or drop.

These measurements overestimate the actual loss. This overestimate results from the fiber attenuation that occurs between the two cursors. As an overestimate, this method is a conservative method.[42]

▶The principle for estimated reflective connection loss measurement is:

➤ Two cursors placed in the backscatter, or straight-line, trace on both sides of the peak, as close to the peak as possible without being in the peak (Figure 13-61).

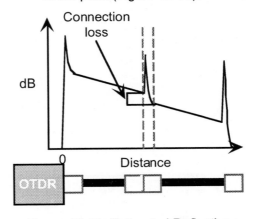

Figure 13-61: Estimated Reflective Connection Loss With Correct Cursor Placement

---

[42] This method is called the two-point method.

If the installer places the cursors away from the peak (Figure 13-62), the measured loss increases. If the installer places the cursors in the peak, the measured loss increases (Figure 13-63) or decreases (Figure 13-64).

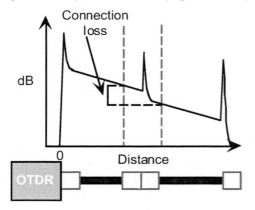

Figure 13-62: Incorrect Cursor Placement

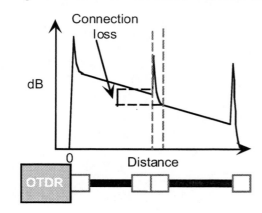

Figure 13-63: Incorrect Cursor Placement

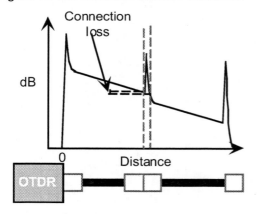

Figure 13-64: Incorrect Cursor Placement

The estimated loss measurement of non-reflective connections requires cursors placed in the backscatter on both sides of the drop off, but as close as possible to the

drop off without being in the drop off (Figure 13-65). If the installer places the cursors away from the drop off (Figure 13-66), the measured loss will increase. If the installer places the cursors in the drop-off, the measured loss will decrease (Figure 13-67).

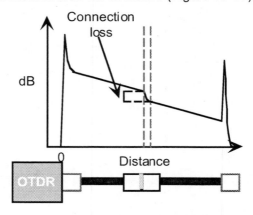

Figure 13-65: Estimated Non-Reflective Connection Loss Measurement

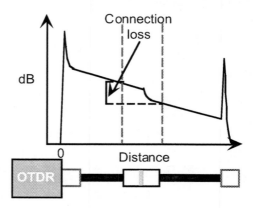

Figure 13-66: Wide Spacing Of Cursors

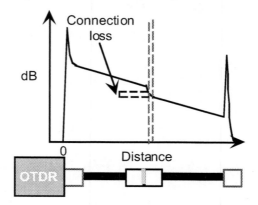

Figure 13-67: Cursors In Drop Off

### 13.3.6.2.2    ACCURATE CONNECTION LOSS MEASUREMENTS

The OTDR can make accurate loss measurements, also called splice loss measurements, automatically. When this measurement method is active, the computer in the OTDR performs a 'least squares analysis' (LSA), also called a 'least squares fit', of the straight-line trace that follows the connection. The computer extrapolates the line defined by the least squares fit equation back to the end of the previous segment. The computer calculates the power drop from the end of the previous segment to the extrapolation of the subsequent segment (Figure 13-68 and Figure 13-69). As this method includes no fiber attenuation in the loss value, this method provides accurate loss values.

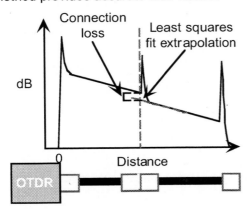

Figure 13-68: Accurate Reflective Loss Measurement

This method requires only that the installer place the curser near the location of the connection. The computer in the OTDR performs the calculation, even without precise curser placement.

### 13.3.6.3    ATTENUATION RATE MEASUREMENTS

Attenuation rate measurements require two cursors: one placed at the beginning of the segment and one placed at the end of the segment. The cursors must be as far apart as possible to create an attenuation rate value that is most representative of the fiber. However, the cursors must not be in or enclose a drop or peak, as such features will create an inaccurate attenuation rate value.

▶The principles for attenuation rate measurement are:

➢ Placement of two cursers as far apart as possible in the same straight line segment (Figure 13-70)

➢ Cursers must not enclose any features such as a drop (Figure 13-71), or a peak (Figure 13-72).

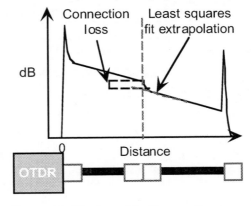

Figure 13-69: Accurate Connection Loss Measurement Of Non-Reflective Event

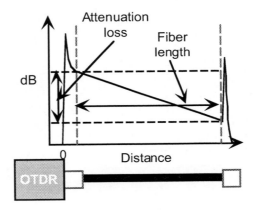

Figure 13-70: Attenuation Rate Measurement

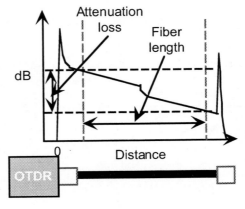

Figure 13-71: Improper Cursor Placement For Attenuation Rate Measurement

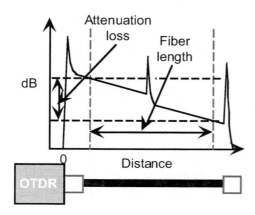

Figure 13-72: Improper Cursor Placement
For Attenuation Rate Measurement

If the backscatter trace is not straight, the attenuation rate measurement is biased higher than the actual value. In this case,[43] the installer makes attenuation rate measurements on each side of the non-uniform event (Figure 13-73).

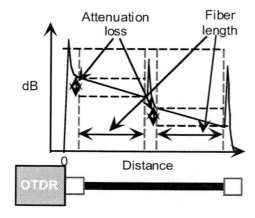

Figure 13-73: Correct Attenuation Rate
Measurement With Non-Uniformity

A common error is placement of cursers in the peaks or drop off than define the ends of the segment. To avoid making this error, the installer can move the two cursors slightly away from peaks or drop offs to ensure that the cursors are properly placed in the straight backscatter trace (Figure 13-74).

Moving the cursors slightly away from peaks or drop offs will change the attenuation rate measurement slightly. However, the interpretation of the attenuation rate measurement will not change. That is,

---

[43] This non-uniformity can result from a violation of any cable performance parameter.

measurements made with both cursor placements will indicate the same interpretation, i.e., an acceptable rate or an unacceptable rate.

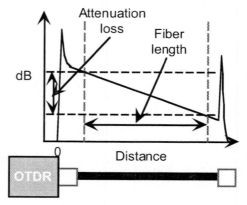

Figure 13-74: Attenuation Rate
Measurement With Reduced Cursor
Separation

#### 13.3.6.4   UNUSUAL TRACES

There are two unusual traces: 'gainers' and 'multiple reflections', also known as 'ghost reflections'.

#### 13.3.6.4.1   GAINERS

Previous measurement sections may create the impression that all OTDR connection losses are negative. Such is not the case. It is possible to measure a positive connection loss, also known as a 'gainer' (Figure 13-75).

Gainers are a phenomenon of OTDR testing. A gainer indicates that more optical power is scattered back from the location after the connection than from before the connection. As such, a gainer is not a real gain in power. Our experience is that gainers occur more frequently in singlemode than in multimode fibers and that the gains are small, 0.1-0.2 dB.

A gainer results from at least two different conditions: different attenuation rates on opposite sides of the connection; and different core diameters, or mode field diameters, on opposite sides of the connection.

To understand how different attenuation rates can create a gainer, we return to the cause of attenuation. At each point along its length, an optical fiber scatters power backwards towards the input end.

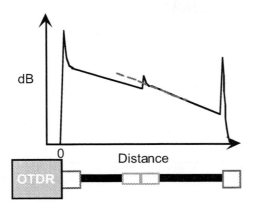

Figure 13-75: Gainer

If we splice two fibers with the same attenuation rate, same core diameter, and same NA with a perfect splice, the splice loss is 0 dB. However, if the attenuation rate of the fiber before the splice is higher than the attenuation rate of the fiber after the splice, the power scattered backwards by the fiber before the splice will be higher than the power scattered backwards by the fiber after the splice.[44] With this difference in attenuation rates, the OTDR trace of the splice will be of a loss. But we have a 0 dB splice! The difference in the attenuation rates and the scattering coefficients will result in a splice with a loss, even though the splice is a 0 dB splice!

However, in the opposite direction, the splice will have a power gain, because there will be more power scattered backwards from after than before the splice. In summary, a gainer can be a splice with a higher attenuation rate after the splice than before.

### 13.3.6.4.2    MULTIPLE REFLECTIONS

'Multiple reflections', also known as 'ghost reflections', occur when optical power makes more than one round trip through the fiber before entering the OTDR.[45] Understanding multiple reflections is necessary, as they appear like a broken fiber.

Imagine that we have a high reflectance connector on the near end of a cable attached to the OTDR. This connector will

reflect light strongly in both directions. The power scattered backwards from the atoms in the core of the fiber and the power reflected back to the OTDR from connectors in the cable under test must travel through this high reflectance connector in order to return to the OTDR. Even if this connector is low loss, this connector will reflect some of the returning power back into the fiber. This power will travel to the far end of the fiber. As it travels on its second trip through the fiber, some of the power will be scattered backwards by the atoms in the core. In addition, the far end connector will reflect some of this power back to the OTDR.

However, the power from the second round trip arrives after the power that returned after the first round trip. Thus, a single segment may create two apparent segments in an OTDR trace (Figure 13-76).

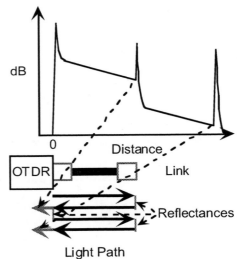

Figure 13-76: Multiple Segments Appear From A Single Segment

The installer identifies multiple reflections as such. If OTDR reflections are not ghosts, they can be broken fibers in tight tube cables.

The installer can identify ghost reflections by three characteristics:

➢ Length

➢ Height of peak

➢ Appearance from opposite end of cable

---

[44] Attenuation rate and backscattered power are directly related.

[45] Ghosts are analogous to echoes in radar.

Imagine a 100 m segment with a ghost reflection. Without a ghost, we would expect to see a trace like that in (Figure 13-77). If we see a second segment (Figure 13-78), we would expect the second segment to have exactly the same length as the first.

As the power entering the OTDR after the second round trip is much lower than that entering after the first round trip, we would expect the height of the second peak to be lower than that of the first. This is the case.

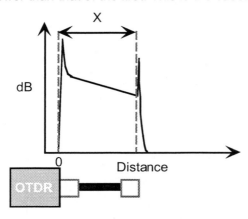

Figure 13-77: Single Segment Trace Expected

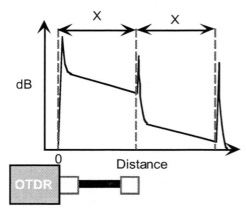

Figure 13-78: Ghost Segment Appears After Actual Segment

Ghosts can appear on a trace from one end of the cable, but not from the other.[46] In this

---

[46] In this case, the connector on the end from which the ghost appears has a loss higher than the loss of the connector on the opposite end. As the ghost reflections have lower power levels than do real reflections, the closer to the OTDR noise floor the signal level is, the more frequently the ghost reflections appear.

case, the reflection is obviously a ghost, as reflections are from fiber ends. A real end in the cable will create a reflection in both directions.

One situation in which a ghost reflection is most troubling is a multi-segment cable with a short segment followed by a long segment. In this case, a ghost reflection from the short segment can appear in the middle of the long segment (Figure 13-79). The installer must identify the origin of this reflection at a distance of 2X, as it could be a broken fiber.

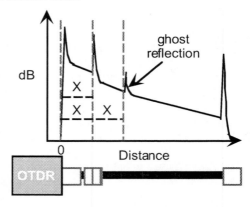

Figure 13-79: Ghost Reflection In Middle Of Segment

One method to determine whether the unknown peak is a ghost reflection is testing from both ends. When the cable is tested from the near end, the unknown reflection occurs at about 2X from the near end. If the reflection is a real end and not a ghost, the reflection will occur at a distance of 2x from the first end when the cable is tested from the second end. If the unknown reflection occurs at 2X from the OTDR at both ends of the cable, the reflection is a ghost.

### 13.3.6.5   DIRECTIONAL DIFFERENCES

From the discussion of gainers (13.3.6.4.1), you can understand how differences in core diameters[47] can result in gainers. If the core diameter of the fiber before the splice is smaller than the core diameter of the fiber after the splice, there will be more atoms scattering power backwards from the fiber after the splice than before the splice, resulting in a gainer. If measured in the

---

[47] The same effect occurs with differences in singlemode mode field diameters.

opposite direction, the splice will exhibit a loss.

Because of these three effects, differences in attenuation rates, differences in core diameters, and differences in mode field diameters,

### 13.3.6.5.1    ▶TRUE SPLICE LOSS IS AN AVERAGE

The true splice loss is the average of the loss measurements in both directions. This averaging eliminates the bias that occurs when the attenuation rates, core diameters, or mode field diameters of the two fibers are different.

# 13.4    REFLECTANCE TESTING

The installer performs reflectance testing of connectors to ensure signal accuracy (5.3.4). Excessive reflectance from connectors can result in multiple pulses reaching the receiver for each pulse created by the transmitter.

The installer performs reflectance testing on pigtails and short patch cords. The installer performs reflectance testing on pigtails prior to their installation on the ends of the main cable. The installer does not perform reflectance testing of connectors installed on a long length of cable because the backscatter from the fiber between the cable ends will result in a high reflectance measurement.

As a practical matter, installers perform reflectance tests on singlemode connectors but not on multimode connectors. There is no field test equipment for such multimode testing.[48] There is singlemode field test equipment (Figure 13-80).

The installer has a choice of two reflectance test methods: FOTP-107 and FOTP-8. The installer uses FOTP-107 to test the reflectance of connectors on patch cords or pigtails. The installer uses an OTDR according to FOTP-8 to test the reflectance of patch cords of at least 10 m.

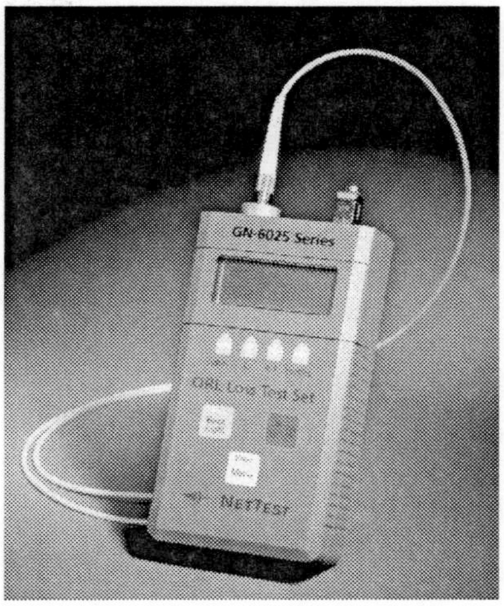

Figure 13-80: Singlemode Reflectance Test Set[49]

## 13.4.1    REFLECTANCE PRINCIPLES

By definition (Equation 5-1), reflection is a measurement of the ratio of incident power to reflected power. By this definition, a reflectance test requires two power measurements. In addition, the reflectance test equipment may have internal reflections that need to be removed from the reflected power calculation.

## 13.4.2    EQUIPMENT REQUIRED

The FOTP-107 reflectance test requires:

➢ A reflectance test set

➢ A reference lead

➢ Low loss, clean barrels

➢ A mandrel with a diameter appropriate to the wavelength of the test

➢ Connector cleaning supplies

The reflectance test sets consists of a high-power, ultra-stable, laser diode, a high sensitivity detector, and two directional couplers (Figure 13-81). The test set must have a high-power laser in order to create measurable reflected signal strength. For example, a 200-microwatt laser diode and a -60 dB reflectance connector will result in a

---

[48] As of May 2005.

[49] Photograph is courtesy of NetTest.

reflected signal strength of 200 nanowatts, an extremely low power level. As result of this low power level, the test set requires a high sensitivity detector.

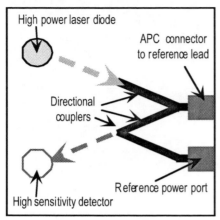

Figure 13-81: Internal Structure Of Reflectance Test Set

The reference lead needs an APC connector on one end, the end to be connected to the laser port and a low reflectance connector on the other end. The APC connector reflects back zero power to the test set.

The low reflectance connector is of the style to be tested, e.g., ST-compatible, SC, LC. The second connector of the reference lead must have reflectance that is 5 to 10 dB below the value used as an acceptance value. A high reflectance reference connector will provide measurements that are higher than reality. With a high reflectance reference lead, the installer will reject low reflectance connectors.

## 13.4.3   EQUIPMENT OPERATION

The typical reflectance test has six steps:

- ➢ Clean all connectors
- ➢ Set a reference power level
- ➢ Null out power from internal reflections in the test set
- ➢ Check the reference lead against a known reflectance reference lead
- ➢ Connect the reference lead to the connector to be tested and
- ➢ If required, wrap the opposite end of the jumper around a mandrel.

### 13.4.3.1   CONNECTOR CLEANING

The installer cleans all connectors to be tested and both connectors on the reference lead. This cleaning needs to be done with a liquid that leaves no residue when it evaporates. If the liquid leaves a residue, the installer must wipe the connector with both a wet lens grade tissue and a dry lens grade tissue. The installer must perform the dry wipe immediately after the wet wipe to prevent the formation of a residue. Without the dry wipe, the residue can result in high reflectance from a low reflectance connector.[50]

### 13.4.3.2   ▶▶MEASURE REFERENCE POWER

The installer connects both connectors of the reference lead to the test set (Figure 13-82), turns on the test set and allows it to stabilize. Light travels from laser diode through the directional coupler to the APC connector, through low reflectance reference connector to the detector. With this set up, the installer determines the reference or incident power, which is the power delivered to low reflectance reference connector.

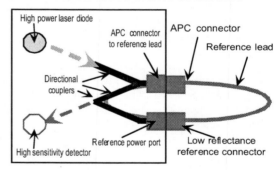

Figure 13-82: Reflectance Reference Configuration

### 13.4.3.3   ▶▶CHECK REFERENCE LEAD

With use, reference leads can become damaged and develop high reflectance. Before performing any reflectance tests, the

---

[50] While 99 %, isopropyl alcohol can be used, it tends to leave a residue on the connectors, resulting in high reflectance. Acetone, an excellent cleaner, is a carcinogen and dangerous to use. Electro-Wash Px, from Chemtronix, Kennesaw, GA, cleans connectors extremely well. It leaves no residue and tends to create a clean connector from the first cleaning.

installer tests the low reflectance reference lead with a known, low reflectance 'master' reference lead. This test will verify the low reflectance of the reference lead.

To verify low reflectance, the installer disconnects the low reflectance reference connector from the reflectance test set and connects it to the master reference connector with known low reflectance (Figure 13-83).

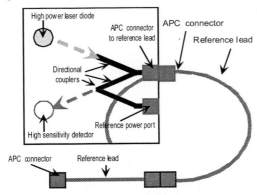

Figure 13-83: Verification of Reference Lead

### 13.4.3.4 ▶▶TESTING REFLECTANCE

To test reflectance, the installer connects the connector under test to the reference connector. If the connector on the opposite end of the cable under test is not an APC connector, the installer wraps that opposite end 10 times around a 10 mm mandrel (Figure 13-84).

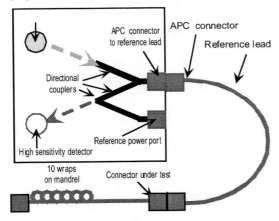

Figure 13-84: Reflectance Test With Mandrel Wrap

This wrap is required to remove any light that is reflected from the connector on the opposite end of the cable under test. If the connector on the opposite end of the cable

is an APC connector, the installer need not wrap the opposite end, as there is no reflectance from an APC connector.

## 13.5  OTHER EQUIPMENT

The installer will perform most of his testing with a power meter, light source, OTDR and reflectance test set. In addition, he can use six other tools to assist in evaluating and troubleshooting links.

> ➢ Fiber identifier
> ➢ Attenuator
> ➢ Visual fault locator
> ➢ Fiber identifier
> ➢ Talk set
> ➢ Microscope

The fiber identifier is a receiver that it placed on a fiber to indicate the presence of a signal. The identifier bends the fiber, allowing light to escape from the core. A typical identifier detects a 2kHz signal, which a source creates on the opposite end of the fiber.

An attenuator is a device that produces a deliberate loss into an optical link. Attenuators can be used to verify the optical power budget available from a transmitter receiver pair, and to verify the sensitivity of a receiver. Attenuators can be fixed or variable, calibrated or uncalibrated.

A visual fault locator or finder, or is a high power visible red laser source. In general, the fault locator is used to find faults in short lengths of fiber or cable. This tool is most useful when the OTDR indicates a problem in the dead zone.

When the installer places this source of a fiber, any light that escapes from the core will be visible. The installer uses this locator to find breaks in a tight tube cable, breaks in a splice tray or splice enclosure, loss in a mechanical splice and in some cleave and leave connectors, and bend radius violations in a splice enclosure.

While most fault locators will not allow light to shine through a dark and thick jacket of an outdoor cable, they are useful for finding breaks and excess loss in light colored indoor cables and 900 µm buffer tubes.

One version of this type of product is a visual fiber tracer. This product detect power in a fiber and can be used to trace circuits, determine polarity, and verify continuity.

A fiber talk set enables voice communication over fiber. Typically, talk sets allow half duplex communication over a single fiber. The talk set can connect to the fiber via a connector or via a mechanism that bends the fiber. By bending the fiber, the talk set does not require the fiber to be terminated.

The microscope enables inspection of connector ends (21). Such inspection reveals defects on polished connectors.

## 13.6    STANDARDS

The Building Wiring Standard, TIA/EIA-568-B.1, requires that multimode insertion loss testing be performed according to Method B of ANSI/TIA/EIA-526-14-A.[51] This same document requires that singlemode insertion loss testing be performed according to Method A.1 of ANSI/TIA/EIA-526-7-A. Both methods are 'single reference lead' methods and require that the reference leads be 1-5 m in length.

TIA/EIA-568-B.3 requires that the multimode light source be a Category 1 source.[52] This same document requires that the source reference cable be wrapped around a mandrel of a specific diameter.

ANSI/TIA/EIA-526-7-A references, but does not require use of, FOTP-171 (EIA/TIA-455-171) for requirements for reference quality cables and connectors. FOTP-171 defines the 2" diameter loop[53] on the singlemode source reference cable.

FOTP-8 presents procedures for measurement of reflectance and connection loss with an OTDR. FOTP-61 presents procedures for measurement of attenuation rate with an OTDR. FOTP-107 presents procedures for measurement of reflectance with a reflectance test set.

---

[51] Clause 11.3.3. This standard is also known as OFSTP-14.

[52] Clause 7.1. This standard is also known as OFSTP-7.

[53] Clause 2.2.2.1.1.2

## 13.7    REVIEW QUESTIONS

### 13.7.1    GENERAL QUESTIONS

1.  True or false: all networks are tested for both power loss and dispersion.

2.  True or false: all data networks are tested for both power loss and dispersion.

### 13.7.2    INSERTION LOSS TESTING

1.  What are the five types of equipment required for an insertion loss test?

2.  What are the two requirements of a light source?

3.  What is the function of these two requirements?

4.  What are the two basic requirements for an optical power meter?

5.  What is the third desirable characteristic of an optical power meter?

6.  What are the five requirements that reference leads must meet?

7.  An alternative name for the Method A insertion loss test is the _____ reference lead test.

8.  An alternative name for the Method B insertion loss test is the _____ reference lead test.

9.  True or false: insertion loss test tells you that all components in a link have been properly installed.

10.  True false: Method A insertion loss test values are higher than Method B insertion loss test values.

11.  What is the numerical difference between a Method A insertion loss test value and a method B insertion loss test value of the same link?

Find and qualify three answers to this question.

12. True or false: insertion loss measurements are always exactly the same in both directions. Explain your answer.

## 13.7.3    OTDR TESTING

1. The attenuation rate in segment A is: ___ higher / ___lower than that in Segment B.

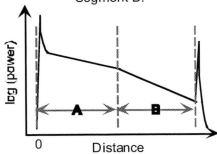

2. Select the best answer. The reflection in the circle of the figure in Question 3 could have:

___ One connector pair
___ Two connector pairs
___ Any number of connector pairs

3. What fact must be true to answer Question 2 (above)?

> For Questions 4-9, multiple answers are possible.

4. The feature(s) in the circle below could be:

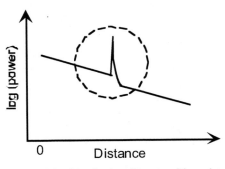

___ Mechanical splice, multimode
___ Mechanical splice, singlemode
___ Fusion splice, multimode
___ Fusion splice, singlemode
___ Fusion splice with gas bubble

___ APC connectors
___ Radiused connectors
___ Single segment
___ Two segments
___ APC connector on cable end
___ Bad cleave on cable end[54]
___ Mechanical splice on cable end
___ Bend radius violation
___ Broken fiber at OTDR
___ Broken fiber in dead zone

5. The feature(s) in the circle below could be:

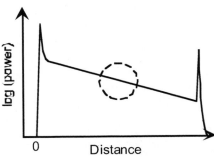

___ Mechanical splice, multimode
___ Mechanical splice, singlemode
___ Fusion splice, multimode
___ Fusion splice, singlemode
___ Fusion splice with gas bubble
___ APC connectors
___ Radiused connectors
___ Single segment
___ Two segments
___ APC connector on cable end
___ Bad cleave on cable end[55]
___ Mechanical splice on cable end
___ Bend radius violation
___ Broken fiber at OTDR
___ Broken fiber in dead zone

6. The feature(s) in the circle below could be:

---

[54] In the context of this question, a bad cleave is a high angle cleave that reflects power outside the critical angle.

[55] In the context of this question, a bad cleave is a high angle cleave that reflects power outside the critical angle.

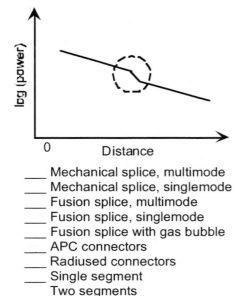

0          Distance

____ Mechanical splice, multimode
____ Mechanical splice, singlemode
____ Fusion splice, multimode
____ Fusion splice, singlemode
____ Fusion splice with gas bubble
____ APC connectors
____ Radiused connectors
____ Single segment
____ Two segments
____ APC connector on cable end
____ Bad cleave on cable end[56]
____ Mechanical splice on cable end
____ Bend radius violation
____ Broken fiber at OTDR
____ Broken fiber in dead zone

7.   The feature(s) in the circle below
     could be:

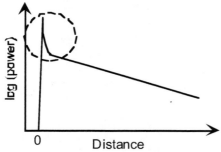

0          Distance

____ Mechanical splice, multimode
____ Mechanical splice, singlemode
____ Fusion splice, multimode
____ Fusion splice, singlemode
____ Fusion splice with gas bubble
____ APC connectors
____ Radiused connectors
____ Single segment
____ Two segments
____ APC connector on cable end
____ Bad cleave on cable end[57]

____ Mechanical splice on cable end
____ Bend radius violation
____ Broken fiber at OTDR
____ Broken fiber in dead zone

8.   The feature(s) in the circle below
     could be:

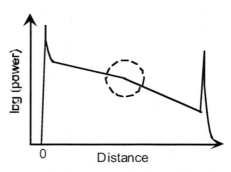

0          Distance

____ Mechanical splice, multimode
____ Mechanical splice, singlemode
____ Fusion splice, multimode
____ Fusion splice, singlemode
____ Fusion splice with gas bubble
____ APC connectors
____ Radiused connectors
____ Single segment
____ Two segments
____ APC connector on cable end
____ Bad cleave on cable end[58]
____ Mechanical splice on cable end
____ Bend radius violation
____ Broken fiber at OTDR
____ Broken fiber in dead zone

9.   The feature(s) in the circle below
     could be:

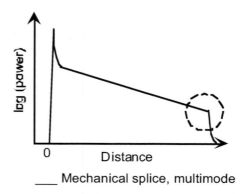

0          Distance

____ Mechanical splice, multimode

---

[56] In the context of this question, a bad cleave is
a high angle cleave that reflects power outside
the critical angle.

[57] In the context of this question, a bad cleave is
a high angle cleave that reflects power outside
the critical angle.

[58] In the context of this question, a bad cleave is
a high angle cleave that reflects power outside
the critical angle.

___ Mechanical splice, singlemode
___ Fusion splice, multimode
___ Fusion splice, singlemode
___ Fusion splice with gas bubble
___ APC connectors
___ Radiused connectors
___ Single segment
___ Two segments
___ APC connector on cable end
___ Bad cleave on cable end[59]
___ Mechanical splice on cable end
___ Bend radius violation
___ Broken fiber at OTDR
___ Broken fiber in dead zone

10. The feature(s) in the circle below could be:

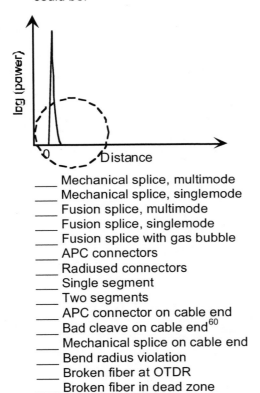

___ Mechanical splice, multimode
___ Mechanical splice, singlemode
___ Fusion splice, multimode
___ Fusion splice, singlemode
___ Fusion splice with gas bubble
___ APC connectors
___ Radiused connectors
___ Single segment
___ Two segments
___ APC connector on cable end
___ Bad cleave on cable end[60]
___ Mechanical splice on cable end
___ Bend radius violation
___ Broken fiber at OTDR
___ Broken fiber in dead zone

11. State the rules of cursor placement for attenuation rate measurements.

12. State the rules of cursor placement for estimated connection loss measurements.

13. State the rules of cursor placement for accurate connection loss measurements.

14. State the rules of cursor placement for segment length measurements.

15. Is the estimated connection loss greater than or less than the accurate connection loss?

16. Explain your answer to the previous question.

For each of the traces below, identify the type of measurement being made.

Use the following codes:

    X= invalid cursor placement
    A= attenuation rate measurement
    C= accurate connection loss measurement
    EC= estimated connection loss measurement
    FS= first segment length measurement
    SS= subsequent segment length measurement
    EC= estimated connector/splice loss
    AC= accurate connector/splice loss
    AR= attenuation rate

17. The type of measurement is _____

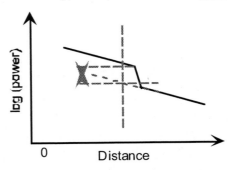

18. The type of measurement is _____

---

[59] In the context of this question, a bad cleave is a high angle cleave that reflects power outside the critical angle.

[60] In the context of this question, a bad cleave is a high angle cleave that reflects power outside the critical angle.

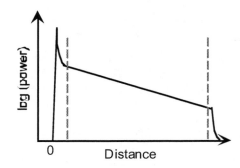

19. The type of measurement is _____

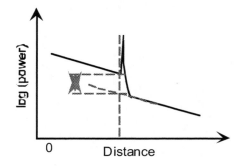

20. The type of measurement is _____

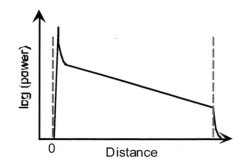

21. The type of measurement is _____

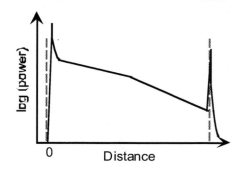

22. The type of measurement is _____

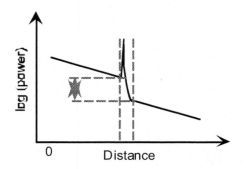

23. The type of measurement is _____

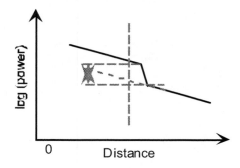

24. The type of measurement is _____

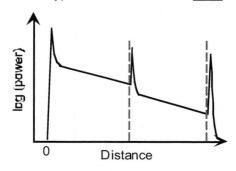

Instructions For Questions 25-30:
identify the features that could be in each of the following traces. If there are specific conditions (singlemode, multimode, APC connector, fusion splice, etc.) that must be met, or locations in which the feature must be located, identify those conditions or locations. Multiple answers are possible.

25. The trace below *could* contain:

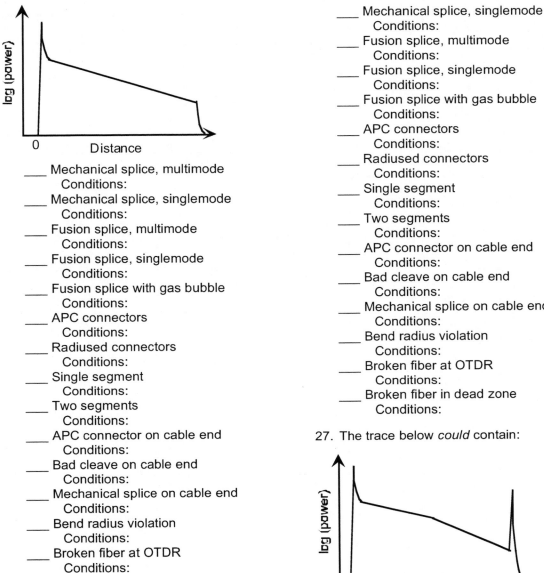

___ Mechanical splice, multimode
Conditions:
___ Mechanical splice, singlemode
Conditions:
___ Fusion splice, multimode
Conditions:
___ Fusion splice, singlemode
Conditions:
___ Fusion splice with gas bubble
Conditions:
___ APC connectors
Conditions:
___ Radiused connectors
Conditions:
___ Single segment
Conditions:
___ Two segments
Conditions:
___ APC connector on cable end
Conditions:
___ Bad cleave on cable end
Conditions:
___ Mechanical splice on cable end
Conditions:
___ Bend radius violation
Conditions:
___ Broken fiber at OTDR
Conditions:
___ Broken fiber in dead zone
Conditions:

26. The trace below *could* contain:

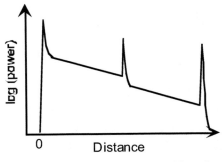

___ Mechanical splice, multimode
Conditions:

___ Mechanical splice, singlemode
Conditions:
___ Fusion splice, multimode
Conditions:
___ Fusion splice, singlemode
Conditions:
___ Fusion splice with gas bubble
Conditions:
___ APC connectors
Conditions:
___ Radiused connectors
Conditions:
___ Single segment
Conditions:
___ Two segments
Conditions:
___ APC connector on cable end
Conditions:
___ Bad cleave on cable end
Conditions:
___ Mechanical splice on cable end
Conditions:
___ Bend radius violation
Conditions:
___ Broken fiber at OTDR
Conditions:
___ Broken fiber in dead zone
Conditions:

27. The trace below *could* contain:

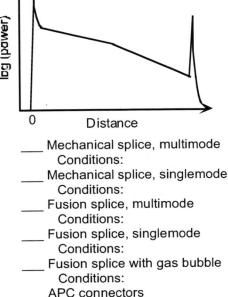

___ Mechanical splice, multimode
Conditions:
___ Mechanical splice, singlemode
Conditions:
___ Fusion splice, multimode
Conditions:
___ Fusion splice, singlemode
Conditions:
___ Fusion splice with gas bubble
Conditions:
___ APC connectors
Conditions:
___ Radiused connectors
Conditions:
___ Single segment

Conditions:
___ Two segments
Conditions:
___ APC connector on cable end
Conditions:
___ Bad cleave on cable end
Conditions:
___ Mechanical splice on cable end
Conditions:
___ Bend radius violation
Conditions:
___ Broken fiber at OTDR
Conditions:
___ Broken fiber in dead zone
Conditions:

28. The trace below *could* contain:

___ Mechanical splice, multimode
Conditions:
___ Mechanical splice, singlemode
Conditions:
___ Fusion splice, multimode
Conditions:
___ Fusion splice, singlemode
Conditions:
___ Fusion splice with gas bubble
Conditions:
___ APC connectors
Conditions:
___ Radiused connectors
Conditions:
___ Single segment
Conditions:
___ Two segments
Conditions:
___ APC connector on cable end
Conditions:
___ Bad cleave on cable end
Conditions:
___ Mechanical splice on cable end
Conditions:
___ Bend radius violation
Conditions:
___ Broken fiber at OTDR
Conditions:

___ Broken fiber in dead zone
Conditions:

29. The trace below *could* contain:

___ Mechanical splice, multimode
Conditions:
___ Mechanical splice, singlemode
Conditions:
___ Fusion splice, multimode
Conditions:
___ Fusion splice, singlemode
Conditions:
___ Fusion splice with gas bubble
Conditions:
___ APC connectors
Conditions:
___ Radiused connectors
Conditions:
___ Single segment
Conditions:
___ Two segments
Conditions:
___ APC connector on cable end
Conditions:
___ Bad cleave on cable end
Conditions:
___ Mechanical splice on cable end
Conditions:
___ Bend radius violation
Conditions:
___ Broken fiber at OTDR
Conditions:
___ Broken fiber in dead zone
Conditions:

30. The trace *could* contain:

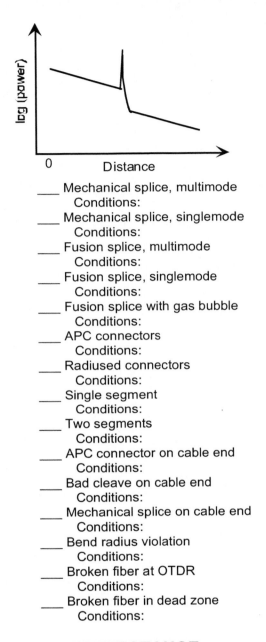

____ Mechanical splice, multimode
  Conditions:
____ Mechanical splice, singlemode
  Conditions:
____ Fusion splice, multimode
  Conditions:
____ Fusion splice, singlemode
  Conditions:
____ Fusion splice with gas bubble
  Conditions:
____ APC connectors
  Conditions:
____ Radiused connectors
  Conditions:
____ Single segment
  Conditions:
____ Two segments
  Conditions:
____ APC connector on cable end
  Conditions:
____ Bad cleave on cable end
  Conditions:
____ Mechanical splice on cable end
  Conditions:
____ Bend radius violation
  Conditions:
____ Broken fiber at OTDR
  Conditions:
____ Broken fiber in dead zone
  Conditions:

## 13.7.4   REFLECTANCE TESTING

1.  True or false: a -45 dB connector has a lower reflectance than a -60 dB connector.

2.  True or false: dirt on a connector results in a reduced reflectance.

3.  True or false: reflectance testing is performed on multimode connectors only.

# 14  CERTIFICATION PRINCIPLES

Chapter Objectives: in this chapter, you will learn how to certify an installed link and network. In addition, you will learn of alternative certification strategies.

## 14.1  INTRODUCTION

Certification is the process of interpreting the testing results. This process has two objectives:

- Verification of sufficiently low loss through the link[1]

- Verification that each component in a link has been properly and reliably installed.

With these two verifications, the link will work properly, i.e., optically accurately. In addition, the link will provide the maximum reliability possible.

In order to certify a link, the installer must choose a certification strategy to interpret the test results. In this chapter, we present the process of interpretation and the advantages of three certification strategies.

The process of certification has three parts:

- Obtaining required information

- Performing insertion loss calculations

- Calculating acceptance values

## 14.2  REQUIRED INFORMATION

In order to certify a network, the installer must make calculations of the power loss that the signal will experience. To make these calculations, the installer requires seven data:

- Accurate map

- Attenuation rate, maximum

- Attenuation rate, typical

- Connector loss, maximum

- Connector loss, typical

- Splice loss, maximum

- Splice loss, typical

These data are available from data sheets for the products or from web pages. With these data, the installer can calculate the maximum loss and the typical loss that each link should experience.

## 14.3  INSERTION LOSS CALCULATIONS

The installer must choose from at least two insertion loss methods, Method B and Method B (13). The insertion loss calculation depends upon the method the installer uses.

For most installers, the choice is determined by the requirement for compliance with TIA/EIA-568-B. With such compliance, the installer must use Method B. Otherwise, the installer could use Method A.

These two methods treat the end connectors differently:

- Method B treats two end connectors as two pairs

- Method A treats two end connectors as one pair

Thus, an insertion loss calculation for Method B will be higher than a calculation for Method A by the loss of one connector pair. As this text has a focus on compliance with TIA/EIA-568-B, we use Method B.

### 14.3.1  OPTICAL POWER LOSS CALCULATION

We present the optical power loss calculation in Table 14-1. The optical power loss is the sum of the losses in all components in the optical path. This loss includes cable loss, connector loss, splice loss, and passive device loss. For reasons that will become apparent, the installer performs this calculation with both the maximum and typical values.

---

[1] The inference is that this condition results in sufficient power at the receiver.

| Loss in | dB/km | | #km | | dB |
|---|---|---|---|---|---|
| Cable | | * | | = | |
| | dB/pair | | #pairs | | |
| Connect or | | * | | = | |
| | dB/splice | | #splices | | |
| Splice | | * | | = | |
| | | | Total | = | |

Table 14-1: The Optical Power Loss Calculation

## 14.4   DEVELOPMENT OF A STRATEGY

We perform a Method B calculation of the link in Figure 14-1. This link consists of two segments, with segment lengths of 1500 m and 500 m. There is a mid span patch panel with single pair at the panel. We present the component specifications in Table 14-2.

With the specifications in this table, the maximum and typical losses are 9.25 dB (Table 14-3) and 6.9 dB (Table 14-4), respectively.

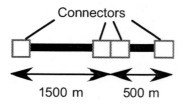

Connectors

1500 m    500 m

Figure 14-1: Map 1

| | Maximum | Typical |
|---|---|---|
| | dB/km | dB/km |
| Attenuation rate | 3.5 | 3.0 |
| | dB/pair | dB/pair |
| Connector loss | 0.75 | 0.30 |
| | dB/splice | dB/splice |
| Splice loss | 0.15 | 0.10 |

Table 14-2: Values For Multimode Components At 850 nm

What happens if the installer were to use the maximum loss as an acceptance value? He would allow up to 2.35 dB of excess loss.[2] Excess loss occurs only through installation errors. Installation errors reduce network reliability.

---

[2] 9.25 dB -6.9 dB= 2.35 dB

➢ The risk of using the maximum loss as an acceptance value is reduced reliability.[3]

| Loss in | dB/km | | #km | | dB |
|---|---|---|---|---|---|
| Cable | 3.5 | * | 2.0 | = | 7.00 |
| | dB/pair | | #pairs | | |
| Connector | .75 | * | 3 | = | 2.25 |
| | dB/splice | | #splices | | |
| Splice | 0.15 | * | 0 | = | 0.0 |
| | | | Total | = | 9.25 |

Table 14-3: Calculation, Maximum Loss

| Loss in | dB/km | | #km | | dB |
|---|---|---|---|---|---|
| Cable | 3.0 | * | 2.0 | = | 6.0 |
| | dB/pair | | #pairs | | |
| Connector | 0.3 | * | 3 | = | 0.9 |
| | dB/splice | | #splices | | |
| Splice | 0.1 | * | 0 | = | 0.0 |
| | | | Total | = | 6.9 |

Table 14-4: Calculation, Typical Loss

If use of the maximum loss value as an acceptance value can result in reduced reliability, the installer might consider using the typical value. However, properly installed cables, connectors and splices can have loss values slightly higher than the typical values.[4] Were the installer to use the typical value as a maximum acceptance value, he would reject properly installed products. Such a rejection would increase the cost of the network without any increase in reliability.

Since the installer does not want to use either the maximum loss or the typical loss as an acceptance value, he can consider an acceptance value mid way between the maximum loss and the typical loss.[5] We call this mid point value the 'acceptance value'. For the link in Figure 14-1, the acceptance value is 8.075 dB.[6]

---

[3] TIA/EIA-568-B allows acceptance of the maximum loss.

[4] For example, the 3M multimode ST® compatible connector has a typical loss of 0.3 dB/pair but can exhibit loss as high as 0.4 dB/pair when installed properly.

[5] There is nothing magic about this approach. However, this approach avoids the problems from using either the maximum or typical losses.

[6] = 1/2 * (6.9+9.25)= 8.075 dB

## 14.4.1 ▶HIGH RELIABILITY INSERTION LOSS ACCEPTANCE VALUE

The acceptance value is halfway between calculated maximum and calculated typical values.

There is nothing magic about this strategy. Use of this mid point value as an acceptance value assumes that the installer will either make minor mistakes or major mistakes. Minor mistakes tend to increase the loss from the typical value to just below the acceptance value. Major mistakes tend to increase the loss to above the acceptance value.

## 14.5   CERTIFICATION

Certification of network links requires two steps: certification of insertion loss tests and certification of OTDR test values. Certification of reflection tests is not required, since the reflection test is a maximum value allowed.

## 14.5.1   INSERTION LOSS CERTIFICATION

The basic strategy (14.4) is designed to avoid acceptance of conditions of reduced reliability. The basic strategy is based on the expectation of typical performance most of the time. With this expectation, the insertion loss strategy has three steps:

> Accept test values less than or equal to the acceptance value

> Investigate test values greater than the acceptance value and less than the calculated maximum value

> Reject test values greater than the calculated maximum value

The first and third of these steps should be obvious. The second step requires some detail.

It is possible that properly installed cables, connectors and splices will have loss values higher than the acceptance value and less than the maximum value.[7] Thus, products with values between these two values must

be investigated to verify proper installation. If installation is proper, the installer accepts these components.

## 14.5.2   OTDR CERTIFICATION

The installer investigates an insertion loss value between the acceptance and the maximum values with OTDR measurements. To interpret these measurements, we follow the same strategy we used with the insertion loss test.

### 14.5.2.1   ▶HIGH RELIABILITY OTDR ACCEPTANCE VALUES

The installer expects that each component will test less than or equal to midway between the typical and the maximum values. With this expectation, the OTDR acceptance values are:

> Attenuation rate acceptance value= (maximum rate + typical rate)/2

> Connector pair acceptance value= (maximum loss + typical loss )/2

> Splice loss acceptance value= (maximum loss + typical loss )/2

In addition to meeting these three acceptance values, the trace must meet a requirement for uniformity:

### 14.5.2.2   ▶UNIFORMITY PRINCIPLE

The OTDR trace for every cable segment must be a straight line.

A straight line indicates uniform loss through the segment. A properly designed, properly manufactured, properly installed cable segment always exhibits a straight-line trace. Any deviation from a straight trace indicates an installation error.

Because it is essentially impossible to violate a cable performance parameter so that the attenuation rate is uniform and excessive, a high attenuation rate cable segment with a straight-line trace indicates a defective cable, not improper installation.[8]

---

[7] Our experience is that this is highly unlikely.

[8] Some things are simpler than you might think!

## 14.6  AN ALTERNATIVE STRATEGY

The mid point strategy allows the installer to identify conditions of reduced reliability. However, this strategy does not guarantee identification of all such conditions.

Another, more expensive, strategy enables identification of conditions of reduced reliability with loss values that would be acceptable by the mid point strategy. This strategy has three steps:

> ➢ Comparison of OTDR attenuation rates of each segment prior to installation to those rates after installation

> ➢ Visual inspection of all connectors with acceptance requirements for the core, cladding, and ferrule surface (21)

> ➢ Use of a maximum connector loss value less than the mid point value

With comparison of the attenuation rate of each segment prior to installation to that after installation, the installer can determine proper installation. With proper installation, there will be no increase in attenuation rate.

With inspection of all connectors prior to testing, the installer can identify conditions of reduced reliability.[9] Acceptance requirements would be:

> ➢ A featureless core

> ➢ A clean cladding and

> ➢ A clean ferrule (Chapter 21)

With these three requirements, the connectors would have close to the maximum reliability possible.

It is possible, and highly likely, that connectors will be improperly installed at the mid point value. Our experience indicates that the mid point value, 0.525 dB/pair, is never reached except when there are installation errors.[10]

Since some reduced reliability can result from use of the mid point value for connector loss, the installer could consider use of a reduced value. To determine an appropriate reduced value, the installer would need to know the statistics of connector loss for the products he intends to use. Such statistics are not readily available. However, were these statistics available, the installer could set a statistical upper limit based on a statistical knowledge of the connector loss.

## 14.7  SUMMARY

In order to certify fiber optics links, the installer must choose a strategy for determining acceptance values. Use of the maximum loss values can result in acceptance of reduced reliability. Use of the typical loss values results in increased cost with no benefit. Use of mid point values results in detection most conditions of reduced reliability with no major disadvantage. Once the installer chooses the mid point strategy, the installer calculates acceptance values according to these simple formulas:

> ➢ Insertion loss= (maximum loss + typical loss)/2

> ➢ Attenuation rate= (maximum rate + typical rate)/2

> ➢ Connector loss= (maximum loss/pair + typical loss/pair)/2

> ➢ Splice loss= (maximum loss/splice + typical loss/ splice)/2

## 14.8  REVIEW QUESTIONS

1. Using Method B, the multimode map (Figure 14-2) and specifications (Table 14-5), calculate the maximum and typical insertion loss, the insertion loss and OTDR acceptance values.

---

[9] Of course, the cleave and leave connectors is an exception to this statement, as loss and reliability depend on the cleave.

[10] From installation of approximately 10,000 connectors, we have observed that the

---

multimode, 3M Hot Melt, ST-™ compatible connectors never exceed 0.40 dB/pair unless there is visible damage on the core. Our experience indicates that properly installed cleave and leave connectors may exceed this value.

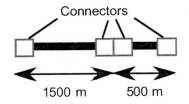

Figure 14-2: Map For Question 1

|  | Maximum | Typical |
|---|---|---|
|  | dB/km | dB/km |
| Attenuation rate | 1.5 | 0.7 |
|  | dB/pair | dB/pair |
| Connector loss | 0.75 | 0.30 |
|  | dB/splice | dB/splice |
| Splice loss | 0.15 | 0.10 |

Table 14-5: 1300 nm Multimode Values

2. Using Method B, the singlemode map (Figure 14-3) and specifications (Table 14-6), calculate the maximum insertion loss, the typical insertion loss, the insertion loss acceptance value and the OTDR acceptance values. You may assume that the patch cord between the two segments is short enough to ignore its length.

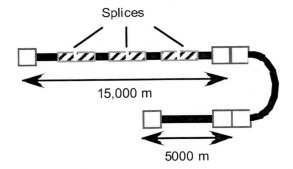

Figure 14-3: Map For Question 2

|  | Maximum | Typical |
|---|---|---|
|  | dB/km | dB/km |
| Attenuation rate | 0.5 | 0.35 |
|  | dB/pair | dB/pair |
| Connector loss | 0.75 | 0.30 |
|  | dB/splice | dB/splice |
| Splice loss | 0.15 | 0.10 |

Table 14-6: 1310 nm Singlemode Values

3. Using Method B, the map below (Figure 14-4) and multimode specifications in Question 1 (Table 14-5), calculate the maximum

insertion loss, the typical insertion loss, the insertion loss acceptance value and the OTDR acceptance values for this collapsed backbone.

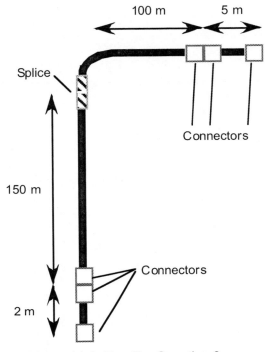

Figure 14-4: Map For Question 3

4. Using Method B, the multimode map below (Figure 14-5) and specifications in Question 1 (Table 14-5), calculate the maximum insertion loss, the typical insertion loss, the insertion loss and the OTDR acceptance values for this building riser backbone.

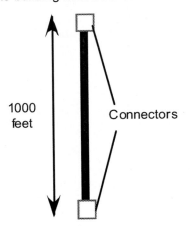

Figure 14-5: Map For Question 4

5. Using Method B, the singlemode map below (Figure 14-6) and specifications

in Question 2 (Table 14-6), calculate
the maximum insertion loss, the
typical insertion loss, the insertion loss
acceptance value and the OTDR
acceptance values.

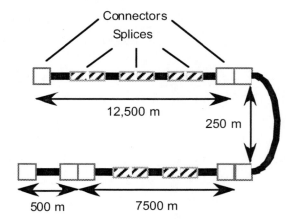

Figure 14-6: Map For Question 5

6.  Using the multimode specifications in
    Table 14-2 and the map in Question 3
    (Figure 14-4), calculate the maximum
    insertion loss, the typical insertion
    loss, the insertion loss acceptance
    value and the OTDR acceptance
    values for the collapsed backbone.

7.  Using the specifications in Table 14-2
    and the map in Question 4 (Figure
    14-5), calculate the maximum
    insertion loss, the typical insertion
    loss, the insertion loss acceptance
    value and the OTDR acceptance
    values for the riser backbone.

8.  Recalculate the Method A insertion
    loss acceptance values for Questions
    1-7.

# PART THREE

# INSTALLATION PROCEDURES

## HOW TO USE THESE PROCEDURES

To develop an overview of the entire process covered by this document, the installer should read the chapter through several times. He should use the One Page Summary to perform the activity.

## SAFETY PRECAUTIONS

For all installation activities that involve the creation and handling of bare fibers, the installer should follow the safety rules and guidelines of 10.6.

# 15   CABLE END PREPARATION

Chapter Objectives: by following the procedures in this chapter, you will be able to prepare the ends of loose tube and tight tube cables for pulling and termination. In addition, you will learn how to handle the 250-μm fiber exposed at the ends of loose tube cables without damage.

## 15.1   INTRODUCTION

The installer handles the fiber in both the cable form and in the fiber form. He handles the fiber, both with and without the primary coating, during splicing and connector installation.

He handles the cable in two different operations: end preparation for pulling and end preparation for termination.

In this chapter, we present the procedures for:

➢ Fiber handling (15.3)

➢ End preparation of loose tube cables for pulling (15.4)

➢ End preparation of tight tube cables for pulling (15.5)

➢ End preparation of loose tube cables for termination (15.6)

➢ End preparation of tight tube cables for termination (15.7)

As these procedures are generic, they apply to many, but not all, cables. For exact instructions, we recommend that the installer review data sheets and installation instructions for the cables he is to install.

## 15.2   TOOLS AND SUPPLIES

➢ Pull rope, installed in conduit or inner duct

➢ Swivel with shear pin rated below installation load rating of cable General Machine Products part number 71406 or equivalent)[1]

➢ Electrician's tape

➢ Jacket removal tool, (Ideal 45-162 or Clauss RCS-20)

---

[1] www.GMtools.com, GMP swivel part numbers are 71399-71406 70188 and 71418.,

➢ Break off blade knife

➢ Kevlar© cutter

➢ Tubing cutter, Ideal part number 45-162[2]

➢ Fiber stripper, Clauss No Nik, 203 or Miller jacket stripper

➢ Fiber optic cable gel/grease remover, D'Gel™ (Polymicro Technologies) or Electrosol™ (American Polywater Corporation)

➢ 98 % isopropyl alcohol

➢ Clean rags or heavy duty paper towels

➢ Unscented talc[3]

➢ Fiber, with primary coating of 245 μm, 3' long

➢ 12' of 3 mm single fiber cable

➢ Matches

➢ Bare fiber collection bottle

➢ Pliers

➢ Disposable gloves

## 15.3   FIBER HANDLING

The activities in this section sensitize the installer to what the fiber will and will not withstand. From these activities, the installer will recognize those steps at which he needs to be careful and those steps at which he needs to be very careful.

### 15.3.1   COATED FIBER

Coated fiber has properties that are different from those of uncoated fiber. These

---

[2] This cutter is for use with loose tubes with a diameter of 2-4 mm. For larger buffer tubes, you will use a different cutter.

[3] This talc is known as 'dry fiber lubricant'.

activities sensitize the installer to the properties of coated fiber.

### 15.3.1.1    TENSILE BEHAVIOR

The installer wraps a fibers around the fingers of both hands. He pulls as hard as he dares.[4] The installer answers the following questions.

#### 15.3.1.1.1    REVIEW QUESTIONS

1.  Is fiber stronger or weaker than expected?

2.  What region of the fiber allows the fiber to retain its intrinsic high strength?

3.  How well does this region function?

### 15.3.1.2    BENDING BEHAVIOR

The installer makes a large loop near the end of the fiber. Slowly, he pulls the loop smaller until the fiber breaks. He estimates the diameter at which the fiber breaks. He repeats this step. He places the fiber in the fiber collection bottle.

With a 3 mm diameter cable, the installer makes a loop at the minimum long term bend radius (10.3.3). He compares this cable diameter to the diameter at which the fiber broke.

#### 15.3.1.2.1    REVIEW QUESTIONS

1.  If the installer respects the minimum bend radius, will he ever experience breakage in bending?

2.  Is the minimum bend radius conservative or realistic?

3.  Was it easier to break the fiber in bending or in tension?

4.  When installing fiber cables, will the installer need to be more careful with tension or with bending?

## 15.3.2    UNCOATED FIBER 1

These activities sensitize the installer to the properties of bare fiber after significant

---

[4] Drawing blood is not a requirement of this activity.

exposure to the air or after damage to the cladding.

### 15.3.2.1    BENDING BEHAVIOR

With a match, the installer burns off 2-3" of the primary coating. He wipes the burnt coating from the fiber with his fingers. He bends the bare fiber. He repeats this step. He places the fiber in the bare fiber collection bottle.

### 15.3.2.2    REVIEW QUESTIONS

1.  What happens to the bend strength of the fiber when the primary coating is removed?

2.  How well does the primary coating function?

3.  Consider fitting a 125 ±0.5 µm fiber into a connector or splice with a 126 µm or 127 µm hole. What might happen?

4.  How can the installer avoid this?

5.  When does the installer need to be careful and when does he need to be very careful?

## 15.3.3    UNCOATED FIBER 2

These activities sensitize the installer to the properties of the fiber after proper removal of the primary coating.

The installer wraps the fiber around one finger 5 times at 12" from the end. Any finger will do. Following the procedure in 15.7.1.3, the installer strips 3" of primary coating from the fiber.

By holding both the bare and coated fiber, the installer bends the bare fiber until it breaks. He estimates the diameter at which it broke. He repeats this step (15.3.3). He places the fiber in the fiber collection bottle.

### 15.3.3.1    REVIEW QUESTIONS

1.  What happens to the bend strength of the fiber when the primary coating is removed correctly?

2.  How well does the primary coating function?

3. The strength the installer observes with flame stripping is the strength he would expect after exposure of the cladding for 12 hours. Should he remove the last layer of protection from the fiber one day and install the connector or splice the next?

## 15.4 LOOSE TUBE END PREPARATION FOR PULLING

### 15.4.1 CHOOSE SWIVEL

The installer chooses a break away swivel rated at a load less than the maximum installation load rating of the cable. The swivel must fit into the conduit into which the cable is to be installed. He follows the directions for installing the shear pin into the swivel (Figure 15-1). With two half hitches, he ties a pull rope to the swivel. With electricians tape, he tapes the loose end of the pull rope back along the rope. He wraps the last layer of tape in the direction away from the end of the rope.

Figure 15-1: Break Away Swivel With Pull Rope

### 15.4.2 SET SLITTER DEPTH

While holding the jacket slitter against the end of the cable, the installer sets the depth of the slitter blade to slightly less than the thickness of the cable jacket (Figure 15-2).

Figure 15-2: Setting Slitter Depth

### 15.4.3 MAKE TEST CUT

The installer places the slitter on the jacket 2" from end. He rotates the slitter around the jacket several times. He removes the slitter. He pulls on the jacket to slide the jacket off the end of the cable (Figure 15-3). The jacket should not slide off. If it does, the slitter was set excessively deep. In addition, the strength members should not be visible (Figure 15-4).

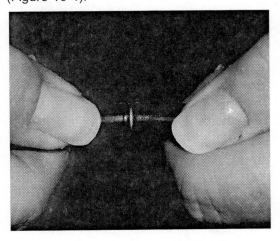

Figure 15-3: Proper Slit Depth

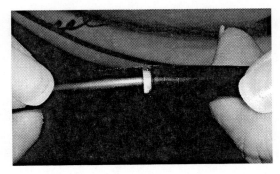

Figure 15-4: Excessive Slit Depth

If the jacket slides off, the installer sets the blade to a shallower depth and makes another test cut on the jacket at a distance of about 2" from the previous cut. He tries to pull the jacket from the cable.

### 15.4.4 REMOVE TEST CUT

The installer bends and rotates the cable at the slit. If the slitter has been set correctly, the jacket becomes fully separated (Figure 15-4). He pulls the jacket from the cable. He examines the strength members[5] and buffer tubes for damage. There should be none.

If there is damage, he sets the blade to a shallower depth and makes another test cut on the jacket at a distance of about 2" from the previous cut.

### 15.4.5    REMOVE JACKET

The installer repeats Steps 15.4.3-15.4.4 at a distance of 18" from the end of the cable. He removes the jacket.

### 15.4.6    GEL/GREASE FILLED

If there is no grease, the installer proceeds to 15.4.7. He dons plastic gloves.

#### 15.4.6.1    REMOVE GEL

The installer moistens paper towels or clean rags with gel/grease remover. He wipes the strength members with the towels until he has removed all the grease.

#### 15.4.6.2    REMOVE GEL REMOVER

The installer moistens paper towels or clean rags with isopropyl alcohol. He wipes the strength members with the paper towels until he has removed all the gel/grease remover.

### 15.4.7    REMOVE CORE MATERIALS

The installer separates the buffer tubes from the strength members. If a binder tape is present, he cuts it off. He cuts the buffer tubes flush with the end of the jacket. He cuts and removes a central strength member[6] at the end of the jacket. He cuts the ripcord 8" from the end of the jacket.

### 15.4.8    ATTACH SWIVEL

The installer twists and feeds the strength members through the lower housing of the swivel. He ties the strength members to the swivel in a double half hitch (Figure 15-6).

He tapes the strength members so the tape ends on the cable.

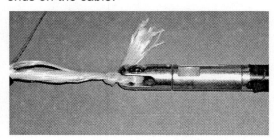

Figure 15-5: Strength Members Attached To Swivel

### 15.4.9    INSTALL CABLE

Following the appropriate procedure, the installer pulls the cable into location. He cuts off 3' from the end of the cable.[7]

## 15.5    TIGHT TUBE END PREPARATION FOR PULLING

### 15.5.1    JACKETED FIBERS

This procedure is for one fiber and two fiber zip cord cables.

#### 15.5.1.1    ATTACH SWIVEL

The installer chooses a swivel that will fit through the conduit into which the cable is to be installed. As in 15.4.1, the installer attaches a pull rope to the swivel.[8]

#### 15.5.1.2    PREPARE END

For a zip cord cable, the installer separates the two channels to a length of at least 5".

As in 15.7.1.2, the installer removes at least 5" of jacket from the fiber or fibers. He separates the fiber(s) from the aramid yarns.[9] He cuts the fiber(s) flush with the jacket.

He twists the aramid yarns and feeds them through the swivel. He ties two half hitches into the aramid yarn. He covers the aramid

---

[5] For most loose tube cables, the strength members are an aramid yarn, such as Kevlar™, or flexible fiberglass rovings.

[6] Usually, the central strength member is a fiberglass epoxy rod.

---

[7] Some installers cut off more than 3' of cable.

[8] Some manufacturers do not warranty their cables if they are installed without a swivel.

[9] We make the assumption that all such cables use Kevlar or a similar aramid yarn.

yarn with 1-3 layers of electricians tape. The tape should cover the end of the jacket. The last layer of tape should end on the jacket.

### 15.5.1.3    INSTALL CABLE

Following the appropriate procedure, the installer pulls the cable into location. He cuts off 3' from the end of the cable.[7]

## 15.5.2    PREMISES CABLE

This procedure is for 2-24 fiber distribution or premises cables.

### 15.5.2.1    ATTACH SWIVEL TO PULL ROPE

As in 15.4.1, the installer attaches a pull rope to the swivel.

### 15.5.2.2    SLIT JACKET

The installer bends the cable at 12" from the end of the cable. He places a sharp knife blade against the outside of the bend (Figure 15-6). Gently, he saws the blade until the jacket cuts through to the strength members. He rotates the bend so that jacket that is not cut is on the outside of the bend. He repeats the sawing action on the outside of the bend until the jacket cuts through. He repeats this step until he has cut the jacket around its circumference.

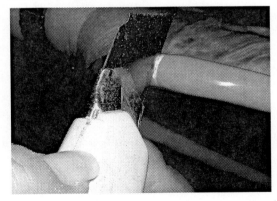

Figure 15-6: Cutting Of Premises Cable Jacket

#### 15.5.2.2.1    REMOVE FIBERS

The installer separates the fibers from the strength members. If a binder tape is present, he cuts it off. He cuts the fibers flush with the jacket.

#### 15.5.2.2.2    REMOVE CENTRAL STRENGTH MEMBER

The installer cuts and removes the central strength member at the jacket.[10]

#### 15.5.2.2.3    INSTALL STRENGTH MEMBERS INTO SWIVEL

The installer twists the strength members and feeds them through the swivel. He ties two half hitches into the strength members (Figure 15-7). He covers the strength members with 1-3 layers of electricians tape. The tape covers the end of the jacket. The last layer of tape ends on the jacket of the cable.

Figure 15-7: Premises Cable Attached To Pull Rope

#### 15.5.2.2.4    PULL CABLE

Following the appropriate procedure, the installer pulls the cable into location. He cuts off 3' from the end of the cable.[7]

## 15.6    LOOSE TUBE END PREPARATION FOR TERMINATION

## 15.6.1    DETERMINE DIMENSIONS

The installer determines the following four dimensional requirements of the enclosure into which the cable is to be installed (Figure 15-8):

➢ Length of jacket to be removed

➢ Length of strength member to be left

---

[10] Some cables may require retention of the central strength member. We recommend that the installer review the manufacturer installation procedure for the cable.

➤ Length of central strength member to be left

➤ Length of buffer tube to be left

The enclosure instruction sheet specifies these lengths.

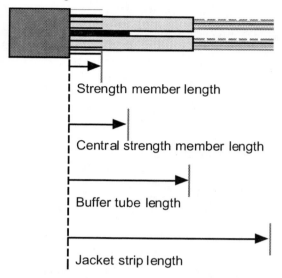

Strength member length

Central strength member length

Buffer tube length

Jacket strip length

Figure 15-8: End Preparation Dimensions

## 15.6.2    PREPARE WORK AREA

The installer sets up a work surface covered with a disposable plastic sheet or newspapers.

## 15.6.3    PRE INSTALL CABLE

If the enclosure allows the cable to be installed into a 'U' shaped cut out, the installer proceeds to Step 15.6.4. If the enclosure requires the cable to be fed through a hole, the installer feeds the cable through the hole and out the front of the enclosure. He pulls enough cable through the hole so that it reaches a work surface that makes the cable relatively easy with which to work.[11]

## 15.6.4    ACCESS RIPCORD

If at least 8" of the ripcord is available, the installer proceeds to 15.6.6.

---

[11] The installer will push back the excess cable through the hole. This excess cable becomes a service loop.

## 15.6.5    REMOVE JACKET

To remove the jacket, the installer performs 15.4.2-15.4.4. He repeats these steps at a distance of at least 8" from the end of the cable. He removes the jacket.

If the cable does not slide off, the installer rotates the blade in the slitter by 90°. While holding the blade in this position, he places the blade in the cut at 8" but not on top of the rip cord. While forcing the blade to stay in the jacket, he pulls the slitter to the end of the jacket. He removes the jacket to access the ripcord.

## 15.6.6    MAKE RING CUT

The installer repeats 15.4.3 at a distance from the end of the cable equal to the length of jacket strip length (Figure 15-8).[12] This is the 'ring cut'.

The installer wraps the exposed ripcord around the plastic covered handle of a pair of pliers. He wraps the ripcord on top of itself. He pulls the rip cord along the cable to the ring cut. He removes the jacket by pulling the cable core through the slit.

## 15.6.7    PREPARE CABLE CORE

The installer separates the strength members from the cable core. He cuts the external strength members[13] to the strength member length e (Figure 15-8). He cuts the rip cord 8" from the end of the jacket.[14] He cuts the binding tape at the jacket. He removes the tape from the core.

He untwists and separates the buffer tubes from the central strength member. He cuts the central strength member to the central strength member (Figure 15-8).

## 15.6.8    CLEAN CABLE CORE

If there is no grease, the installer proceeds to 15.6.9.

---

[12] A typical jacket removal length is 8'.

[13] The external strength members are strength members external to the cable core and under the jacket.

[14] Leave this ripcord for future use.

### 15.6.8.1    REMOVE GEL

The installer dons plastic gloves.[15] The installer moistens paper towels or clean rags with gel/grease remover. He wipes the buffer tubes and strength members with the towels until the buffer tubes begin to squeak. After the squeaking begins, he wipes the buffer tubes and strength members with gel/grease remover one more time.

### 15.6.8.2    REMOVE GEL REMOVER

The installer moistens paper towels or clean rags with isopropyl alcohol. He wipes the buffer tubes and strength members with the paper towels until the buffer tubes begin to squeak. After the squeaking begins, he wipes the buffer tubes and strength members with isopropyl alcohol two more times.

## 15.6.9    PREPARE FIBERS

The installer performs this step on one buffer tube at a time.

### 15.6.9.1    REMOVE BUFFER TUBE

The installer places the tubing cutter on one buffer tube at the buffer tube length (Figure 15-8).[16] Without applying pressure to the tubing cutter, he rotates the cutter 30° in one direction and 30° back (Figure 15-9).[17]

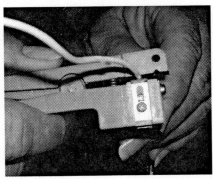

Figure 15-9: Cutter On Buffer Tube

---

[15] The gel/grease remover is dermatologically safe. However, the isopropyl alcohol tends to remove moisture from skin.

[16] Some gels are thick enough to prevent removal of the buffer tube in a single length. For cables with such gel, the installer removes the buffer tube in several segments.

[17] This action will score, but not cut through the buffer tube.

With his thumb on the buffer tube opposite to the score, he rapidly bends ('snaps') the buffer tube until it breaks. Slowly, he pulls the buffer tube from fibers. While pulling the buffer tube from the fibers, he drags a paper towel along the fibers to remove some of the water blocking compound.[18]

### 15.6.9.2    CLEAN FIBERS

If there is no gel, the installer proceeds to 15.6.9.3.

With a paper towel or clean rag moistened with water blocking compound/gel remover, the installer wipes the fibers from the end of the buffer tube to the end of the fibers repeatedly until the fibers begin to squeak. When wiping, he squeezes the fibers lightly. He repeats this wiping two more times.

### 15.6.9.3    LUBRICATE AND SEPARATE FIBERS[19]

The installer places approximately 1/2 teaspoon of 'dry fiber lubricant' (talc) in the palm of one hand. With the thumb of his other hand, he forces the fibers into the talc and draws the entire length through the talc. He repeats this step two more times. The fibers will automatically untwist and separate themselves.

He counts the fibers in each buffer tube. The number of fibers should be 6 or 12.[20] If the installer broke a fiber, he cuts all the fibers at the end of the cable. He repeats the process from Steps 15.6.6-15.6.9.3.

## 15.6.10    ATTACH CABLE

If the installer has fed the cable been through an access hole in the enclosure, he feeds the excess cable back through the hole and arranges the extra cable as a service loop. If appropriate, he attaches the cable strength members to the enclosure.

---

[18] The installer removes whatever gel comes off with this one wipe. He does not attempt to remove all the gel.

[19] If the installer is preparing this cable for splicing, this step is optional. If he plans to install these fibers into a furcation kit, this step is essential.

[20] If the cable is a central buffer tube design, there can be as many as 216 fibers in the buffer tube.

## 15.7    TIGHT TUBE END PREPARATION FOR TERMINATION

### 15.7.1    JACKETED FIBERS

These instructions are for end preparation for termination of one fiber, two fiber zip cord cables and break-out cables.

#### 15.7.1.1    INSTALL CABLE INTO ENCLOSURE

As in 15.6.3, the installer pre-installs the cable.

#### 15.7.1.2    REMOVE JACKET

If the cable is a break out cable, the installer removes the jacket (15.6.1-15.6.4 and 15.6.6). If the cable is a zip cord duplex, the installer separates the two channels to a length of 10-12 ".

For each fiber, the installer places a tubing cutter on the jacket at the length specified in the connector installation instructions (Figure 15-10). He rotates the cutter around the jacket once or twice (Figure 15-11). He removes the jacket from the cable.

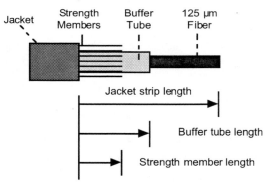

Figure 15-10: End Preparation Template For 3 mm Cables

Figure 15-11: Tubing Cutter Placement

#### 15.7.1.3    STRIP BUFFER TUBE

If he is to terminate the cable at this time, the installer strips the buffer tube from the fiber(s) with the Clauss stripper. He cleans the stripper by holding the stripper open and snapping each cap once (Figure 15-12).[21] The installer grips the cable or buffer tube firmly. The installer can grip the cable by wrapping the cable around one finger 5 times (Figure 15-13) or by weaving the cable through his fingers.

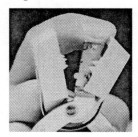

Figure 15-12: Cleaning of Clauss Stripper

The installer places the stripper on the buffer tube at the marked distance (Figure 15-10) or 1/2" from the end of the buffer tube, whichever is shorter.[22] While holding the stripper at 90° to the fiber (Figure 15-13), the installer pulls the stripper towards the fiber end slowly. He allows the buffer tube and primary coating to slide from the fiber. He does not force the buffer tube and primary coating from the fiber.

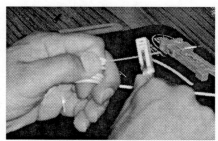

Figure 15-13: Fiber Straight In Stripper

---

[21] Occasionally, this method does not work. In that case, the installer may clean the stripper with lens grade gas.

[22] This instruction indicates a maximum strip length of 1/2". US-made fiber optic cables can be stripped to at least this distance. Some US-made cables allow a longer strip length without breakage. For such cables, you may strip to that increased distance. Few cables allow a single strip length of more than 1.5 ".

### 15.7.1.4    TRIM STRENGTH MEMBERS

The installer separates the fiber from the aramid yarns. He twists the aramid yarns. He cuts the aramid yarns (Figure 15-14) to the strength member length (Figure 15-10).

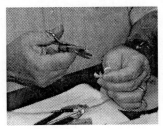

Figure 15-14: Cutting Aramid Yarn To Length

### 15.7.1.5    ATTACH CABLE TO ENCLOSURE

When the termination is complete, the installer places the cable in the enclosure, according to the instructions for the enclosure. He coils the service loop in a convenient location.

## 15.7.2    PREMISES CABLE

These instructions are for 2-24 fiber premises or distribution cables.

### 15.7.2.1    DETERMINE DIMENSIONS

The installer determines the following four dimensional requirements of the enclosure into which the cable is to be installed (Figure 15-8):

➢ Length of jacket to be removed

➢ Length of strength member to be left

➢ Length of central strength member to be left

➢ Length of buffer tube to be left

### 15.7.2.2    INSTALL CABLE INTO ENCLOSURE

As in 15.6.3, the installer pre-installs the cable.

### 15.7.2.3    SLIT JACKET

The installer bends the cable at the jacket strip length (Figure 15-8). As in 15.5.2.2, he removes the jacket.

### 15.7.2.4    SEPARATE FIBERS

If a binder tape is present, the installer cuts it off at the end of the jacket. He separates the fibers from the central strength member.

### 15.7.2.5    TRIM FLEXIBLE STRENGTH MEMBERS

The installer separates the fiber(s) from the aramid yarns. He twists and cuts the aramid yarns to the proper length (Figure 15-8).

### 15.7.2.6    TRIM CENTRAL STRENGTH MEMBER

The installer cuts the central strength member at the distance indicated for the enclosure (Figure 15-8).

### 15.7.2.7    STRIP BUFFER TUBE

Shortly before installing the connector, the installer strips the buffer tube from each fiber, as in 15.7.1.3.

### 15.7.2.8    ATTACH CABLE TO ENCLOSURE

When the termination is complete, the installer places the cable in the enclosure, according to the instructions for the enclosure. He coils the service loop of buffer tube inside the enclosure. He coils the service loop of cable in a convenient location.

## 15.8    ONE PAGE SUMMARY

## 15.8.1    LOOSE TUBE END PREPARATION FOR PULLING

Choose a swivel

Set slitter blade depth

Make a test cut

Remove test cut

Remove jacket

Remove gel

Remove gel remover

Remove core materials

Attach swivel

Install cable

Cut off cable end

## 15.8.2   TIGHT TUBE END PREPARATION FOR PULLING

15.8.2.1   JACKETED FIBERS

Attach swivel

Remove jacket and fibers

Install cable

15.8.2.2   PREMISES CABLE

Attach swivel to pull rope

Slit jacket

Remove fibers

Remove central strength member

Attach cable to swivel

Pull cable

Cut off cable end

## 15.8.3   LOOSE TUBE END PREPARATION FOR TERMINATION

Determine dimensions

Prepare work area

Pre-install cable

Access ripcord

Set slitter depth

Make test cut

Remove test cut

Remove jacket

Make ring cut

Prepare cable core

Clean cable core

Remove Gel

Remove Gel remover

Remove buffer tube

Clean fibers

Lubricate and separate fibers

Attach cable

## 15.8.4   TIGHT TUBE END PREPARATION FOR TERMINATION

15.8.4.1   JACKETED FIBERS

Determine dimensions

Install cable into enclosure

Remove jacket

Strip buffer tube

Trim strength members

Attach cable to enclosure

15.8.4.2   PREMISES CABLE

Determine dimensions

Install cable into enclosure

Slit jacket

Separate fibers

Trim flexible strength members

Trim central strength member

Strip buffer tube

Attach cable to enclosure

# 16   CONNECTOR INSTALLATION: EPOXY

Chapter Objectives: by following the procedures in this chapter, you will install epoxy SC connectors with low loss and high reliability. In addition, you will achieve singlemode reflectance below -50 dB.

## 16.1   INTRODUCTION

This chapter applies to the installation of one specific connector onto four types of jacketed cables. Three of the cables, a single fiber, a zip cord duplex and a break out, have a with 3 mm jacket on each fiber. The fourth type of cable is a premises cable with a 900 μm tight buffer tube.

These instructions may apply to other connectors with changes to the dimensions (Figure 16-1 and Figure 16-2) and to the crimp nest diameter(s).

The method of connector installation is epoxy. The epoxy requires heat curing for 10 minutes at 85° C.

These instructions will enable the novice installer to achieve low loss and high reliability.

## 16.2   MATERIALS AND SUPPLIES[1]

For installation of these connectors, the installer requires a connector installation tool kit, which includes the following:[2]

> Multimode or singlemode SC connectors[3]

> Work mat (Clauss Fiber-Safe™)

> Tubing cutter (Ideal 45-162)

> Kevlar scissors (with ceramic blade)[4]

> Miller buffer tube and primary coating stripper (FO-103-S) or Clauss NoNik stripper (NN203)

> Syringe (Fiber Optic Center Inc., FOCI)

> Epoxy (FIS part number H05-100-R2 or equivalent; FOCI part number AB9112)

> 85° C. connector curing oven (FIS part number F1-9772)

> Lens grade tissue (Kim-Wipes™ or equivalent)

> 98% isopropyl alcohol (Fiber Instrument Sales (FIS))[5]

> Alternative to isopropyl alcohol: Alco pads or Opti-Prep Pads

> Connector cleaner (Electro WashPx, from ITC Chemtronics)

> Wedge scriber (Corning Cable Systems Ruby Scribe, 3233304-01)

> Small plastic bottle (for bare fiber collection)

> Lens grade compressed gas (Stoner part number 94203 or equivalent)

> SC polishing tool6 (FIS or FOCI)

> Two or more hard rubber polishing pads, one pad for each polishing film, except for the air polish film (FIS part number PP 575)

> 12 μm polishing film (FOCI part number AO-12-F-91-3N)

> 3 μm polishing film (FOCI part number AO-3-T-91-3N)

---

[1] We have chosen some of these tools and supplies on the basis of their superior performance. We have chosen others, on the basis of their price. Finally, we have chosen some of these tools and supplies based on their convenience.

[2] Sources of equipment and supplies are: Fiber Optic Center Inc. (FOCI) 800-ISFIBER and Fiber Instrument Sales (FIS), 800-5000-FIS.

[3] from Crystal Tech (770-957-8027)

---

[4] Scissors with ceramic blades provide the best results, but have the highest cost.

[5] Do not use rubbing alcohol, as it contains oil that can interfere with adhesion of the epoxy.

[6] The polishing tool is also called a fixture and a puck.

---

➢ 1 μm polishing film[7] (FOCI part number AO-1-T-91-3N)

➢ Optional: for multimode polishing: 0.5 μm polishing film (FOCI part number AO-05-T-91-3N)

➢ Crimper for the connectors to be installed (0.137" and 0.190")

➢ 400 x connector inspection microscope with ST-compatible or SC fixture (Westover Scientific)

➢ 1 μm diamond polishing film (Fiber Optic Center Inc., part number D1RG0403N1)[9]

➢ 0.5 μm diamond polishing film (Fiber Optic Center Inc., part number D05FN403N1)[9]

➢ 0.3 μm alumina polishing film (Fiber Optic Center Inc., part number D5RG0403N1)[9]

➢ Polishing extender solution (Fiber Optic Center Inc.)[8]

## 16.3   PROCEDURE

### 16.3.1   SET UP OVEN

The installer plugs in the oven. If the oven has a temperature adjustment, he sets the temperature to that appropriate for the epoxy to be used.[9] He allows the oven to heat up for at least 15 minutes or for the length of time indicated in the oven instruction sheet.

### 16.3.2   PREINSTALL CABLE

The installer installs the cable into the enclosure without permanently attaching the cable to the enclosure. He pulls the cable out of the enclosure to a work surface near the enclosure.

### 16.3.3   REMOVE OUTER JACKET

By the appropriate procedure, the installer removes the outer jacket of a premises

---

[7] Multimode polishing requires these materials.

[8] Singlemode polishing requires these materials.

[9] These instructions are for an epoxy that cures in 10 minutes at 85° C.

cable (15.7.2) or of a breakout cable (15.7.1). At this step, the installer does not remove the jacket of 3 mm simplex or 3 mm zip cord duplex.

### 16.3.4   INSTALL BOOTS AND SLEEVES

#### 16.3.4.1   PREMISES CABLE

The installer installs the 0.9 mm boot on each buffer tube. He pushes the boot approximately 12" away from end of buffer tubes. He marks the length of buffer tube to be removed (Figure 16-1).

Strip this much bare fiber

█████████    0.688"

Figure 16-1: Template for Length Bare

#### 16.3.4.2   BREAKOUT AND SIMPLEX CABLE

The installer installs the boots on all fibers to be terminated. The cable enters the small end of the boot. He pushes the boots approximately 12" away from end of cable.

The installer installs the crimp sleeves on all fibers to be terminated. The cable enters the small end of the crimp sleeve. He pushes the crimp sleeve approximately 12" away from end of cable. He does not push the crimp sleeve under the boot.

#### 16.3.4.3   ZIP CORD DUPLEX

The installer separates the two channels by pulling the channels apart. If necessary, the installer can cut the thin web that connects the channels. He installs a boot and crimp sleeve as in 16.3.4.2.

### 16.3.5   PREPARE END

The installer repeats this step for all fibers to be terminated at this location.

#### 16.3.5.1   PREMISES CABLE

If the installer uses a No Nik Stripper, he cleans the stripper by holding the stripper open and snapping each cap once (Figure 16-2).[10] The installer grips the cable or

---

[10] Occasionally, this method of cleaning the Clauss stripper does not work. In that case, the

buffer tube firmly. The installer can grip the cable by wrapping the cable around one finger 5 times (Figure 16-3) or by weaving the cable through his fingers.

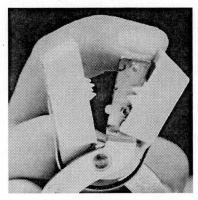

Figure 16-2: Cleaning of Clauss Stripper

The installer places the stripper on the buffer tube at the marked distance (Figure 16-1) or 1/2" from the end of the buffer tube, whichever is shorter.[11]

While holding the stripper at 90° to the fiber (Figure 16-3), the installer pulls the stripper towards the fiber end slowly. He allows the buffer tube and primary coating to slide from the fiber. He does not force the buffer tube and primary coating from the fiber.

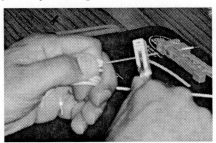

Figure 16-3: Fiber Straight In Stripper

If the installer uses a Miller Stripper, he cleans the stripper with lens grade gas. He grips the cable or buffer tube firmly. He can grip the cable by wrapping the cable around

one finger 5 times (Figure 16-4) or by weaving the cable through his fingers.

The installer places the stripper on the buffer tube at the marked distance or at 1/2" from the buffer tube end, whichever is shorter.[13] He holds the stripper at 45° to the fiber. He pulls the stripper slowly towards the end of the fiber, allowing the buffer tube to slide from the fiber. He does not force the buffer tube and primary coating from the fiber.

If necessary, the installer repeats this step until the length of bare fiber is as indicated in Figure 16-2. He inspects the fiber to ensure that there is no buffer tube or primary coating remaining on the fiber.

### 16.3.5.2     JACKETED FIBERS

#### 16.3.5.2.1     REMOVE JACKET

The installer removes the inner jacket by placing the tubing cutter at the distance from the cable end indicated in Figure 16-4 (Figure 16-5). He rotates the cutter around the cable once or twice. He removes the cutter[12] and slides the jacket from the buffer tube and aramid yarn.

Remove this much jacket; 0.137" crimp die

███████████  1.25"

Leave this much buffer tube

██████  0.625"

Leave this much aramid yarn; 0.190" crimp die

███  0.313"

Figure 16-4: Template of Strip Lengths[13]

Figure 16-5: Tubing Cutter On Cable

installer may blow out the stripper with lens grade gas.

[11] This instruction indicates a maximum strip length of 1/2". US-made fiber optic cables can be stripped to at least this distance. Some US-made cables allow a longer strip length without breakage. For such cables, you may strip to that increased distance. Few cables allow more than 1.5 ".

[12] The installer does not pull the jacket from the cable with the jacket cutter.

[13] Figure is to scale. We recommend use of a template for all connector installation activities.

### 16.3.5.2.2    STRIP BUFFER TUBE

The installer holds the aramid yarns back against the remaining jacket. He marks the buffer tube length of to be left (Figure 16-4). He strips the buffer tube and primary coating as in 16.3.5.1.

### 16.3.5.2.3    TRIM STRENGTH MEMBERS

The installer separates the aramid yarn from the buffer tube. He twists the yarn. He cuts the yarn to the length in Figure 16-4 (Figure 16-6).[14]

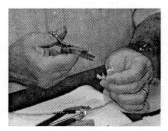

Figure 16-6: Cutting Aramid Yarn To Length

### 16.3.5.3    CABLE CONTINUITY TEST

The installer holds a high intensity light source close to the fibers in one end of the cable. An associate at the opposite end views the fibers. Each fiber should glow, indicating continuity.[15]

### 16.3.5.4    FIBER STRENGTH TEST

This step is optional. The installer performs this step to troubleshoot fiber breakage. The installer performs this step for each fiber just prior to inserting a it into a connector.

The installer pushes each fiber against a lens grade tissue on the work surface.[16] If the fiber bends without breaking, the installer has not damaged the cladding. If there is a single defect on the cladding, the fiber will break.

---

[14] Some connectors allow trimming the strength member as the second step. For such connectors, the strength member length must be less than the buffer tube length.

[15] This test is optional, but recommended. This test works on both multimode and singlemode fibers to several thousand feet.

[16] The installer should not push a bare fiber against his finger. Doing so can result in the fiber penetrating the skin and breaking.

## 16.3.6    PREPARE EPOXY

The installer twists a needle onto the barrel of a syringe until the needle resists additional twisting. He removes the plunger from the barrel.

He checks the expiration date of the adhesive and primer. If the date has not passed, he uses the epoxy.

He mixes the two-part epoxy by removing the separator and rubbing the package with a mixing roller. As an alternative method, the installer can rub the package over a dull edge, such as the edge of a table. While mixing, he moves all of the epoxy components from one end of package to the other a minimum of 15 times or until the color of the mixture is uniform.

The installer squeezes all the epoxy into one end of the package. He squeezes the epoxy away from one corner of package. He cuts off 1/8" of the corner. He squeezes as much epoxy as possible into the barrel of the syringe.

He inserts the plunger into the barrel 1/8" - 1/4". He points the needle up, allowing all of the epoxy to run onto plunger. He presses the plunger into the barrel until all the air passes through the needle. He pulls the plunger back about 1/8", so that epoxy does not 'weep' from the needle. He places the needle on a non-absorbent material.[17]

## 16.3.7    CLEAN FIBER

The installer performs this step for each fiber prior to inserting it into a connector. The installer moistens a lens grade tissue with isopropyl alcohol. He folds the moist area around the fiber (Figure 16-7). He pulls the fiber through the fold twice. He inspects the fiber for particles on the cladding. If necessary, he cleans the fiber repeatedly until the cladding is free of all visible particles. He repeats this step for each fiber just prior to inserting a it into a connector.

---

[17] The epoxy packaging material is non absorbent.

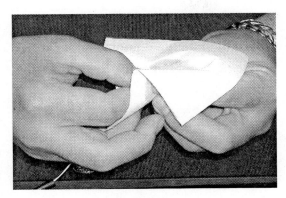

Figure 16-7: Cleaning of Fiber

## 16.3.8    CONNECTOR TESTS

Both tests are optional for novice installers and for troubleshooting fiber breakage. In addition, the dry fit test is a troubleshooting step for failure of fibers to fit into connectors. If necessary for troubleshooting or desirable for practice, the installer repeats these steps for all connectors.

### 16.3.8.1    WHITE LIGHT TEST

While aiming the ferrule towards a light source, such as a window or ceiling light, the installer looks into the back shell of a connector. He should see a sparkle that indicates the presence of a fiber hole and the absence of contamination in the connector. Such contamination could block the path of the fiber.

### 16.3.8.2    DRY FIT TEST

While resting his hands together, the installer feeds the fiber into central tube in the back shell of the connector (Figure 16-8). As soon as the fiber enters the back shell, he twists the connector back and forth. As long as the fiber continues feeding into the back shell without bending, he continues twisting the connector and inserting the fiber. If the fiber bends, he withdraws the fiber approximately 1/8", twists the connector back and forth and feeds the fiber into the back shell.

The installer must see the fiber protruding beyond the tip of the ferrule. This protrusion indicates that the fiber and the hole are compatible, that the fiber is sufficiently long and that there is nothing blocking the fiber path through the ferrule. The installer removes the fiber from the connector and places that connector near that fiber.

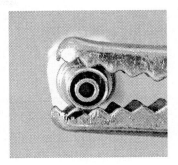

Figure 16-8: Central Tube Of SC Connector

## 16.3.9    INJECT EPOXY

Before each use, the installer wipes the epoxy from the outside of the needle. He places the needle into the connector back shell until the needle butts against the inside end of the ferrule. While maintaining pressure on the needle, he presses the plunger until the adhesive flows through the fiber hole in the end of the ferrule. As soon as the adhesive flows through the fiber hole, he removes the needle from the connector. He pulls the plunger 1/8" out of the barrel of the syringe to prevent 'weeping'. He can repeat this step for up to 12 connectors.[18]

With lens grade tissue, the installer wipes the tip of the ferrule to remove all of the epoxy from the tip.[19]

## 16.3.10    INSTALL CONNECTOR

The installer inserts the fiber into the center tube in the back shell of a filled connector. As soon as the fiber enters the back shell, he twists the connector back and forth. As long as the fiber continues into the back shell without bending, he continues twisting the connector and inserting the fiber. If the fiber bends, withdraws the fiber 1/8", twists

[18] You may experiment with filling more than 12 connectors. However, all epoxies have a useful life, called the pot life. Should the epoxy harden excessively, you will not be able to feed the fiber through the ferrule the breaking the fiber losing the connector.

[19] Some installers will benefit from leaving the epoxy on the tip of the ferrule. This epoxy provides additional support for the fiber during polishing. However, this epoxy increases polishing time.

the connector back and forth and feeds the fiber into the back shell.

When the buffer tube stops further motion of the fiber into the ferrule, he inspects the tip of the ferrule. He should see the fiber protruding beyond the tip of the ferrule. The amount of protrusion is not critical. If he does not see the fiber protruding beyond the tip of the ferrule, he removes and cuts off the fiber. [20] He repeats end preparation (16.3.5). If the time to prepare a new end is short, the installer can insert the new end into the same connector.

The installer may tape the cables to the work surface so that the connectors do not slide off. Should the cables slide, the fibers protruding beyond the end of the ferrule may break.

## 16.3.11 CRIMP SLEEVE

The installer repeats this step for each connector that has epoxy and has fiber protruding beyond the tip of the ferrule. He slides the crimp sleeve up to and over the back shell of the connector. While sliding the sleeve over the back shell, he rotates the sleeve back and forth. He crimps the crimp sleeve with the appropriate crimp nest or nests (Figure 16-4 and Figure 16-9). For most connectors, he crimps the large diameter of the sleeve over the back shell of the connector and the small diameter of the crimp sleeve over the jacket.

After completing this step for all connectors that are filled with epoxy, the installer re-prepares any ends that did not have a fiber protruding beyond the tip of the ferrule.

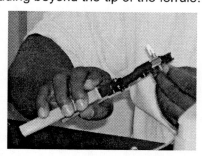

Figure 16-9: Crimping Crimp Sleeve

---

[20] If you cannot see the fiber protruding beyond the end of the ferrule, the fiber was not stripped to a long enough length or the fiber broke during insertion.

## 16.3.12 INSERT CONNECTOR

### 16.3.12.1 JACKETED FIBERS

While holding onto the back shell of the connector, the installer centers the connector over the oven port (Figure 16-10). Slowly, he lowers the connector into the port. If he feels any 'springiness' or resistance, the fiber is off center and touching the inside of the oven. If he detects such resistance, he lifts the connector 1/4", re-centers the connector in the oven port and reinserts slowly.

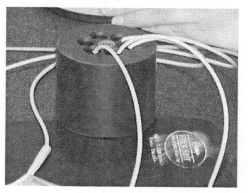

Figure 16-10: Connectors In Curing Oven

### 16.3.12.2 PREMISES CABLES

The installer inserts the connector into the oven without placing tension on the fiber.[21] While squeezing the boot, the buffer tube and the back shell of the connector, he inserts the connector into the oven port as in 16.3.12.1.

The installer repeats this step for all connectors. He records the cure start time for each connector or batch of connectors. He removes each connector from the oven after the specified minimum cure time. The cure time for the epoxy in this procedure is ten minutes. If no oven position is available for a new connector, the installer places the connector horizontally on the work surface in such a manner to avoid tension on the fiber.

> Do not pause or delay installing fibers into filled connectors because the epoxy hardens continuously after being mixed.

---

[21] With no crimp sleeve on the connector, tension can cause the fiber to withdraw into the ferrule.

You may cure the epoxy for more than the minimum curing time as excessive cure time causes not problems.[22]

Repeat this step until you have cured and allowed to cool all connectors. Do not force cool connectors.

## 16.3.13  REMOVE EXCESS FIBER

While resting his hands together, the installer places the wedge surface[23] of a scriber onto the end of the ferrule (Figure 16-11). He moves the blade of the scriber up to the fiber so that the scriber gently touches the fiber at the top of the bead of epoxy. The fiber should not move or bend.

The installer moves the scriber back and forth along the fiber 1/16" once. He should not break the fiber with the scriber. He should not 'saw' the fiber with the scriber.

The installer holds the connector with the fiber pointing up. He grips the connector with his thumb and forefinger lightly. He slides his thumb and forefinger up the connector towards and over the fiber. He grips and pulls the fiber away from the tip of the connector. The fiber should break easily. He places of the fiber in the fiber collection bottle.

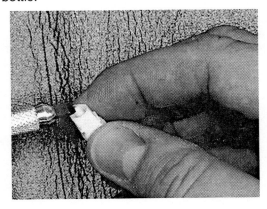

Figure 16-11: Scribing the Excess Fiber

If the fiber does not break, the installer scribed epoxy on the fiber and not the fiber. He repeats this step until the fiber breaks.

---

[22] Excessive temperature can cause cracking of the fiber.

[23] The installer should not place the flat surface of the scriber against the tip of the ferrule.

## 16.3.14  AIR POLISH

The installer holds the connector with the ferrule pointing up. He holds a 12 μm polishing film at one edge with the abrasive side[24] down. He places the opposite edge of the film above the connector. He curls the front and back edges of the film down. With a light pressure, he rubs the film against connector until the fiber is flush with the bead of epoxy (Figure 16-12).[25] If he scribed the fiber just above the surface of the adhesive bead, this step will take less than 10 seconds. The installer does not remove all the epoxy.

The installer checks the fiber by bringing a finger down onto the tip of the ferrule from the top.[26] If he cannot feel the fiber, the fiber is flush, or nearly flush, with the epoxy.

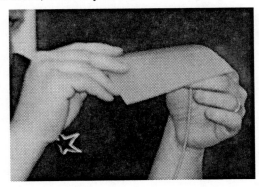

Figure 16-12: Air Polishing of Fiber

## 16.3.15  MULTIMODE POLISH

### 16.3.15.1  CLEAN EQUIPMENT

The installer moistens a lens grade tissue with isopropyl alcohol. He wipes the ferrules of all connectors with this moistened tissue.

The installer can clean his polishing equipment with either lens grade gas or isopropyl alcohol. With lens-grade compressed gas, he cleans off the top surface of the polishing pads, both sides of the polishing films and the polishing tool. With isopropyl alcohol and lens grade

---

[24] The abrasive side is dull.

[25] Do not remove all the adhesive.

[26] Do not rub a finger across the tip of the ferrule. If the fiber is not flush with the epoxy, the installer may snag and break the fiber. In addition, the broken fiber may pierce the installer's skin.

tissues, the installer cleans his equipment in a similar manner. He places the polishing films, dull side up, on the pads.

### 16.3.15.2    FIRST POLISH

The installer places the tool on the 3 μm film.[27] He inserts the connector into the polishing tool. While holding both the connector and the tool (Figure 16-13), he moves the tool in a ½" high, figure-8 pattern slowly. If he feels scratchiness, the fiber is not flush with the adhesive. He maintains a light pressure[28] and a slow, ½" high figure-8 pattern until the scratchiness ceases.

Figure 16-13: Polishing

After the scratchiness ceases, the installer increases the size of the figure-8 pattern to cover the entire film. He does not increase the pressure. He continues polishing until the adhesive is completely removed.

The installer may detect a change in the friction of the connector on the film. This change indicates the removal of the last of the adhesive. If he does not detect this change, he removes the connector from the tool periodically. He views the tip of the ferrule by reflecting light off the tip. When the adhesive is completely removed, the tip of the ferrule will be glass smooth and shiny. The tip will have the same appearance as that of the side of the ferrule.

---

[27] If you install the connector into the tool and slap the tool against the film, you may break the fiber.

[28] Light pressure means that the installer holds the connector against the film without compressing the spring inside the SC connector.

### 16.3.15.3    CLEANING

With lens grade compressed gas or isopropyl alcohol and lens grade tissues, the installer cleans the connector and the tool.

### 16.3.15.4    SECOND POLISH

'High pressure' for polishing means holding the connector in the polishing tool and pushing down the inner housing until the internal spring is fully compressed. The installer need not increase the pressure beyond the level at which the spring is fully compressed.

The installer places the polishing tool on the 1 μm film and applies high pressure to the connector for ten, large figure-8 patterns. Large means using the full area of the film.

### 16.3.15.5    THIRD POLISH

This polish is optional.[29] The installer cleans the connector and polishing tool (16.3.15.3). The installer places the polishing tool on the 0.5 μm film. He inserts the connector in the tool and applies high pressure to the connector for ten, large figure-8 patterns.

## 16.3.16    FINAL CLEANING

The installer slides the boot over the back shell. He cleans the connector with one of the following methods.[30]

### 16.3.16.1    BEST METHOD

The installer moistens a lens grade, lint free tissue with isopropyl alcohol. He wipes the sides and tip of the ferrule with this tissue. He sprays a one-inch diameter area of connector cleaner, such as ElectroWash Px, onto a small pad of lens grade tissues. He wipes the tip of the ferrule from the wet area to the dry area three times.

---

[29] Some connector manufacturers recommend this third polish. We have found no improvement in multimode loss from this polish. We have found only minor improvement in the microscopic appearance. For that reason, we do not recommend it.

[30] Do not use lens grade gas for final cleaning of the connector. This gas tends to leave water marks that can increase loss and reflectance.

### 16.3.16.2   METHOD B

The installer moistens a tissue with isopropyl alcohol. He wipes the sides and the tip of the ferrule. Immediately he wipes the tip of the ferrule with a dry tissue.

### 16.3.16.3   METHOD C

The installer wipes the sides and the tip of the ferrule with a pre-moistened lens grade tissue (Alco Pad or OptiPrep Pad). Immediately, he wipes the tip of the ferrule with a dry tissue. The installer blows out the connector cap and installs the cap.

## 16.3.17   INSPECT CONNECTOR

After polishing each connector, the installer inspects and rates the connector according to the connector inspection procedure (21). If the connector is good, he installs the cap. If the connector is not good, he attaches a label to indicate a potential problem and installs the cap. If the problem is severe enough to indicate unacceptable loss, he replaces the connector.

## 16.3.18   WHITE LIGHT TEST

When the installer has installed all connectors on the one end of a cable, he performs a white light, continuity test as in 16.3.5.3 (Figure 16-14). The installer does not install connectors on the opposite end until all of the fibers have passed this continuity test. If one or more connectors fail this test, he troubleshoots these connectors to identify the problem. An OTDR test may be required.

The installer replaces the caps on all connectors that pass this test. He repeats the continuity test after he installs all connectors on the opposite end of the cable.

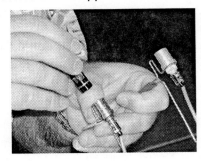

Figure 16-14: White Light Test

## 16.3.19   FINAL ASSEMBLY

The installer slides the boot over the back shell of the connector. The top of the inner housing has missing corners (Figure 16-15). The top of the outer housing has the key. He holds the top of the inner housing and the top of the outer housing up. He inserts the inner housing into the end of the outer housing that is opposite the end with the key (Figure 16-16). He wiggles the inner housing until it snaps through the outer housing (Figure 16-17).

Figure 16-15: Alignment of Inner and Outer Housings For Final Assembly

Figure 16-16: Insertion of Inner Housing

Figure 16-17: Inner Housing Fully Inserted

## 16.3.20   SINGLEMODE POLISHING

Singlemode polishing can be used for initial installation and for restoration of low reflectance. Because of high cost, field polishing of singlemode connectors by hand is done rarely. Pigtail splicing is preferred.

We provide this procedure, with the recommendation that it be used for initial installation when no other options are available. This procedure can be used for restoring a singlemode connector to low reflectance by replacing the 3 μm film with a diamond film of 3 μm.[31]

### 16.3.20.1 CLEANING

As in 16.3.15.3, the installer cleans the polishing pads, the polishing tool and the following films:

> 3 μm

> 1 μm diamond

> 0.5 μm diamond

> 0.3 μm

### 16.3.20.2 FIRST POLISH

The installer polishes the connector as in 16.3.17.2.

### 16.3.20.3 CLEANING

With isopropyl alcohol and lens grade tissues, the installer cleans the connector. He scrubs the tool with lens grade tissues moistened with isopropyl alcohol at least twice.

### 16.3.20.4 SECOND POLISH

'High pressure' for polishing means holding the connector in the polishing tool and pushing down the inner housing until the internal spring is fully compressed. The installer need not increase the pressure beyond the level at which the spring is fully compressed.

The installer places the polishing tool on the 1 μm diamond film and applies high pressure to the connector for 20 to 40, large figure-8 patterns. Large means using the full area of the polishing film.

The installer polishes for 20 strokes for new diamond film. He polishes 40 strokes after he has polished five connectors on the film. He can use the same film for at least 10 connectors.

### 16.3.20.5 CLEANING

The installer cleans the connector and polishing tool as in 16.3.15.3.

### 16.3.20.6 THIRD POLISH

With a high pressure, the installer polishes the connector for 20-40 large figure 8 strokes on the 0.5 μm film. The installer polishes for 20 strokes for new diamond film. He polishes 40 strokes after he has polished five connectors on the film. He can use the same film for at least 10 connectors.

### 16.3.20.7 CLEANING

The installer cleans the connector and polishing tool as in 16.3.15.3. There must be no residue on the tool from previous polishing steps.[32]

### 16.3.20.8 FOURTH POLISH

The installer adds two drops of the polishing extender liquid to the film. With a high pressure, he polishes the connector for 20 large figure 8 strokes.

He replaces this film after five connectors.

## 16.3.21 FINAL CLEANING

As in 16.3.16, the installer cleans the connector with isopropyl alcohol and lens grade tissue three times.

## 16.3.22 INSPECTION

The installer inspects the connector as in 16.3.16. In addition, he inspects the cladding for uniformity of appearance (Figure 21-7).

## 16.4 TROUBLESHOOTING

## 16.4.1 INSTALLATION

### 16.4.1.1 FIBER BREAKAGE DURING INSERTION

Potential cause: dirt or buffer coating on fiber
Action: clean fiber

---

[31] Our assumption is that the defects causing high reflectance are less than approximately 4 μm deep. Although defects deeper than 4 μm can be remove with 5 μm diamond film, we recommend connector replacement.

[32] If the installer uses a single polishing tool for all films, he scrubs the tool with a toothbrush and isopropyl alcohol before each use on the 0.3 μm film. Failure to do so will degrade the condition of the core to worse than that after the 0.5μm film.

Potential cause: debris in connector
Action: perform white light check of connector[33]

### 16.4.1.2    FIBER BREAKS OR DOES NOT FIT INTO CONNECTOR

Potential cause: buffer coating not completely removed
Action: restrip fiber

### 16.4.1.3    FIBER BREAKS OR DOES NOT FIT INTO CONNECTOR

Potential cause: epoxy has partially hardened
Action: replace connector

## 16.4.2    POLISHING

### 16.4.2.1    NON-ROUND CORE[34]

Potential cause: fiber broken during first polishing due to incomplete air polishing
Action: replace connector and perform complete air polish

Potential cause: excessive pressure during first pad polishing[35]
Action: reduce polishing pressure

### 16.4.2.2    EXCESSIVE POLISHING TIME

Potential cause: large bead of epoxy due to failure to remove epoxy from tip of ferrule prior to insertion of fiber
Action: remove all epoxy from tip of ferrule after injecting epoxy

Potential cause: film worn out
Action: replace film

Potential cause: insufficient polishing pressure
Action: increase polishing pressure

### 16.4.2.3    NO APPARENT REDUCTION OF BEAD SIZE

Potential cause: dirt in ferrule hole of polishing tool[36]
Action: clean hole in polishing tool with lens grade air or with pipe cleaner dipped in isopropyl alcohol.

### 16.4.2.4    FEW CORE AND CLADDING SCRATCHES

Potential cause: contamination of film by environment.
Action: replace film[37]

### 16.4.2.5    EPOXY SMEARS ON FIBER DURING POLISHING

Potential cause: uncured or incompletely cured epoxy due to insufficient time
Action: increase curing time. Monitor dwell time in oven with written log.

Potential cause: low curing temperature
Action: check oven temperature

Potential cause: epoxy used past its expiration date
Action: discard epoxy

Potential cause: epoxy allowed to freeze
Action: discard epoxy[38]

### 16.4.2.6    CRACKED FIBER

Potential cause: excessive pressure during scribing
Action: scratch fiber lightly during scribing

Potential cause: excessive temperature during curing
Action: replace oven

### 16.4.2.7    EPOXY FLOWS FROM BACK SHELL

Potential cause: excessive epoxy in back shell
Action: replace connector; after filling fiber hole in ferrule, immediately withdraw needle

---

[33] If the connector fails this test, the installer blows out connector with lens grade gas. If the connector still fails this test, he flushes the connector with isopropyl alcohol injected through the connector with a syringe needle. If the connector fails this step, he replaces the connector.

[34] Chapter 21

[35] In this case, polishing sheared of the epoxy bead. This bead may be found on the first film.

[36] This dirt prevents the tip of the ferrule from passing through the tool and contacting the film.

[37] The installer cleans the film only if no replacement film is available. He can move the polishing location away from air vents and any other source of airborne dust.

[38] Some epoxy loses its ability to cure after it has been frozen. Store such epoxy so that it does not freeze.

### 16.4.2.8 EPOXY ON OUTSIDE OF BACK SHELL.

Potential cause: failure to wipe needle before each use.
Action: wipe epoxy from outside of needle before each use

### 16.4.2.9 EPOXY ON OUTSIDE OF INNER TUBE

Potential cause: failure to wipe needle before each use
Action: discard connector; wipe epoxy from outside of needle before each use

See 16.4.2.7

## 16.4.3 SINGLEMODE POLISHING

### 16.4.3.1 PITS REMAIN AFTER FIRST 20 STROKES ON NEW 1 µm FILM

. Potential cause: insufficient polish pressure
Action: increase pressure as described in procedure

### 16.4.3.2 PITS REMAIN AFTER FIRST 20 STROKES ON 'OLD' 5 µm FILM.

Potential cause: film worn out
Action: replace film

### 16.4.3.3 HIGH REFLECTANCE WITH NO APPARENT FEATURES IN CORE AND SOME NEAR CORE BOUNDARY

Potential cause: features create roughness
Action: repolish starting with 3 µm diamond film

### 16.4.3.4 HIGH REFLECTANCE WITH NO APPARENT FEATURES IN CORE OR CLADDING

Potential cause: roughness not visible at 400 x.
Action: repolish starting with 1 µm film

### 16.4.3.5 HIGH REFLECTANCE

Potential cause: dirt on connector outside of field of view
Action: re-clean and retest

### 16.4.3.6 PITS APPEAR AFTER POLISHING ON 0.3 µm FILM[39]

Potential cause: the puck was contaminated with debris from the prior polishing films
Action: thoroughly clean the puck prior to polishing on 0.3 µm film

## 16.5 SUMMARY

This summary is in three parts, one each for connector installation, multimode polishing and singlemode polishing.

## 16.5.1 INSTALLATION

Set up oven. Plug in. Allow to preheat.

Install cable through enclosure.

Pull cable through enclosure to work surface.

If necessary, remove jacket, Kevlar and central strength member to proper lengths.

Install boots on all buffer tubes.

Remove buffer tubes with Miller stripper to proper lengths. Clean fiber with lens grade tissue and isopropyl alcohol.

Mix epoxy thoroughly and fill syringe.

Optional Step: give all connectors a white light test.

Optional Step: give all connectors a dry fit.

For up to 12 connectors, inject epoxy through fiber hole and a small amount into back shell.

Optional Step: Wipe all epoxy off tip of ferrules.

Insert fiber into back shell with rotation until fiber bottoms out against ferrule. Do not allow fiber to bend.

For jacketed fiber, slide crimp sleeve over back shell and crimp sleeve. For premises cable, bring boot over back shell.

While keeping connector centered over curing position, insert connector into curing oven without breaking fiber. Allow to cure 10 minutes.

Remove connector from oven and allow to cool. Do not force cool in any way.

---

[39] See Figure 21-6.

Scribe and remove excess fiber.

Air polish excess fiber flush with epoxy.

Proceed to multimode or singlemode polishing procedure.

## 16.5.2   MULTIMODE POLISH

Clean all connectors.

Clean connector, pads, films and tool. Place 3 µm film on pad and tool on film.

Install connector into tool.

Polish in small figure 8 pattern with light pressure until scratchiness ceases.

When scratchiness ceases, polish in large figure 8 pattern with slightly higher pressure until all the epoxy is gone. Polish the connector using the entire area of the film.

Clean the 1 µm film, the tool and the connector.

Install the connector into the tool. With moderate pressure, make 10 large figure 8 motions.

Clean the side and tip of the connector.

Proceed to connector inspection procedure (21).

Perform a white light continuity test after you install connectors on the first end of the cable.

Perform a white light continuity test after you install connectors on the second end of the cable.

Install outer housing.

Clean and install cap on ferrule.

## 16.5.3   SINGLEMODE POLISH

Scribe and air polish the fiber flush with the epoxy.

Clean the ferrules of all connectors.

Clean off the polishing pad, the polishing films and the polishing tool.

Polish on the 3 µm film to remove the epoxy.

Clean the connector, pad, tool and the 1 µm film with a lens grade gas.

With a heavy pressure, polish the connector on the 1 µm film for 20-40 large figure 8 strokes.

Clean the connector, pad, tool and the 0.5 µm film with a lens grade gas.

With a heavy pressure, polish the connector on the 0.5 µm film for 20-40 large figure 8 strokes.

Clean the connector, pad, tool and the 0.3 µm film with a lens grade gas.

Place two or three drops of the polishing liquid on the film. With a heavy pressure, polish the connector on the 0.3 µm film for 20 large figure 8 strokes.

Clean the connector with alcohol and lens grade tissue three times.

Proceed to connector inspection (21).

Perform a white light continuity test after you install connectors on the first end of the cable.

Perform a white light continuity test after you install connectors on the second end of the cable.

Install outer housing.

Clean and install cap on ferrule.

For jacketed fibers, slide the boot up over the back shell.

# 17  CONNECTOR INSTALLATION: QUICK CURE ADHESIVE

Chapter Objectives: by following the procedures in this chapter, you will install SC connectors with quick cure adhesive and achieve low loss and high reliability.

## 17.1  INTRODUCTION

This chapter applies to the installation of an SC connector with adhesive onto four cable types. Three of the cables, single fiber, zip cord duplex and break out, have a 3 mm jacket on each fiber. Because of this jacket, we refer to these cables as having 'jacketed fibers'. The fourth type of cable, a premises cable, has a 900 µm tight buffer tube.

The method of connector installation is quick cure adhesive. Such adhesives do not require power to be cured. Such adhesives cure rapidly, resulting in relatively short installation time.

However, the adhesive creates a very small bead on the tip of the ferrule. This small bead provides limited support for the fiber during polishing. This limited support increases the difficulty of polishing.

In addition, quick cure adhesives may harden prior to full insertion of the fiber. In this situation, there is bare fiber inside the connector, a condition of reduced reliability.

## 17.2  MATERIALS AND SUPPLIES[1]

For installation of these connectors, the installer requires a connector installation tool kit, which includes the following:[2]

> - Multimode or singlemode SC connectors[3]
> - Work mat (Clauss Fiber-Safe™)

> - Tubing cutter (Ideal 45-162)
> - Kevlar scissors (with ceramic blades)[4]
> - Miller buffer tube and primary coating stripper (FO-103-S) or Clauss NoNik stripper (NN203)
> - Syringe (Fiber Optic Center Inc., FOCI)
> - Quick cure adhesive, Locktite part number 6805
> - Quick cure primer, Locktite part number 7649
> - Lens grade tissue (Kim-Wipes™ or equivalent)
> - 98% isopropyl alcohol (Fiber Instrument Sales (FIS))[6]
> - Alternative to isopropyl alcohol: Alco pads or Opti-Prep Pads
> - Connector cleaner (Electro WashPx, from ITC Chemtronics)
> - Wedge scriber (Corning Cable Systems Ruby Scribe, 3233304-01)
> - Small plastic bottle for bare fiber collection
> - Lens grade compressed gas (Stoner part number 94203 or equivalent)
> - SC polishing tool[7] (FIS or FOCI)
> - Two or more hard rubber polishing pads, one pad for each polishing film[8] (FIS part number PP 575)

---

[1] We have chosen some of these tools and supplies on the basis of their superior performance. We have chosen others, on the basis of their price. Finally, we have chosen some of these tools and supplies based on their convenience.

[2] Sources of equipment and supplies: Fiber Optic Center Inc. (FOCI) 800-ISFIBER and Fiber Instrument Sales (FIS), 800-5000-FIS.

[3] The connector used in this chapter is from Crystal Tech (678-957-8027).

[4] Scissors with ceramic blades provide the best results, but have the highest cost.

[5] You may use other quick cure adhesives, as long as you follow the instructions.

[6] Do not use rubbing alcohol, as it contains oil that can interfere with adhesion of the adhesive.

[7] The polishing tool is also called a fixture and a puck.

[8] No pad is required for the 12 µm air polish film.

---

➤ 12 µm polishing film (FOCI part number AO-12-F-91-3N)

➤ 3 µm polishing film[9] (FOCI part number AO-3-T-91-3N)

➤ 1 µm polishing film[9] (FOCI part number AO-1-T-91-3N)

➤ Optional: 0.5 µm polishing film[9] (FOCI part number AO-05-T-91-3N)

➤ Crimper for the connectors to be installed (0.137" and 0.190")

➤ 400 x connector inspection microscope with ST-compatible or SC fixture (Westover Scientific)

## 17.3   PROCEDURE

### 17.3.1   PREINSTALL CABLE

The installer installs the cable into the enclosure without permanently attaching the cable to the enclosure. He pulls the cable out of the enclosure to a work surface near the enclosure.

### 17.3.2   REMOVE OUTER JACKET

By the appropriate procedure, the installer removes the outer jacket of a premises cable (15.7.2) or of a breakout cable (15.7.1). At this step, the installer does not remove the jacket of 3 mm simplex or 3 mm zip cord duplex.

### 17.3.3   INSTALL BOOTS AND SLEEVES

#### 17.3.3.1   PREMISES CABLE

The installer installs the 0.9 mm boot on each buffer tube. He pushes the boot approximately 12" away from end of buffer tubes. He marks the length of buffer tube to be removed (Figure 17-1).

Strip this much bare fiber

█████████    0.688"

Figure 17-1: Template of Strip Length For Premises Cable[10]

---

[9] Multimode polishing requires these materials.

#### 17.3.3.2   BREAKOUT AND SIMPLEX CABLE

The installer installs the boots on all fibers to be terminated. The cable enters the small end of the boot. He pushes the boots approximately 12" away from end of cable.

The installer installs the crimp sleeves on all fibers to be terminated. The cable enters the small end of the crimp sleeve. He pushes the crimp sleeve approximately 12" away from end of cable. He does not push the crimp sleeve under the boot.

#### 17.3.3.3   ZIP CORD DUPLEX

The installer separates the two channels by pulling the channels apart. If necessary, the installer can cut the thin web that connects the channels. He installs a boot and crimp sleeve as in 17.3.3.2.

### 17.3.4   PREPARE END

The installer repeats this step for all fibers to be terminated at this location.

#### 17.3.4.1   PREMISES CABLE

If the installer uses a No Nik Stripper, he cleans the stripper by holding the stripper open and snapping each cap once (Figure 17-2).[11] The installer grips the cable or buffer tube firmly. The installer can grip the cable by wrapping the cable around one finger 5 times (Figure 17-3) or by weaving the cable through his fingers.

The installer places the stripper on the buffer tube at the marked distance (Figure 17-1) or 1/2" from the end of the buffer tube, whichever is shorter.[12]

While holding the stripper at 90° to the fiber (Figure 17-3), the installer pulls the stripper towards the fiber end slowly. He allows the

---

[10] These dimensions are to scale.

[11] Occasionally, this method of cleaning the Clauss stripper does not work. In that case, the installer may blow out the stripper with lens grade gas.

[12] This instruction indicates a maximum strip length of 1/2". US-made fiber optic cables can be stripped to at least this distance. Some US-made cables allow a longer strip length without breakage. For such cables, you may strip to that increased distance. Few cables allow more than 1.5 ".

buffer tube and primary coating to slide from the fiber. He does not force the buffer tube and primary coating from the fiber.

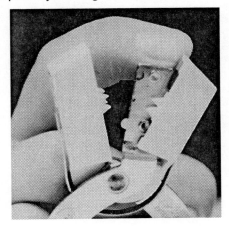

Figure 17-2: Cleaning of Clauss Stripper

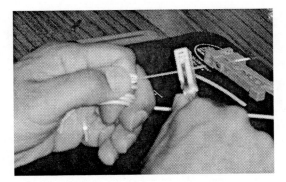

Figure 17-3: Fiber Straight In Stripper

If the installer uses a Miller Stripper, he cleans the stripper with lens grade gas. The installer grips the cable or buffer tube firmly. The installer can grip the cable by wrapping the cable around one finger 5 times (Figure 17-3) or by weaving the cable through his fingers.

The installer places the stripper on the buffer tube at the marked distance or at 1/2" from the buffer tube end, whichever is shorter.[13] He holds the stripper at 45° to the fiber. He pulls the stripper slowly towards the end of the fiber, allowing the buffer tube to slide from the fiber. He does not force the buffer tube and primary coating from the fiber.

If necessary, the installer repeats this step until the length of bare fiber is as indicated in Figure 17-1. He inspects the fiber to ensure that there is no buffer tube or primary coating remaining on the fiber.

### 17.3.4.2    JACKETED FIBERS

#### 17.3.4.2.1    REMOVE JACKET

The installer removes the inner jacket by placing the tubing cutter at the distance from the cable end indicated in Figure 17-4 (Figure 17-5). He rotates the cutter around the cable once or twice. He removes the cutter[13] and slides the jacket from the buffer tube and aramid yarn.

Remove this much jacket; 0.137" crimp die

▬▬▬▬▬▬▬▬▬ 1.25"

Leave this much buffer tube

▬▬▬▬▬ 0.625"

Leave this much aramid yarn; 0.190" crimp die

▬▬ 0.313"

Figure 17-4: Template of Strip Lengths For Jacketed Fiber[14]

Figure 17-5: Tubing Cutter On Cable

#### 17.3.4.2.2    STRIP BUFFER TUBE

The installer holds the aramid yarns back against the remaining jacket. He marks the buffer tube length of to be left (Figure 17-4). He strips the buffer tube and primary coating as in 17.3.4.1.

#### 17.3.4.2.3    TRIM STRENGTH MEMBERS

The installer separates the aramid yarn from the buffer tube. He twists the yarn. He cuts the yarn to the length in Figure 17-4 (Figure 17-6).[15]

---

[13] The installer does not pull the jacket from the cable with the jacket cutter.

[14] These dimensions are to scale.

[15] Some connectors allow trimming the strength member as the second step. For such connectors, the strength member length must be less than the buffer tube length.

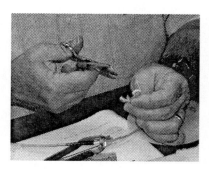

Figure 17-6: Cutting Aramid Yarn To Length

### 17.3.4.3    CABLE CONTINUITY TEST

The installer holds a high intensity light source close to the fibers in one end of the cable. An associate at the opposite end views the fibers. Each fiber should glow, indicating continuity.[16]

### 17.3.4.4    FIBER STRENGTH TEST

This step is optional. The installer performs this step to troubleshoot fiber breakage. The installer performs this step for each fiber just prior to inserting a it into a connector.

The installer pushes each fiber against a lens grade tissue on the work surface.[17] If the fiber bends without breaking, the installer has not damaged the cladding. If there is a single defect on the cladding, the fiber will break.

## 17.3.5    PREPARE ADHESIVE

The installer twists a needle onto the barrel of a syringe until the needle resists additional twisting. He removes the plunger from the barrel.

He checks the expiration date of the adhesive and primer. If the date has not passed, he uses both.[18]

---

[16] This test is optional, but recommended. This test works on both multimode and singlemode fibers to several thousand feet.

[17] The installer should not push a bare fiber against his finger. Doing so can result in the fiber penetrating the skin and breaking.

[18] Here's a trick for training: adhesives can be used past their expiration date. The curing time increases as the adhesive ages. Such increase a) allows the trainee increased time for insertion of the fiber and b) reduces the frequency of premature hardening. We have used adhesives

He squeezes the adhesive bottle so that the adhesive runs onto the side of the inside of the barrel without running onto the needle. He needs no more than 1-2 cc of adhesive.

He inserts the plunger into the barrel 1/8" - 1/4". He points the needle up, allowing all of the adhesive to run onto plunger. He presses the plunger into the barrel until all the air passes through the needle. He pulls the plunger back about 1/8", so that adhesive does not 'weep' from the needle.

## 17.3.6    CLEAN FIBER

The installer performs this step for each fiber prior to inserting it into a connector. The installer moistens a lens grade tissue with isopropyl alcohol. He folds the moist area around the fiber (Figure 17-7). He pulls the fiber through the fold twice. He inspects the fiber for particles on the cladding. If necessary, he cleans the fiber repeatedly until the cladding is free of all visible particles.

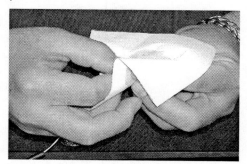

Figure 17-7: Cleaning of Fiber With Moist Tissue

## 17.3.7    CONNECTOR TESTS

Both tests are optional. These tests are for novice installers and for troubleshooting fiber breakage problems. In addition, the dry fit test is a troubleshooting step for failure of fibers to fit into connectors. If necessary for troubleshooting or desirable for practice, the installer repeats these steps for all connectors.

### 17.3.7.1    WHITE LIGHT TEST

While aiming the ferrule towards a light source, such as a window or ceiling light, the

---

for up to three years past their expiration date. Eventually, the adhesives ceases to cure.

installer looks into the back shell of a connector. He should see a sparkle that indicates the presence of a fiber hole and the absence of contamination in the connector. Such contamination could block the path of the fiber.

### 17.3.7.2   DRY FIT TEST

While resting his hands together, the installer feeds the fiber into central tube in the back shell of the connector (Figure 17-8). As soon as the fiber enters the back shell, he twists the connector back and forth. As long as the fiber continues feeding into the back shell without bending, he continues twisting the connector and inserting the fiber. If the fiber bends, he withdraws the fiber approximately 1/8", twists the connector back and forth and feeds the fiber into the back shell.

The installer must see the fiber protruding beyond the tip of the ferrule. This protrusion indicates that the fiber and the hole are compatible, that the fiber is sufficiently long and that there is nothing blocking the fiber path through the ferrule. The installer removes the fiber from the connector and places that connector near that fiber.

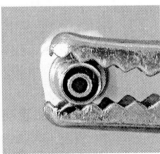

Figure 17-8: Central Tube Of SC Connector

## 17.3.8   INJECT ADHESIVE

Before each use, the installer wipes the adhesive from the outside of the needle. He places the needle into the connector back shell until the needle butts against the inside end of the ferrule. While maintaining pressure on the needle, he presses the plunger until the adhesive flows through the fiber hole in the end of the ferrule. As soon as the adhesive flows through the fiber hole, he removes the needle from the connector. He pulls the plunger 1/8" out of the barrel of

the syringe to eliminate 'weeping'. He can repeat this step for up to 6 connectors.[19]

## 17.3.9   INSTALL CONNECTOR

With the brush from the primer bottle, the installer wipes the fiber and the last 2 mm of the buffer tube with the primer. Immediately, he feeds the fiber into the center tube in the back shell of a filled connector. As soon as the fiber enters the back shell, he twists the connector back and forth. As long as the fiber continues into the back shell without bending, he continues twisting the connector and inserting the fiber. If the fiber bends, withdraws the fiber 1/8", twists the connector back and forth and feeds the fiber into the back shell.

When the buffer tube stops further motion of the fiber into the ferrule, he inspects the tip of the ferrule. He should see the fiber protruding beyond the tip of the ferrule. The amount of protrusion is not critical. If he does not see the fiber protruding beyond the tip of the ferrule, he removes and discards the connector.[20]

| Caution |
|---|
| After wiping the fibers with primer, do not delay inserting the fiber.  Excessive time allows the primer to harden, making the fiber too large to fit in the ferrule.[21] |

The installer may need to tape the cables to the work surface so that the connectors do not slide off. Should the cables slide, the fibers protruding beyond the end of the ferrule may break.

## 17.3.10   CRIMP SLEEVE

The installer repeats this step for each connector that has adhesive and has fiber protruding beyond the tip of the ferrule. He slides the crimp sleeve up to and over the

---

[19] If excessive time passes between injection of the adhesive and insertion of the fiber, the adhesive can harden in the fiber hole.

[20] If you cannot see the fiber protruding beyond the end of the ferrule, the fiber was not stripped to a long enough length or the fiber broke during insertion.

[21] New adhesive cures faster than old adhesive.

back shell of the connector. While sliding the sleeve over the back shell, he rotates the sleeve back and forth. He crimps the crimp sleeve with the appropriate crimp nest or nests (Figure 17-9). For most connectors, he crimps the large diameter of the sleeve over the back shell of the connector and the small diameter of the crimp sleeve over the jacket. After completing this step for all connectors that are filled with adhesive, the installer re-prepares any ends that did not have a fiber protruding beyond the tip of the ferrule.

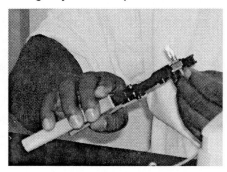

Figure 17-9: Crimping Crimp Sleeve

## 17.3.11    CREATE BEAD

The installer dips the primer brush into the primer. While holding a connector with the fiber pointing up, he wipes the brush against the fiber. He allows primer to run down the fiber onto the bead of adhesive on the tip of the ferrule. With a lens grade tissue, he wicks excess primer from the tip of the ferrule. He does not touch or break the fiber.

## 17.3.12    REMOVE EXCESS FIBER

While resting his hands together, the installer places the wedge surface[22] of a scriber onto the end of the ferrule (Figure 17-10). He moves the blade of the scriber up to the fiber so that the scriber gently touches the fiber at the top of the bead of adhesive. The fiber should not move or bend.

The installer moves the scriber back and forth along the fiber 1/16" once. He should not break the fiber with the scriber. He should not 'saw' the fiber with the scriber.

---

[22] The installer should not place the flat surface of the scriber against the tip of the ferrule.

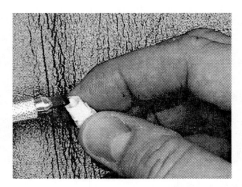

Figure 17-10: Scribing the Excess Fiber

The installer holds the connector with the fiber pointing up. He grips the connector with his thumb and forefinger lightly. He slides his thumb and forefinger up the connector towards and over the fiber. He grips and pulls the fiber away from the tip of the connector. The fiber should break easily. He places of the fiber in the fiber collection bottle.

If the fiber does not break, the installer scribed adhesive on the fiber and not the fiber. He repeats this step until the fiber breaks.

## 17.3.13    AIR POLISH

The installer holds the connector with the ferrule pointing up. He holds a 12 μm polishing film at one edge with the abrasive side[23] down. He places the opposite edge of the film above the connector. He curls the front and back edges of the film down. With a light pressure, he rubs the film against connector until the fiber is flush with the bead of adhesive (Figure 17-11).[24] If he scribed the fiber just above the surface of the adhesive bead, this step will take less than 10 seconds. The installer does not remove all the adhesive.

The installer checks the fiber by bringing a finger down onto the tip of the ferrule from the top.[25] If he cannot feel the fiber, the fiber is flush, or nearly flush, with the epoxy.

---

[23] The abrasive side is dull.

[24] Do not remove all the adhesive.

[25] Do not rub a finger across the tip of the ferrule. If the fiber is not flush with the epoxy, the installer may snag and break the fiber. In addition, the broken fiber may pierce the installer's skin.

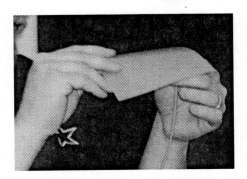

Figure 17-11: Air Polishing of Fiber

## 17.3.14    MULTIMODE POLISH

### 17.3.14.1    CLEAN EQUIPMENT

The installer moistens a lens grade tissue with isopropyl alcohol. He wipes the ferrules of all connectors with this moistened tissue.

The installer can clean his polishing equipment with either lens grade gas or isopropyl alcohol. With lens-grade compressed gas, he cleans off the top surface of the polishing pads, both sides of the polishing films and the polishing tool. With isopropyl alcohol and lens grade tissues, the installer cleans his equipment in a similar manner. He places the polishing films, dull side up, on the pads and the tool on the 3 μm film.[26]

### 17.3.14.2    FIRST POLISH

The installer inserts the connector into the polishing tool. While holding both the connector and the tool (Figure 17-12), he moves the tool in a ½" high, figure-8 pattern slowly. If he feels scratchiness, the fiber is not flush with the adhesive. He maintains a light pressure[27] and a slow, ½" high figure-8 pattern until the scratchiness ceases.

After the scratchiness ceases, the installer increases the size of the figure-8 pattern to cover the entire area of the film. He does not increase the pressure. He continues polishing until the adhesive is completely removed.

---

[26] If you install the connector into the tool and slap the tool against the film, you may break the fiber.

[27] Light pressure means that the installer holds the connector against the film without compressing the spring inside the SC connector.

Figure 17-12: Polishing

The installer may detect a change in the friction of the connector on the film. This change indicates the removal of the last of the adhesive. If he does not detect this change, he removes the connector from the tool periodically. He views the tip of the ferrule by reflecting light off the tip. When the adhesive is completely removed, the tip of the ferrule will be glass smooth and shiny. The tip will have the same appearance as that of the side of the ferrule.

### 17.3.14.3    CLEANING

With lens grade compressed gas or isopropyl alcohol and lens grade tissues, the installer cleans the connector and the polishing tool.

### 17.3.14.4    SECOND POLISH

'High pressure' for polishing means holding the connector in the polishing tool and pushing down the inner housing until the internal spring is fully compressed. The installer need not increase the pressure beyond the level at which the spring is fully compressed.

The installer places the polishing tool on the 1 μm film and applies high pressure to the connector for ten, large figure-8 patterns. Large means using the full area of the polishing film.

### 17.3.14.5    THIRD POLISH

This polish is optional.[28] The installer cleans the connector and polishing tool (17.3.14.3).

---

[28] Some connector manufacturers recommend this third polish. We have found no improvement in multimode loss from this polish. We have found only minor improvement in the microscopic

The installer places the polishing tool on the 0.5 μm film. He inserts the connector in the tool and applies high pressure to the connector for ten, large figure-8 patterns.

## 17.4    SINGLEMODE POLISHING

Use the procedure in 16.3.20.

## 17.5    FINAL CLEANING

The installer slides the boot over the back shell. He cleans the connector with one of the following methods.[29]

### 17.5.1.1    BEST METHOD

The installer moistens a lens grade tissue with isopropyl alcohol. He wipes the sides and tip of the ferrule with this tissue. He sprays a one-inch diameter area of connector cleaner, such as ElectroWash Px, onto a small pad of lens grade tissues. He wipes the tip of the ferrule from the wet area to the dry area three times.

### 17.5.1.2    METHOD B

The installer moistens a lens grade tissue with isopropyl alcohol. He wipes the sides and the tip of the ferrule. Immediately he wipes the tip of the ferrule with a dry lens grade tissue.

### 17.5.1.3    METHOD C

The installer wipes the sides and the tip of the ferrule with a pre-moistened lens grade tissue (Alco Pad or OptiPrep Pad). Immediately, he wipes the tip of the ferrule with a dry lens grade tissue. The installer blows out the connector cap and installs the cap on the ferrule.

## 17.5.2    INSPECT CONNECTOR

After polishing each connector, the installer inspects and rates the connector according to the connector inspection procedure (21). If the connector is good, he installs the cap.

---

appearance. For that reason, we do not recommend it.

[29] Do not use lens grade gas for final cleaning of the connector. This gas tends to leave water marks that can increase loss and reflectance.

If the connector is not good, he attaches a label to indicate a potential problem and installs the cap. If the problem is severe enough to indicate unacceptable loss, he replaces the connector.

## 17.5.3    WHITE LIGHT TEST

When the installer has installed all connectors on the one end of a cable, he performs a white light, continuity test as in 17.3.4.3 (Figure 17-13).

The installer does not install connectors on the opposite end of the cable until all of the fibers have passed this continuity test. If one or more connectors fail this test, he troubleshoots these connectors to determine the problem. An OTDR test may be required.

The installer replaces the caps on all connectors that pass this test. He repeats the continuity test after he installs all connectors on the opposite end of the cable.

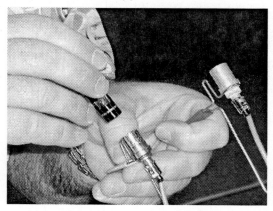

Figure 17-13: White Light Test

## 17.5.4    FINAL ASSEMBLY

The installer slides the boot over the back shell of the connector. The top of the inner housing has missing corners (Figure 17-14). The top of the outer housing has the key. He holds the top of the inner housing and the top of the outer housing up. He inserts the inner housing into the end of the outer housing that is opposite the end with the key (Figure 17-15). He wiggles the inner housing until it snaps through the outer housing (Figure 17-16).

Figure 17-14: Alignment of Inner and Outer Housings For Final Assembly

Figure 17-15: Insertion of Inner Housing

Figure 17-16: Inner Housing Fully Inserted Into Outer Housing

# 17.6   TROUBLESHOOTING

## 17.6.1   INSTALLATION

### 17.6.1.1   FIBER BREAKAGE

Multimode fiber breaks upon insertion or does not fit into connector

Potential cause: dirt or buffer coating on fiber
Action: clean fiber

Potential cause: debris in connector
Action: replace connector[30]

Potential cause: buffer coating not completely removed

---

[30] Prior to injection of adhesive, the installer performs a white light check of connector. If the connector fails this test, he blows out the connector with lens grade gas. If the connector still fails this test, he flushes the connector with isopropyl alcohol injected through connector with a syringe. If connector fails a white light test after being flushed, the installer replaces the connector.

Action: if the fiber appears slightly larger than other fibers, re-strip the fiber

Potential primer has dried
Action: do not delay inserting fiber into connector after wiping primer on fiber

Potential cause: adhesive has partially hardened
Action: fill fewer connectors

### 17.6.1.2   ADHESIVE FLOWS FROM BACK SHELL

Potential cause: excessive adhesive in back shell
Action: after adhesive flows from fiber hole in ferrule, immediately withdraw needle from connector

### 17.6.1.3   ADHESIVE ON OUTSIDE OF BACK SHELL

Potential cause: failure to wipe needle before each use
Action: wipe adhesive from outside of needle before each use

## 17.6.2   POLISHING

### 17.6.2.1   NON-ROUND CORE

Potential cause: incomplete air polishing and abrasive torn from film backing
Action: increase air polish time

Potential cause: excessive pressure during polishing one first film and small bead of adhesive on first film
Action: reduce polishing pressure

Potential cause: all adhesive removed by excessive air polishing and ferrule tip is mirror smooth without any dull or colored film or bead of adhesive
Action: reduce air polish time

### 17.6.2.2   EXCESSIVE POLISHING TIME ON FINAL FILM

Potential cause: film worn out
Action: replace film

### 17.6.2.3   EXCESSIVE POLISHING TIME

Potential cause: insufficient polishing pressure
Action: increase polishing pressure

Potential cause: film worn out
Action: replace film

#### 17.6.2.4    NO APPARENT REDUCTION OF BEAD SIZE

Potential cause: dirt in ferrule hole of polishing tool

Action: clean hole in polishing tool with lens grade air or with pipe cleaner dipped in isopropyl alcohol

#### 17.6.2.5    A FEW CORE AND CLADDING SCRATCHES

Potential cause: contamination of film by environment

Action: replace film; move polishing location away from air vents or any other source of airborne dust

Potential cause: incomplete polishing
Action: complete polishing

#### 17.6.2.6    ADHESIVE SMEARS ON FIBER DURING POLISHING

Potential cause: adhesive past its expiration date

Action: replace adhesive

#### 17.6.2.7    CRACKED FIBER

Potential cause: excessive pressure during scribing

Action: scratch fiber lightly during scribing

### 17.6.3    SINGLEMODE POLISHING

See 16.4.3.

## 17.7    SUMMARY

This summary is in three parts, one each for connector installation, multimode polishing and singlemode polishing.

### 17.7.1    INSTALLATION

Install cable through enclosure

Pull cable through enclosure to work surface

Remove jacket

Install boots

Install crimp sleeves on jacketed fibers

Trim strength members to proper lengths

Strip buffer tube

Perform cable continuity test

Transfer adhesive to syringe

Clean the fiber

Optional step: perform a white light test

Optional step: perform a dry fit

Inject adhesive

Wipe primer onto fiber and end of buffer tube

While twisting, insert fiber into connector

Slide crimp sleeve over back shell

Crimp crimp sleeve

Wipe fiber with primer

Scribe fiber

Remove excess fiber

Air polish excess fiber flush with adhesive bead

### 17.7.2    MULTIMODE POLISH

Clean connector

Clean pads, films and polishing tool

Polish on 3 µm film

Clean connector and polishing tool

Polish on 1 µm film

Clean connector and polishing tool

Optional: polish on 0.5 µm film

### 17.7.3    FINISH INSTALLATION

Clean connector

Inspect connector

White light cable test

Install outer housing

Clean and install cap

# 18 CONNECTOR INSTALLATION: HOT MELT ADHESIVE

Chapter Objectives: by following the procedures in this chapter, you will install multimode, Hot Melt adhesive, ST-compatible connectors with low loss and high reliability on either jacketed fibers or premises cable.

## 18.1 INTRODUCTION

This chapter applies to the installation of multimode, Hot Melt ST-™ compatible connectors onto four types of cables. Three of the cables, single fiber, zip cord duplex and break out, have a 3 mm jacket on each fiber. Because of this design characteristic, we refer to these cables as having 'jacketed fibers'. The fourth type of cable, a premises cable, has a 900 μm tight buffer tube.

This method of connector installation is a hot melt adhesive that is preloaded into the connector. The connector requires pre-heating prior to and cooling after installation. This method reduces installation time. This method allows for salvage of damaged connectors through reheating. In addition, the preloaded adhesive creates a bead of adhesive on the tip of the ferrule with a predetermined size. These latter two characteristics enable the novice installer to achieve high process yield.[1]

## 18.2 MATERIALS AND SUPPLIES[2]

For installation of these connectors, the installer requires a Hot Melt connector installation tool kit, which includes the following:[3]

> - 3M HOT MELT, ST-compatible multimode connectors, part number 6100

- Work mat (Clauss Fiber-Safe™)
- Tubing cutter (Ideal 45-162)
- Kevlar scissors (with ceramic blade)[4]
- Miller buffer tube and primary coating stripper (FO-103-S) or Clauss NoNik stripper (NN203)
- Hot Melt™ cooling stand
- Hot Melt™ holders for ST™-compatible connectors
- Hot Melt™ oven
- 2 μm polishing film for Hot Melt™ connectors (FIS, 3M part number 51144 85932, 254X Imperial, 6192A)
- Lens grade tissue (Kim-Wipes™ or equivalent)
- 99% isopropyl alcohol (Fiber Instrument Sales (FIS))
- Alternative to isopropyl alcohol: Alco pads or Opti-Prep Pads
- Connector cleaner (Electro WashPx, from ITC Chemtronics)
- Wedge scriber (Corning Cable Systems Ruby Scribe, 3233304-01)
- Small plastic bottle (for bare fiber collection)
- Lens grade compressed gas (Stoner part number 94203 or equivalent)
- ST-compatible polishing tool (FIS or FOCI)
- Two hard rubber polishing pads,[5] (FIS part number PP 575)

---

[1] Typical yield by first-time installers is 90 %.

[2] We have chosen some of these tools and supplies on the basis of their superior performance. We have chosen others on the basis of their prices. Finally, we have chosen some of these tools and supplies based on their convenience.

[3] Sources of equipment and supplies: Fiber Optic Center Inc. (FOCI), 800-ISFIBER and Fiber Instrument Sales (FIS), 800-5000-FIS.

[4] Scissors with ceramic blades provide the best results, but have the highest cost.

[5] Use one pad for each polishing film, except for the air polish film.

---

➢ 12 µm polishing film (FOCI part number AO-12-F-91-3N)

➢ For multimode polishing: 1.0 µ polishing film (FOCI part numbers AO-1-T-91-3N)

➢ 400 x connector inspection microscope with ST-compatible or SC fixture (Westover Scientific)

## 18.3    PROCEDURE

### 18.3.1    PREINSTALL CABLE

The installer installs the cable into the enclosure without permanently attaching the cable to the enclosure. He pulls the cable out of the enclosure to a work surface near the enclosure.

### 18.3.2    SET UP OVEN

The installer turns on the preheating oven and allows it to heat up for at least 15 minutes. He assembles the cooling stand (Figure 18-1).

Figure 18-1: Hot Melt Cooling Stand

### 18.3.3    LOAD HOLDERS

The installer removes the connector parts from the packages. He aligns the key of a connector with the slot in a connector holder. He slides the connector into the holder. He rotates the retaining nut so that the holder retains the connector (Figure 18-2). The installer loads 4-6 connectors into holders. He places the holders into the cooling stand.

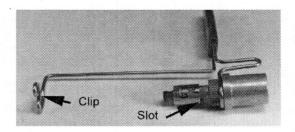

Figure 18-2: Loaded Connector Holder

## 18.3.4    REMOVE OUTER JACKET

#### 18.3.4.1    PREMISES CABLE

The installer removes the outer jacket of a premises cable (15.7.2).

#### 18.3.4.2    BREAKOUT CABLE

The installer removes the outer jacket of a breakout cable (15.7.1). [6]

## 18.3.5    INSTALL BOOTS

#### 18.3.5.1    PREMISES CABLE

The installer installs the boot and a clear flexible tubing on each buffer tube. He pushes the boots and tubes approximately 12" away from end of buffer tubes. He marks the length of buffer tube to be removed (Figure 18-3).

▬▬▬▬▬▬▬

Strip this much bare fiber (1.06")

Figure 18-3: Template of Strip Length For Premises Cable[6]

#### 18.3.5.2    BREAKOUT AND SIMPLEX CABLE

The installer installs the boots on all fibers to be terminated. The installer installs the small end of the boot first. He pushes the boots approximately 12" away from end of cable.

#### 18.3.5.3    ZIP CORD DUPLEX

The installer separates the two channels by pulling the channels apart. If necessary, the installer can cut the thin web that connects the channels.

---

[6] This figure is to scale.

## 18.3.6    PREPARE END

The installer repeats this step for all fibers to be terminated at this location.

### 18.3.6.1    PREMISES CABLE

The installer can use a No Nik Stripper. The installer cleans the stripper by holding the stripper open and snapping each cap once (Figure 18-4).[7] The installer grips the cable or buffer tube firmly. The installer can grip the cable by wrapping the cable around one finger 5 times (Figure 18-5) or by weaving the cable through his fingers.

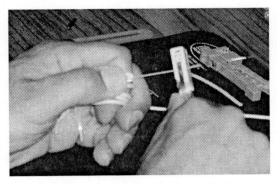

Figure 18-5: Fiber Straight In Stripper

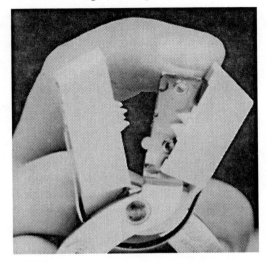

Figure 18-4: Cleaning of Clauss Stripper

The installer places the stripper on the buffer tube at the marked distance (Figure 18-3) or 1/2" from the end of the buffer tube, whichever is shorter.[8]

While holding the stripper at 90° to the fiber (Figure 18-5), the installer pulls the stripper towards the end of the fiber slowly. He allows the buffer tube and primary coating to slide from the fiber. He does not force the buffer tube and primary coating from the fiber.

The installer can use a Miller Stripper. The installer cleans the stripper with lens grade gas. The installer grips the cable or buffer tube firmly. The installer can grip the cable by wrapping the cable around one finger 5 times (Figure 18-5) or by weaving the cable through his fingers.

The installer places the stripper on the buffer tube at the marked distance or at 1/2" from the end of the buffer tube, whichever is shorter.[10] He holds the stripper at 45° to the fiber. He pulls the stripper slowly towards the end of the fiber, allowing the buffer tube to slide from the fiber. He does not force the buffer tube and primary coating from the fiber.

If necessary, the installer repeats this step until the length of buffer tube is as indicated in Figure 18-6 or the length of bare fiber is as indicated in Figure 18-3. He inspects the fiber to ensure that there is no buffer tube or primary coating remaining on the fiber.

### 18.3.6.2    JACKETED FIBERS

### 18.3.6.2.1    REMOVE JACKET

The installer removes the inner jacket by placing the tubing cutter at the distance from the cable end (Figure 18-7). He rotates the cutter around the cable once or twice. He removes the cutter[9] and slides the jacket from the buffer tube and aramid yarn.

---

[7] Occasionally, this method of cleaning the Clauss stripper does not work. In that case, the installer may blow out the stripper with lens grade gas.

[8] This instruction indicates a maximum strip length of 1/2". US-made fiber optic cables can be stripped to at least this distance. Some cables allow a longer strip length without breakage. For such cables, you may strip to that increased distance. Few cables allow more than 1.5 ".

---

[9] The installer does not pull the jacket from the cable with the jacket cutter.

Remove 1.25" of jacket

Leave 0.1875" of buffer tube beyond jacket

Leave 0.1875" of aramid yarn beyond jacket

Figure 18-6: Template of Strip Lengths For
Jacketed Fiber[10]

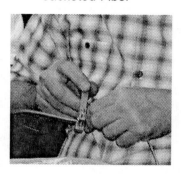

Figure 18-7: Tubing Cutter On Cable

### 18.3.6.2.2    STRIP BUFFER TUBE

The installer holds the aramid yarns back
against the remaining jacket. He marks the
buffer tube length of to be left (Figure 18-6).
He strips the buffer tube and primary coating
as in 18.3.6.1.

### 18.3.6.2.3    TRIM STRENGTH MEMBERS

The installer separates the aramid yarn from
the buffer tube. He twists the yarn. He cuts
the yarn to the length in Figure 18-6 (Figure
18-8).[11]

### 18.3.6.3    CABLE CONTINUITY TEST

The installer holds a high intensity light
source against one end of the cable. An
associate at the opposite end views the
fibers. Each fiber should glow, indicating
continuity.[12]

---

[10] These dimensions are to scale.

[11] Some connectors allow trimming the strength
member as the second step. For such
connectors, the strength members are shorter
than the buffer tube.

[12] This test is optional, but recommended. This
test works on both multimode and singlemode
fibers to several thousand feet.

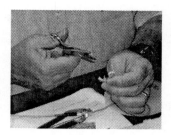

Figure 18-8: Cutting Aramid Yarn To Length

### 18.3.6.4    FIBER STRENGTH TEST

The installer pushes each fiber against a
lens grade tissue on the work surface.[13] If
the fiber bends without breaking, the
installer has not damaged the cladding. If
there is a single defect on the cladding, the
fiber will break.

## 18.3.7    CLEAN FIBER

The installer performs this step for each fiber
just prior to inserting it into a connector. The
installer moistens a lens grade tissue with
isopropyl alcohol. He folds the moist area of
the tissue around the fiber. He pulls the fiber
through the fold twice (Figure 18-9). He
inspects the fiber for particles on the
cladding. There should be none. If
necessary, he cleans the fiber until the
cladding is free of all visible particles.

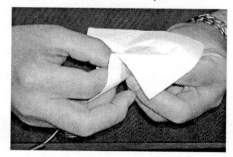

Figure 18-9: Cleaning of Fiber With Moist
Tissue

## 18.3.8    INSTALL
CONNECTOR

The installer repeats this step for all fibers at
this location. He places the connector
holders into the oven so that the wide flange
of the holder rests against the oven-heating

---

[13] The installer should not push a bare fiber
against his finger. Doing so can result in the fiber
penetrating the skin and breaking.

block (Figure 18-10). If the hot melt adhesive bubbles out of the back shell, he discards the connector.[14] After allowing the connector to heat for one minute, he removes one holder from the oven. He verifies that the boot and clear tubing are still on the jacket or buffer tube.

> Caution: the holders are hot enough to burn your fingers severely!

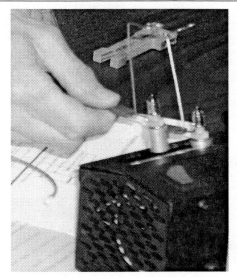

Figure 18-10: Connectors In Preheating Oven

The installer holds the connector holder so that he can insert the cable into the back shell of the connector. He holds the cable near the end of the jacket or the end of the buffer tube. While twisting the cable or buffer tube back and forth slowly, he inserts the end of the fiber into the back shell of the connector. As long as the fiber continues feeding into the back shell without bending, he continues twisting and inserting the fiber into the connector.

For a jacketed fiber, the jacket will enter the back shell. The aramid yarn will fold over the jacket and enter the back shell. A small drop of hot melt adhesive may come out of the back shell.

If the fiber bends, the installer withdraws the fiber 1/8", twists the fiber back and forth and inserts the fiber into the back shell. When the buffer tube stops further motion of the

---

[14] The connector has absorbed excessive moisture.

fiber into the ferrule (Figure 18-11), he presses the cable into a 'V' area of the holding clip (Figure 18-12).

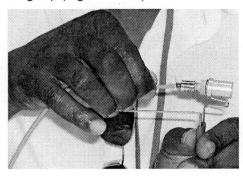

Figure 18-11: Cable Inserted Into Connector

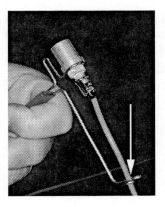

Figure 18-12: Cable in Clip

For a premises cable, the installer slides the clear tubing into the back shell and the boot over the tubing and back shell. Without putting tension on the buffer tube, he places the holder in the cooling stand.

## 18.3.9  REMOVE EXCESS FIBER

The installer touches the holder carefully to ensure that it is cool enough to handle. Without breaking the fiber protruding beyond the bead of adhesive, the installer removes the connector from the holder. He should see the fiber protruding beyond the bead of adhesive.

While resting his hands together, he places the wedge surface of a scriber onto the end of the ferrule (Figure 18-13). He moves the blade of the scriber up to the fiber so that the scriber gently touches the fiber. The fiber should not move or bend.

Figure 18-13: Scribing the Excess Fiber[15]

The installer moves the scriber back and forth along the fiber 1/16" once. He should not break the fiber with the scriber. He should not 'saw' the fiber with the scriber.

The installer holds the connector with the fiber pointing up. He grips the ferrule with his thumb and forefinger lightly. He slides his thumb and forefinger up the ferrule towards and over the fiber. He grips and pulls the fiber away from the tip of the connector. The fiber should break easily. He places of the fiber in the fiber collection bottle.

If the fiber does not break, the installer scribed the hot melt adhesive on the fiber and not the fiber. He repeats this step until the fiber breaks.

## 18.3.10    AIR POLISHING

The installer holds the connector with the ferrule pointing up. He holds a 12 µm polishing film at one edge with the abrasive side[16] down. He places the opposite edge of the film above the connector. He curls the front and back edges of the film down. He rubs the film against connector until the fiber is flush with the bead of adhesive (Figure 18-14).[17] If he scribed the fiber just above the surface of the adhesive bead, this step will take less than 10 seconds.

---

[15] We have shown the SC connector.

[16] The abrasive side is dull.

[17] Do not remove all the adhesive.

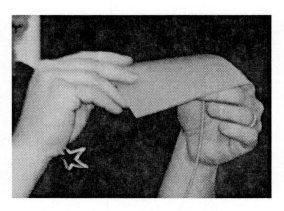

Figure 18-14: Air Polishing of Fiber

The installer checks the fiber by bringing a finger down onto the tip of the ferrule from the top.[18] If he cannot feel the fiber, the fiber is flush, or nearly flush, with the epoxy.

## 18.3.11    MULTIMODE POLISHING

### 18.3.11.1    CLEAN EQUIPMENT

The installer moistens a lens grade tissue with isopropyl alcohol. He wipes the ferrules of all connectors with this tissue.

The installer can clean his polishing equipment with either lens grade gas or isopropyl alcohol. With lens-grade compressed gas, he cleans off the top surface of the polishing pads, both sides of the 2 µm and 1 µm polishing films and the polishing tool. With isopropyl alcohol and lens grade tissues, the installer cleans his equipment in a similar manner. He places the polishing films, dull side up, on the pads and the tool on the 2 µm film.[19]

### 18.3.11.2    FIRST POLISH

The installer inserts the connector into the polishing tool. While holding both the connector and the tool (Figure 18-15), he moves the tool in a ½" high, figure-8 pattern slowly. If he feels scratchiness, the fiber is not flush with the adhesive. He maintains a

---

[18] Do not rub a finger across the tip of the ferrule. If the fiber is not flush with the epoxy, you may snag and break the fiber. In addition, the broken fiber may pierce your skin.

[19] If you install the connector into the tool and slap the tool against the film, you may break the fiber.

light pressure and a slow, ½" high figure 8 pattern until the scratchiness ceases.

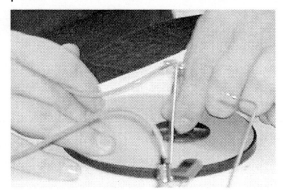

Figure 18-15: Polishing

After the scratchiness stops, the installer increases the size of the figure-8 pattern to cover the entire area of the film. He does not increase the pressure or the speed. He continues polishing until the adhesive is completely removed.

The installer may detect a change in the friction of the connector on the film. This change indicates the removal of the last of the adhesive. If he does not detect this change, he removes the connector from the tool periodically. He examines the tip of the ferrule by viewing it with light reflecting off the tip. When the adhesive is completely removed, the tip of the ferrule will be glass smooth and shiny, with the same appearance as that of the side of the ferrule.

### 18.3.11.3   CONNECTOR CLEANING

With lens grade compressed gas or isopropyl alcohol and lens grade tissues, the installer cleans the connector, and the polishing tool.

### 18.3.11.4   OPTIONAL SECOND POLISH[20]

'High pressure' for polishing means holding the connector by its retaining nut and pushing down the retaining nut[21] until the

---

[20] We recommend this optional second polish, because it will improve the microscopic appearance of the connector and simplify microscopic inspection. This second polish but will not reduce multimode loss.

[21] For an SC connector, the installer pushes the inner housing down until the inner spring is fully compressed.

internal spring is fully compressed. The installer need not increase the pressure beyond the level at which the spring is fully compressed.

The installer applies high pressure to the connector for ten, large figure 8 patterns. Large means using the full area of the polishing film.

## 18.4   FINAL CLEANING

The installer cleans the connector with one of the following methods.

### 18.4.1.1   BEST CLEANING METHOD

The installer moistens a lens grade tissue with isopropyl alcohol. He wipes the sides and tip of the ferrule with this tissue. He sprays a one-inch diameter area of connector cleaner, such as ElectroWash Px, onto a small pad of lens grade tissues. He wipes the tip of the ferrule from the wet area to the dry area three times.

### 18.4.1.2   CLEANING METHOD B

The installer moistens a lens grade tissue with isopropyl alcohol. He wipes the sides and the tip of the ferrule. Immediately he wipes the tip of the ferrule with a dry lens grade tissue.

### 18.4.1.3   CLEANING METHOD C

The installer wipes the sides and the tip of the ferrule with a pre-moistened lens grade tissue (Alco Pad or OptiPrep Pad). Immediately, he wipes the tip of the ferrule with a dry lens grade tissue.

## 18.4.2   INSPECT CONNECTOR

After cleaning, the installer blows out the connector cap. He places the cap on the ferrule. For a jacketed fiber, he slides the boot over the back shell.

The installer inspects and rates the connector according to the connector inspection procedure (21). If the connector is good, he installs the cap. If the connector is not good, he attaches a label to indicate a potential problem, or he replaces it. After inspection, he installs the cap.

### 18.4.3 WHITE LIGHT TEST

When the installer has installed all connectors on the one end of a cable, he performs a white light, continuity test as in 18.3.6.3 (Figure 18-16).

The installer does not install connectors on the opposite end until all of the fibers have passed this continuity test. If one or more connectors fail this test, he troubleshoots these connectors to determine the problem. An OTDR test may be required.

The installer replaces the caps on all connectors that pass this test. He performs a second continuity test after he installs connectors on the opposite end.

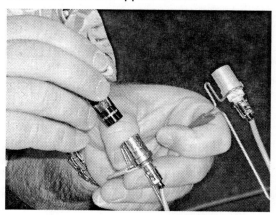

Figure 18-16: White Light Test

## 18.5 SALVAGE

### 18.5.1 PROCEDURE

When the installer installs the Hot Melt, ST™-compatible and SC connectors onto premises cables or the ST-™ compatible on 3 mm jacketed cables, he can reheat the connector to repair damage.

To salvage a damaged fiber end, the installer reheats the connector, removes the cable, re-prepares the cable end, and inserts the new end. A new end is ready for polishing.

This salvage procedure requires a subtle change to the scribing technique. When scribing, the installer holds the scriber so that the blade touches the fiber slightly above the surface of the ferrule. After scribing, he repeats the procedure (18.3.9-18.4.3).

This salvage procedure requires a subtle change to the polishing procedure. The installer uses a very light pressure, a ½" high 'figure 8' movement, and a very slow 'figure 8' movement. This new end may have a very small adhesive bead to support the fiber during polishing.

### 18.5.2 ALTERNATE FIBER INSERTION METHOD

The installer can eliminate the re-preparation for salvage by modifying the technique in 18.3.8. Instead of fully inserting the cable, he inserts the cable fully, and then withdraws the cable by approximately 1/16". This modification leaves extra bare fiber buried in the adhesive. After reheating, he pushes this extra fiber through the ferrule to create a new end for polishing.

With this alternate method, the installer must use an extremely light polishing pressure and slow polishing movement, since there will be essentially no adhesive on the ferrule tip for support of the fiber.

## 18.6 TROUBLESHOOTING

### 18.6.1 INSTALLATION

#### 18.6.1.1 FIBER BREAKAGE

Multimode fiber breaks upon insertion into connector
Potential cause: dirt or buffer coating on fiber
Action: clean fiber

Fiber breaks or does not fit into connector

Potential cause: buffer coating not completely removed
Action: if the fiber appears larger than other fibers, restrip the fiber[22]

Fiber breaks or does not fit into connector.
Potential cause: adhesive is too cool for insertion.
Action: reheat connector

#### 18.6.1.2 ADHESIVE FLOWS FROM BACK SHELL

Potential cause: moisture in adhesive

---

[22] In this case, the inner of the two primary coatings has not been removed.

Action: discard connector

## 18.6.2    POLISHING

### 18.6.2.1    NON-ROUND CORE

Potential cause: broken fiber due to excessive polishing pressure
Action: check the 2 µm polishing film. If abrasive has been torn from backing, fiber protruding above adhesive snagged on film and broke. Increase air polish time

Potential cause: excessive pressure during polishing sheared off bead of adhesive
Check 2 µm film for small bead of adhesive
Action: reduce polishing pressure

Potential cause: all adhesive removed by excessive air polishing
Action: check the connector before final polishing. If the tip of the ferrule is mirror smooth without any dull or colored film or bead of adhesive, no adhesive remains
Action: reduce air polish time

### 18.6.2.2    EXCESSIVE POLISHING TIME ON EITHER FILM

Potential cause: film worn out
Action: replace film

### 18.6.2.3    EXCESSIVE POLISHING TIME

Potential cause: insufficient polishing pressure
Action: increase polishing pressure

Potential cause: film worn out
Action: replace film

### 18.6.2.4    NO APPARENT REDUCTION OF BEAD SIZE

Potential cause: dirt in ferrule hole of polishing tool prevents tip of ferrule from contacting film
Action: clean hole in polishing tool with lens grade air or with pipe cleaner dipped in isopropyl alcohol

### 18.6.2.5    A FEW CORE AND CLADDING SCRATCHES

Potential cause: contamination of film by environment
Action: replace film.[23]

---

[23] Clean film only if no replacement film is available.

Action: move polishing location away from air vents or any other source of airborne dust

### 18.6.2.6    A FEW SCRATCHES ON CORE

Scratches extend across core and cladding

Potential cause: contamination of film
Action: replace film

Potential cause: incomplete polishing
Action: complete polishing

### 18.6.2.7    CRACKED FIBER

Potential cause: excessive pressure during scribing
Action: scratch fiber lightly during scribing

### 18.6.2.8    HIGH LOSS

With no cause apparent from microscopic inspection

Potential cause: over polished on either film.
Action: polish of 2 µm film only until adhesive is gone. Polish on the 1 µm film for 10 strokes

## 18.7    ONE PAGE SUMMARY

This summary is in two parts, one each for connector installation and multimode polishing

## 18.7.1    INSTALLATION

Install cable through enclosure

Pull cable through enclosure to work surface

Set up oven and cooling stand

Load connectors into holders

Remove jacket, Kevlar and central strength member to proper lengths

Install boots on all buffer tubes

Remove buffer tubes with Miller stripper to proper lengths

Preheat connector

Perform cable continuity test

Preheat connector

Clean the fiber with lens grade tissue and isopropyl alcohol

With rotation connector, insert fiber into back shell until fiber bottoms out against ferrule

Do not allow fiber to bend

For jacketed cable and SC connectors, slide the crimp sleeve or boot over back shell [24]

For jacketed fibers, press the jacket into the clip of the connector holder

Crimp the crimp sleeve with the crimper

Scribe and remove the excess fiber

Air polish the excess fiber flush with the adhesive

Proceed to multimode or singlemode polishing procedure

## 18.7.2    MULTIMODE POLISHING

Clean all connectors

Clean the connector ferrule, pad, film and tool Place 2 μm film on the pad and the tool on the film

Install the connector into the tool

Polish in a ½" high figure 8 pattern with light pressure until the scratchiness ceases

When scratchiness ceases, polish in large figure 8 pattern with light pressure until all the adhesive is gone Polish the connector using the entire area of the film

Clean the 1 μm film, the tool and the connector

Install the connector into the tool With high pressure, make 10 large figure 8 motions

Clean the side and tip of the connector

Clean and install the cap

Inspect the connector

Perform a white light test of the cable

After installing connectors on the second end, perform a white light test of the cable

---

[24] For premises cable, insert the clear tubing into the back shell and slide the boot over the back shell.

# 19 CONNECTOR INSTALLATION: CLEAVE AND CRIMP #1

Chapter Objectives: from this chapter, you will learn how to install a 'cleave and crimp, SC connector on 62.5 µm, premises cable and achieve low loss and low cost.

## 19.1   INTRODUCTION

The 'cleave and leave' method, otherwise know as the 'cleave and crimp' method, requires neither adhesive nor polishing. As a result, this no epoxy, no polish method has the lowest installation time and the simplest installation procedure. However, this simplicity conceals the subtleties that, when ignored, can result in high power loss and high installation cost.

This connector is known as the LightCrimp Plus™ SC Simplex Multimode connector. TYCO/AMP NETCONNECT manufactures this connector.

## 19.2   TOOLS AND SUPPLIES REQUIRED

The installer needs a connector installation tool kit that includes the following items:

- Premises cable with 62.5 µm fiber[1]
- SC connectors with 62.5 µm fiber, TYCO/AMP NETCONNECT SC connectors, 62.5 µm, part number 492643-1
- Work mat (Clauss Fiber-Safe™)
- Tubing cutter (Ideal 45-162)
- Kevlar scissors (with ceramic blade)[2]
- Miller buffer tube and primary coating stripper (FO-103-S) or Clauss NoNik stripper (NN203)
- Cable holder assembly, part number 1278023-1 (Figure 19-1)

---

[1] The installer may use 50 µm cable as long as he uses the 50 µm connectors. The TYCO/AMP NETCONNECT SC connector with standard 50 µm fiber is part number 1278079-(1). The part number for laser optimized 50 µm fiber is 1588291-1.

[2] Scissors with ceramic blades provide the best results, but have the highest cost.

- Lens grade tissue
- 98% isopropyl alcohol
- Small plastic bottle (for bare fiber collection)
- Lens grade compressed gas (Stoner 94203 or equivalent)
- Crimper/ installation tool, TYCO/AMP NETCONNECT part number 492782-1 (Figure 19-2)
- Optional: Alco pads or Opti-Prep Pads

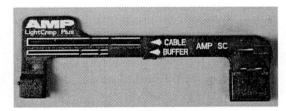

Figure 19-1: LightCrimp™ Holder Assembly

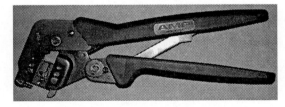

Figure 19-2: LightCrimp™ Crimper Tool

## 19.3   PROCEDURE

For field installation, the installer repeats this procedure for all connectors to be installed at this location. He repeats this procedure for all connectors on the opposite end. For training, the installer performs this procedure for one connector. He repeats this procedure on the same color buffer tube at the opposite end of the cable.

### 19.3.1   INSTALL CABLE

The installer installs the cable into the enclosure without attaching the cable to the enclosure. He pulls the cable out through

---

the front of the enclosure to a horizontal work surface. He removes the jacket and trims both the central and flexible strength members to the lengths specified in the instructions for the enclosure (15). If necessary, he untwists the buffer tubes.

## 19.3.2 PREPARE BUFFER TUBES

The installer installs boots on all buffer tubes. He pushes the boots 10-12" from the ends of the buffer tubes. He places one buffer tube into the groove labeled 'buffer' of the cable holder assembly. He marks the buffer tube at the two locations of the cross grooves (Figure 19-3).

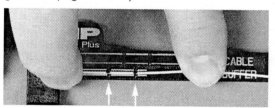

Figure 19-3: Marked Buffer Tube

## 19.3.3 STRIP BUFFER TUBE

To strip the buffer tube and primary coating to the mark closest to the end of the fiber (15.7.2), the installer wraps the buffer tube around one finger several times, or weaves it through the fingers of one hand. He cleans the stripper. He places the stripper on the buffer tube at no more than ½" from the end of the buffer tube. He holds the Miller stripper at an angle of about 45°.[3] He pulls slowly, allowing the buffer tube to slide from the fiber. He repeats this stripping procedure in ½" increments until he has stripped the buffer tube to the mark closest to the end of the fiber.

## 19.3.4 LOAD HOLDER

The installer empties the contents of the connector package. He removes the covers from the ferrule and the back shell of the connector. He places the connector in the 'U' shaped end of the cable holder with the flat side of the connector facing away from the holder. He slides the connector into the holder as far as possible (Figure 19-4).

---

[3] For the procedure, see 15.7.1.4.

Figure 19-5 and Figure 19-6 illustrate improper placement of the connector the holder.

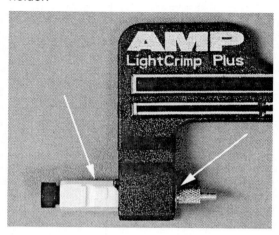

Figure 19-4: Properly Inserted Connector

Figure 19-5: Incompletely Inserted Connector

Figure 19-6: Connector Upside Down In Holder

## 19.3.5 PREPARE CLEAVER

The installer opens the two covers of the CT07 cleaver (Figure 19-7). Before the first and after every tenth cleave,[4] he blows out the grooves of the cleaver with lens grade gas.

The installer lifts the breaking arm (Figure 19-7) and moves the scribing blade to the start position (Figure 19-8), which is close to the hinge of the outer cover.

---

[4] This cleaning frequency is suggested. Choose the frequency that provides consistent low angle cleaves.

### 19.3.6    CLEAN FIBER

The installer moistens a lens grade tissue with isopropyl alcohol. He drags the fiber through a fold in the moistened area twice. After cleaning the fiber, he does not touch it (16.3.7).

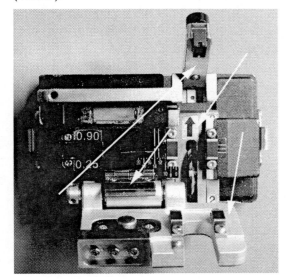

Figure 19-7: Cleaver Set Up

### 19.3.7    CLEAVE FIBER

The installer places the end of the buffer tube at the cleave length of 8.0 ± 0.5 mm (Figure 19-9). He closes the inner cover. If necessary, he adjusts the end of the buffer tube to 8 ± 0.5 mm. He closes the outer cover (Figure 19-10). He lowers the breaking arm.[5]

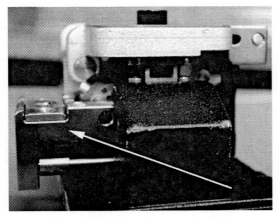

Figure 19-8: Scribing Arm In Starting Position

---

[5] Do not drop the breaking arm.

The installer pushes the scribing blade under the fiber once in the direction of the arrow (Figure 19-9). With the tip of his finger, he pushes down on the breaking arm (Figure 19-11) until the outer cover pops up (Figure 19-12).

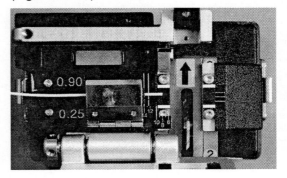

Figure 19-9: Cleaver With Fiber At 8 mm

Figure 19-10: Outer Cover Closed

Figure 19-11: Proper Method Of Pushing Breaking Arm

The installer holds the buffer tube. He lifts the outer cover. He places the broken fiber in the fiber collection bottle. He opens the inner cover. He removes the cleaved fiber from the cleaver.[6]

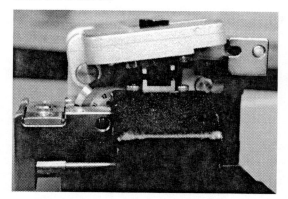

Figure 19-12: Outer Cover Position After Fiber Cleaved

## 19.3.8    INSTALL BUFFER TUBE IN HOLDER

The installer opens the cable clamp of the cable holder assembly. He positions the buffer inside the clamp with the cleaved end facing the connector. He moves the buffer tube so that the end of the fiber is even with the front of the arm of the cable holder assembly (Figure 19-13). While holding the buffer in place, he closes the clamp.

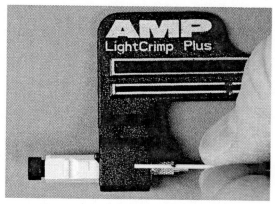

Figure 19-13: Position Of Buffer Tube In Holder Assembly

## 19.3.9    INSTALL FIBER IN CONNECTOR

While holding the fiber near the end of the buffer tube, and without hitting the end of the

fiber against anything,[7] the installer feeds the fiber into the plunger tube at the end of the back shell until the fiber butts against the internal fiber (Figure 19-14).

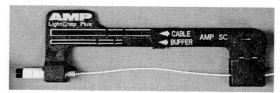

Figure 19-14: Initial Appearance Of Buffer Tube In Connector

The installer checks the mark on the buffer tube: it should be inside the back shell. If the mark does not enter the back shell or if the fiber does not seem to bottom against the internal fiber, he withdraws the fiber 1/8". Then, while rotating the fiber, he re-inserts the fiber. If this reinsertion does not result in the mark entering the plunger, he cuts off the fiber and repeats the end preparation and cleaving.

| Caution |
| --- |
| Do not remove the connector from the cable holder until after the two crimping actions. |

The installer opens the clip slightly. He pulls the buffer tube through the clip on the holder towards the connector until the buffer tube bends and is against the cable holder (Figure 19-15).

Figure 19-15: Bent Buffer Tube Before Crimping

## 19.3.10   CRIMP CONNECTOR

The installer fully compresses and releases the crimper. He closes the tool handles slowly until he hears two clicks from the ratchet. With one hand, he holds the crimper open fully. With his other hand holding the cable holder, he guides the ferrule of the

---

[6] If the installer drops the fiber or places the fiber onto any surface, he repeats the end preparation and cleaving process.

[7] Do not touch the end of the fiber against the connector. Doing so may contaminate the end, resulting in an unacceptable, high loss connector.

connector into the right cavity of the crimper (Figure 19-16).

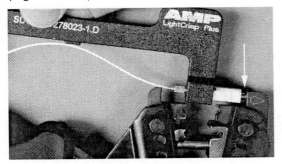

Figure 19-16: Initial Position Of Connector In Crimper

The installer positions the back shell of the connector between the sides of the left jaw of the crimper. He pushes the buffer tube gently into the connector to make sure the fiber remains fully inserted in the plunger.

Without catching the knurled area of the connector back shell with the sides on the crimper (Figure 19-17), the installer squeezes the tool handles together slowly (Figure 19-18) until the ratchet releases and the tool handles open.

The installer removes the connector from the crimper. He places the plunger (with the knurled region) into the crimp nest with two diameters (Figure 19-19). This nest is closest to the open end of the crimper jaws. He closes the crimper slowly until the ratchet releases. He allows the handles to open fully. He removes the connector assembly from the crimp nest.

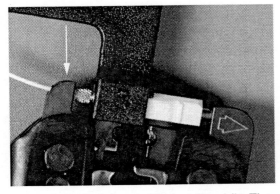

Figure 19-17: Crimper 'Wings' Straddle The Back Shell

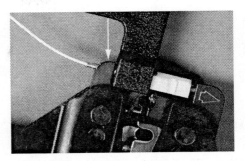

Figure 19-18: First Crimp Completed[8]

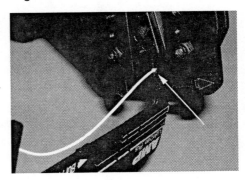

Figure 19-19: Second Crimp

## 19.3.11   FINISH ASSEMBLY

He slides the boot up the buffer tube and over the back shell of the connector until the boot butts against the inner housing (Figure 19-20).

The installer removes the connector from the cable holder. He holds the connector with the chamfered edges up and the outer housing with the key up (Figure 19-20). He slides the inner housing into the outer housing from the end of the outer housing opposite the end with the key. He slides the inner housing into the outer housing until the inner housing snaps through the opposite end of the outer housing (Figure 19-21). With lens grade air, the installer blows out the ferrule cap. He installs the cap onto the ferrule.

Figure 19-20: Boot Installed and Outer Housing Aligned

---

[8] Note: The arrows marked on the front die indicate the direction that the ferrule must point when the connector is positioned in that cavity.

Figure 19-21: Assembled Connector

## 19.4    TROUBLESHOOTING

### 19.4.1    PROCESS MARK OUTSIDE LEAD IN TUBE

Potential cause: broken fiber
Action: pull fiber through stripper without bending fiber

Potential cause: dirty fiber
Action: clean fiber before cleaving; do not clean fiber after cleaving; do not place fiber on any surface prior to inserting fiber into connector;

### 19.4.2    HIGH LOSS

Potential cause: contamination of fiber from placing of surface or touching fiber after cleaving
Action: do not place fiber on any surface or touch fiber after cleaving
Symptom: high loss

Potential cause: dirty, worn or damaged scribing blade
Action: clean blade; if problem persists, replace blade

Potential cause: dirt on end of fiber
Action: install in environment which does not have floating dust or particles in air; do not touch end of fiber; do not clean fiber after cleaving; do not place fiber on any surface prior to inserting fiber into back shell

Potential cause: dirt on fiber
Action: clean fiber prior to cleaving; clean cleaver grooves

## 19.5    SUMMARY

Install cable into enclosure

Prepare cable end

Install boots

Using cable holder, mark the buffer tubes in two locations

Strip the buffer tube and primary coating to the first mark

Remove the two caps from the connector

Install the connector into the cable holder

Clean the cleaver before the first cleave and after every tenth cleave

Clean the bare fiber

Install the fiber into the cleaver with the end of the buffer tube at 8 ±0.5mm

Scribe and cleave the fiber at 8 ±0.5mm

Install the buffer tube into the clip of the cable holder so that the end of the fiber is at the opposite end of holder from the clip

Insert the fiber into the lead in tube

Feed additional buffer tube into the clip so that the buffer tube bows to contact the cable holder

Using the cable holder, install the ferrule of the connector into crimp tool

Without catching the knurled area of the back shell, crimp the connector

Remove the connector from the crimp tool

Reinstall the back shell of the connector into the crimp tool in the area with two diameters

Crimp the back shell of the connector

Slide the boot over the back shell

Align the beveled surface of the connector and the key of the outer housing in the up position

Feed the connector into the outer housing from the end opposite the end with the key

Cap the ferrule

Repeat all instructions on the buffer tube at the opposite end of the cable

Repeat all instructions on all buffer tubes in the cable

Finish installing the cable in accordance with the instructions for the enclosure

Test all connectors

# 20  CONNECTOR INSTALLATION: CLEAVE AND CRIMP #2

Chapter Objectives: from this chapter, you will learn how to install SC and ST-™ compatible connectors by a second 'cleave and crimp' method and achieve low loss and low cost.

## 20.1  INTRODUCTION

This product, the UNICAM™, requires no adhesive and no polishing.[1] This installation method has the lowest time of all the connector installation methods. While this method is fast, its' apparent simplicity hides subtleties. These subtleties determine the insertion loss, the process yield, and the total installed cost. Attention to these subtleties results in consistent and acceptable results.

The procedure herein is based on a high quality cleaver, the Alcoa Fujikura CT07. This cleaver is different from one of the cleavers recommended by the manufacturer. The CT07 produces low cleave angles, low loss connectors, high yield, low total installed cost and high consistency in loss.[2]

## 20.2  TOOLS AND SUPPLIES REQUIRED

➢ Jacket stripper, Ideal tool (45-162)

➢ Tight tube and primary coating stripper (Clauss 203 µm or Miller stripper)

➢ Kevlar® cutters

➢ cleaver (Alcoa Fujikura CT 07 or later recommended, Figure 20-1)

➢ Premises cable[3]

➢ Unicam connectors with the same core diameter as in the cable above: 95-000-50 (ST-™ compatible, 62.5 µm, composite ferrule); 95-000-40 (SC, 62.5 µm, composite ferrule); 95-050-51 (ST-™ compatible, 50 µm, zirconia ferrule); 95-050-41 (SC, 50 µm, zirconia ferrule); 95-000-51 (ST-™ compatible, 62.5 µm, zirconia ferrule); 95-000-41 (SC, 62.5 µm, zirconia ferrule)

➢ 99% isopropyl alcohol or Electrowash Px

➢ Lens grade tissues

➢ Connector installation tool (Figure 20-2)

➢ Fiber collection bottle

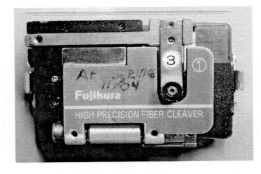

Figure 20-1: CT07 Cleaver

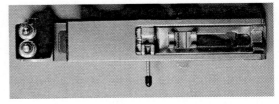

Figure 20-2: SC and ST-™ Compatible UniCam Installation Tool

---

[1] These connectors are manufactured by Corning Cable Systems.

[2] The Corning Inc. instruction sheet, SRP 006-083, includes instructions for two cleavers, one high cost and one low cost. We expect the results from the high cost cleaver to be equivalent to those from the CT07. The results from the CT07 cleaver are superior to those obtained from the low cost cleaver. See Eye On Fiber, Vol. 1, Issue 3 for the data that demonstrate these results 2 (Pearson Technologies Inc.).

[3] We recommend a 10' length for training purposes and for simulating field installation.

---

## 20.3   SC PROCEDURE

For field installation, the installer repeats this procedure on all connectors on one end of the cable. He repeats this procedure on all connectors on the opposite end.

For training, the installer installs a connector on one buffer tube. He repeats this procedure on the same color buffer tube at the opposite end of the cable.

### 20.3.1   REMOVE JACKET

For field installation, the installer prepares the cable end to the dimension specified for the enclosure. For training, the installer prepares the cable ends to expose a minimum buffer tube length of 18" (15.7.2).

### 20.3.2   LOAD TOOL

The installer opens the installation tool by pivoting the top crimping handle so that the handle is off the tool (Figure 20-3). He rotates the cam wrench handle to the vertical position (Figure 20-4).

Figure 20-3: Open UniCam Installation Tool

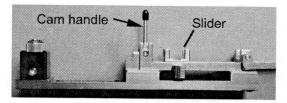

Figure 20-4: Starting Position Of Cam Handle

He removes the cap from the lead-in tube of the back end of the connector (Figure 20-5).

If necessary, he adjusts the position of the cam: it should be at 90° to the date code surface (Figure 20-6)

The installer positions the connector so that 'UP' label (for ST-™ compatible connector) or date label (for the SC connector) is up (Figure 20-5). He pulls the slider towards the right end of the installation tool (Figure 20-4). He places the tip of the connector into the slider.

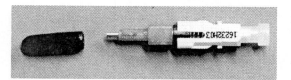

Figure 20-5: Date Code On Top Surface

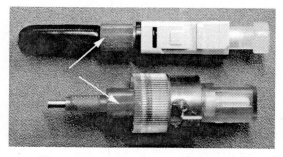

Figure 20-6: Proper Cam Positions

While guiding the lead in tube into the cam wrench, he allows the slider to push the connector into and through the cam wrench until the connector is fully seated. The connector is fully seated when the lead in tube extends beyond the edge of the crimping surface (Figure 20-7 and Figure 20-8).

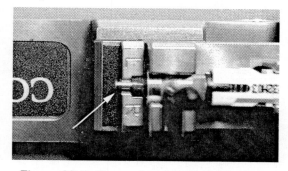

Figure 20-7: Proper Lead In Tube Position

Figure 20-8: Improper Lead In Tube Position

### 20.3.3    PREPARE CABLE END

The installer installs a boot on the buffer tube. He marks the buffer tube at 40 mm and 52 mm from the end of the fiber. In increments 1/2" (12.7 mm) or less, he strips the buffer tube and primary coating to expose 40 mm of bare fiber (15.7.1.3).

### 20.3.4    PREPARE CLEAVER

The installer lifts the cleaver outer cover, the inner cover and the breaking arm (Figure 20-9 to Figure 20-11). He moves the scribing arm to the same side of the cleaver as the outer cover hinge (Figure 20-12). Before the first and after every tenth cleave,[4] he blows out the grooves of the cleaver with lens grade gas.

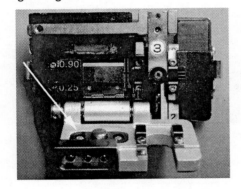

Figure 20-9: Outer Cover Open

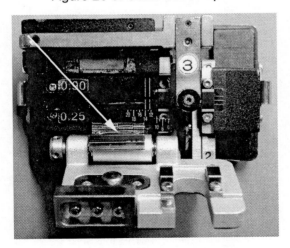

Figure 20-10: Inner Cover Open

[4] This cleaning frequency is suggested. Choose the frequency that provides consistent low angle cleaves.

### 20.3.5    CLEAN FIBER

The installer moistens a lens grade tissue with isopropyl alcohol. He folds the moist area of the tissue around the fiber. He pulls the fiber through the fold twice. He inspects the fiber to verify lack of contamination of the fiber surface.

| Caution |
| --- |
| Do not place the fiber down. |

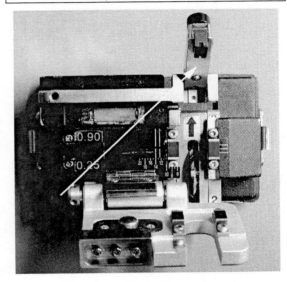

Figure 20-11: Breaking Arm Up

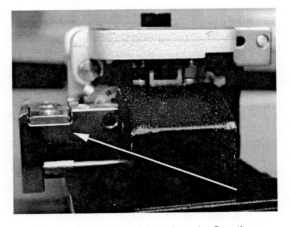

Figure 20-12: Scribing Arm In Starting Position

### 20.3.6    CLEAVE FIBER

The installer places the buffer tube in the 0.9 groove of the cleaver so that the end of the buffer tube aligns at the 8.5 mm mark.[5] He closes the inner cover (Figure 20-13). If necessary, he readjusts the position of the end of the buffer tube to the 8.5 mm cleave length.

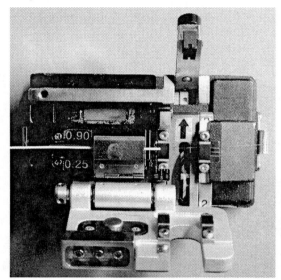

Figure 20-13: Closed Inner Cover

He closes the outer cover (Figure 20-14). He slides the scribing arm in the direction of the arrow on the scribing arm (Figure 20-14 and Figure 20-15).

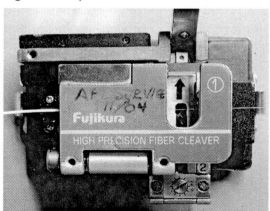

Figure 20-14: Closed Outer Cover

He lowers the breaking arm, labeled 3. With the tip of his finger (Figure 20-16), he pushes down the black tab of the breaking arm until the outer cover pops up (Figure 20-17).

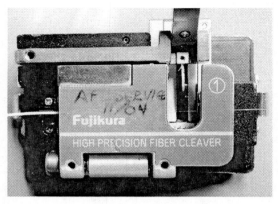

Figure 20-15: Cleaver After Scribing Operation

Figure 20-16: Proper Activation Of Breaking Arm

Figure 20-17: Cleaver Cover Popped After Fiber Broken

He holds the buffer tube, lifts the breaking arm, the outer cover and the inner cover. He places the broken fiber in the fiber collection bottle.

---

[5] The tolerance on the cleave length is +1.5 mm, -0.5 mm.

> **Caution**
>
> Do not place the cleaved fiber onto any surface. Do not touch the sides or the end of cleaved fiber against anything. Do not delay the next step.

## 20.3.7 INSTALL FIBER

While rotating the fiber, the installer inserts the cleaved fiber into the lead-in tube until the fiber butts against the internal fiber (Figure 20-18). He checks the process control mark to ensure that it is within 2 mm of lead-in tube. If the process control mark is closer than 2 mm to the lead in tube, the fiber has broken. He replaces the connector, restrips and recleaves the fiber.

Figure 20-18: Fiber Inserted Into Feed In Tube

The installer inserts the buffer tube into the clip at the end of the installation tool so that the buffer tube bows down by 0.5" from its straight position (Figure 20-19). He rotates the cam wrench to the horizontal position (Figure 20-20).

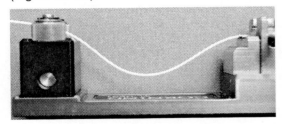

Figure 20-19: Buffer Tube in Rear Clip

To crimp the lead in tube, the installer flips the top crimping handle over onto the lead-in tube and presses firmly (Figure 20-21). The lead in tube will be flat (Figure 20-22).

He flips open the crimping handle. He pulls the slider towards the right end of the installation tool. He removes the connector

from the installation tool. He pushes the boot over the lead-in tube and back shell (Figure 20-23).

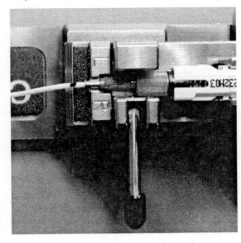

Figure 20-20: Rotated Cam Lever

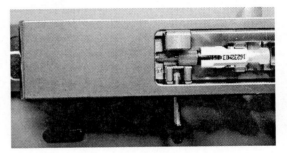

Figure 20-21: Crimping Of Lead In Tube

Figure 20-22: Appearance Of Lead In Tube After Crimping

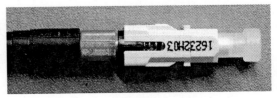

Figure 20-23: Boot Installed Over Lead In Tube

The installer aligns the date code and the key on the outer housing in the up position (Figure 19-24). He inserts the connector into the outer housing from the end opposite the key. He inserts the inner housing into the end of the outer housing until the inner housing snaps through the opposite end of the outer housing (Figure 20-25). He places a cap onto the ferrule end of the connector.

Figure 20-24: Proper Alignment Of Date Code and Key

Figure 20-25: Inner Housing Fully Inserted Into Outer Housing

## 20.4    ST-™ COMPATIBLE PROCEDURE

Installation of the ST-™ compatible connector is almost the same as that of the SC connector. The only difference is in the connector and its orientation in the installation tool. You will install the ST-™ compatible connector in the tool with the cap on the ferrule. The date code and the word 'UP' on the cap will be up (Figure 20-26).

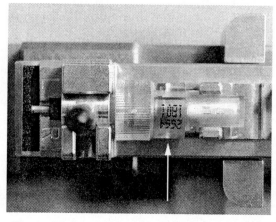

Figure 20-26: ST-™ Compatible Connector Properly Installed In Tool

## 20.5    TEST LOSS

When he has installed connectors on both ends of a buffer tube or on both ends of all buffer tubes, the installer tests the insertion loss (13.2.4.1).

## 20.6    TROUBLESHOOTING

### 20.6.1    50 mm MARK CLOSER TO LEAD IN TUBE THAN 2 mm

Potential cause: broken fiber due to damage during stripping
Action: pull fiber through stripper without bending fiber

### 20.6.2    HIGH LOSS

Potential cause: contamination of fiber from placing of surface or touching fiber after cleaving
Action: do not place fiber on any surface or touch fiber after cleaving

Potential cause: dirty, worn or damaged scribing blade
Action: clean blade; if problem persists, replace blade

Potential cause: dirt on end of fiber
Action: install in an environment that does not have floating dust or particles in air

Potential cause: bad cleave due to dirt on fiber
Action: clean fiber prior to cleaving

### 20.6.3    IDENTIFYING HIGH LOSS END

If a link is high loss, the installer places a visual fault locator on one end. Often, the end with the high loss will glow. He replaces the connector that glows.

## 20.7    SUMMARY

Open crimping handle

Rotate cam lever to vertical position

If necessary, adjust cam position of connector

Load connector into tool so that lead in tube is beyond edge of crimping surface

Prepare cable end to expose buffer tube

Install boot on buffer tube

Mark buffer tube at 40 mm and 52 mm

Strip the buffer tube to the 40 mm mark

Open cleaver

Clean cleaver before first and after each tenth cleave

Set scribing arm in starting position

Clean the fiber

Cleave the fiber at 8.5 mm

Insert the fiber into lead in tube

Verify proper location of second mark

Bow fiber 0.5"

Rotate cam lever to horizontal position

Crimp lead in tube

Remove connector from tool

Slide boot over lead in tube

Install connector into outer housing

If necessary, install cap on connector

When connectors are installed on both ends, test cable

# 21   CONNECTOR INSPECTION

Chapter Objectives: from this chapter, you will learn how the inspect and rate the appearance of a connector. You will learn how to interpret the appearance of 'bad' connectors in order to identify the appropriate corrective actions during installation and maintenance.

## 21.1   APPLICABILITY

This chapter applies to the inspection of all fiber optic connectors. For all connectors except the 'cleave and crimp' products, the condition of the end face of the connector correlates highly with the power loss of the connector. That is, a 'good' appearance of the end face correlates highly with low loss. Because the 'cleave and crimp' products include a mechanical splice in the back shell, the correlation between end face appearance and power loss is not as high as in connectors that use epoxy or an adhesive.

## 21.2   EQUIPMENT REQUIRED

➢ A 400-magnification[1] connector inspection microscope with an IR filter (Westover Scientific, www.westoverscientific.com)

➢ Lens grade tissues (Kim wipes or equivalent, FIS[2])

➢ 98% isopropyl alcohol (FIS)

➢ ElectroWash Px (FIS)

## 21.3   PROCEDURE

### 21.3.1   GENERAL INSTRUCTIONS

The installer performs these steps on each connector with a connector inspection microscope that has an adapter that will accept the connector ferrule.

---

[1] Some fiber optic professionals recommend magnifications of 100 x and 200x. These lower magnification microscopes allow the installer to miss features that increase loss and reflectance. The 400-magnification microscope enables installers to see all features of concern, and, unfortunately, some features that are irrelevant.

[2] Fiber Instrument Sales, 800-5000FIS.

➢ Remove the cap from the connector.

➢ Install the connector into the microscope.

➢ Turn on and focus the microscope.

➢ View and evaluate the connector (Figure 21-1).

Figure 21-1: Use Of Connector Inspection Microscope

### 21.3.2   EVALUATION CRITERIA

A connector looks 'good', that is, will have low loss, if it has a

➢ Round

➢ Clear

➢ Featureless

➢ Flush core

➢ A clean cladding and

➢ A clean ferrule surface

If the core is round, clear and featureless, there is nothing to block or divert the light from its normal path. Thus, low loss will result. This description defines a properly installed connector (Figure 21-2 to Figure 21-8). If there is any deviation from this description, the installer rates the connector 'bad' (Figure 21-9 to 21-21).

---

For maximum reliability, the fiber needs to be flush with the ferrule. This condition is evident when the ferrule surface and the fiber are in the focus at the same time. Occasionally, this condition is evident when adhesive remains on the ferrule due to inadequate polishing time (Figure 21-20).

Features are scratches (Figure 21-9 and Figure 21-11), cracks, missing glass (Figure 21-13, Figure 21-17, and Figure 21-21) or dirt and dust.

If the cladding and ferrule surfaces are not clean, the cores will not contact each other fully. The air gap so created will result in increased loss (Figure 21-10, Figure 21-11, Figure 21-14, and Figure 21-15).

With the exception of dirt and dust, features in the cladding or on the surface of the ferrule do not block or divert light from its normal path through the connector. Therefore, with such features are irrelevant (Figure 21-4, Figure 21-6 and Figure 21-8).[3]

If the connector has a problem that the installer can easily correct, such as dirt on surface, water stains or polishing grit on surface, he cleans and inspects the connector.

The cladding need not be perfectly round for the connector to exhibit low loss (Figure 21-4). Because the light travels through the core (3), defects in the cladding will not interfere with the normal light path.[4]

However, defects in the cladding can create surface roughness and high reflectance. It appears that defects in the cladding that are closer to the core than to the outer diameter of the cladding can result in increased reflectance (Figure 21-6).[5]

---

[3] Such features indicate less than perfect polishing. Perfect polishing is easily achieved during factory installation of connectors. Perfect polishing during field installation is difficult due to lack of control of the environment in which the connectors are polished.

[4] A round cladding results from most factory installation, because such installation involves grinding off ferrule and fiber. Such grinding removes chipped glass at the outside of the cladding.

[5] This is the author's experience.

Most scratches are from contamination of the polishing film from the environment. Contamination of polishing film is common in field polishing. Such scratches can be in the core (Figures 21-9 and 21-11), cladding (Figure 21-9 and Figure 21-11) and ferrule (Figure 21-2 and Figure 21-8).

Finally, connectors need not be exactly centered in the fiber hole. While centering usually results from twisting the fiber during insertion, fibers can be slightly off center, as indicated by the uneven thickness of the ring of adhesive (Figure 21-5, Figure 21-6, Figure 21-7, and Figure 21-12). Such connectors will exhibit acceptable low loss. However, as the centering improves, the loss becomes lower.

## 21.3.3    BACK LIGHT INSPECTION

The installer performs the microscopic inspection both without and with backlighting. To inspect with back lighting, another person holds a light source to the connector on the same fiber at the opposite end of the cable. The core should light up. If the core does not light up, the fiber is broken. The installer inspects and evaluates the connector as in Step 21.3.2.

The installer performs connector inspection both with and without back light. Backlight can both reveal and conceal features in the core.

> ➢ The installer rates the connector 'good' if it is 'good' both with and without back light.

If the cladding lights up during back lighting, the fiber is broken in the connector, usually in the ferrule. While infrequent with adhesive connectors, back light in the cladding is not unusual in 'cleave and crimp' connectors (19, 20) installed by novices.

During back lighting, multimode cores can exhibit concentric rings. These rings result from the multiple layers in the core (3.2.2).

## 21.3.4    CONNECTOR DISPOSITION

The installer does not replace a 'bad' connector immediately. Instead, he places a label on the connector to indicate the possibility that the connector will have high loss. If the connector tests low loss, the installer removes the label. If the connector tests high loss, the installer leaves the label in place to indicate the need for connector replacement. After inspecting the connector, the installer replaces the cap.

In reality, the definition of a 'good' connector is that of a perfect connector. Small scratches, cracks or contamination in the core may not divert enough light to cause the connector to exhibit high loss (Figure 21-9 and Figure 21-11).

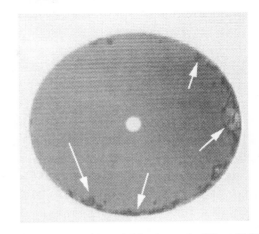

Figure 21-4: A Good Singlemode Fiber With Cladding Features

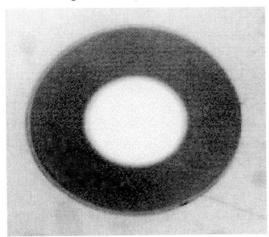

Figure 21-2: A Good Back Lit Multimode Connector With Back Light

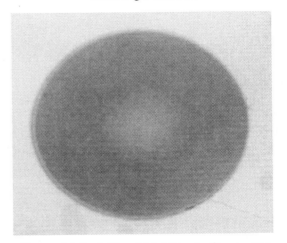

Figure 21-5: A Good Multimode Connector

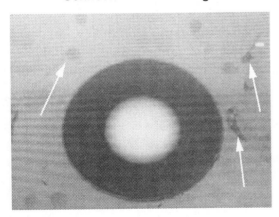

Figure 21-3: Good Back Lit Multimode Connector With Ferrule Features[6]

Figure 21-6: A Good Singlemode Connector With Cladding Features

---

[6] This ferrule is a LCP, or composite, ferrule.

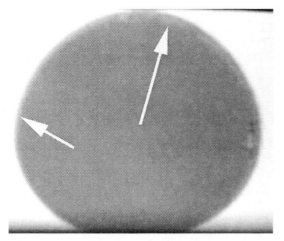

Figure 21-7: Good Connector With Uneven Adhesive Ring

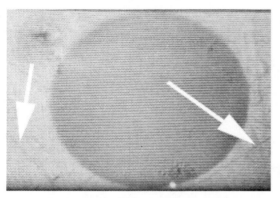

Figure 21-8: Good Connector With Scratches On Ferrule And Features In Cladding

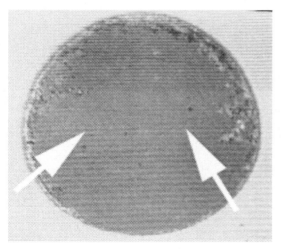

Figure 21-9: A Singlemode Connector With Scratches In The Core

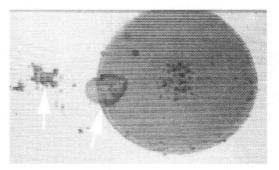

Figure 21-10: Bad Connector With Dirt On The Core And Cladding

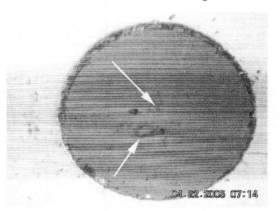

Figure 21-11: Bad Connector With Dirt On The Core

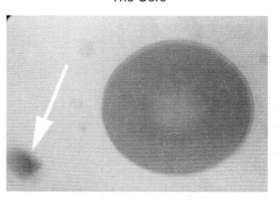

Figure 21-12: Bad Connector With Dirt On The Ferrule Surface

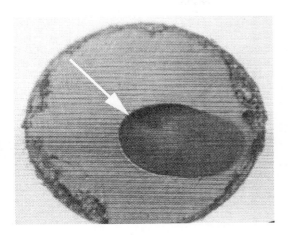

Figure 21-13: Bad Connector With Defect In The Core And Cladding

Figure 21-16: Dirt Particles On The Cladding

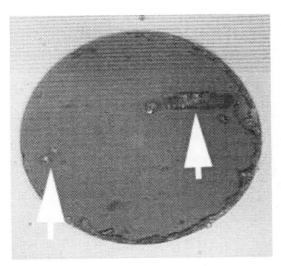

Figure 21-14: Bad Connector With Dirt On The Cladding

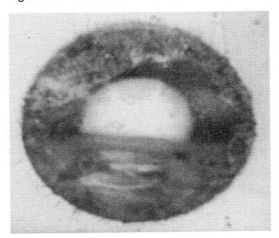

Figure 21-17: Non-Round Core[7]

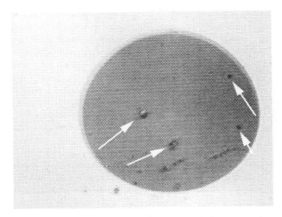

Figure 21-15: Bad Singlemode Connector With Dirt On The Cladding

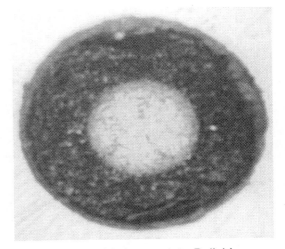

Figure 21-18: Incomplete Polishing

[7] The fiber is broken below the surface of the ferrule.

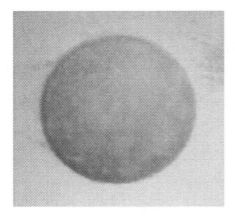

Figure 21-19: Epoxy On Fiber[8]

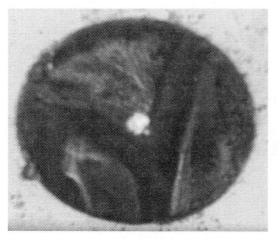

Figure 21-20: Fiber Not Flush With Ferrule
Due To Adhesive On Ferrule

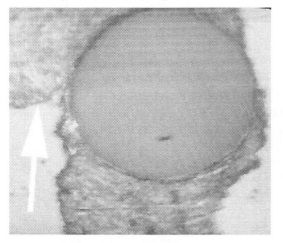

Figure 21-21: Badly Shattered Fiber

## 21.4  TROUBLESHOOTING

Symptom: dirt on connector that does not disappear when connector cleaned
Potential cause: dirt on microscope lens
Action: clean lens; or, rotate connector in microscope; if dirt does not move, dirt is on lens. Clean lens if possible.

Symptom: faint stains on connector
Potential cause: moisture stains from alcohol
Action: dry wipe immediately after cleaning with alcohol; or clean with ElectroWash Px

Symptom: no fiber found
Potential cause: out of focus
Action: move focusing ring through entire range of motion; or, back light connector and move focusing ring through entire range of motion

Symptom: no fiber found
Potential cause: connector not completely inserted into microscope
Action: insert connector into microscope adapter

Symptom: core does not light up when connector backlit

Potential cause: broken fiber
Action: locate break with fault indicator or faultfinder

---

[8] This photograph is courtesy of Dominick Tambone of Crystal Tech.

# 22   MID SPAN SPLICING

Chapter Objectives: in this chapter, you will learn how to perform all the activities of mid span splicing. You will learn how to make fusion and mechanical splices. You will learn how to make splices on both multimode and singlemode fibers. Finally, you will learn how to install the splices in splice trays and the trays and cable into an enclosure.

## 22.1   INTRODUCTION

In this chapter, we present procedure for single fiber, field, mid span splicing.[1] The procedure is for fusion (22.9.1) and mechanical splicing (22.9.2) of either singlemode or multimode fiber.

Mid span splicing requires ten steps:

> Cable end preparation
> Enclosure preparation
> Cable attachment
> Buffer tube attachment
> Splicing
> Fiber coiling
> Buffer tube coiling
> Tray attachment
> Enclosure finishing
> Testing

## 22.2   TOOLS AND SUPPLIES REQUIRED[2]

> Jacket slitter tool (Clauss RCS-20)
> Tight tube and primary coating stripper (Clauss 203 µm or Miller stripper)
> Kevlar® cutters
> High performance cleaver, Fujikura CT07, CT04 or CT20
> Two loose tube cables[3]

> Gel/grease remover
> Paper towels or clean rags
> Fusion splicer
> Heat shrink oven for splice covers, or adhesive splice covers
> Splice covers, either heat shrink (FIS[4] P/N F1-1002 or F1-100240) or adhesive (FIS P/N F1-FS40, F1-FS60)
> 3M Fibrlok™ II splices (P/N 2529)
> Fibrlok™ assembly tool (P/N 2501)
> 98% isopropyl alcohol
> Lens grade tissues
> Foam fiber optic swabs (FIS P/N F1-0005)
> Lens grade gas (Stoner 94203 or equivalent)
> An OTDR
> A launch cable
> An outdoor fiber optic splice enclosure (FIS P/N 1120-F, 2000-F)
> Two splice trays
> Splice holders compatible with splice trays
> Cable ties for buffer tubes and for pigtails
> Visible Feature Finder (Advanced Fiber Solutions, Model OS405)[5]
> Optional: index matching gel
> Optional: 0.004" piano wire

---

[1] In Chapters 23, and 24, we present the procedures for single fiber pigtail splicing, and mid span ribbon splicing, respectively.

[2] See 16.4 for sources of items not identified in this section.

[3] To perform mid span splicing, the installer needs two cables. The cables must be longer than the dead zone of the OTDR. For practical

purposes, this length should be at least three times the dead zone. For training, we recommend cables with at least 12 fibers in two buffer tubes.

[4] Fiber Instrument Sales, 800-5000FIS

[5] www.advancedfibersolutions.com

---

➤ Optional: reusable mechanical splice, Elastomeric splice, (FIS)

A mechanical splice or a connector of the same type as that on the end of the cable will be on the end of the launch cable.

The splice trays will be compatible with the enclosure. The splice holders will be compatible with the trays and the splice cover or mechanical splice.

## 22.3   CABLE END PREPARATION

### 22.3.1   DIMENSIONS

From the enclosure instructions, the installer identifies the following dimensions (Figure 22-1):

➤ Length of jacket to be removed

➤ Length of strength member to be left

➤ Length of central strength member to be left

➤ Length of buffer tube to be left

### 22.3.2   END PREPARATION

The installer prepares the cable end to those dimensions (22.3.1), according to the procedure in Chapter 15. This process may include replacement of the buffer tube with a tubing material than is compatible with the bend radius of the enclosure.

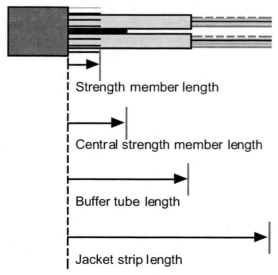

Figure 22-1: Cable End Preparation Dimensions

Before cutting and removing the first buffer tube, the installer verifies the buffer tube length. The installer marks the buffer tube at the distance indicated in the enclosure instructions. The installer places the cable into the enclosure. He routes one buffer tube from the cable entrance to the opposite end of the enclosure, back to the entrance end and into the location of the splice tray. If the buffer tube length is correct, the mark on the buffer tube will be inside the tray by approximately 1" (Figure 22-2). If the mark on the buffer tube is inside the tray by more than 1", he reduces the buffer tube length dimensions by the appropriate amount.

If the mark is outside the tray, the installer adjusts the loop of buffer tube until the mark is inside the tray. He checks the buffer tube to ensure that there are no sharp bends in the buffer tube. If there are no sharp bends, he uses the buffer tube length indicated in the enclosure instructions. If the buffer tube has a sharp bend, the installer increases the buffer tube length by the amount necessary to eliminate all sharp bends.

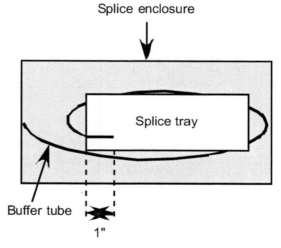

Figure 22-2: Proper Buffer Tube Length

## 22.4   ENCLOSURE PREPARATION

The installer prepares the enclosure according to the instructions for that enclosure. These instructions will address at least the following aspects:

➤ Moisture seals around the cables

➤ Moisture seals for the enclosure

> ➤ Grounding and bonding hardware

There are at least three configurations of cable moisture seals. The seal may consist of a plug with an inner diameter equal to the outer diameter of the cable (Figure 22-3). This seal may consist of parts assembled to create a seal (Figure 22-4). This seal may consist of a solid rubber plate, through which the installer drills holes for the cables (Figure 22-5).

In addition, the moisture seal(s) for the enclosure may include plugs for unused cable entrances (Figure 22-6) and gasket material for use between the enclosure halves.

Figure 22-5: End Cap Requiring Drilling[8]

Figure 22-3: 7 and 12mm Plugs For Starfighter™ 2000-F Enclosure[6]

Figure 22-6: Enclosure Plugs

If splice holders are not installed in the trays, the installer installs the holders. Finally, the enclosure may include hardware for grounding or bonding (Figure 22-7). If the cables contain conductive materials, the installer bonds the cables with such hardware.

Figure 22-4: Moisture Seal Components For Lightlinker Enclosure[7]

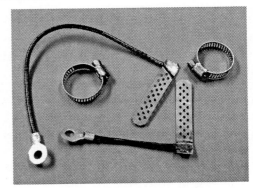

Figure 22-7: Grounding And Bonding Hardware

---

[6] This enclosure is a product of Multilink.

[7] This enclosure is a product of 3M.

---

[8] This enclosure is product number CAP6S2-531-0-0 from the Dulmisson Telecommunications Division.

## 22.5   CABLE ATTACHMENT

The installer attaches the cable strength members of both cables to the same end of the enclosure[9] according to the instructions for that enclosure. We present an example of such hardware for attachment in Figure 22-8.

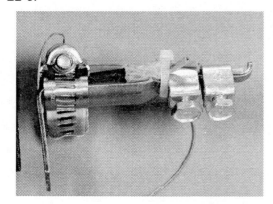

Figure 22-8: Strength Member Attachment Hardware

## 22.6   BUFFER TUBE ATTACHMENT

The installer selects the same color buffer tube from each cable.[10] He straightens both buffer tubes to eliminate any twisting. While straight, he routes one buffer tube[11] from each cable to the same end of one splice tray.

The installer feeds one buffer tube from each cable into the same end of one tray. By the method specified in the instructions for the enclosure and/or the splice tray, he attaches both buffer tubes to the tray (Figure 22-9). Some trays require pinching of a tab over the buffer tube. Other trays require a cable tie around the buffer tube and a portion of the tray (Figure 22-9).

With a separate tray for each pair of buffer tubes from the two cables, the installer repeats this step.

---

[9] This procedure is for the preferred configuration of butt splicing (12.4.1).

[10] Unless there is an overriding reason, use the same color buffer tube from both cables.

[11] Hereafter, we will use the term buffer tube with the understanding that a furcation tube or spiral wrap may replace the buffer tube.

Figure 22-9: Buffer Tubes Attached To Tray

## 22.7   FIBER LENGTH VERIFICATION

The installer routes the fibers from the splice tray to the splicer. If the fibers reach the splicer, the fibers are sufficiently long. If they do not, he adjusts the location of the splicer so that the fibers reach the splicer without any tension or sharp bends.

The installer coils the fibers from one buffer tube inside the tray so that the size of the coil is as large as possible. The input side of the splice holder is the side opposite to the side of the tray at which the buffer tube enters the tray. The installer compares the location of the end of the fibers to the location of the input side of the splice holder. If the fiber ends are between the ends of the splice holder,[12] the fiber length is adequate (Figure 22-10).

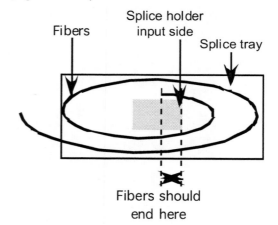

Figure 22-10: Proper Fiber Length

---

[12] This dimension assumes a fiber strip length of 1.5-2". If the cleaver requires a fiber strip length in excess of 2", the fibers can extend past the splice holder by the amount in excess of two inches. For example, if the cleaver requires a strip length of 6", the fibers can extend beyond the splice holder by 4".

If the fibers are long, the installer trims them so that they are at the splice holder.[13] If the fiber ends do not reach the input side of the splice holder, the installer tightens the coil of fibers until the ends reach the input side of the splice holder. He checks the bend radius of the fibers. If the fibers do not exhibit any tight bend radius in the tray, he uses this fiber length.

If the fibers appear to take a tight bend radius, the installer lengthens fibers from both buffer tubes by removing additional buffer tube and jacket. If the installer lengthens the fibers, he will recheck the buffer tube length (22.3.2).

The installer routes the fibers out of the tray. He untwists all fibers from each other. Without twisting or crossing the fibers, he routes the fibers from each buffer tube to opposite sides of the splicer or splicing tool.

## 22.8   OTDR SET UP

The installer sets up the OTDR at the end of one of the cables. He attaches the launch cable to the OTDR. He enters the index of refraction, the maximum length of the cable to be tested,[14] the time of the test, the wavelength of the test, and the pulse width necessary to obtain a loss measurement in an acceptable time.[15]

The installer connects the OTDR to the first fiber to be spliced. He can make this connection with a launch cable with the same connector style as on the end of the cable. Alternatively, he can make this connection to the cable with a reusable mechanical splice.[16]

---

[13] If the installer trims the fiber, he may need to readjust the location of the splicer.

[14] To measure the splice loss, this length must be more than the length of the cable plus at least three times the width of the dead zone.

[15] As the pulse width increases, the time required to obtain a noise free splice loss measurement becomes less. However, as the pulse width increases, the dead zone becomes longer and launch cable length must be increased.

[16] We suggest use of the Elastomeric Lab Splice (Fiber Instrument Sales). For repeated use of the same splice, you will need a vial of index matching gel and a 0.004" piano wire to remove broken fibers from the splice.

The installer makes a trace of the first fiber to be spliced in order to determine the distance to the cable end. He records that distance.

## 22.9   SPLICING

## 22.9.1   FUSION SPLICING

### 22.9.1.1   SPLICER SET UP

The installer plugs in and turns on the splicer. He opens all covers. He inspects the grooves. With a dry, lint free, fiber optic swab, he cleans the grooves by swabbing from the inside end of the grooves to the outside end (Figure 22-11).[17,18]

Figure 22-11: Splicer Grooves

### 22.9.1.2   SPLICE MENU

The installer examines the active menu in the splicer (Figure 22-12). If the active menu is the one the installer wants, he proceeds. If the desired menu is not active, he activates the appropriate menu according to the instructions for the splicer.

---

[17] If the installer swabs in the opposite direction, he may contaminate the mirrors and optics with dust. If he uses a swab moistened with isopropyl alcohol, the isopropyl alcohol may contaminate the mirrors and optics with water marks. If he uses lens grade gas, the cold gas may create water marks on the mirrors and optics. Such contamination can result in error messages from the splicer software.

[18] If the installer has problems with fiber alignment, he will clean the grooves until he eliminates this problem

Figure 22-12: Active Fiber Menu[19]

### 22.9.1.3   MAXIMUM CLEAVE ANGLE

The installer examines the maximum acceptance angle for cleaves (Figure 22-13). If the value is the installer wants, he proceeds. If not, he enters the appropriate value according to the instructions for the splicer.

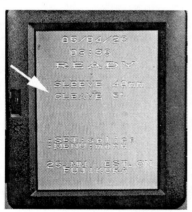

Figure 22-13: Cleave Angle Setting

### 22.9.1.4   SPLICE COVER LENGTH

The installer examines the splice cover length (Figure 22-14). If the value is the one the installer wants, he proceeds. If not, he enters the appropriate value according to the instructions for the splicer.

### 22.9.1.5   OPTICS CHECK

The installer checks the screen image. The image should be free from spots. If spots or

---

[19] Multimode menu 25 with splice loss estimation is active.

dust exist, he cleans the mirrors according to the instructions for the splicer.

Figure 22-14: Splice Cover Length Setting

### 22.9.1.6   CLEAVER PREPARATION

The installer opens, cleans and sets up the cleaver according to the instructions for that cleaver. For the CT04, CT07 cleavers, the installer follows the instructions in 19.3.5-19.3.6.

### 22.9.1.7   COVER INSTALLATION

If the installer uses an adhesive splice cover, he ignores this step. The installer places a heat shrink splice cover on one fiber.

### 22.9.1.8   FIBER STRIPPING

The cleaver determines the strip length. The installer follows the instructions for the cleaver. The CT04 and CT07 require a strip length of 1.5-1.75". In a single strip, the installer strips the appropriate length of primary coating from the fiber (15.7.1.3).

The installer moistens a lens grade tissue with isopropyl alcohol. He makes a fold in the tissue. He pulls the fiber through the fold at least twice. He examines the fiber to ensure that there are no particles on the cladding. If necessary, he re-cleans the fiber.

### 22.9.1.9   FIBER CLEAVING

From the splicer instructions, the installer determines the cleave length. The installer uses the appropriate cleave length. For the

Alcoa Fujikura splicers, he cleaves the fibers at 12 mm (19.3.5-19.3.7).[20]

| Caution |
|---|
| After cleaving, do not clean the fiber.[21] |

### 22.9.1.10   PLACE FIBER IN SPLICER

Following the instructions for the splicer, the installer resets the splicer to 'start'. From its side of the splicer, he places the first cleaved fiber in the holders so that the fiber is on its side of the electrodes (Figure 22-15).

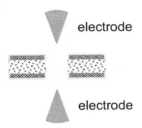

electrode

electrode

Figure 22-15: Proper Fiber Location For Splicing

### 22.9.1.11   SECOND FIBER

The installer repeats Steps 22.9.1.8-22.9.1.10 with the fiber from the second buffer tube.

### 22.9.1.12   FUSING

To begin the splicing process, the installer pushes the fuse button. Some splicers allow the option of reviewing and accepting the cleave angles and alignment prior to fusing. If this option is active, the installer pushes the fuse button several times.

### 22.9.1.13   ESTIMATED LOSS REVIEW

If the splicer has a splice loss estimation feature, the splicer will display the estimated splice loss. If this estimation correlates with OTDR splice loss measurement,[22] and if the

---

[20] The Alcoa Fujikura model numbers are FSM30S and FMS20CSII.

[21] In fusion splicing, cleaning the fiber after cleaving may not create 'fatal' contamination of the fiber. However, such cleaning and contamination can result in excessive loss in a mechanical splice.

[22] For simplicity, we have assumed that such correlation exists. If such correlation does not exist, the installer will measure the loss of each

value is acceptable, the installer proceeds to 22.9.1.14. If the value is not acceptable, the installer breaks the splice and repeats Steps 22.9.1.8-22.9.1.12.

### 22.9.1.14   COVER INSTALLATION

For heat shrinkable splice covers, the installer follows the instructions in 22.9.1.14.1. For adhesive covers, he follows the instructions in 22.9.1.14.2.

### 22.9.1.14.1   HEAT SHRINK COVER

The installer slides the splice cover up to the fiber holder. He opens both fiber holders. While holding the fiber at the holder opposite to the splice cover, he slides the cover over the bare fiber gently so that the bare fiber is centered in the cover.

The installer places the cover in the cover-heating oven (Figure 22-16). He gently tubs on both fibers to ensure that the fibers are straight in the cover. He closes the oven covers. He turns on the oven. He allows the oven to run its heating cycle. While waiting for the end of this cycle, the installer prepares the next two fibers for splicing.

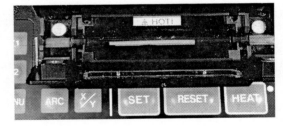

Figure 22-16: Splice Cover In Heating Oven

After the heating cycle is complete, the installer uses a toothpick or tweezers to move the splice cover towards one side of the heating oven. This action will cause the cover to become free from the oven surface.[23] With pair of tweezers, he removes the splice cover from the oven. He transfers the splice to the splice tray.

---

splice after he makes the splice and after he shrinks the splice cover.

[23] The splice cover may stick to the inside of the oven. If you try to remove the splice from the oven without removing this sticking, you may break the fiber inside the cover.

> **Caution**
>
> Do not grip the splice cover tightly with the tweezers. Do not grip the splice cover on the area of the bare glass. Doing so may break the fiber inside the cover.

#### 22.9.1.14.2 ADHESIVE SPLICE COVER

The installer removes the protective tape from the adhesive surface of the cover (Figure 22-17, Top). With both hands, the installer holds the fiber above the center of the cover. He lowers the fiber to the adhesive surface slowly (Figure 22-17, Middle). He folds the second side of the cover over the first (Figure 22-17, Bottom).

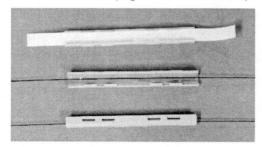

Figure 22-17: Adhesive Splice Cover

After each splice, the installer proceeds to 22.10 or to 22.11, depending on the experience of the installer. The installer repeats 22.9.1.7-22.9.1.14 until he has spliced all fibers in one tray.

## 22.9.2 MECHANICAL SPLICE

These instructions are for the Fibrlok™ splice from 3M (P/N 2529). If the installer uses a different mechanical splice, he modifies the procedure in this section.

#### 22.9.2.1 SPLICE TOOL PREPARATION

The installer cleans the 'feed in' grooves of the holder with a fiber optic swab moistened with isopropyl alcohol (Figure 22-18). He lifts the closing arm (Figure 22-19). With the closing button of the mechanical splice up (arrow in Figure 22-20), he inserts the mechanical splice into the tool (Figure 22-20). He sets the position of the side clamps for 250 μm primary coated fiber (Figure 22-19) or for 900 μm tight tube (Figure 22-21).[24]

---

[24] For splicing of a 250 μm fiber to a 900 μm pigtail, the installer will set one clamp in each of

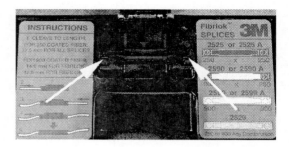

Figure 22-18: 3M FIBRLOK™ Splice Tool Feed In Grooves

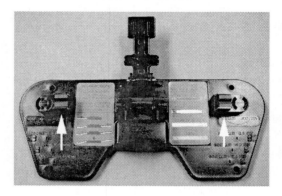

Figure 22-19: Position of Holders For 250 μm Primary Coating

Figure 22-20: Open FIBRLOK™ Splice In Tool

Figure 22-21: Position of Holders For 900 μm Tight Tube

---

the positions indicated in Figure 22-20 and Figure 22-21.

## 22.9.2.2    CLEAVER PREPARATION

The installer opens, cleans and sets up the cleaver according to the instructions for that cleaver. For the CT04, CT07 cleavers, he follows the instructions in 19.3.5-19.3.6.

## 22.9.2.3    FIBER STRIPPING

The cleaver determines the strip length. The installer follows the instructions for the cleaver. Many strippers require a strip length of 1.5-1.75". The installer strips the appropriate length of primary coating from the fiber (19.3.5-19.3.6).

The installer moistens a lens grade tissue with isopropyl alcohol. He makes a fold in the tissue. He pulls the fiber through the fold at least twice. He examines the fiber to ensure that there are no particles on the cladding. If necessary, he re-cleans the fiber.

## 22.9.2.4    CLEAVE FIBER

For the Fibrlok™, the installer uses a cleave length of 12.5 mm. For a different mechanical splice, the installer cleaves to the length indicated in the instructions for that splice.

---

**Caution**

After cleaving, the installer does not clean the fiber, does not place fiber on any surface and does not wait to insert the fiber into the splice.

---

## 22.9.2.5    FIBER INSERTION

The installer inserts the first fiber into one side of the mechanical splice until the fiber stops. The installer places the primary coating in the foam of the holder so that the fiber is straight (Figure 22-22).

Figure 22-22: First Fiber In Splice Tool

The installer cleaves and inserts the second fiber into the other end of the mechanical splice until the fiber stops. The installer places the primary coating in the foam of the holder so that the fiber is straight (Figure 22-22). The first fiber will be bowed.

While holding the first fiber between the holder and the splice, the installer pushes the first fiber into the splice until the amount of bow of both fibers is equal (Figure 22-23).

Figure 22-23: Fibrlok™ II Splice With Even Bows

The installer lowers the tool arm onto the splice button (Figure 22-24). He pushes the arm so that the button moves into the splice and is level with the rest of the splice (Figure 22-25).

Figure 22-24: 3M Arm In Closing Position

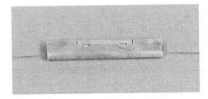

Figure 22-25: Closed Fibrlok™ Splice

After each splice, the installer proceeds to 22.10. The installer repeats this step until he has spliced all fibers in the tray.

## 22.10  TEST LOSS

The installer can perform splice loss testing at various times:

 ➢ After splicing,
 ➢ After installation of the splice cover

➤ After installation of the splice in the splice tray, or

➤ After closing the enclosure

The most meaningful time for testing is the last, after closing the enclosure. This time of testing is appropriate for experienced installers, who are able to perform the entire procedure without making errors.

As long as the fusion splicer loss estimation value correlates well with OTDR loss measurements, this time of testing is appropriate for fusion splicing. For mechanical splicing, the installer will test the loss after installing the splice and after closing the enclosure.

For training, the trainee can perform testing at any or all of the times indicated. Such testing can indicate the step at which an error has occurred.

## 22.10.1    FUSION SPLICES

The installer tests the loss with an OTDR. If the loss is acceptable, the installer proceeds to 22.11. If the loss is not acceptable, the installer cuts the fibers and makes a new splice, starting at 22.9.1.7. For final testing, the installer tests the splice in both directions (13.3.6.4.2).

If the splice loss is positive, the installer tests in the opposite direction and averages the two loss measurements.

## 22.10.2    MECHANICAL SPLICES

### 22.10.2.1    THE FIBRLOK™ SPLICE

The installer tests the loss with an OTDR. If the loss is acceptable, he proceeds to 22.11. If the loss is not acceptable, he cuts the fibers and replaces the splice.

### 22.10.2.2    RE-ENTERABLE SPLICES

If the installer uses a splice that allows opening of both ends, he may tune the splice to achieve acceptable loss. To tune, the installer opens one side of the splice, rotates one of the fibers, closes the splice, and tests the splice. He repeats this process until he obtains the lowest loss measurement.

If this lowest loss is not acceptable, the installer repeats this tuning on the second fiber until he achieves the lowest loss measurement. If this measurement is not acceptable, he replaces the splice.

If the installer has a visible feature finder and a mechanical splice that lets him see the fiber ends, he can tune the splice without multiple OTDR tests. To tune the splice, he connects a visible feature finder to the end of one of the cables being spliced. The installer observes the glow at the mechanical splice. As described above, he tunes one or both of the fibers until there is no glow.

## 22.11    FIBER COILING

The installer holds the splice so that the fibers are parallel to both sides of the tray (Figure 22-26). He lays the fibers in the tray from the input end to the second end.

Figure 22-26: Fibers Parallel To Tray Sides

He twists the fibers at the second end. He lays the fibers in the tray from the second end to the input end. He twists the fibers in the direction opposite to that of the first twist (Figure 22-27).

Figure 22-27: Twisted Fibers At Second End

The installer repeats this process until almost all the fiber is in the tray (Figure 22-28).

The first position is the position on either end of the splice holder (Figure 22-28). The installer places the splice cover, or mechanical splice, in the first position. He places additional splices in the tray in sequence from that position.

Figure 22-28: Fibers Reversed Twisted At Input End

Figure 22-29: Fibers In Holder

Figure 22-30: Starting Positions Of Splice Holder

The installer repeats this step for all fibers in the tray. He places the cover on the splice tray (Figure 22-31).

Figure 22-31: Full Splice Holder With Cover

## 22.12  BUFFER TUBE COILING

After the installer has installed all splices in a tray,[25] he moves the tray so that the buffer tubes run parallel to the sides of the enclosure (Figure 22-32).

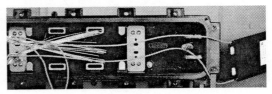

Figure 22-32: Starting Position

He places the buffer tubes into the enclosure, under any structure that supports the trays. He twists the tray upside down (Figure 22-33). He places the tray on its support structure (Figure 22-34).

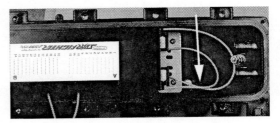

Figure 22-33: Twisted Buffer Tubes

Figure 22-34: Tray Support Structure

If the length of buffer tube requires more than routing the buffer tubes from one end to the opposite end, the installer places the buffer tubes parallel to the sides of enclosure back towards the input end of the enclosure (Figure 22-34).

## 22.13  TRAY ATTACHMENT

After the installer has installed all trays onto the support structure, he attaches the trays to that structure in the manner indicated by the enclosure instructions.

---

[25] The common numbers are six and twelve.

Some trays attach to the enclosure by a bolt, which feeds through a bolt hole in the tray (Figure 22-35). Some trays attach with Velcro™ bands (Figure 22-36). Finally, Some trays attach with rubber holders (Figure 22-37).

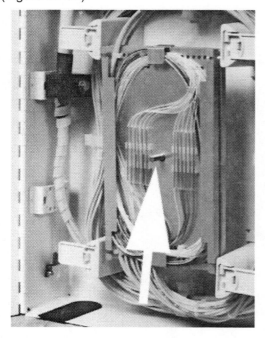

Figure 22-35: Bolt Hole For Tray Attachment

Figure 22-36: Attachment With Velcro Bands

Figure 22-37: Tray Attachment With Rubber Holders

## 22.14  ENCLOSURE FINISHING

The installer performs the following steps, in accordance with the instructions for the enclosure. He verifies that the buffer tubes

are restricted to the inside of the enclosure. He cleans all moisture seal surfaces. He installs moisture seals and gaskets. He assembles the enclosure housing parts. If the enclosure instructions require use of a specific torque, he tightens the bolts with a torque wrench. He tests moisture seals for leaks by pressurizing the enclosure. If so instructed, he releases the pressure.

The installer installs the enclosure in its location. If the enclosure has weep holes, he installs the enclosure so that the weep holes are on the bottom of the enclosure.

## 22.15  TROUBLESHOOTING

### 22.15.1  BAD CLEAVES

Potential cause: dirt on scribing blade
Action: clean blade with swab and isopropyl alcohol.

Potential cause: dirt in alignment grooves
Action: clean grooves with lens grade gas

Potential cause: fiber from previous cleave is on pads on underside of the outer cover
Action: inspect and clean pads with isopropyl alcohol and lens grade tissue

Potential cause: loose alignment pad
Action: tighten screws on alignment pad

Potential cause: worn scribing blade[26]
Action: rotate blade to next position

Potential cause: missing or misplaced alignment shim
Action: return cleaver to factory for service

Potential cause: worn bearings in scribing arm
Action: return cleaver to factory for service

### 22.15.2  FUSION SPLICING

22.15.2.1  HIGH LOSS SPLICE

Potential cause: high cleave angle
Action: reset cleave angle value on splicer

Potential cause: incorrect menu active
Action: reset menu for fibers being spliced

---

[26] When the cleaver produces five bad cleaves in sequence, the blade is worn. If the bad cleaves are erratic, there is a problem different from a worn scribing blade.

## 22.15.2.2  NON UNIFORM SPLICE DIAMETER

Potential cause: overrun set incorrectly
Action: reset overrun in menu

## 22.15.2.3  WEAK SPLICE

Potential cause: arc current and/or time set low
Action: increase overrun value or change menu to that for a different fiber

## 22.15.2.4  ROUND BALL ON FIBER ENDS

Potential cause: arc current and/or time set high
Action: reduce value or change menu to that for different fiber

## 22.15.2.5  ALIGNMENT FAILURE

Potential cause: dirt in fiber holders
Action: clean holders with fiber optic swab or fine paintbrush; brush from center towards outside of holder.

Potential cause: cleave length below minimum value
Action: check cleave length; recleave

Potential cause: primary coating in final alignment groove
Action: reposition fiber so that cladding is in final groove (Figure 22-11)

## 22.15.3  MECHANICAL SPLICING

### 22.15.3.1  HIGH LOSS SPLICE

Potential cause: fiber not in center of splice
Action: ensure equal amount of bow on both fibers

Potential cause: bad cleave
Action: see 22.15.1

Potential cause: dirt on fiber end
Action: review procedure to ensure no contamination of end between cleaving and insertion; see Caution in 22.9.2.4

Potential cause: incorrect cleave length
Action: correct cleave length

# 22.16  SUMMARY

## 22.16.1  CABLE END PREPARATION

Determine the end preparation dimensions

Prepare the cable end

If necessary, replace the buffer tubes

## 22.16.2  ENCLOSURE PREPARATION

Install moisture seals

Install bonding

Verify buffer tube length

Attach the buffer tubes to tray

Attach the cables to enclosure

Verify the fiber length

## 22.16.3  SET UP OTDR

Set OTDR parameters

## 22.16.4  FUSION SPLICING

Set up the splicer

Activate the appropriate splice menu

Set the maximum cleave angle

Set the splice cover length

Check the optics

Prepare the cleaver

Install the splice cover

Strip and clean the fiber

Cleave the fiber

Place the fiber in the splicer

Strip, clean and cleave the second fiber

Place second fiber in splicer

Fuse the fibers

Review the estimated loss

Shrink the splice cover

## 22.16.5  MECHANICAL SPLICE

Prepare the splice tool

Prepare the cleaver

Strip and clean the fiber

Cleave the fiber

Place the first fiber in the mechanical splice

Strip, clean and cleave the second fiber

Place the second in the mechanical splice

Make the bows equal

Close splice

**22.16.6   TEST LOSS**

**22.16.7   COIL FIBER**

**22.16.8   COIL BUFFER TUBE**

**22.16.9   ATTACH TRAY**

**22.16.10  FINISH ENCLOSURE**

# 23   PIGTAIL SPLICING

Chapter Objectives: in this chapter, you will learn how to perform all the activities of pigtail splicing. You will learn how to make fusion and mechanical pigtail splices. You will learn how to make splices on both multimode and singlemode fibers. Finally, you will learn how to install the splices in splice trays and the trays and cable into an indoor enclosure.

## 23.1   INTRODUCTION

In this chapter, we present procedure for single fiber, field, pigtail splicing. The procedure is for fusion (23.9.1) and mechanical splicing (23.9.2) of either singlemode or multimode fiber.[1] The pigtail can be either longer or shorter than the dead zone of the OTDR.

Pigtail splicing differs from mid span splicing is three aspects:

 ➤ Coiling of fiber and pigtail

 ➤ Cleave length of pigtail

 ➤ Measurement of splice loss

When coiling the fiber, the installer need not use the reverse twist. Instead, he can coil the fiber and pigtail in the tray.

The cleave length of the pigtail tends to be longer than that of the fiber. This difference is due to the fusion splicer holders. Usually, these holders are sized for the 250 μm diameter of the fiber primary coating. If the 900 μm pigtail diameter of the buffer tube rests in the holder, the cladding may be out of the range of motion of the splicer. In this case, the splicer will be unable to align the two fibers. To avoid this potential limitation, the cleave length must be long enough to allow the cladding to be positioned in the appropriate groove (Figure 22-11).

A potential consequence of this increased cleave length is increased splice cover length. It is possible that a 40 mm splice cover will not cover and support the bare fiber and the increased length of the bare fiber of the pigtail. In this case, the installer will use the 60 mm splice cover.

The measurement of pigtail splice loss can be different from that of the mid span splice. If the length of the pigtail is shorter than the width of the dead zone, it will not be possible to measure the loss of the splice (13.3.6.2 and Figure 13-41). In this case, the installer measures the total loss of the splice and the connector on the pigtail.[2] This measurement requires a launch cable attached to the pigtail instead of the end of the cable being spliced.

If the pigtail is longer than the dead zone of the OTDR, the installer can measure the splice loss of the pigtail separately from the that of the connector.

Pigtail splicing requires ten steps, many of which are identical, or almost identical, to those of mid-span splicing (22):

 ➤ Cable end preparation

 ➤ Enclosure preparation

 ➤ Cable attachment

 ➤ Buffer tube attachment

 ➤ Splicing

 ➤ Fiber coiling

 ➤ Buffer tube coiling

 ➤ Tray attachment

 ➤ Enclosure finishing

 ➤ Testing

---

[1] Mechanical splicing of pigtails is rare, as it reduces, and can eliminate, the cost advantage of pigtail splicing.

[2] In this case, it is possible to estimate the loss of the pigtail splice by performing a single end test of a jumper that is twice the length of the pigtail.

## 23.2    TOOLS AND SUPPLIES

➤ One loose tube cable with at least 6 fibers[3]

➤ Six 200 ' lengths of 2 mm or 3 mm pigtails [4] or three 2 m patch cords with a diameter of either 3 mm or 900 µm[5]

➤ All items listed in 22.2, except cable

## 23.3    END PREPARATION

### 23.3.1    CABLE

The installer prepares the end of the cable by the procedure in 22.3.

### 23.3.2    PIGTAIL

#### 23.3.2.1    LONG PIGTAIL

A long pigtail is longer than the dead zone of the OTDR. Long pigtails require no qualification.[6]

#### 23.3.2.2    SHORT PIGTAIL

A short pigtail is shorter than the width of the OTDR dead zone. As such, the OTDR splice loss includes the connector loss. Short pigtails require qualification of the connector.[7]

---

[3] To perform pigtail splicing, the installer needs a cable longer than the dead zone of the OTDR. A practical length is greater than three times the length of the dead zone. For 12 fibers per buffer tube, double the number of pigtails and patch cords. The quantity of six fibers is recommended for training.

[4] The 200' length is for training purposes and is convenient for simulating field installation The 200' length enables separate measurement of the splice loss and the pigtail connector loss. The fiber should be the same type as in the cable.

[5] We suggest a pigtail length of 1 m and a jumper length of 2 m.

[6] Because of this length, the pigtail splice loss and the connector loss will be measurable separately.

[7] Professional installers may not perform this qualification. Instead, they assume that the connector is low loss and assume a value for the connector loss. They calculate an OTDR splice

To qualify the connector, the installer starts with a patch cord that is double the length of the pigtail. He performs a single-end loss test as described in 23.3.2.3 or 23.3.2.4 and in Figures 13-8 to 13-10.

#### 23.3.2.3    SINGLEMODE QUALIFICATION

The installer makes a two-inch diameter loop[8] in a qualified reference lead with the same MFD as in the cable and pigtail. He measures the launch power as in Figure 13-8. He inserts the patch cord (the 'B' lead in Figure 13-9) between the qualified reference lead and the power meter. The loss should be less than 0.5 dB.[9] If that loss is less than 0.5 dB, the installer records that value on a label. He attaches that label to end 1. If not, he rejects this patch cord and attempts to qualify a different patch cord.

The installer inserts the patch cord between the reference lead and the power meter in the direction opposite to that of the first test (Figure 13-10). The loss should be less than 0.5 dB. If that loss is less than 0.5 dB, he records that value on a label. He attaches that label to end 2. If not, he rejects this patch cord and attempts to qualify a different patch cord. If both ends exhibit loss less than 0.5 dB, the installer cuts the patch cord in half for use as pigtails.

#### 23.3.2.4    MULTIMODE QUALIFICATION

Follow the procedure in 23.3.2.3 with a Category 1 source (13.3.1) without the two-inch loop but with a qualified reference lead with the same core diameter as in the cable and pigtail.[10]

#### 23.3.2.5    PREPARATION

The installer removes the jacket and strength members from the pigtail to the length required by the tray. If the tray instructions do not include these

---

loss acceptance value by adding that value to the splice loss. This procedure risks increased cost.

[8] This loop eliminates high order modes that can create high connector loss measurements.

[9] We make the assumption of factory installed, adhesive connectors. When properly installed, such connectors rarely exceed 0.5 dB loss.

[10] This test does not require a mandrel on the A lead. Use of the mandrel reduces connector loss measurements.

dimensions, the length of jacket removed is sufficient to allow the 900 μm buffer tube to make at least one circumference in the tray (Figure 23-1).

## 23.4    ENCLOSURE PREPARATION

The installer prepares the enclosure (22.4).

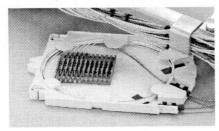

Figure 23-1: Pigtail Length[11]

## 23.5    CABLE ATTACHMENT

The installer attaches the cable strength members of the cable to the enclosure (22.5).

For an indoor enclosure, the attachment will be different from that for an outdoor enclosure (Figure 23-2). At this time, the installer does not attach the pigtails to the enclosure or to the tray.

## 23.6    BUFFER TUBE ATTACHMENT

The installer attaches one buffer tube from the cable to the splice tray (22.6). With a new tray for each buffer tube, the installer repeats this step for each buffer tube.

Figure 23-2: Cable Attachment To Enclosure

---

[11] Photograph is courtesy of Preformed Line Products.

## 23.7    FIBER LENGTH VERIFICATION

The installer verifies the fiber length (22.7).

## 23.8    OTDR

### 23.8.1    SET UP

The installer connects the OTDR launch cable to the OTDR. He enters the index of refraction, the maximum length of the cable to be tested,[12] the time of the test, the wavelength of the test, and the pulse width necessary to obtain a loss measurement in an acceptable time.

### 23.8.2    PIGTAIL CONNECTOR LOSS MEASUREMENT

Using the OTDR launch cable as the A lead and the double length pigtail as the B lead, the installer performs a single end test of the pigtail in both directions (Figures 13-8 to 13-10).[13] He labels the connectors and records the pigtail connector losses in both directions. The installer will use these values to evaluate the OTDR splice loss measurements.

## 23.9    SPLICING

The installer repeats this step for each fiber in the tray.

### 23.9.1    FUSION SPLICING

#### 23.9.1.1    FIBER FROM CABLE

The installer follows the procedure in 22.9.1-22.9.10 for the fiber from the cable.

#### 23.9.1.2    PIGTAIL

The installer repeats 22.9.1.8-22.9.1.10 for the pigtail. The cleave length will be appropriate for the splicer. For example, the

---

[12] To have a measurable splice loss, this pigtail length must be more than three times the width of the dead zone.

[13] Though not rigorous for multimode pigtails, this method is reasonably accurate for singlemode pigtails.

Fujikura FSM-30S splicer requires a cleave length of 18 mm.

### 23.9.1.3   FUSE AND COVER INSTALLATION

The installer performs the steps in 22.9.1.12 to 22.9.1.14.2.

## 23.9.2   MECHANICAL SPLICE

The installer repeats this step for each fiber in the tray. The installer follows the procedure in 22.9.2. After each splice, the installer proceeds to 23.10.

## 23.10 TEST LOSS

### 23.10.1   PIGTAIL SPLICE LOSS

The installer connects the OTDR launch cable to the spliced pigtail. The installer makes a trace of the spliced fiber. If the pigtail is longer than the dead zone of the OTDR, the installer measures the splice loss.

If the pigtail is shorter than the dead zone of the OTDR, the loss at the end of the launch cable is the total of the connector loss and the splice loss. The installer subtracts the measured pigtail connector loss (23.8.2) from the splice loss measured on the OTDR. This difference is the splice loss. If this loss is acceptable, the installer proceeds to 23.11.

### 23.10.2   RETESTING

This section applies to short pigtails. If the splice loss is higher than the splice acceptance value,[14] the installer inspects the connectors on the launch cable and on the pigtail with a microscope. Both cores should be free of features (21). The installer cleans the connectors on the pigtail and the launch cable. The installer makes a repeat trace of

---

[14] The installer obtains the splice acceptance value from the splicer or from the mechanical splice data sheet. The installer can use the TIA/EIA-568-B value of 0.3 dB. The installer can use the FOA certification value of 0.15 dB. Finally, The installer can use the typical splice acceptance value calculated from the strategy in Chapter 14, which is 0.125 dB.

the spliced fiber. Finally, the installer repeats the steps in 23.10.1. If the splice loss is unacceptably high, the installer replaces the splice.

## 23.10.3   RE-ENTERABLE SPLICES[15]

If the splice allows multiple uses, the installer can open the splice, rotate one of the fibers, close the splice and test the splice. The installer repeats this process until he achieves the lowest loss measurement.

If this lowest loss is not acceptable, the installer repeats this process on the second fiber until he achieves the lowest loss measurement. If this measurement is not acceptable, the installer replaces this splice.

## 23.11 FIBER COILING

The installer repeats this process for all pigtails in the tray (Figure 23-3).

No reverse twisting (22.11) is required for a pigtail splice. As in 22.11, the installer coils the fiber and pigtail into the splice tray until the splice cover or the mechanical splice is at the splice holder. He places the splice into the appropriate position of the splice holder (22.11). He coils the pigtail inside the splice tray for one full circumference. He attaches the pigtail to the splice tray according to the instructions for the splice tray.

If the jacket is not present on the pigtail, the installer coils all the buffer tube except the length necessary to feed the connector to the appropriate barrel in the patch panel (Figure 23-3).

If the instructions require use of a cable tie, the installer tightens the cable tie over the jacket tightly enough to prevent the jacket from slipping out from under the cable tie.

## 23.12 BUFFER TUBE COILING

The installer coils the buffer tube (22.12).

---

[15] It is possible to open the 3M splice, remove the fibers and reuse the splice. We have not tested such reuse.

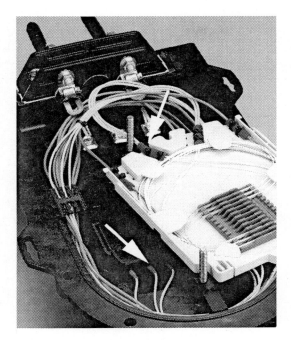

Figure 23-3: Pigtails In Enclosure

## 23.13  TRAY ATTACHMENT

The installer attaches the trays to the enclosure (22.13).

## 23.14  ENCLOSURE FINISHING

The installer finishes the enclosure (22.14).

## 23.15  TROUBLESHOOTING

See 22.15.

## 23.16  SUMMARY

### 23.16.1   END PREPARATION

Determine end preparation dimensions

Prepare cable end

Qualify short pigtail

Prepare pigtail end

### 23.16.2   ENCLOSURE PREPARATION

If required, replace buffer tubes (22.3.2)

Attach cable to enclosure

Verify fiber length

Attach buffer tube to tray

### 23.16.3   OTDR

Set OTDR parameters

Qualify the connector on the end of the launch cable

### 23.16.4   FUSION SPLICING

Set up splicer

Activate appropriate splice menu

Set maximum cleave angle

Set splice cover length

Check optics

Prepare cleaver

Install splice cover

Strip and clean fiber

Cleave fiber

Place fiber in splicer

Strip, clean and cleave pigtail

Place pigtail in splicer

Fuse

Review estimated loss

Shrink splice cover

### 23.16.5   MECHANICAL SPLICE

Prepare splice tool

Prepare cleaver

Strip and clean fiber

Cleave fiber

Place fiber in mechanical splice

Strip, clean and cleave pigtail

Place pigtail in splice

Make the bows equal

**23.16.6    TEST LOSS**

**23.16.7    COIL FIBER**

**23.16.8    COIL BUFFER TUBE**

**23.16.9    ATTACH TRAY**

**23.16.10  FINISH ENCLOSURE**

# 24  RIBBON SPLICING

Chapter Objectives: in this chapter, you will learn how to perform the activities of ribbon splicing for multimode or singlemode ribbons.

## 24.1  INTRODUCTION

Ribbon splicing is similar to single fiber splicing, but different in seven important details.

> Furcation tubing

> Thermal ribbon stripper

> Ribbon Cleaver

> Cleaves

> Holders

> Splice covers

> Splice loss

The installer uses furcation tubing (Figure 24-1) to route each ribbon from the end of the cable to the splice tray. This necessity results from the fact that multiple ribbons are in a single buffer tube and must be protected as they are routed from the cable end to the splice tray.[1]

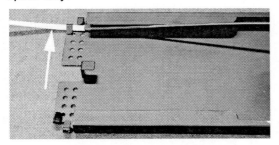

Figure 24-1: Ribbon Furcation Tubing

The installer uses a thermal stripper to remove the ribbon and primary coatings. The thermal stripper strips the ribbon and the primary coatings from all fibers without damage.

The installer uses a ribbon cleaver, which is a modification of a single fiber cleaver. The ribbon cleaver scribes and breaks all fibers simultaneously.

All cleaves must the same length. This requirement is a significant difference from single fiber cleaving, in that single fiber fusion splicers can compensate for different cleave lengths of the two fibers. In comparison, ribbon splicer cannot compensate for different cleave lengths in the same ribbon.

To achieve proper cleave lengths, ribbon splicers have holders, which are used during stripping, cleaving and splicing. The use of holders significantly simplifies the handling of the ribbon.

The splice covers are ribbon splice covers, which are larger than single fiber, splice covers.

Not all splices need meet the same low loss requirement imposed on single fiber splices. Since the ribbon fibers are aligned as a group, it is possible that one splice will have a loss higher than the maximum acceptance value because each fiber is not optimally aligned. This situation may be acceptable as long as the end-to-end loss is sufficiently low. In fact, this situation may be unavoidable due to fiber-to-fiber variations in core diameter, MFD, core offset and cladding non-circularity.

Mid span ribbon splicing requires ten steps:

> Cable end preparation

> Enclosure preparation

> Cable attachment

> Furcation tube attachment

> Splicing

> Ribbon coiling

> Furcation tube coiling

> Tray attachment

> Enclosure finishing

> Testing

---

[1] While possible, it is unusual for a single ribbon to be in a buffer tube.

## 24.2 TOOLS AND SUPPLIES REQUIRED[2]

- Jacket slitter
- Kevlar® cutters
- Two ribbon cable ends[3]
- Gel/grease remover
- Paper towels or clean rags
- Ribbon splice covers
- Ribbon fusion splicer with holders for the number of fibers in the ribbon
- Ribbon thermal stripper which accepts holders from the splicer
- Ribbon cleaver which accepts holders from the splicer
- Heat shrink oven for splice covers or adhesive splice covers
- Ribbon furcation tubing
- 98% isopropyl alcohol or Electrowash Px
- Lens grade tissues
- An OTDR
- A launch cable; the launch cable will need either a mechanical splice or have a connector of the same type as that on the end of the cable
- An outdoor splice enclosure
- One splice tray with splice holder suitable for the ribbon splice cover per ribbon to be spliced
- Cable ties for buffer tubes and for pigtails
- Optional: index matching gel
- Optional: 0.004" piano wire
- Optional: reusable mechanical splice, Elastomeric splice, (FIS)

- Lint free swabs

## 24.3 CABLE END PREPARATION

### 24.3.1 DIMENSIONS
From the enclosure instructions, identify the following dimensions

- Length of jacket to be removed
- Length of strength member to be left
- Length of central strength member to be left
- Length of buffer tube to be left
- Length of furcation tube to be installed on ribbons

### 24.3.2 END PREPARATION
The installer prepares the cable end to those dimensions (24.3.1). The installer follows the cable end preparation procedure (15).

Following the instructions for the enclosure, the installer installs the specified length of furcation tubing on each of the ribbons.[4] If required, the installer installs spiral wrap over the cable buffer tube and the furcation tubes.[5]

## 24.4 ENCLOSURE PREPARATION
The installer prepares the enclosure according to the instructions for that enclosure (22.4).

## 24.5 CABLE ATTACHMENT
The installer attaches the cable strength members of both cables to the same end of the enclosure according to the instructions for that enclosure (22.5).

[2] See Chapters 15, 16, 17, and 22 for sources of materials.

[3] To perform mid span splicing, you will need two cables. The cables must be longer than the dead zone of the OTDR. For practical purposes, this length should be at least three times the width of the dead zone.

[4] The furcation tubing will be long enough to create a loop of ribbon inside the enclosure. This loop will make a single circuit around the inside of the enclosure before entering the splice tray. The furcation tubing will enter the tray for approximately 1".

[5] The spiral wrap (Figure 22-35) attaches the furcation tubing to the end of the cable.

## 24.6  FURCATION TUBE ATTACHMENT

The installer repeats this step with a separate tray for each pair of furcation tubes.

The position of the ribbon is its number in the stack. Arbitrarily, we call the top of the ribbon the side that has primary coating exposed. Arbitrarily, we call the top ribbon in the stack the number one ribbon.

The installer selects the same ribbon position from each cable.[6] The installer straightens out both furcation tubes to eliminate all twisting. While maintaining straight furcation tubes, the installer routes one furcation tube from each cable to the same end of the same splice tray (Figure 24-2).

Figure 24-2: Attached Furcation Tubes

By the method specified in the instructions for the splice tray, the installer attaches both furcation tubes to the tray. Some trays require pinching of a tab over the furcation tube (Figure 24-2). Other trays require a cable tie around the furcation tube and a portion of the tray (Figure 12-11).

## 24.7  FIBER LENGTH VERIFICATION

The installer verifies the length of the ribbons (22.7).

The installer routes the ribbons out of the tray. Without twisting or crossing the ribbons, the installer routes the ribbons from each furcation tube to opposite sides of the splicer (Figure 24-3).

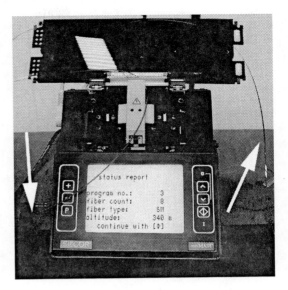

Figure 24-3: Ribbons Routed To Splicer

## 24.8  OTDR SET UP

The installer sets up the OTDR (22.8). The installer connects the OTDR to the first fiber to be spliced. The installer can make this connection with a launch cable with the same connector style as on the end of the cable. Alternatively, the installer can make this connection to a cable with a reusable mechanical splice.[7]

The installer runs a trace of the first fiber to be spliced in order to determine the distance to the cable end. The installer records that distance.

## 24.9  FUSION SPLICING[8]

The installer performs this step for each pair of ribbons.

### 24.9.1  SPLICER SET UP

The installer plugs in and turns on the splicer. The installer opens all covers. The installer inspects the grooves. With a lint

[6] Unless there is an overriding reason, use the same position ribbon from both cables.

[7] We suggest use of the Elastomeric Lab Splice (Fiber Instrument Sales). For repeated use of the same splice, the installer will need a vial of index matching gel and a 0.004" piano wire to remove broken fibers from the splice.

[8] This procedure is based on the Corning Cable Systems (formerly Siecor®) miniMASS™ Fusion Splicer, model C752. Other splicers have similar procedures. This splicer is a system, with integrated holders, cleaver and thermal stripper.

free, fiber optic swab, the installer cleans the grooves by swabbing from the inside end of the fiber grooves to the outside end (Figure 24-4).[9,10]

Figure 24-4: Ribbon Splicer Grooves

## 24.9.2 SPLICE MENU

The installer examines the active menu in the splicer (Figure 24-5). If the active menu is the one the installer wants, he proceeds. If it is not, the installer activates the appropriate menu according to the instructions for the splicer.

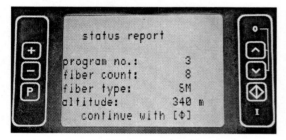

Figure 24-5: Active Menu

The installer examines the number of fibers in the active program. If the active number is the one the installer wants, he proceeds. If not, the installer activates the appropriate

---

[9] If the installer swabs in the opposite direction, he may contaminate the mirrors and optics with dust. If the installer uses a swab moistened with isopropyl alcohol, the isopropyl alcohol may contaminate the mirrors and optics with water marks. If the installer uses lens grade gas, the cold gas can cause water marks on the mirrors and optics. Such contamination can result in error messages from the splicer software.

[10] If the installer has repeated problems with fiber alignment, he will clean out the grooves until he eliminates the problem.

---

number according to the instructions for the splicer.

### 24.9.2.1 MAXIMUM CLEAVE ANGLE[11]

If required, the installer examines and, if necessary changes, the maximum cleave acceptance angle.

## 24.9.3 COVER LENGTH[14]

If required, the installer examines and, if necessary changes, the splice cover length.

## 24.9.4 OPTICS CHECK

The installer checks the screen image. The image should be free from spots. If spots or dust exist, the installer cleans the mirrors in accordance with the instructions for the splicer.

## 24.9.5 PREPARE CLEAVER

The installer opens, cleans and sets up the cleaver according to its instructions.

## 24.9.6 INSTALL SPLICE COVER

If the installer is using adhesive splice covers, he ignores this step. The installer places a heat shrink splice cover on one of the ribbons.

## 24.9.7 RIBBON STRIP

The installer pre-heats the thermal stripper for the length of time indicated in the stripper instructions.

The installer determines a ribbon orientation: he chooses one of the fiber colors on the edge of the ribbon to be the 'top' fiber. He places the ribbon in the holder so that that color is on top. He installs all ribbons into the holders with the chosen color on top.

He places the ribbon in the holder with 1.25" -1.5" of ribbon exposed (Figure 24-6).[12] He places the ribbon in the pre-heated thermal stripper and closes the stripper (Figure 24-7 and Figure 24-8).

---

[11] This step is not required for the miniMASS™ splicer.

[12] The ribbon stripper determines the strip length.

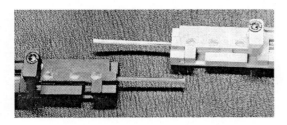

Figure 24-6: Ribbon In Holder

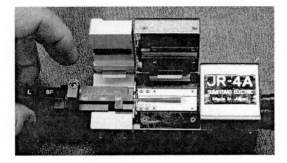

Figure 24-7: Ribbon In Open Thermal
Stripper

He allows the ribbon to soften for one to two
minutes. While holding both covers against
the ribbon, the installer slowly pulls the cool
end of the stripper away from the hot end.[13]

Figure 24-8: Ribbon In Closed Thermal
Stripper

If the installer has allowed sufficient heating
time and used enough pressure on the hot
cover, the fibers will appear without the
ribbon and the primary coatings (Figure
24-9). If the primary coating or ribbon
remains on the fibers, the installer wipes the
fibers with a lens grade tissue and isopropyl
alcohol. He places the fibers into the thermal
stripper for one to two minutes. As before,
he pulls the cool end of the stripper away
from the hot end.

---

[13] To prevent burnt fingers, the installer can place
a piece of heavy card stock on top of the hot
section of the stripper.

Figure 24-9: Properly Stripped Fibers

The installer moistens a lens grade tissue
with isopropyl alcohol. He makes a fold in
the tissue. He pulls the fiber through the fold
at least twice. He examines the fibers: he
should see no particles on the cladding
(Figure 24-10) .

Figure 24-10: Cleaned Fibers

## 24.9.8    FIBER CLEAVING

The installer places the holder with the clean
fibers in the cleaver (Figure 24-11). He
slowly presses the cleaver arm down and
releases the arm. He disposes of the broken
fibers.

Figure 24-11: Ribbon In Cleaver

He examines the fibers. All lengths should be the same (Figure 24-12). If all fibers do not have the same length, the installer cuts off the bare fibers and repeats 24.9.7 and 24.9.8.

Figure 24-12: Improperly Cleaved Fiber

## 24.9.9    FIBER PLACEMENT

Following the instructions for the splicer, the installer resets the splicer to start. From its side of the splicer, the installer places the first ribbon holder into the splicer. The installer evaluates the cleaved fibers for proper fiber placement in grooves, quality of cleaves and equality of cleave lengths. If placement is improper (Figure 24-13) or if the lengths are unequal or if one or more cleaves are bad (Figure 24-14), he repeats 24.9.7-24.9.9.

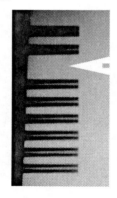

Figure 24-13: Improperly Seated Fibers

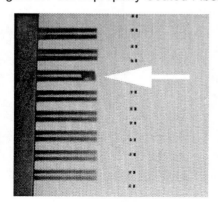

Figure 24-14: Fiber With Bad Cleave

## 24.9.10    SECOND FIBER

The installer verifies that the color of the fiber on the top of the second ribbon is correct. He repeats 24.9.7-24.9.9 for the second fiber. If the installer has prepared and installed both fibers correctly, the fibers will appear as in Figure 24-15.

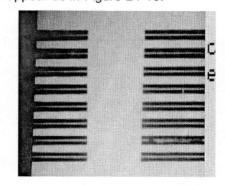

Figure 24-15: Ribbons Ready For Splicing

## 24.9.11    FUSING

To begin the splicing process, the installer pushes the fuse button. Splicers may allow the installer the option of reviewing and accepting the cleave angles and alignment prior to proceeding to the next step. If this option is active, the installer pushes the fuse button several times. The splicer will cycle through the steps of fusing, such as those in Figure 24-16 to Figure 24-19.

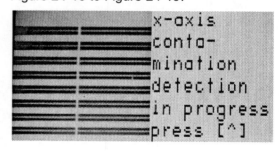

Figure 24-16: Contamination Check

Figure 24-17: Core Offset Check

Figure 24-18: Appearance During Fusing

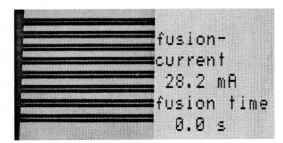

Figure 24-19: Appearance After Fusing

## 24.9.12  ESTIMATED LOSS REVIEW

If the splicer has a splice loss estimation feature, the splicer will display the estimated splice loss. If this estimation correlates with OTDR splice loss measurements,[14] and if the value is acceptable (Figure 24-20), the installer proceeds to 24.9.13. If not, the installer breaks the splice and repeats Steps 24.9.7-24.9.11.

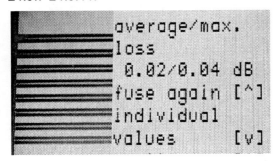

Figure 24-20: Estimated Loss Values

## 24.9.13  COVER SHRINKING

The installer repeats this step for all ribbons in the cables.

The installer slides the splice cover up to the fiber holder. He opens both fiber holders. While holding the ribbon from the holder opposite to the splice cover, he slides the cover over the bare glass gently so that the bare glass is centered in the cover.

The installer opens the oven cover and the two fiber holders on either side of the oven. He places the cover in the oven. He rechecks the ribbon to ensure that the splice is in the center of the cover. He closes the cover (Figure 24-21).[15] He allows the heating cycle to complete. During this cycle, he prepares the next two ribbons for splicing.

Figure 24-21: Oven Covers Closed

After the heating cycle is complete, the installer uses a toothpick or tweezers to move the splice cover towards one side of the heating oven. This will cause the cover to become free from the oven surface.[16] With pair of tweezers, he removes the splice cover from the oven. He transfers the splice to the splice tray.

| Caution |
|---|
| Do not grip the splice cover with the tweezers tightly. Do not grip the splice cover on the area of the bare glass. Doing so may break the fiber inside the cover. |

After each splice, proceed to 24.9.14.

## 24.9.14  TEST LOSS

The installer tests the splice losses with an OTDR. If the loss is acceptable, he transfers

[14] For simplicity, we have assumed that such correlation exists. If such correlation does not exist, the installer will measure the loss of each splice after he makes the splice and after he places the tray in the enclosure.

[15] On some ovens, closing the cover starts the heating cycle.

[16] The splice cover may stick to the inside of the oven. If the installer tries to remove the splice from the oven without eliminating this sticking, he may break the fiber inside the cover.

the ribbon to the splice tray. If not, he breaks the splice and repeats 24.9.7 to 24.9.14.[17]

## 24.10  PROCESS COMPLETION

The installer completes the splicing process (22.11-22.14).

## 24.11  TROUBLESHOOTING

### 24.11.1  STRIPPING

#### 24.11.1.1  RIBBON AND COATING NOT STRIPPED

Potential cause: insufficient pressure on hot section of stripper
Corrective action: increase pressure on hot section

Potential cause: excessively rapid stripping rate
Corrective action: pull the hot and cold ends of the stripper slowly apart. Allow primary coating and ribbon to be removed

Potential cause: insufficient time in stripper
Corrective action: increase time from previous value

Potential cause: low temperature
Corrective action: increase temperature

Potential cause: stripper unplugged
Corrective action: plug in stripper and allow stripper to pre-heat

### 24.11.2  CLEAVING

#### 24.11.2.1  OCCASIONAL BAD CLEAVE

Potential cause: fibers in cleaver from previous cleave
Corrective action: clean the holding pads of the cleaver and the ribbon holder recessed area before each use

Potential cause: dirt on scribing wheel
Corrective action: clean scribing wheel with isopropyl alcohol

Potential cause: dirt or dust on gripping pads

Corrective action: clean the gripping pads with isopropyl alcohol

#### 24.11.2.2  FREQUENT BAD CLEAVE

Potential cause: dirt on scribing wheel
Corrective action: clean scribing wheel with isopropyl alcohol

Potential cause: worn scribing wheel
Corrective action: rotate scribing wheel to next position

Potential cause: completely worn scribing wheel
Corrective action: replace scribing wheel

#### 24.11.2.3  UNEQUAL CLEAVE LENGTHS

See 24.11.2.1 and 24.11.2.

Potential cause: excessively rapid lowering of cleaver arm
Corrective action: lower arm slowly[18]

### 24.11.3  SPLICING

#### 24.11.3.1  IMPROPER FIBER SPACING

Potential cause: fiber in wrong groove
Corrective action: remove fibers and replace fibers

Potential cause: dirt in grooves
Corrective action: clean grooves with soft brush. Brush grooves away from the center of the splicer

Potential cause: dirt on cladding
Corrective action: inspect fibers for dirt on cladding. Clean fibers with lens grade tissue and isopropyl alcohol

Potential cause: damaged grooves
Corrective action: send splicer to manufacturer for replacement of grooves

#### 24.11.3.2  CONSISTENT HIGH LOSS ON THE SAME FIBER

Potential cause: dirty of worn[19] electrodes
Corrective action: clean or replace electrodes

---

[17] This step has no error in sequence. To arrive at this step, the splicer loss estimations indicated an acceptably low splice loss on all fibers.

[18] Rapid lowering of cleaver arm is similar to use of a hand stapler.

[19] Some manufacturers recommend cleaning or replacement of electrodes after 1000 arcs. We have found electrodes produce low loss splices to a much higher number of arcs.

Potential cause: mismatch of core diameter, MFD, NA, offset or non-circularity
Corrective action: there is no appropriate corrective action

### 24.11.3.3  OCCASIONAL HIGH LOSS ON ONE FIBER

Potential cause: high, but acceptable, cleave angle
Corrective action: remake splice

Potential cause: mismatch of core diameter, MFD, NA, offset or non-circularity
Corrective action: there is no appropriate corrective action

## 24.11.4  FINISHING

### 24.11.4.1  RIBBONS DO NOT LIE FLAT IN TRAY

Potential cause: twist on ribbons present prior to splicing
Corrective action: break splice, remove twist, and make new splice

Potential cause: ribbons placed in tray without the reverse twist (22.11)
Corrective action: remove ribbons from tray; re-install ribbons with reverse twist

## 24.12  SUMMARY

### 24.12.1  CABLE END PREPARATION

Determine the end preparation dimensions

Prepare the cable end

### 24.12.2  ENCLOSURE PREPARATION

Install new buffer tubes or furcation tubes

Attach the cable to the enclosure

Attach the buffer tubes to trays

Verify the ribbon lengths

### 24.12.3  SET UP OTDR

Set OTDR parameters

### 24.12.4  FUSION SPLICING

Set up the splicer

Activate the appropriate splice menu

Set the maximum cleave angle

Set the splice cover length

Check the optics

Prepare the cleaver

Install the splice cover

Install ribbons in holders

Strip the ribbon

Clean the ribbon

Cleave the ribbon

Place the ribbon in the splicer

Check cleave lengths, cleave angles, and fiber spacing

Strip, clean and cleave the second ribbon

Place the second ribbon in the splicer

Fuse the ribbons

Review the estimated loss

Shrink the splice cover

Test the losses

### 24.12.5  COIL RIBBONS

### 24.12.6  COIL BUFFER TUBES

### 24.12.7  ATTACH TRAYS

### 24.12.8  FINISH ENCLOSURE

# 25   APPENDICES

## 25.1   INDICES OF REFRACTION

### 25.1.1   SINGLEMODE

| Supplier | Product | 850 nm | 1300 nm | 1310 nm | 1550 nm |
|----------|---------|--------|---------|---------|---------|
| Alcatel | 6901 | | | 1.4640 | 1.4640 |
| Alcatel | 6900 | | | 1.4640 | 1.4645 |
| Corning Inc. | SMF-28 | | | 1.4677 | 1.4682 |
| Corning Inc. | SMF-28e | | | 1.4677 | 1.4682 |
| Corning Inc. | NexCor | | | 1.4670 | 1.4677 |
| Corning Inc. | MetroCor | | | | 1.469 |
| Corning Inc. | Leaf™ | | | | 1.469 |
| OFS | TruWave Reach | | | 1.471 | 1.470 |
| OFS | TruWave RS | | | 1.471 | 1.470 |
| OFS | AllWave ZWP | | | 1.466 | 1.467 |
| OFS | Matched Clad | | | 1.466 | 1.467 |
| Plasma | ESMF G.652.D | | | 1.467 | 1.468 |
| Plasma | G.652.B | | | 1.466 | 1.467 |
| Plasma | TeraLight Metro | | | 1.469 | 1.4692 |

### 25.1.2   50 µm

| Supplier | Product | 850 nm | 1300 nm | 1310 nm | 1550 nm |
|----------|---------|--------|---------|---------|---------|
| Alcatel | 6930 | 1.482 | 1.480 | | |
| Alcatel | 6931 | 1.482 | 1.480 | | |
| Corning Inc | InfiniCor | 1.481 | 1.476 | | |
| Corning Inc. | 50/125 | 1.490 | 1.486 | | |
| OFS | LaserWave 550 | 1.483 | 1.479 | | |
| OFS | LaserWave 300 | 1.483 | 1.479 | | |
| OFS | LaserWave G+ | 1.483 | 1.479 | | |
| Plasma | Maxcap 550 | 1.482 | 1.477 | | |
| Plasma | Maxcap 300 | 1.482 | 1.477 | | |
| Plasma | 50 | 1.482 | 1.477 | | |
| Plasma | Hicap 50 | 1.482 | 1.477 | | |

### 25.1.3   62.5 µm

| Supplier | Product | 850 nm | 1300 nm | 1310 nm | 1550 nm |
|----------|---------|--------|---------|---------|---------|
| Alcatel | 6932 | 1.497 | 1.492 | | |
| Corning, Inc. | Infincor | 1.496 | 1.491 | | |
| Corning Inc. | Infincor CL1000 | 1.496 | 1.487 | | |
| Corning Inc. | 62.5 | 1.496 | 1.487 | | |
| OFS | 62.5/62.5XL | 1.496 | 1.491 | | |
| Plasma | Hicap | 1.496 | 1.491 | | |
| Plasma | 62.5 | 1.496 | 1.491 | | |

## 25.2 GLOSSARY

905 SMA: see SMA 905

adapter: a device for mating two connectors. Also known as mating adapter, barrel, bulkhead and feed through

APD: avalanche photodiode. This device converts an optical signal to an electrical signal. It operates to lower optical power levels and to higher speeds than does its cousin, the photodiode.

armor: a layer of material, usually stainless steel, which is placed around a cable core to prevent damage from gnawing rodents. The armor is corrugated and covered with a layer of plastic. The plastic is heat sealed to itself.

attenuation: the loss of optical power or intensity as light travels in a fiber. It is expressed in units of decibels. When used to describe fibers or cables, it is expressed as a rate in decibels/kilometer. It is specified at a specific wavelength under precisely defined test conditions. The usual method of measurement used by fiber manufacturers is called the 'cut-back' test method. Attenuation or attenuation rate can be determined with an OTDR. In this book, attenuation refers to reduction in signal strength in the fiber or cable.

back reflection: an outdated term that was used to mean return loss or reflectance. See reflectance and return loss.

back shell: the portion of a connector in back of the retaining nut or latching mechanism.

bandwidth: a measure of the transmission capacity of an analog transmission system.

bandwidth-distance product: the product of the length of a fiber and the analog bandwidth that the fiber can transmit over that length. It is specified at a specific wavelength under precisely defined test conditions. It is expressed in units of MHz-km for multimode fibers. It is not the relevant parameter for laser optimized fibers. It is not used for singlemode fibers. Instead, the term 'dispersion rate' is used.

bend radius, long term: see bend radius, minimum unloaded.

bend radius, minimum loaded: the smallest radius to which a cable can be bent during installation at the maximum recommended installation load without any damage to either the fiber or the cable materials. Typically, this radius is 20 times the diameter.

bend radius, minimum recommended: the smallest radius to which a cable can be bent without any damage to either the fiber or the cable materials.

bend radius, minimum unloaded: the smallest radius to which a cable can be bent without any damage to either the fiber or the cable materials while the cable is unloaded. Typically, this radius is 10 times the diameter for the life of the cable.

bend radius, short term: see bend radius, minimum loaded.

biconic: a style of connector.

binding tape: a cable component. This tape holds buffer tubes together during jacket extrusion.

binding yarn: a cable component. This yarn holds buffer tubes together during jacket extrusion.

bit error rate: a measure of the accuracy of a digital fiber optic system. The BER is the rate of errors produced by the optoelectronics. Abbreviated as BER.

bit rate: the data transmission rate of a digital transmission system.

boot: a plastic device that slides over the cable and the back shell. It serves to limit the radius of curvature of the cable as the cable exits the back shell.

break out: a style of cable composed of sub cables, each of which contains a single fiber.

buffer coating: a layer of plastic placed around the clad by the fiber manufacturer.

buffer coating diameter: the diameter of the layer of plastic that is placed around the fiber by the fiber manufacturer. Typical diameters are 250 and 500 µm.

buffer tube: a layer of plastic that surrounds a fiber or a group of fibers.

bulkhead: see adapter.

butt coupling: a method of transmitting light from one fiber to another by precise mechanical alignment of the two fiber ends without the use of lenses.

BWDP: bandwidth-distance product.

cable: the structure that protects an optical fiber or fibers during installation and use.

cable core: the structure of fibers, buffer tubes, fillers and strength members that reside inside the inner most jacket of a cable.

cable end boxes: the enclosures placed on the end of a cable to protect the buffer tubes and fibers.

cap: a plastic structure that protects the end of a connector ferrule from dust and damage when the connector is not in use.

CBT: see central buffer tube

central buffer tube: a cable design in which all fibers reside in a single, centrally located buffer tube.

central strength member: a strength member that resides in the center of a cable.

chromatic dispersion: the spreading of pulses of light due to rays of different wavelengths traveling at different speeds through the core.

clad diameter: the outer diameter of the clad. It is measured in micrometers.

clad non-circularity: the degree to which the clad and the core deviate from perfect circularity.

clad, cladding: the region of an optical fiber that confines the light to the core and provides additional strength to the fiber.

cleaver: device to create a flat and perpendicular surface on end of a fiber.

cleaving: the process of creating a fiber end that is flat and perpendicular to the axis of the fiber.

coating: see buffer coating

concentricity: the degree to which the core deviates from being in the exact center of the clad.

cone of acceptance: the cone defined by the critical angle or the numerical aperture. This is also the cone within which all of the light exits a fiber.

core diameter: the diameter of the region in which most of the light energy travels. It is measured in micrometers.

core offset: see concentricity.

core: the region of an optical fiber in which most of the light energy travels.

coupler: a device that allows two separate optical signals to be joined for transmission on a single fiber.

crimp ring: the device that is deformed around the back shell of a connector. The crimp ring traps the strength member of the cable, providing acceptable cable-connector strength.

critical angle: the maximum angle to the axis of a fiber at which rays of light will enter a fiber and experience total internal reflection at the core-clad boundary.

crush load, maximum recommended: the recommended maximum load that can be applied to a fiber optic cable without any permanent change in the attenuation of the cable. This can be specified as either or both of a long-term or a short-term crush load.

cut-off wavelength: the wavelength, below which a singlemode fiber will not transmit a singlemode. Below this wavelength, the singlemode fiber will transmit multimode light, at an attenuation rate that is higher than that when transmitting singlemode light.

D4: a connector style

design: used in this text to refer to a cable

dielectric: having no components that conduct electricity in the cable.

differential modal attenuation: the mechanism by which rays in multimode fibers experience differing attenuation rates due to their mode, or location in the core.

differential modal delay: the measurement of dispersion in a multimode fiber that is optimized for use with a laser source.

dispersion: the spreading of pulses in fibers. There are three types of dispersion: modal, spectral, and material.

ESCON™: a connector style.

expanded beam coupling: a method of transmitting light from one fiber to another with lenses.

FC: a connector style.

FC/PC: a connector style.

FDDI: fiber data distributed data interface.

feed through: see adapter.

ferrule: that portion of the connector with which a fiber is aligned

fiber: the structure that guides light in a fiber optic system.

Fiber Jack: see Opti-Jack™.

filled and blocked cable : a type of cable in which all empty space is filled with compounds to prevent two situations: first, the filling and blocking compounds prevent the movement of water along the axis of the cable; second, the compounds prevent water from coming into contact with the fibers. Such contact will result in a degradation of both

mechanical and optical properties of the fibers.

fillers: cable structures that fill otherwise empty space in a cable.

Fresnel reflection: the reflection that occurs when light travels between two media in which the speed of light (or index of refraction) differs.

FRP strength member: a fiberglass reinforced plastic or epoxy rod that is used as a dielectric strength member in cables. The term 'plastic' may refer to either a polymer plastic or an epoxy.

fusion splice: a splice made by melting two fibers together.

gel-filling compound: a compound placed inside a loose buffer tube to prevent water from contacting the fiber(s) in that buffer tube.

graded index: a type of multimode fiber, in which the chemical composition of the core is not uniform.

HCS™: a hard clad silica fiber.

heat shrink tubing: tubing placed on the back shell of a connector.

HiPPI: high speed, parallel processor interface.

index of refraction (IR, h): the ratio of the speed of light in the material to the speed of light in a vacuum. This is a dimensionless number, with typical values of 1.46-1.51 in communication fibers.

inner duct: a corrugated plastic pipe in which fiber optic cables are placed.

inner jacket: any layer of jacketing plastic that is not the outer-most layer.

installation strength, maximum recommended: the maximum load that can be applied along the axis of a cable without any breakage of fibers and without any permanent change in attenuation.

installation temperature range: the temperature range within which a cable can be installed without damage. The plastics used in the cable usually determine this range.

jacket: a layer of plastic in a cable. It can be an outer jacket or an inner jacket.

jumper: a short length of a single fiber cable with connectors on both ends.

Kevlar®: an aramid yard produced by Dupont Chemical. It is used to provide strength in fiber optic cables.

keying: a mechanism in connectors by which ferrules are prevented from

laser diode: a semiconductor that converts electrical signals to optical signals.

Laser optimized: a type of multimode fiber that is designed to enable long transmission distance at 1 Gb/s and 10 Gbps; long distance means in excess of those distances stated in the 802.3.

latching mechanism: device that retains a connector to a receptacle or to an adapter .

LC: a SFF connector with a 1.25 mm ferrule.

LX.5: a SFF connector with a 1.25 mm ferrule and a built-in dust cover.

LED: light emitting diode. A semiconductor that converts electrical signals to optical signals.

lensed coupling: see expanded beam coupling.

loose buffer tube: a buffer tube with space between the outer diameter of the buffer coating and the inner diameter of the buffer tube.

loose tube: a cable design in which the fiber floats loosely inside an oversized tube. The tube does not contact the entire circumference of the fiber. A loose tube can contain either 1 or more than one fiber.

loss: the end to end reduction in optical power as light travels through a fiber, connectors or splices. In this book, the 'loss' refers to reduction of optical power at a splice or a connector pair.

material dispersion: the spreading of pulses of light due to rays of light traveling through different regions of the core. These different regions have slightly different compositions. In each of these different compositions, light travels at slightly different speeds.

maximum recommended installation load: see installation strength, maximum recommended.

mechanical splice: a mechanism that aligns two fiber ends precisely for efficient transfer of light from one fiber to another.

MFPT: a multiple fiber per (buffer) tube cable design. This design usually has 6 or 12 fibers per loose buffer tube.

mini-BNC: a connector style.

minimum recommended long term bend radius: see bend radius, minimum unloaded.

minimum recommended short term bend radius: see bend radius, minimum loaded.

MPO: the generic term for a 4-12 fiber, ribbon connector with a single ferrule.

MPT: the proprietary term for a 4-12 fiber, ribbon connector with a single ferrule.

modal dispersion: the spreading of pulses of light due to rays traveling different paths through the core. Modal dispersion occurs in multimode fibers.

modal pulse spreading: see modal dispersion.

mode: one of the paths in which light can travel in a fiber core. Mode translates roughly to 'path.' A ray of light can travel in a path in a fiber core.

mode field diameter: the diameter within which the light energy field actually travels in a singlemode fiber. The mode field diameter is slightly larger than the core diameter.

monomode: a method of light transmission in which all rays of light act as though they are traveling parallel to the axis of the fiber.

MT-RJ: a duplex SFF connector with a single ferrule.

MU: a SFF connector with a size of approximately half that of the SC connector

multimode: a method of propagation of light in which all of the rays of light do not travel in a path parallel to the axis of the fiber. These rays travel paths that result in differences in time of transit for different rays. This difference in transit times result in the limitation in bandwidth which any given multimode fiber can transmit.

NA: see numerical aperture.

numerical aperture (NA): the sine of the critical angle. The NA is a measure of the solid angle within which rays of light will enter the fiber and be transmitted along the fiber.

offset, core: see core offset.

optical amplifier: a device that increases the signal strength without an optical to electrical to optical conversion.

optical coupling: see expanded beam coupling.

optical power budget: the maximum loss of optical power which a

transmitter-receiver pair can withstand while still functioning at the specified level of accuracy.

Opti-Jack™: a duplex SFF connector.

optical return loss: see return loss.

optical rotary joint: a rotating joint that allows transmission of light from a stationary fiber to a rotating fiber.

optical switch: a switch that can direct light to more than one output path.

optical time domain reflectometer: a test device that creates a map of the loss of signal strength of a passive optical path.

optical waveguide: another term for an optical fiber.

optoelectronic device: any device that converts a signal from electrical to optical domain or vice versa.

optoelectronics: see optoelectronic device.

OTDR: optical time domain reflectometer or optical time domain reflectometry.

ovality: a measure of the degree to which a fiber deviates from perfect circularity. See clad non-circularity.

passive component: a device that manipulates light without requiring an optical signal to electrical signal conversion.

patch panel: a sheet of material that contains adapter(s).

PCS: a plastic clad silica fiber.

PD: photodiode. This device converts an optical signal to an electrical signal.

pigtail: a length of fiber or cable that is permanently attached to a connector or an optoelectronic device.

ping pong: a type of transmission that results from using a single LED as both a transmitter and receiver. During one cycle, the bias on the LED is reversed from its normal bias so that it will behave as a photo diode. Use of an LED reduces its potential bandwidth due to the time required to reverse the bias completely.

plug: another term for connector.

POF: plastic optical fiber. A fiber with a plastic core and a plastic clad.

polishing fixture: device to hold connector perpendicular to fiber; for use in creating flat and perpendicular fiber surface

pull-proof: a performance characteristic of connector styles. A connector style is pull-proof when tension on the cable attached to the connector does not produce an increase in the loss of the connector pair.

pulse dispersion: see dispersion.

pulse spreading: see dispersion.

receptacle: the device within which an active device is mounted. The receptacle is designed to mate with a specific connector style. Otherwise, a pigtail is connected to the receptacle.

reflectance: the ratio of reflected power to incident power for a single device, such as a connector or mechanical splice. Reflectance is measured in units of dB.

reinforced jacket: two layers of plastic that are separated by strength members. Strength members are usually Kevlar® or fiberglass in cables not made by AT&T. Cables made by AT&T can contain steel wires as strength members.

repeatability: the maximum change in loss between successive measurements of two connectors.

retaining nut: device that retains connector to receptacle or to adapter

return loss: the ratio of reflected power to incident power for an entire link or cable system. In the past, return loss was used to refer to reflectance.

ribbon: a structure on which multiple fibers are precisely aligned.

SAP: see super absorbent polymer

Super absorbent polymer: a material that absorbs moisture by converting the moisture to a gel; used in fiber optic cables to provide moisture resistance; incorporated into cables as tapes, yarns, threads and powders.

SC: a connector style.

SFF: see 'small form factor'.

shrink tubing: plastic that covers back shell of connector

simplex: a single fiber cable.

singlemode: a method of propagation of light in which all of the energy of light arrives at the fiber at the same time. A simplistic, but technically inaccurate, explanation is that all rays of light behave as though they are traveling in a path parallel to the axis of the fiber.

slotted core: a cable design with a core containing helical slots.

SMA 905: a connector style.

SMA 906: a connector style.

small form factor: a type of connector with the characteristic of small size that enables doubling of density in patch panels, enclosures, and switches.

spectral width: the measure of the width of the output power-wavelength curve at a power level equal to half the peak power.

splice enclosure: a structure that encloses and protects splice trays and cable ends.

splice tray: a structure that encloses and protects fibers.

splice: a device for permanent alignment of two fiber ends.

splitter: a device that creates multiple optical signals from a single optical signal.

spot size: the size of the area of an LED or laser diode from which light is produced.

ST®: the first of a series of connector styles designed by ATT. Other styles from ATT are the ST-II and the ST-II+.

star core: see slotted core.

ST-compatible: a connector with a style which is compatible with the ST® connector.

step index: a type of multimode fiber, in which the chemical composition of the core is uniform. This uniform composition results in a uniform index of refraction. This uniform index of refraction allows rays of light to travel in straight lines until they are reflected from the core-clad interface. This type of reflection results in a lower bandwidth-distance than that attainable from a graded index fiber.

storage temperature range: the temperature range within which a cable can be stored without damage.

strength members: those elements of a cable design that provide strength.

style: the sum of characteristics that differentiates one connector style from another style.

TECS™: a technically enhanced clad fiber similar to hard clad silica fiber.

temperature operating range: the range of temperature within which the cable can be operated during its lifetime without degradation of either mechanical of optical properties.

tight tube: a design in which the tube does contact the entire circumference of the fiber. A tight tube can contain only 1 fiber.

total internal reflection: the mechanism by which optical fibers function. Internal reflection results from a difference in the speed of light in the core and clad. This difference results in reflection at the core-clad boundary if the angle of a ray of light to the axis of the fiber is less than or equal to the critical angle.

type: used in this text to refer to a fiber

use load, maximum recommended: the maximum longitudinal load that can be applied to a cable during its entire lifetime without increase in attenuation and without breakage of fibers. This load is typically about 10% of the maximum recommended installation load.

VCSEL: a type of relatively low cost light source that transmits at 1 Gbps and 10 Gbps; multimode VCSELs enable 1 Gb and 10 Gb Ethernet implementation; singlemode VCSELs exist.

Volition™: a duplex SFF connector with no ferrules.

water blocking compound: a compound placed in the interstices between buffer tubes or between jackets in a cable.

wavelength division multiplexer: a passive device that combines light signals with different wavelengths on different fibers light onto a single fiber. The wavelength division demultiplexer performs the reverse function.

wavelength: a measure of the color of the light for which the performance of the fiber has been optimized. It is a length stated in nanometers (nm) or in micrometers (μm).

wiggle proof: a connector performance characteristic. A connector style is wiggle proof if lateral pressure on the back shell does not produce an increase in the loss.

window: the wavelength range within which a fiber is designed to provide optimum performance. A single window product is designed for optimum performance at a single wavelength. A dual or double window product is designed for acceptable performance at two discrete windows. Typical windows for multimode fibers are 850 nm and/or 1300 nm. Typical windows for singlemode fibers are 1310 nm and/or 1550 nm.

Zip cord®: a two-fiber cable with a figure 8 cross-section that allows each of the two fibers to be separarted in the same manner as a lamp cord.

## 25.3    ACRONYMS

| | |
|---|---|
| ADSS | all dielectric self support |
| APC | angled physical contact connector |
| ATM | Asynchronous Transfer Mode |
| BER | bit error rate |
| CATV | Cable TV |
| CWDM | coarse wavelength division multiplexing |
| D4 | a connector |
| DAC | dual attachment concentrator |
| DAS | dual attachment station |
| DS | dispersion shifted |
| DS-NZD | dispersion shifted, non-zero dispersion |
| DWDM | dense wavelength division Multiplexing |
| EDFA | erbium doped fiber amplifier |
| ESCON | Enterprise System Connectivity |
| FC | a connector type |
| FDDI | fiber data distributed interface |
| FOLS | Fiber Optic LAN Section of the TIA |
| FTTD | fiber to the desk |
| FTTH | fiber to the home |
| FTTP | fiber to the premises |

| FTTX | any of the above three |
| GI | graded index |
| HDPE | high density polyethylene |
| IP | Internet Protocol |
| LAN | local area network |
| LD | laser diode |
| LEAF™ | large effective area fiber (Corning Inc.) |
| LED | light emitting diode |
| LSA | least squares analysis |
| LX.5 | a connector type |
| MFPT | multiple fiber per tube |
| MIC | media interface connector |
| MM | multimode |
| MT-RJ | a duplex connector type |
| MU | a SFF connector type |
| NA | numerical aperture |
| NDS | non dispersion shifted |
| NEC | National Electrical Code |
| NIST | National Institute of Science and Technology |
| OFC | optical fiber cable, conductive, horizontal rated |
| OFCP | optical fiber cable, conductive, plenum rated |
| OFCR | optical fiber cable, conductive, riser rated |
| OFN | optical fiber cable, non conductive, horizontal rated |
| OFNP | optical fiber cable, non conductive, plenum rated |
| OFNR | optical fiber cable, non conductive, riser rated |
| OPBA | optical power budget available |
| OPBR | optical power budget requirement |
| PC | physical contact |
| PMD | polarization mode dispersion |
| PON | passive optical network |
| SAN | storage area network |
| SAP | super absorbent polymer |
| SAC | single attachment concentrator |
| SAS | single attachment station |
| SC | a connector type |
| SDH | Sychronous Digital Hierarchy |
| SI | step index |
| SM | singlemode |
| SONET | synchronous optical network |
| STP | shield twisted pair |
| UPC | ultra physical contact |
| UTP | unshielded twisted pair |
| VCSEL | vertical cavity, surface emitting laser |
| WDM | wavelength division multiplexing |
| ZDW | zero dispersion wavelength |

## 25.4  CHAPTER 12 ANSWERS

The supervisor rents the splicer with the estimation feature. At three days, or 24 man hours, the cost of the OTDR operator will be $1200, if the splicer has no estimation feature. Each splice will need to be tested prior to installing the splice in the splice tray. The OTDR technician will sit idle while the splicing technician makes the splices. With the estimation feature, the OTDR technician can test the splices after they are all complete in one day. With the estimation feature, the cost of the OTDR technician will be $400, which is an $800 reduction in labor cos., for a net savings of $300.

## 25.5  CHAPTER 14 ANSWERS

1. Insertion loss acceptance value= 3.775 dB[1]

   OTDR acceptance values
   Attenuation rate: 1.1 dB/km
   Connector loss: 0.525 dB/pair
   Splice loss: 0.125 dB/splice

| Loss in | dB/km | | #km | | dB |
|---|---|---|---|---|---|
| Cable | 1.5 | * | 2.0 | = | 3.00 |
| | dB/pair | | #pairs | | |
| Connector | .75 | * | 3 | = | 2.25 |
| | dB/splice | | #splices | | |
| Splice | 0.15 | * | 0 | = | 0.0 |
| | | | Total | = | 5.25 |

Table 25-1: Calculation, Maximum Loss

| Loss in | dB/km | | #km | | dB |
|---|---|---|---|---|---|
| Cable | 0.7 | * | 2.0 | = | 1.4 |
| | dB/pair | | #pairs | | |
| Connector | 0.3 | * | 3 | = | 0.9 |
| | dB/splice | | #splices | | |
| conductive | 0.1 | * | 0 | = | 0.0 |
| | | | Total | = | 2.3 |

Table 25-2: Calculation, Typical Loss

2. Insertion loss acceptance value= 10.975 dB

   OTDR acceptance values
   Attenuation rate: 0.425 dB/km

---

[1] To avoid all confusion, we have included all decimals. As a matter of practice, field installers need not measure to better than 0.1 dB.

Connector loss: 0.525 dB/pair
Splice loss: 0.125 dB/splice

| Loss in | dB/km | | #km | | dB |
|---|---|---|---|---|---|
| Cable | 0.5 | * | 20.0 | = | 10.0 |
| | dB/pair | | #pairs | | |
| Connector | .75 | * | 4 | = | 3.0 |
| | dB/splice | | #splices | | |
| Splice | 0.15 | * | 3 | = | 0.45 |
| | | | Total | = | 13.45 |

Table 25-3: Calculation, Maximum Loss

| Loss in | dB/km | | #km | | dB |
|---|---|---|---|---|---|
| Cable | 0.35 | * | 20.0 | = | 7.0 |
| | dB/pair | | #pairs | | |
| Connector | 0.3 | * | 4 | = | 1.2 |
| | dB/splice | | #splices | | |
| Splice | 0.1 | * | 3 | = | 0.3 |
| | | | Total | = | 8.5 |

Table 25-4: Calculation, Typical Loss

3. Insertion loss acceptance value=
   2.5077 dB

   OTDR acceptance values
   Attenuation rate: 3.25 dB/km
   Connector loss: 0.525 dB/pair
   Splice loss: 0.125 dB/splice

| Loss in | dB/km | | #km | | dB |
|---|---|---|---|---|---|
| Cable | 3.5 | * | .257 | = | .900 |
| | dB/pair | | #pairs | | |
| Connector | .75 | * | 4 | = | 3.0 |
| | dB/splice | | #splices | | |
| Splice | 0.15 | * | 1 | = | 0.15 |
| | | | Total | = | 3.536 |

Table 25-5: Calculation, Maximum Loss

| Loss in | dB/km | | #km | | dB |
|---|---|---|---|---|---|
| Cable | 0.7 | * | .257 | = | .180 |
| | dB/pair | | #pairs | | |
| Connector | 0.3 | * | 4 | = | 1.2 |
| | dB/splice | | #splices | | |
| Splice | 0.1 | * | 1 | = | 0.1 |
| | | | Total | = | 1.48 |

Table 25-6: Calculation, Typical Loss

4. Insertion loss acceptance value=
   1.3849 dB

   OTDR acceptance values
   Attenuation rate: 1.1 dB/km
   Connector loss: 0.525 dB/pair
   Splice loss: 0.125 dB/splice

| Loss in | dB/km | | #km | | dB |
|---|---|---|---|---|---|
| Cable | 3.5 | * | .304 | = | .457 |
| | dB/pair | | #pairs | | |
| Connector | .75 | * | 2 | = | 1.5 |
| | dB/splice | | #splices | | |
| Splice | 0.15 | * | 0 | = | 0.0 |
| | | | Total | = | 1.957 |

Table 25-7: Calculation, Maximum Loss

| Loss in | dB/km | | #km | | dB |
|---|---|---|---|---|---|
| Cable | 0.7 | * | .304 | = | .2128 |
| | dB/pair | | #pairs | | |
| Connector | 0.3 | * | 2 | = | 0.6 |
| | dB/splice | | #splices | | |
| Splice | 0.1 | * | 0 | = | 0.0 |
| | | | Total | = | .8128 |

Table 25-8: Calculation, Typical Loss

5. Insertion loss acceptance value=
   12.06875 dB

   OTDR acceptance values
   Attenuation rate: 0.425 dB/km
   Connector loss: 0.525 dB/pair
   Splice loss: 0.125 dB/splice

| Loss in | dB/km | | #km | | dB |
|---|---|---|---|---|---|
| Cable | 0.5 | * | 20.750 | = | 10.375 |
| | dB/pair | | #pairs | | |
| Connector | .75 | * | 5 | = | 3.75 |
| | dB/splice | | #splices | | |
| Splice | 0.15 | * | 5 | = | 0.75 |
| | | | Total | = | 14.875 |

Table 25-9: Calculation, Maximum Loss

| Loss in | dB/km | | #km | | dB |
|---|---|---|---|---|---|
| Cable | 0.35 | * | 20.750 | = | 7.2625 |
| | dB/pair | | #pairs | | |
| Connector | 0.3 | * | 5 | = | 1.5 |
| | dB/splice | | #splices | | |
| Splice | 0.1 | * | 5 | = | 0.5 |
| | | | Total | = | 9.2625 |

Table 25-10: Calculation, Typical Loss

6. Insertion loss acceptance value=
   3.06025 dB

   OTDR acceptance values
   Attenuation rate: 3.25 dB/km
   Connector loss: 0.525 dB/pair
   Splice loss: 0.125 dB/splice

| Cable | 3.5 | * | 0.257 | | .900 |
|---|---|---|---|---|---|
| | dB/pair | | #pairs | | |
| Connector | .75 | * | 4 | = | 3.0 |
| | dB/splice | | #splices | | |
| Splice | 0.15 | * | 1 | = | 0.15 |
| | | | Total | = | 4.05 |

Table 25-11: Calculation, Maximum Loss

| Loss in | dB/km | | #km | | dB |
|---|---|---|---|---|---|
| Cable | 3.0 | * | 0.257 | = | .77 |
| | dB/pair | | #pairs | | |
| Connector | 0.3 | * | 4 | = | 1.2 |
| | dB/splice | | #splices | | |
| Splice | 0.1 | * | 0 | = | 0.10 |
| | | | Total | = | 2.07 |

Table 25-12: Calculation, Typical Loss

7. Insertion loss acceptance value= 2.038 dB

   OTDR acceptance values
   Attenuation rate: 1.1 dB/km
   Connector loss: 0.525 dB/pair
   Splice loss: 0.125 dB/splice

| Loss in | dB/km | | #km | | dB |
|---|---|---|---|---|---|
| Cable | 3.5 | * | 0.304 | = | 1.06 |
| | dB/pair | | #pairs | | |
| Connector | .75 | * | 2 | = | 1.5 |
| | dB/splice | | #splices | | |
| Splice | 0.15 | * | 0 | = | 0.0 |
| | | | Total | = | 2.56 |

Table 25-13: Calculation, Maximum Loss

| Loss in | dB/km | | #km | | dB |
|---|---|---|---|---|---|
| Cable | 3.0 | * | 0.304 | = | .912 |
| | dB/pair | | #pairs | | |
| Connector | 0.3 | * | 2 | = | 0.6 |
| | dB/splice | | #splices | | |
| Splice | 0.1 | * | 0 | = | 0.0 |
| | | | Total | = | 1.512 |

Table 25-14: Calculation, Typical Loss

8. Method A insertion losses are one connector pair, or 0.525 dB, lower than Method B losses. Reducing the answers from Questions 1-7 by 0.525 dB gives us:

| Question | Loss, dB |
|---|---|
| 1 | 3.2500 |
| 2 | 10.4500 |
| 3 | 1.9827 |
| 4 | 0.8599 |
| 5 | 11.5438 |
| 6 | 1.8577 |
| 7 | 0.8594 |

Table 25-15: Method A Acceptance Values For Questions 1-7

## 25.6  THE AUTHOR

Mr. Eric R. Pearson has been involved in fiber optic communications for the last 28 years. This involvement includes a wide variety of activities, as is detailed below.

Mr. Pearson has developed and run two fiber optic cable manufacturing facilities and organizations (Manufacturing Manager, Times Fiber Communications and Business Manager, Whitmor Waveguides). In these positions, Mr. Pearson developed cable designs, manufacturing techniques and qualified designs against performance specifications. As business manager, he was responsible for developing a profitable multi-million dollar business unit.

Mr. Pearson managed two fiber manufacturing facilities, one for Corning Glass Works and for Times Fiber Communications.

Mr. Pearson has delivered more than 432 training presentations and trained more than 6800 personnel in proper installation procedures. Between his field installations and training, he has made and supervised more than 38,000 connectors. From both field experience and training, Mr. Pearson gained sufficient experience to write two definitive texts on cable and connector installation, The Complete Guide to Fiber Optic Cable Installation (Delmar Publishers, 1997, ISBN #0-8273-7318-X) and Successful Fiber Optic Network Installation.

He has written the books: Fiber Optic Network Design, Practical Fiber Optic System Design and Implementation, How to Specify and Choose Fiber Optic Cables, and How to Specify and Choose Fiber Optic Connectors.

Mr. Pearson was the technical expert for a patent infringement suit, four legal suits between installers and end users, a fifth suit regarding apparent technical fraud in fiber optic cables, and a sixth suit regarding fiber optic cable performance specifications.

Mr. Pearson is a Director and the Director of Certification, of the Fiber Optic Association (FOA). As the latter, he is responsible for developing requirements and examinations for basic and advanced certification of fiber optic installer personnel. These activities require an in depth knowledge of all aspects of cable and connector installation.

From the Fiber Optic Association, he has received all three advanced Certified Fiber Optic Specialist certifications (CFOS/T, CFOS/S, CFOS/C).

Since 1986, he has been a Member, Editorial Advisory Board, Fiberoptic Product News.

The Academy of Professional Consultants & Advisors (APCA) has certified him as a Certified Professional Consultant (CPC).

Mr. Pearson is a Master Instructor for the Building Industry Consultants Services International (BICSI), and the developer of the BICSI fiber optic network design program.

He has over 100 articles, reports and presentations to his credit. He is frequently quoted in fiber optic and related trade journals, most recently in the Editorial column of the January, 2002 issue of Lightwave.

He has been selected to speak at three Newport Fiber Optic Marketing Conferences.

He is listed in: Who's Who Worldwide, Who's Who of Business Leaders, Who's Who in Technology and Who's Who in California.

Mr. Pearson has provided consulting services to several hundred companies in the areas of fiber network design and specification, technical and marketing evaluations.

Mr. Pearson received his education at Massachusetts Institute of Technology (BS, 1969) and Case-Western Reserve University (MS, 1970). Both degrees are in Metallurgy and Materials Science.

Mr. Eric R. Pearson, CPC, CFOS

# INDEX